Comi

MW01284171

In which I make several attempts to float from Albany to Manhattan between 2006 and 2010, with a miscellany of characters, family, and friends, and the trials and tribulations which ensued from the act.

By Dallas K. Trombley

Prologue

This book began as an effort to do something: to float to Manhattan on a boat I built myself that didn't use a gas motor. The goal became an entity, striving for realization. We obtained a kind of symbiosis: it could not be completed without me, and through realizing it, I accrued experiences, acquaintances, and wisdom that I otherwise would not have. The book argues that individuals should *do things* which require thought and action constantly.

The following narrative does not contain explosions, violence, or gratuitous sexual behavior or drug use. It is not a political manifesto, a romance novel, a history, nor a philosophical or sociological tract, but it contains elements of each of those genres. I intended the book to be entertaining but primarily thought-provoking.

I have changed the names of most of the characters, if only because the conversations took place in what was assumed a private sphere, many years ago, and are reconstructed from my notes and memories. I am indebted to all of the people I have met, even those whose foibles I noted because it affected the plot.

I hope the reader can bear occasional foul language. To edit some but not other language would be discriminatory toward youth and a particular sociological and geographical strata of the population, which I inhabit(ed). I hope this does not prohibit recommendation of the book to adolescents, juveniles, teens — young *adults* — because it contains insights into sociological relationships, carpentry, Hudson River history, philosophy, the soul, electricity, political and bureaucratic functions, music, language, depression, nautical construction and piloting, sailing, bartending, painting, loneliness and virtue.

Planning, constructing and piloting the boats took me five years and $20,000. It took me five months of 3-18 hour days to write the original draft of this book, between November and May of 2013. I edited the book seven times, hand-drew the maps and formatted the margins and pictures. After each draft I distributed copies for friends to proofread. This book represents thousands of hours I've spent in pursuit of the publication of a book about this particular goal. I hope the reader savors it, allows her or his mind to dwell here and there, as though listening to a conversation among friends.

Dallas Trombley

November 16th, 2016

Table of Contents

Book I: July, 2005- August, 2006. A Piece of Floating Driftwood

In the summer of 2005 I turned 21. It seemed like a big deal at the time.

Mike was my friend of eleven years, who was born one day after me. We had a joint birthday party at his parent's house on Indian Fields Road in rural Albany County. There was a bonfire with a keg that got thrown around after it was empty. We made a mess playing drinking games and celebrating our entree to an age when *We Can Drink Now*. Then we were 21 years old and one day, picking up sticky *Solo Cups* and musing mildly maudlinly, "Well, there's nothing to look forward to now."

A piece of driftwood, on the tidal waters of the Hudson River, will take six months to float between Albany and New York City. At least that is what a middle-aged man who called himself Kayak Guy, who paddled more than 5,000 miles on the estuaries of the East Coast as a way to quit smoking, once told me.

Driftwood is a limb from a cadaver. It has no motivation. Eventually, it is used by plants the way that all once-living things are used, when they settle in one spot, break down, and become the matter from which more recently-living things grow. Driftwood doesn't care if it tangles in a thicket in Greene County, or floats with the current through The Narrows between Brooklyn and Staten Island, out to sea.

People move, but driftwood *is* moved. In many ways, without admitting it, we train people to act like driftwood, until a certain age. Then we expect them to act like people. From the perspective of the person trained to act like driftwood, this can be a jarring experience. Perhaps the kind of experience that determines a person's life-trajectory and perspective.

It's easy to see how or why driftwood moves. It is either carried by a fluid which itself is tugged by gravity, or it lays on land, which doesn't move in any way appreciable to human senses, and it just sits there.

People have *minds*, on the other hand. Minds understand the movement of bodies along a fourth dimension called *time*. In our minds are ambitions, goals, and fears. People picture where they will be, and what their surroundings will look like, in the future, and we move toward our goals and away from our fears. People have *agency* or *capability* because we have minds. But that capability or agency is limited by the mind of each person, just as the speed of driftwood is determined by the water it floats in.

When I turned 21 I was not very concerned with law, the workings of society, the life-cycle of towns and cities, the way decisions are made and executed when they involve groups of people with different needs and objectives. That curiosity came later, because I did something. At the time I wanted to travel and make love and drink and write and make love and have adventures and see new places.

The natural niche of restlessness is the breasts of young people. In America, in this millennium, it is pent-up and poured out when one obtains the arbitrary age of Twenty-One, which signifies Adulthood, or the acquisition or rights, or something. Twenty-One has a lot of meaning, at least until you get there.

From birth until Twenty-One, modern American society treats young people like Pavlov's dogs: five days per week, a person rises to an alarm in the dark of the morning. She or he travels to a large building where bells signal when to enter and leave various rooms. This repeats between eight and ten times. The person arrives home, performs mental tasks related to school, and perhaps participates in extracurricular physical or religious activity. There follows a few hours of leisure. Then the person sleeps and repeats the process 180 out of 365 days. This format repeats in four-year blocks encompassing elementary school, primary school, secondary school, and college. During the first three of four blocks one obtains no rights, by virtue of her or his minor status. Nor, during this period, does one accrue much responsibility or discretion. Completion of the third block coincides with the rights to drive a vehicle, purchase tobacco and vote in political contests. Completion of three-quarters of the fourth block, *college*, coincides with the right to purchase alcohol. During this time the measurements are tangible: *tests*. And the result more or less predictable: *success* following a modicum of effort.

Having had one's meaningful movements managed during the first two decades of life, a person grows conditioned, as the behavioral psychologists would say, to anticipate some current to push them toward the next steps of personal development. But at Twenty-One it changes. Immediately, one is expected to *prosper*— while never having been trained to manage, having had no real responsibility; and to *speculate*—by investing time and wages efficiently—while lacking *capital* by virtue of only recently joining the job market. Newly-arrived at the stage of *liberty*, with all of the magic that that word conjures, young, working-class people have few options other than to seek a job, where one can expect to spend the next forty years in much the same fashion as the first twenty.

None of this, of course, is *natural*, and it is in the history of human evolution extremely *new*. And people, possessing not just minds for making sense of their world, but also emotions, *feel* that this is unnatural, somehow weird, like they are being shanghaied, even if they cannot articulate the feeling. At any rate that is how I felt, and how most of my friends felt, and we were not in any hurry to get to the next stage of scheduled-work-for-someone-else. We wanted to pause there at the point where our rights and our youth intersected. Some of us would pause there indefinitely, becoming, like a navigational beacon, a point by which others judged their forward movement. For some of my friends pausing was worse than monotony: they would make the best out of their first employment opportunity. Over the next few years, like the tides of the Hudson, I would ebb and flow.

***

I was raised in a rural town called New Baltimore, in Greene County, "Upstate" New York. New Baltimore is situated on the west bank of the Hudson River about 17 miles, or a 25-minute drive, south of Albany, or 130 standard miles north of New York City.

Although we lived in New York State, my family never travelled to New York City. My classmates and I made a school trip in coach busses there in sixth grade, just as we made a class trip to Boston the year before, both being three hours away and the closest big cities.

My father worked in Albany, and we sometimes made trips there as a family, to go to Easter dinner with my aunts and uncles, or to go buy, as a family, some piece of furniture which my parents had budgeted and saved for a year to purchase. Mostly, though, we travelled to Ravena, a village two miles north of New Baltimore, and that was where we did things like go to school and church, go to parades, go to dinner, shop, and visit the members of my mother's large family (she had eleven brothers and sisters). The majority of my time as a child and teenager were spent within a five-mile radius of my boyhood home, surrounded by woods, small buildings, relatives and, eventually, friends from school.

No one really knows how the place came to be called New Baltimore, according to Clesson Bush, the town historian. He wrote a book called "Episodes from a Hudson River Town" in which he says that New Baltimore is pretty unexceptional, but ought to be read about anyway, because most places in America are pretty unimportant except to the people who live there, so it is representative.[1]

In New Baltimore rises the Kalkbergs, which are like small mountain ridges. These eventually become the Catskill Mountains in the south of Greene County. You get your first look at these worn but majestic mountains as you pass Catskill and Hudson on the Amtrak Hudson River Railroad Line. (Or, if you're coming up from New York City, I suppose you get your *last* look at them as you pass those places.) The Catskills are not as big as the Rockies or as long as the Appalachians but they were the first muses for American artists. After the Revolution the country had no artistic tradition, no unique national identity outside of the institutions inherited from Europe. The Catskills were the setting for Washington Irving's Headless Horseman and Rip Van Winkle stories, where Coopers' characters scouted, where Thomas Cole, Frederick Church and the painters of the Hudson River School drew inspiration in the early Republic. Later, the Catskills were the playground of affluent New York City tourists on trips to the country by steamboat and locomotive, as well as the source of food and milk for city-dwellers and employment for Hudson Valley locals, until the Erie Canal made it as cheap to get grain from the Midwest as it was from Hudson Valley fields, and until cars and air travel made it as easy for city folks to visit Tampa as it was to visit Hudson. At that point the cities, towns and villages of the Catskills began to crumble into the ghost towns they are today. But none of that affected New Baltimore much, since the place never was a tourist destination, like the towns in the Catskills, to begin with.[2] New Baltimore is just to the north, in the Kalkbergs, which no one has ever heard of.

But there were wonderful things to see and do for a boy growing up in the woods. New Baltimore is rocky, populated with coniferous and deciduous trees, full of deer and birds and frogs and raccoons and berries and fireflies. It is transected by numerous winding "cricks," as my grandfather called them, and sports natural vistas which you can climb to the top of and smell the peaty air blowing from below. There is movement there in the woods,

---

[1] Bush, C. S., Episodes from a Hudson River Town (New Baltimore, New York), State University of New York Press, Albany, New York, 2011, pp 1-4.

[2] *Ibid.* pp 5-6; Stradling, D., Making Mountains (New York City and the Catskills), University of Washington Press, Seattle, 2007; Lewis, T., The Hudson (A History), Yale University Press, New York, 2005.

springing from the life-stuff. Being a human, and having not just a mind to calculate but also emotions to feel with, I *felt*, as a boy on adventures into the forest, surrounded by life and forces and elemental power. When I was wading down the Hannacroix Creek, and a thousand trees were blowing in the gusts of wind, and the sky between the rows of trees to the right and left became gray and black bubbling, and the current of the water pushed me stumbling and slipping over mossy smooth stones, and I found myself at the top of the Hannacroix Falls, with the white water rushing over, and the big cold drops started to fall as I climbed out on a tree trunk which extended over the falls like a plank on a pirate ship, and I looked down and saw the water churning below, the water falling above me — mist mixed with rain — the smell of mud and marsh, the leaves shaking on the branches, orange, green, yellow, gray sky and thunder and wind water rushing in my ears blowing — that was a *feeling*! The whole package, all of the sensations at once, experienced, not discretely, but totally, in cumulative effect, with nothing else around except the noise and the smells and the trees moving older than anyone growing out of mountains older than countries, standing in the middle of a stream that flows and always flowed and always will flow — that is a *feeling*! So early on I took these adventures in the woods to experience sensations like these, in order to feel them all at once, in order to feel what it felt like to feel them all at once, and having a mind for thinking in addition to emotions for feeling, I thought, "I like this feeling," and it was probably back then at 8, 9, and 10 that I started feeling calm in the middle of big, dynamic, dramatic systems. When things are crashing and cracking and moving, moving, moving — that is when I feel and have always felt *alive*.

Nothing was moving when I pulled into my parent's driveway that July afternoon in 2005, after our birthday party at Mike's. I parked "my" car — my parent's car — on the lawn, never on the driveway, per my father's instructions. The afternoon was muggy, gray, and stagnant. Outside the car I listened to the engine click and cool. I scanned the yard for my cats, but they were in the woods. I looked across the yard toward my grandparent's house, but I knew they were sleeping, because it was between "dinner" and "supper" times. My parent's jeep was not in the driveway.

The house was shut up and dark because it was supposed to rain. I went into the bathroom and washed the hangover off my face. I looked at the lines under my eyes. I ran hot water, rubbed some shaving cream in my hands, and shaved off the mustache and goatee

I'd worn for three years, since the start of college, to look older so I could get into bars. Then I said aloud to my mirror self, "Yesterday was the last time you will ever want to look older, for the rest of your life."

The second chapter of David Herbert Donald's biography of Abraham Lincoln is titled "A Piece of Floating Driftwood." This was the way Lincoln described his early twenties in Illinois, living in a small town, working first as a laborer, then as a grocery clerk, trying and failing to open his own store, trying and failing to be a flatboat man on the Ohio and Mississippi, thinking of studying law but deciding it would be too hard and cost too much money, trying and failing to run for government office, spending his time reading, like George Bailey, imagining greater and more interesting things that he would rather have been doing, but which were beyond his means; wearing old and awkwardly fitting hand-me-down clothing, never having any money, having no romance, living a listless existence. Driftwood floating place to place with no plan, no propulsion, passively acted upon instead of acting. It was a great analogy from a man known for great analogies.[3]

I descended into the basement of my parent's house which I used for an office and reading space. I pushed a button on the back of the tower of my PC and waited for it to start. On a hook beside my desk hung my old, awkwardly fitting hand-me-down blazer which I wore every day to school the winter before, because I didn't own a heavy coat. It had been a rough semester. I'd broken up with my girlfriend of two years and laid around unhappy until I had only a week to finish 60 pages of final papers. Then I'd barricaded myself in the basement, saw no one, and worked until I was sick and exhausted, with bushy eyes, a beard and pale skin. Then in a personal protest against such a lifestyle, I'd cleaned for days, shaved, spent what little money I had on a new outfit, and for the next month I drank with friends every night until almost dawn.

When the computer warmed I opened Microsoft Word and a file named "Chronicles." This was a prose description of the parties, road trips, stoned sessions, jokes, anecdotes, and slices of conversation I kept as of an electronic journal. I was trying to learn to write better dialogue by inscribing conversations verbatim. I fantasized that I would someday be "The Chronicler of '84," the

---

[3] Donald, D. H., <u>Lincoln</u>, Simon and Shuster Inc., New York, 1995, pp. 38-65.

writer who captured what it was like to have been born in my birth year.

I tapped the spacebar a few times, then rose from my desk and walked to a table where I'd laid a number of half-finished short stories. I lifted one, read a paragraph, put it down. Then I opened *Kazaa*, played some solitary Sinatra music and poured myself a Highball. To inject some levity, I raised the glass, said, "Hello old friend!" and smirked sardonically.

***

Mike asked me to help him move into a new apartment down in New Paltz. In August I borrowed my parents' fourteen-year-old Ford pickup truck for the trip. It was an old white junker speckled with sap and dirt; one fender looked like crumpled aluminum foil. It had a leaky gas tank and the rear cab window wouldn't close. Still, when I hopped onto the pleather bench seat and took off for Mike's parent's house I felt great. It was right at that point in the day when you'd have to flip a coin to decide whether it was late afternoon or early evening. Only one speaker worked in the old truck, but it blasted *American Gold*, Dick Bartley's Saturday night classic oldies show. They were highlighting 1969 and I belted the lyrics to *Hair*, *Windy*, and *Bad Girls* as I drove toward Mike's under the pine trees and the descending summer sun. Out the open window the Alcove Reservoir reflected the oranges and yellows through the spaces between the trees, flashing like an old movie reel. Warm air swirled into the cab, danced around my face and up my nose smelling of musky soil and cut grass. I was so excited to be getting out of town that I nearly jumped out of the seat shouting the songs:

"Gimme a head with hair! *Hair*! Shoulder length or longer! *Hair*! Blah blah blah blah screamin' flaxen waxin'! *Hair*!"

I met a girl that night. After moving Mike's furniture into his dirty 5-bedroom apartment, we went to a bar called *Oasis*. It was exotic to my experience. *Oasis* had a sake bar, a traditional bar, a bunch of modern-looking couches with tea lights burning on end tables, and a pool table and dance floor. The walls were moody maroons and indigos. The lighting was intimate. The milieu was trippy, because the band, which consisted of five middle-aged guys, were jamming to *Grateful Dead* and Tom Petty songs. The most interesting sight to me was the carnival of drunken dancing hippies. At the underage bars and "clubs" I'd frequented in Albany, the dance floor was usually a pit of sweating, wasted teens "grinding" like animals in heat. In New Paltz there were middle-aged hippies, young kids probably in high school or their freshman year of college, young professionals in button-up shirts, even blue-collar workers. Instead of forming sub-groups, they danced together in a way you might label "Art," or an imitation of the characters in *Charlie Brown's Christmas Special*. I could tell after my first White Russian that it was going to be an interesting night, because it was new and people were moving.

A tall guy in business attire sauntered up to me and said,

"Wow there's a lot of hippies around here, huh?" I smiled as we perused the crowd. We calibrated our ocular lenses on one particular young lady. She wore tight, dark jeans, brown boots, and a long tank-top that hung down half-covering her ass. Over the tank-top she donned a brown belt to accentuate her slim waist. She was dancing more provocatively than the other hippies, but not quite showing off.

A couple of seats cleared up closer to the dance floor so I snatched one next to a mid-thirties-looking woman. She was a right-wing newspaper editor, she said. She made me guess her age and told me I was way wrong and she was forty-two, although she'd only just graduated from New Paltz the year before. A couple of her (to me) older friends were dancing with the cute brunette so I figured I'd stick around and maybe fall into some kind of introduction. But the woman kept talking bullshit, like she was trying to get a reaction out of me by telling egregious lies. When Mike came back from the bathroom I introduced them to each other and I was glad when they struck up a conversation because they had had a class together or something, and I excused myself. When I turned back toward the dance floor the brunette had disappeared.

I suddenly felt low. Bars or clubs can be hollow. I looked at all the people dancing, not talking.

Male friends talked about sex as a commodity you could gain if you entered the right code. Like love and romance were the levels you had to fight through to defeat the big boss and win a video game. I sat on a couch and thought about how different guys and girls are today, compared to old movies.

From the corner of my eye I saw the middle-aged woman's friends sitting at a table a few feet away; the cute brunette was sitting there, too. I crossed my legs and with my wine glass in my hand I tried to look disinterested and sophisticated. The brunette waved at me and yelled across the table from 20 feet away,

"Hey! Do you wanna be my partner at pool?" When I realized she was speaking to me I nodded quickly.

"Yeah, definitely, yeah. That sounds like fun to me," I shouted back, "I'm not that good…"

"I'm fucking awesome," she laughed. I couldn't tell if she was serious. "Why don't you come over here and sit with us?"

This I did immediately. She introduced me to her friends. She told me her name was Cadance, but everyone called her Cady. I introduced myself to her friends, who were in their late 30s or early 40s, and told a couple of jokes.

Soon we were at the pool table. Mike spotted us and watched from across the room, rooting for me. Cady paid for the game and then broke because I told her I was no good at that. She left me a lot of easy shots, so right off the bat I threw the stick behind my back and made a fancy pocket.

"Oh you're a hustler, eh Dallas?"

"Nah I'm just fooling around," I said.

"Okay Dallas. Dallas Dallas Dallas. I can't stop saying your name. Dallas Dallas. Are your parents from Dallas?" She leaned over the table. The skin of her chest was silky white. She sunk one of my balls by mistake. I was stripes.

"My dad is a big *Cowboys* fan," I said, sinking the fourteen-stripe and lining up another ball by accident.

"I love that you're drinking wine," she said. "I love wine."

"We should have a glass after this game," I suggested.

"I think so Dallas."

We finished the game and bought glasses of merlot. We played another game and both did terribly. Then I bought us each another glass of merlot. As we stood at the bar she asked if I wanted to be pen pals, and I said sure. So she started writing her info on a napkin. I wrote Coolnphat2@aol.com on another napkin and handed it to her. To my surprise she had written her mailing address, in Long Island.

"What's this?" I asked.

"Well, I don't check my email very often so this is really the fastest way to get in touch with me. Oh! Except my cell phone. I'll write that too. I'll give you my email and screen name but I'm not on much. Are you on Myspace? I'll write my username for that here too."

When she was done I had two cocktail napkins of her contact information. Then I bought us each another glass of wine and we started dancing to a psychedelic *Shakedown Street* cover. We danced together like we were in a teen movie or a Broadway musical. We danced crazy to see how crazy we could get the other to dance; neither of us wanted to be outdone. Cady trotted backward with high strides while I loped toward her singing the lyrics. Then, back to the wall, she pushed forward and sent me cantering backwards as she sang, shaking a finger at me. We bumped hips pretending to be disco stars. Then she shouted over the music,

"So, you're gay right?"

"What? No," I said. "Why would you ask me that?"

"Come on you're obviously gay."

"Why do you think that?" She smirked as though it was obvious. "What, is it my jeans? Or my good dancing? It must be my incredible good looks."

"Tell me the truth," she slurred. "You're gay, aren't you."

"No."

"You can admit it."

"Yo," I shouted over the music, "gimme a break, man."

"I'm not a man. Let's go outside."

We went outside and sat on a concrete half-wall. We bummed two cigarettes off a girl going into the bar. Cady picked up with the same conversation.

"You're the kind of person who gives girls a bad name," I said.

"Why?"

"Because girls always complain," I mimicked a whiny voice, "'I wish guys were sensitive. I wish guys weren't such assholes,' but when you see a guy that's nice and sensitive and a good dresser you say 'Oh he must be gay.' Screw that, man."

"Am I a man?" she said. "Let's talk over there."

We strolled to the side of the building and I pulled down the tailgate of a truck so we had a seat. It was a clear night. Crickets chirped like cymbals above the bass notes muted by the bar's walls. It smelled and felt like eighth grade, playing Truth-or-Dare in Kara Richenbach's barn, drinking *Dr. Pepper*. Here was this short girl with big brown eyes and brown hair that straightened down to her shoulders and curled in with little turns around her chin and neck. She wore at least a dozen bracelets and five shell necklaces. She spoke confidently, even assertively. She talked like she was cat-and-mousing me. She smelled like someone I would have a crush on.

"Is this your truck?" she asked.

"No."

"Tell me the truth now, are you gay?"

"Man, screw this," I said and jumped up. She hurriedly added —

"If you wanna make out with me you can."

What a great compliment! It was a relief not to have to choose between longing and awkwardness. For the next ninety seconds I experienced fun, passionate, soft, cuddly, lovely, poetic kissing with Cady from Massapequa Park way out on Long Island. Then suddenly she pushed away from me, stood up, and said, "Well, we better go back inside before my step-mom and my aunt start asking questions."

When we danced again it was less foolish. We couldn't keep our eyes off each other. Twice Mike called to tell me he'd gone home and was waiting for me to get back. When the bartenders called Last Call, Cady's step-mom and aunts offered me a ride. They declined an invitation to hang out with Mike and I. It was sad watching the Subaru with Cady inside driving away, though I felt pretty cool bragging to Mike that I'd "got my make-out on."

After a while I crashed upstairs on the couch we'd just brought down from our hometown. The sun was rising. Birds chirped through a window. The veil of night was drawing back, and here was the approach of just another day, hanging on the hazy purple skirts of a dream I'd just wandered into. I drifted asleep on my back, lonely, but thinking of Cady, and smiling.

That fall it rained a lot. It rained every day, as I remember it. In the morning the rain slapped the shingles, gurgled in the gutters and patted the window panes. Waking up, warm, almost womb-like under a comforter, was the worst part of the day. It was almost torturous. It rained as I ran to my car, soaking my hand-me-down blazer. It rained on the windshield as the wiper squeaked. It fogged the windshield and the air from the defroster set me sneezing. It rained as I ran from the pothole-pocked parking lot to the office I was I employed in. It rained all day outside as I answered telephone calls, shielding my boss from customers.

"Is Maureen there today? I'd like to speak to her."

"She's not in today, can I take a message?"

"This is the third time I've called and left a message. Are you giving her the messages? I really need to talk to her..."

My boss was never there. She was depressed because her relationship of several years recently dissolved. She owned several insurance offices and lived in a big house in the country with six golden retrievers as her companions in middle age.

"I'll make sure she gets the message, ma'am."

"Well, good. I am very unhappy right now. Please make her aware."

"I will convey your unhappiness, ma'am."

The other person in the office was a militant lesbian feminist vegan. I drank a lot of tea with honey because I got a sore throat every fall. My co-worker said I was a thief, because I stole the honey which rightfully belonged to bees. She lectured about the insidiousness of prosthetic breasts.

"If women united and stopped wearing fake breasts after mastectomies, then people would be aware of the scope of the problem, how many women are affected by cancer, and the government would do something about it."

My boss and my coworker: two more representatives of the adult world who were weird.

It rained as I ran across the potholed parking lot to my car. It rained as I drove up to the State University at Albany for two or three afternoon and evening classes. It rained as I parked in the university parking lot, and it rained as I walked for ten minutes to the Humanities building, soaking my hand-me-down wool blazer. As I drove home at nine o'clock it rained, the air from the heating vents making me sneeze. After I parked my car, off the driveway, per my father's instructions, it rained as I ran into the house. Cold and damp, I'd descend into the basement each night, hanging my damp wool blazer on a hook next to my desk. I'd play Tommy Dorsey songs and pour myself a Highball. That was the beginning of the part of the day I enjoyed. I would work on a short story, update my chronicles, chat on AIM, and after three or four cocktails I'd find myself smiling and singing. Sometimes one of my cats walked across the keyboard and typed a line of nonsense letters, or laid on the desk listening to Billie Holiday with me. Perhaps I would chat with Alan, who was studying medicine at CASE Western, about Platonic philosophy, with Jacquelyn up at Niagara University about the literalness of Christian parables, or with Jess out at Ithaca about the meaning of Truth. My creative writing would grow disjointed, experimental, like E. E. Cummings poetry. Around three a.m. I'd head upstairs to try to sleep. As I drifted off, the rain slapped the shingles and gurgled in the gutters. It was important to fall asleep quickly in order not to remember that in a few hours the routine would start again, and repeat into the future, as far as I could imagine.

Fortunately, I could read my college textbooks at work between phone calls and policy endorsements. If I didn't have a job where I could do schoolwork and earn money at the same time, I don't know how I'd have graduated. The most important lesson I took away from a bartending course I'd attended the summer after high school was the importance of performing multiple tasks at once. Don't waste steps.

That fall term I read two books which opened my mind to two ideas—or ways of thinking about life and society—which changed my life.

The first was a textbook, "Biopsychology" by John P. J. Pinel. It introduced me to the overlap between life functions and cognition. It combined chemistry and psychology to show how *thought*, or at least the firing of neurons, occurs because of the electrical properties of the chemicals of which living tissues are composed.[4] The idea that mental activity was the result of physical laws was a mind-blowing epiphany. This electro-chemical-biological spectrum I would remember years later when studying the physics of batteries.

At the same time, I took a *Philosophy of Law* class. I'd never supposed that Law was based on a philosophy—that there were good laws with specific characteristics. I'd always assumed that laws were based on the whims of whoever holds power, like how you can get away with more or less depending on who your teacher or babysitter is. The textbook for this class traced the evolution of legal theory (the word I learned was "jurisprudence") from John Austin to Ronald Dwarkin and Antonin Scalia.[5] So simultaneously that fall I found myself considering that there are *rules*, not magic, that underlie thought and human behavior; and *rules*, not the arbitrary exercise of power, that underlie the laws, which regulate human behavior. Rules and organization: things a person like me could come to understand, rather than randomness. For me at Twenty-One, this was a re-affirmation of the principles of enlightenment, which I'd questioned as I entered the brave new world of irrational adulthood. It seemed to indicate that laborious study *would* pay off by giving me an understanding of the laws of life and living. It suggested that, with enough study, over years, perhaps, I might come to understand the ways that the rules of law and of life and of everything else were related. It even suggested the possibility of *meta-rules*—rules governing the constitution of rules themselves. That kind of understanding, if possible, seemed similar to seeing the world in

---

[4] Pinel, J. P. J., <u>Biopsychology (Sixth Edition)</u>, Pearson, New York, 2006. For example, a neuron will fire when the electrical potential of the chemicals inside versus outside of the neural wall reach a certain voltage differential.

[5] Feinberg, J. and Coleman, J., <u>Philosophy of Law</u>, Seventh Edition, Wadsworth/Thompson Learning, Belmont, Ca., 2004.

zeroes and ones, like when Neo sees the coding that controls The Matrix.

The fall is a hard time if you live in the country. You have to get the house and the property ready for winter. My parents owned two acres and my grandparents, who lived next door, owned eight acres. In total there were about three or four acres of hills and yards to clear of leaves, the rest were forest. My sister and her husband helped, but mostly the upkeep fell on myself and my parents, my grandparents being in their nineties, too old for physical labor. My grandmother by this point was unable to care for herself, so my grandfather spent the whole of his day looking after her. My parents and I cleaned their house, my mother cooked their meals, and in the fall we took care of both parcels of land in addition to our jobs and school.

We had a riding tractor to help pick up the leaves, at least in the flat portions of the property, but it broke down all of the time, or it would clog. When working optimally we could pick up a one-hundred-foot row of leaves before driving the tractor to a hill on the cusp of the woods. There we emptied the leaf pieces in a pile which grew five feet high before we knocked it down and started piling it up again. We couldn't use the tractor on a lot of the land because there were roots and rocks, or the ground was too steep. In those places we had to rake the leaves and nuts and branches and either burn them in a pile, if they were dry, or put them in 30-gallon trash cans, load them into the back of the pickup truck, drive to the hill on the cusp of the woods, and empty them. To get all of the leaves picked up once took about 50 man-hours, or 16 hours apiece, and then it was time to start over again, more leaves having fallen as the first round was being picked up. In the fall we also had to clean out the chimney by climbing on the roof and dropping a claw-like contraption down and pulling it up by a rope to knock the soot off the flue, and then take apart the furnace pipes and vacuum them out, coughing and getting black from the dust. We cleaned the gutters of both houses by climbing on a ladder and scooping them out by hand. And wood had to be brought from the woodpile by stacking rows on the tailgate of the truck, driving to the cellar door, carrying the wood down the cellar steps and stacking them on pallets in the basement. If we got an early start and the weather was dry, this could all be done if my mother, father and I worked a few hours after work each day and all day on the weekends, and on Election Day. But of course as this was being done my mother had to go in early to make the meals for my grandparents and we had to schedule time to clean their house. It was physical, tiring labor. As I helped with it, I would think about the reading I needed to finish for school. Generally I had about 250 pages a week. I could read about 15 pages per hour, meaning I needed to spend about 16.5 hours per week reading. It was especially frustrating because my father, who attended college for only two years and would say that he'd never read a whole book in his life, thought that once I was out of class and work, my obligations to institutions were over. My mother was more sympathetic. Yet it was irksome to work, attend class, toil around the house, then read...and then be accused of laziness because I wanted to spend Friday or Saturday night in Albany or New Paltz with my friends getting drunk.

This seasonal obligatory unpaid work was educational in its own way. Good experiences are gained from wisdom, which is gained from unpleasant experiences. Having to do such things, each discrete, being evaluated for each individually by someone who didn't care about the other things I had to do, made me plan and schedule so that I had very little idle time. Over years, I grew to dislike idleness, I found it chafing, my time-use became efficient, I planned better, and it bothered me less when people didn't empathize with my workload. None of those important lessons could've been learned from a textbook. Experiential wisdom: it isn't learned by rote, but by *doing*. And it often sucks while you're doing it.

"Peace," said Jared in mock-falsetto voice. He wrinkled his forehead and arched his throwing hand over his spiky hair like he was having an action photo taken. Then he brought his hand down on my open palm and told me, "Alright buddy I sank mine, now it's your turn." So I lined up my elbow and gripped the Ping-Pong ball with my thumb and first two fingers. I visualized the cups at the other end of the table as whirlpools waiting to suck in my ball. A crowd watched around the table with red Solo cups in their hands. Jared was considered one of the kings of Beer Pong and I didn't want to let my good friend down by missing. We'd been covering each other's misthrows with complementary successes. That's a good team. I tossed the ball and it slipped exactly into the center of the cup to the left of the cup I was aiming for. The crowd cheered as our opponents rolled us back the balls.

It was the fourth kegger Mike had thrown at his house in New Paltz since the beginning of school almost three months before. He was the only one in the house old enough to buy beer. For the first couple of parties, Mike collected five-dollar bills from people as they came into the house. When he'd made enough money to cover the cost of the beer and cups, he said to hell with it and let everybody else drink for free. But then one day a kid who called himself Willow — an albino drug-head who was a friend of a friend of someone living in the house — took him aside and said,

"Listen Mike, I know you feel like you've broken even and everybody's having a good time and you might as well just let people have fun and drink for free and everything. But that's a lot of hippy bullshit man! These fuckers are in *your* house, breakin' *your* shit, makin' a mess outta' *your* belongings, spillin' shit on *your* floor...if the cops come and anybody gets in trouble, it's *your* ass. That's *your* money. Now, you tell everybody when they come in that it's five dollars or they can get the fuck out. That's *your* money, man!" After that Mike always collected the money before a stranger got a cup, and started making a small profit off of each party.

Mike had several accidental roommates. He'd been the last to move into the house. The other tenants had moved in two months before I helped him transport his belongings in August, and they'd been doing a good job of filling the house with garbage, putting holes in the walls, accumulating dishes in the sink and broken furniture in the back yard, and other such charming behavior. One was a tall, menacing-looking kid who had his jaw wired shut after he'd been in a fight. Another was a beady-eyed short guy who always seemed to be twitching and itching. As I stood in the center of the Beer Pong crowd I watched Mike sitting on a wooden table in the kitchen by the keg. He wore a Boston hat and a red hooded sweatshirt, holding out cups to a group of nervous, geeky-looking freshmen, one who still had braces. He tucked their dollar bills in a wad in his pocket, then reached behind himself and got four cups for the next people in line. Somebody had to run the show, but I couldn't help but feel that Mike was missing the party.

Jared was about to shoot and I was getting nervous because I was at least eight beers deep and it was almost nine o'clock. Cady's bus was due in at any moment and I couldn't leave her at the Greyhound station alone. But Jared was in his glory running the Beer Pong table. With every shot his smile shined as people watched to see if he could sink another ball and make our opponents choke down another half-cupful of nickel-tasting beer. The road trip was coming off a great success. We felt young and full of potential like back in high school. Then my phone rang — it was Cady telling me she'd just gotten into town. I told her I'd meet her at the bus station in ten minutes and flipped my phone closed.

"Dude we can't go now!" Jared protested. "We're right in the middle of our sixth win in a row!"

"I can't leave her waiting at the bus station."

"Dude, that's so weak. I'm disappointed in you."

"Well, I don't know what to say, man. I like this girl; I can't leave her sitting outside the bus station in the dark with killers and rapists and shit running around."

"Okay, but we gotta finish this game at least." So that's what we did. We won the game and then took off. We'd planned to borrow two bicycles we'd seen leaning against the wall outside Mike's house but both bikes had flat tires so we had to hoof it double-time. I pictured Cady shivering alone on a bench under a streetlight with bugs buzzing and shadows creeping.

We power-walked past set-back houses with front porches. Our feet pat-patted on the sidewalk. I walked balance-beam style on the curb while Jared rubbed his hands together to keep warm. Jared said,

"I'm glad you started coming out with us again. I felt like you and Lindsay were married."

"Did you like Lindsay, though?" Jared's opinion of my girlfriends always mattered to me. He was circumspect.

"I liked Lindsay. I thought she was really nice, but not for you. You drop off the face of the earth when you have a girlfriend, man."

"Was she your favorite ex-girlfriend of mine?"

"No, believe it or not my favorite was Tiffany. You could joke around with her and she didn't stop you from going out and having fun with your friends."

I started feeling pretty nervous because Cady came all the way up from Massapequa Park on the Long Island Railroad and then took a three-hour bus from the Port Authority by herself just to spend one night in New Paltz with me. Here I was in New Paltz with Jared, and neither me or Jared or Cady had a place of our own but had to sleep at Mike's where people didn't crash 'til cocks crowed. This was only my third time seeing Cady, and the first time she would be stone sober. So I started thinking about the six million things that could go wrong with [my perception of] a Long Island girl mixing with me and my friends. But then I thought how odd and unlikely the whole situation was to begin with, that I'd met Cady at a hippy bar and sent her a postcard of Albany, and then met up with her a month later while Mike and I and she were drunk and all happened to be in New Paltz again, and how for the hell of it she decided to come up and meet some of my drunk friends on this particular night.

"She must be a pretty interesting girl to make a road trip all the way up here just to see you for one night, dude," Jared said. "She must be pretty spontaneous and shit."

When Jared said that, all of my anxiety turned into anticipation like the first incline on a roller coaster, when you've *click-click-click*ed to the top and start falling, gaining speed—when you can't help but hang on and maybe throw your hands up and just let go and let whatever is happening happen and maybe even open your eyes and see it racing toward you and there she was with a big suitcase sitting under a naked light-bulb on the bus station porch, waving across the empty lot.

"That's her," I said to Jared.

"I figured."

The three of us converged in the middle of the parking lot, smiling, and I looked at Cady wondering whether to extend my hand. But we hugged each other. Then we talked at once.

"Cady this is Jared; Jared, Cady."

"Sorry I'm late, I missed the bus and had an hour-and-a-half with nothing to do in the Port Authority. So I had three Jack and Cokes and *weeow*, I was feeling it for a little while you know?" Jared smiled at me and she started talking to him at a mile a minute as I dragged her suitcase. I had a feeling everything was going to be alright with those two. On the walk back to Mike's I clinked a stick along a chain-link fence and jumped on benches and curbs spinning and talking. Maybe we even sang a Sinatra song all three of us together. Mostly Jared and Cady did the talking because they were feeling each other out.

"So, Mike's house isn't exactly the *Hilton*," I felt the need to insert.

"Oh it's okay, I've slept in some pretty sketchy places," Cady said.

"Oh...good."

When we got back to the party a wall of cigarette smoke hit us in the face. There were about fifty more people in the kitchen than when we'd left. When I brought Cady's stuff up to Mike's room, we had to practically elbow our way through the crowd. A group were funneling beers off the staircase, another were playing Flipcup, there were tokers lighting up around a coffee table, even a fat guy walking around with a white mouse in his hand showing everybody and making the girls scream. I did the introduction thing which got old fast but before I knew it Cady was having a conversation with two girls that neither of us knew and she gave me a look that said *Go have fun you don't have to baby-sit me I can make friends* and I left her there and it was spectacular. I got in with Jared on another game of Beer Pong, now and then throwing Cady a wave. She'd wave back with a cigarette in her hand and sixteen bracelets on her arm, with a smile on her face having a good ole time.

And the evening wore on. Everybody sucking up the nectar of new experience. At one point Jared grabbed me and, with a very serious expression on his face, said, "Dude what I said before about Tiffany I gotta change. This is my new favorite of your girlfriends." I was tempted not to correct him—Cady was not my girlfriend—and I gave in to the temptation and didn't.

We all ended up in Mike's room watching Mike's favorite episodes of *Saved by the Bell*. At that point I found myself sitting on the floor with a girl I was trying to impress and I couldn't get Mike or Jared away from the computer to hit up the bars.

"Come on, this is lame," I complained.

"Relax. I'm having fun," Cady assured me.

But I didn't want to sit on Mike's dirty floor watching bad television. I got Cady to leave and apologized for the night being boring. As we fell out the door into the early-morning night I wanted to grab her and squeeze her and spend all night wrapped up someplace enveloped in hot breath. Who knows what happened at the bar. When we got back everybody was asleep and we found a pull-out couch downstairs to lie on. I wanted to pull that girl through my skin and bones down to the cornerstones of my nerves. She changed into a pair of shorts in front of me. Soon we fell asleep together, just kissing and running our fingers through each other's hair, her left arm over my shoulder and our hearts lined up, feeling each other beating through our chests, beating because there were now reasons to beat with enthusiasm. I felt I was lying on the very threshold precipice of the present, with a life-changing possibility in the crook of my neck, smelling of *Herbal Essence* with traces of Jack and Coke.

I woke up in the morning because a blonde girl who looked like she'd slept in a make-up container was standing outside the bathroom door, and the bathroom door was right beside our pull-out couch. I laid in my boxer shorts with the covers pulled up around my chest, freezing, with Cady's head on the nape of my neck. After we lay there for a while Cady started making snorting noises and thrashing around because she wanted to get up. I would've laid there until I got bed sores. She surprised me, then. She shot her hand up out of the covers and, with her camera phone, snapped a picture of the two of us right as I was nibbling her earlobe. Later, Jared would look at that grainy photo and tell me Cady looked like she was crying.

We got off the futon and dressed. Cady donned a pair of pink and camo pants with a tank top, about a dozen necklaces of plastic pearls and wood beads hanging to various lengths, and her sixteen colorful bracelets. I donned my outfit from the night before: an old pair of jeans I'd borrowed from Jared and a shirt with a pool ball over the left breast. The house was quiet. But we were rearing to go with the melancholy knowledge that Cady had to leave in a few hours. So we hopped into my car and started driving around. It was just a little chilly that October morning, just a little moist with dew. We drove down route 32 toward a mountain Cady had climbed earlier in the year and blasted *Me and Bobby McGee* with all the windows down. We blasted that song as loud as my car speakers could handle. Without worrying how our voices sounded we sang out—yelled out the lyrics at the tops of our lungs—*Freedom's just another word for*—then dropped our voices low and pulled up from our stomachs—*nothin' left to lose*—and up again, screaming, hollering now—*nothing! A'int nothing hun if it a'int free!* Stopped at a red-light we continued blasting and singing that song. We took off down a pavement path that seemed to extend forever as Janis began all of those *nah-nah-nah-nahs* at the end of the song, and I listened to see if Cady knew all the ups and downs and notes of that crazy last part (because I did) and sure enough she knew every one of them too so that by the end of the song we were both out of breath and laughing and thinking to ourselves, "I have never met anyone like this person sitting next to me."

We picked up Jared and had some breakfast at Micky-D's as Cady and he talked up a storm. The McDonalds had dispensers for the honey mustard and the barbeque sauce and I told Cady I was going to design my own house someday with barbeque sauce dispensers in it and faucets that soda came out of. Jared suggested they be beer faucets. Back out in the parking lot as we walked to my car the clouds cleared and the sun shined down on us suddenly like a cathedral. Along the wall of McDonalds, through a layer of wood chips, delicate flowers sprouted with purple and red swirls adorning their petals. So Cady, Jared and I, a trio of wandering poets now, walked over to these flowers and admired them for being the most ancient pieces of Art to decorate the world. Cady picked a flower and put it in her hair. I speculated that flowers and young women are the two prettiest things that nature created. All the philosophical talk, and the sun breaking through and burning off the morning dew, made us want to see more of nature. So we doubled back to Mike's and picked him up and drove to a little park on the banks of the Wallkill River.

Beneath our feet dry leaves crackled. From the riverbank we gazed at the water slowly floating downstream. It smelled of peat moss and mud. Birds tweeted and flitted from one branch to another. A driftwood tree limb bobbed; it had four green leaves. Jared remarked,

"It would be so awesome to take a boat all the way down to the city and shit."

In the moment, we all imagined our imagination's version of what a trip down the whole Hudson River to New York City would entail.

"Yeah," I said, feeling sort of anxious at idly imagining something we couldn't do, "but where're *we* going to get a boat?"

"True," Jared said, deflated. "Did you see that movie with Will Smith where they take two jet skis to the city?"

Everybody said yeah except me. Cady looked over the water as Mike observed,

"You know, you could canoe all the way to the city if you wanted."

Jared and I sighed. That wasn't the same as having a boat that you could float and relax on with friends. Canoeing seemed like a lot of work and I didn't know how to do it. I'd never been in a canoe.

We sighed some more, then we were silent for a second. We were all sad for different reasons, because Cady was leaving and Jared and my road trip was over, and nobody knew the next time we would see anyone else in our little bevy of new friends. Even our idle conversation was premised on the impossible.

"Man…" Jared stared across the muddy water and trailed off.

"How hard do you think it would be to like, build a raft or something and float down the river?" I asked.

Jared and Cady laughed as Mike scratched his face.

"I think we could do it." Jared and Cady chuckled. Mike continued, "Well I mean, it could be done. We could do it if we wanted to."

"Why don't we do it?" I asked, sort of egging on Mike but also feeling like we could do such a thing easily if we felt like it. I wanted to shift the conversation to something that was potentially fun. Sensing my enthusiasm Mike adopted a cautious tone.

"Well, what would we do, what are we going to build it out of?"

Jared and Cady forced a "*Ha.*"

"Well, it'd be easy," I answered evenly, so that Jared and Cady would see that Mike and I were honestly exploring a potentiality rather than being flippant. That way they might contribute to the conversation. "All you'd need is some wood and a bunch of like, you know, floaty shit. And you could just float down the river when the tide was going out, and tie up when the tide came back in. Then when it goes out again, just untie and keep going. It would be easy."

"The tide changes twice a day," said Mike, who'd been a Boy Scout. "It comes up for six hours and goes out for six hours. Comes up and goes out. And the time it changes changes every day."

Now Jared and Cady were silent.

"So what? You'd have to tie off twice a day. Easy." I said.

"Well I suppose we *could* do it," said Mike, almost cynically, "but why would we *want* to?"

"To go to New York City."

"I'm down," Jared declared.

Mike turned toward Jared and displayed surprised remonstrance. Then he turned back toward me, taking a deep breath, and arched one eyebrow higher than the other. "Have you heard of a train or a car or any of the other means of transportation that exist that aren't ridiculous?"

"Yes yes, but I want to go to New York on a raft," I affirmed. "It would be fun. We could do it. I mean, it would be pretty easy and it's just a raft, we could like, party on it and see the whole river."

"Count me in," said Jared. Mike smiled as if to say *Okay, I understand you're baiting me, I'm going to take the bait and see where this leads.*

"Well, what are we going to build it out of?"

"You know, stuff that floats," I said to Mike.

"And where will we get this stuff that floats?"

"You know, people, businesses."

"So we're just going to float down the river on a bunch of — pretty much other people's garbage?"

"It wouldn't have to be other people's garbage. We could, like, get donations from businesses," I said. Jared added,

"I bet mad businesses would give you like, barrels and shit if you asked. Dusty's father is a member of the Coxsackie Yacht Club. Maybe like, *Saratoga Springwater* would give you a coupla 5-gallon things if you asked."

"Exactly. I have mad old pallets and wood and nails. We could build it at my house which is a mile from the river," I said.

"I bet the local newspaper would come. There's nothing else going on in Ravena," Jared said. Still visibly deciding if we were serious, Mike inquired,

"And what are we going to say when people ask us what we're doing?"

"We'll tell everyone we're protesting America's reliance on fossil fuels," I said, and everyone laughed.[6]

Now a grin swept over Mike's face. We gave in to speculating what we would need as though we were *definitely* planning the trip, laughing as everyone else played along.

"We *should* do this. How hard would it be? We get a bunch of wood and floaty shit and tie it together and if it's ugly who cares it'll be fun." We laughed and Mike added, "The more shitty the thing looks the better. Like, milk cartons and fucking, I donno, barrels and shit, ha ha!"

"You guys won't do it," Cady interjected. The males turned to her with snide smirks. That was all we needed to hear. We were pouncing on the idea and piggy-backing off each other's contributions by this point.

"Oh, we'll do it!" I said.

"I've got a big American flag we can bring," Mike said.

"We'll dress up in like, pirate costumes!" I said.

"We can put up a giant pirate flag!" Jared suggested.

"Arrr me hearty!" I mimicked. "This'll be awesome!" Jared laughed,

"Protesting America's reliance on fossil fuels, that's funny man."

We chuckled and said words like "excellent" while rubbing our hands.

"You guys are full of shit," Cady said. "But I hope you do it."

"Oh," Mike and I warned simultaneously, "we *will*."

Possibly, that was the most significant conversation of my life.

---

[6] In 2005 only a 'crazy granola liberal' might suggest a protest of America's reliance on foreign fossil fuels. Generally the public was apathetic. The suggestion was so silly as to make the project a *happening*; we might as well have said that we were doing it for no purpose at all, except that we thought we would be clever and provide the cheeky answer to the *News Herald*, our hometown newspaper.

II. Flood Tide

Just like that—*poof!*—Cady was gone, chugging along on that big rectangle bus headed south. Jared and I bade farewell to Mike and hopped onto the Thruway for an hour's drive back to New Baltimore. By that point the morning gray had evaporated into a sunny afternoon. Jared rolled down the passenger window, reclined his seat, and crossed his legs at the ankles under the dash. I pushed a CD into the console. It was the mix for the trip—a road trip tradition—with some easy Sunday morning artists like Jack Johnson, Dispatch, and Janis Joplin. Mostly a lot of acoustic stuff to help with headaches and nausea. Jared pulled a piece of crumpled yellow paper from a pocket in his jeans.

"What's that?" I switched the track to *Badfish* as Jared scanned the sheet.

"Some stuff I wrote last night after you and Cady went to the bar. I hung around with Mike. We chilled. He's a pretty interesting guy." While Mike and Jared were two of my closest friends, the two had never hung out *mono y mono* before. It piqued my interest that Jared would keep notes about his conversation with Mike. I'd carried a *Moleskine* notebook to record pieces of conversations, songs to download, books to read, and so forth for three years, but Jared had never adopted the habit. Now he had crumpled notes on a piece of paper, and was joining in on this new river raft adventure, which was also out of character. The sight of Jared reviewing his notes from the night before made me realize there were aspects to his personality a lot of people didn't see because he had spiked hair and wore collared, brand-named shirts. It was something I suppose I'd perceived, but never really noticed. It was warming to remember we were friends partly because we shared this curiosity, which he hid in mixed company. "I think I'm gonna start carrying around paper to write shit on," Jared said.

"Oh yeah?"

"Yeah, Mike said a bunch of interesting stuff." He scanned the yellow scrap, "Like about the News being like a prime-time TV show with a theme song and characters and plot developments and everything." His eyes moved down the page. "I've got a bunch of new song names written here too."

"Good for you man." The CD skipped so I hit the button that looked like two triangles in a conga line and the intro to the next song began. It was Peggy Lee's version of *Why Don't You Do Right*, with a slow, jive, stand-up-bass progression. It was the only bluesy song on the mix so I moved my hand toward the "skip" button but Jared stopped me.

"Hold up, I wanna hear this song."

"Okay." After two measures of bluesy bass, Lee began, as slow and syncopated as the instrumental melody, saucing out the lyrics. I imagined a woman crooning to a smoky cocktail lounge.

"Is this jazz?"

"Yeah, I think you could call it jazz," I mused. As we listened, the song picked up tempo and added more instruments, I mused more. "I feel like the slow pace at the beginning of the song adds to the suspense that gets built up as the song goes on, getting faster and adding more instruments."

"Yeah it's cool. I like this. I feel like you don't hear shit like this in music these days. It's almost like…the instruments are more important or something. Mad relaxing."

"It's like the singer's voice is just another instrument, and all the instruments, including the singer's voice, are all playing different melodies. And the way the melodies mix together is what's most interesting, and the lyrics themselves are almost coincidental. Whereas today it's like we expect lyrics to be the defining part of the song, and the music is more background."

"Yeah, exactly. Yo you got a pen? I wanna write this song down and download it."

"In the glove compartment."

"Thanks."

"No problem. I'm surprised you like it."

"Dude I wanna hear more of this kinda shit. Like, how do you even know this kind of music? Like, how would I know what to even look up to hear this kind of shit? I feel like no one else listens to this stuff."

"I only know it because it's what my grandparents listened to. It's funny because like, when I started hanging out with you senior year of high school, I didn't know any of the songs you guys were playing, like, *Sublime* and *Third Eye Blind* and *Green Day* and shit, and I didn't understand how you guys knew all those songs. My dad listened to records of 50's music all the time at home, and 50's and 60's music in the car, so I knew all that stuff. But then, at Grandma's house—I used to go over every day as a kid—she had a phonograph and used to play records. I loved this three-record set called "Three Great Big Bands of Our Time" – I still have it and play them. They were Tommy Dorsey, Glen Miller and Benny Goodman. Anyhow I was a kid, right? And I didn't know what music I was *supposed* to listen to, just what I *liked*. So I'd want to play Tommy Dorsey sometimes at my parent's house, and my dad would be like 'Yo why we gotta listen to this old shit, can't we play 50's music?' ha ha. And then when I went to college I'd play 50's music and my friends would be like 'Yo why we gotta listen to this old shit, can't we hear 90's music?' So I feel like I can't win."

"Yeah and in a couple of years, we'll probably play *Sublime* at a party and the kids who're ten right now will be like, 'Yo why can't we listen to 2000's shit?'"

"Yeah and it'll probably be like, computers singing or something."

"Yeah. I like this shit though. I wanna hear more jazz. Let's go to see jazz someplace. Where do we go?"

"I donno. I bet we can find someplace. Now that I'm 21 we can get in. We can wear suits and stuff. Dude I would love that. We can visit Pritesh in New York City and go to the *Blue Note*."

"Yeah, I'm down. Man, mad new shit. Now I'm friends with Mike, we're gonna go hear some new music, we're gonna go down the Hudson River, ha ha. This is what life's all about, buddy."

In a little while Jared fell asleep in the passenger seat, and I pretended I was Dean Moriarty from *On the Road* sailing my Chrysler Cirrus around the bends like a boat, as Kerouac described it. The tips of the leaves were turning colors in the bustling clouds of trees to the right and left. The foliage was Beautiful-Sad, which should be a color in a crayon box. Fifty miles away Cady was on the same highway moving at seventy miles an hour in the opposite direction. Together we were moving apart at a hundred and forty. I knew it was going to be a lonely, hard, long winter, as they all are, so I turned up the easy music. I looked over at Jared who was snoring just a little. I noted the end of a successful road trip.

Probably like most people, when I pictured a raft I pictured the raft from *Huck Finn*. That was a driftwood raft, more or less. I think it was made of tree trunks lashed together. But how could I build a raft of lashed logs? I didn't have land by the riverside where I could cut logs so they fell into the water. My parents of course had lots of trees on their property, about a mile from the river, but if I were to ask my father if I could cut ten trees in order to build a raft he would say (correctly) that trees are more valuable as firewood, and to cut ten trees would degrade the property value. And besides, even if I could cut trees down at my parent's house, how would I then get them to the river? They wouldn't fit in the pickup truck, like so many 30-gallon garbage cans full of leaves. And then how would I unload them at the river, and where? No, logs wouldn't work for our raft. We'd have to think of something else.

Perhaps because I spent so much time alone, especially while driving to work and school and back, I started to think about how we could build a raft every day. *If the Indians could do it, I can do it*, I thought. *After all, the Indians didn't have any of the technology we have today.* Driving from the country to Albany I noted a hollow door out for "Free" along the road. *Would that float? That could make a good platform to stand on.* A local warehouse had pallets stacked up for free in their parking lot. *Four or eight of those would make an excellent, and free, frame to hold the floaty shit.*

It had to be free, of course, because I was broke, and it showed.

"Are you on drugs or something?" my father asked one night as I read *Biospsychology* at the kitchen counter.

"What?"

"You work but you never have any money. You look like shit, tired. I'm just making sure you're not addicted to dope or something."

"No, I'm not on drugs."

I was broke because my sister and I were planning a secret twenty-fifth wedding anniversary for my parents and I was giving her some money each week as soon as I got paid. After taxes I brought home about $150 for working 20 hours a week, $50 of that went to my sister for the party, another $30 to gas. Then my cell phone bill. I was lucky if I had $20 at the end of the week. So any raft components had to be, as the hipsters call it, "found" or "reclaimed" material.

As a last hurrah before the winter, Mike, Jared, me and eight others made a road trip to western New York to watch the annual *Cortaca* game between Ithaca and the State University at Cortland, in mid-November. It's a big festival day; Ithaca was filled with tens of thousands of people celebrating. We started drinking around 7:30 in the morning and I was buzzed by the time of the game. Mike and I got separated from the rest of Jared's friends but found a spot on the bleachers on the fifty-yard line. Midway through the first quarter, my mind started wandering from the *action* to the *rules* of the game.

"Huh," I shouted to Mike amidst the din of the crowd. "You know, I never really thought about it before. The end 'zones' are zones — physical spaces, and if the football enters one of those zones, points accumulate."

"Yeah."

"And the two teams, they have various ways of getting the ball there. I mean there are thousands or hundreds of thousands of permutations that can be deployed to convey the ball in remembered patterns down the field. And the other team has to guess which permutation will be employed in a given tactical situation, and they have hundreds of thousands of permutations that their players can deploy to prevent the movement of the ball in one direction. Fascinating!"

"That's football, Dallas."

"Right. But the referee. That's the really interesting part. I guess I always thought of a referee as like, secretly cheering for one side, and the reason you had to have several referees was to make sure that each side had a couple of referees on its side. But that's not how it is at all. The referee's job is just to make sure that the rules are followed, because you can't have a game unless you have rules. Without rules it's just people fighting, chaos, a state of nature. The rules are what make it interesting because it limits the activity to certain movements. It gives people something to expect, provides a framework, but there's still enough creativity that a play can be made within the rules and still be a surprise to the observers."

"Hey, you know, there's a game going on..."

At an after-party I found myself with Mike and Jared standing around the keg. I touched my *Solo Cup* to Mike's and Jared's and I brought up the raft for the first time since we'd had the idea two months before.

"I have a bunch of old tires in the woods at my house," I said. "We could take those and build a platform on top of it." Mike stared at me vacantly. "I mean for the raft."

"Wow, jeeze, I forgot all about that," Mike said. "You're serious about doing that?"

I was a shocked to hear that Mike hadn't been thinking about how we could build the raft every day. Maybe we'd been jocular at the river when we'd first discussed the idea, but I thought the jocularity was to hide what might be called *nerdishness* — excitement at doing a strange and esoteric thing with two other guys — in front of Cady. To each other, I thought, we knew we were sincere.

"Of course I'm serious about it. I think it would be a hell of a time. Don't you think it would be fun to see the whole river from New Baltimore to New York City?"

That suspicious look, as though he was being baited, crossed Mike's face, but quickly faded.

"Yeah, it would be fun. But it'd be a lotta work, too. And we'd look a little silly." I blinked.

"Silly? So what?" I pointed at Mike's head. "You're wearing a yellow wig [Ithaca's colors are purple and yellow] in front of all these people. And work...I don't think it'll be that much work. You built a treehouse by yourself at your parent's house two years ago. I think we could build a platform and tie some water jugs or something underneath it."

Across the room two males bellowed and three girls screeched and laughed at a table playing Quarters. We instinctively looked toward the noise, then back at one another. Mike extended his hand with his palm toward the ceiling and arched his head to the side.

"Okay, but I'm going to be in New Paltz until I graduate, and then I want to look for a job. I can't help at all with building the thing until I'm done with school."

"Obviously," I said. "I have so much shit going on it's ridiculous too."

"Yeah," Jared cut in, (I was waiting for his support), "but you have all that land and junk and shit at your parent's house. I could help you like, get floaty stuff and bring it to New Baltimore. I mean how hard can it be? It's not like it's gonna be pretty. It won't take long to build, right?"

"Wow so you're serious about this too?" Mike asked Jared.

"Yeah man I'm always down for an adventure. I think it'd be mad *kewl*." Mike and I laughed. Jared was good at saying silly things to dissipate tension. He continued, "But I mean, I like to camp. I like to booze. I think it would be cool to see the river and shit and have a story to tell people. I mean who else has gone from our town to New York City, even on a boat, that we know? No one. It'll be like a road trip, except on a piece of shit raft. We might meet a bunch of people. Maybe some bitches will want to come with us." Mike adopted a cut-the-bullshit tone,

"I think it's pretty unlikely that girls are going to see us floating on garbage and want to join us. 'Hey Jen, check out these guys on their sweet raft. Fuck this 35-foot Bayliner that goes 70 miles an hour. I wanna hang out with *these* guys!'"

"Ha, ha, true," Jared conceded. "But maybe they'd want to chill with us like, at night if we're tied up on some beach and have a bonfire and beers."

"And if not, fuck em," I said. "I think it'll be exciting just to see all the big boats and bridges and stuff. The river part is the nicest part of town in New Baltimore and Coeymans. The architecture and the old docks. I wonder the last time anyone has floated on a raft from upstate to New York City." Mike was outnumbered two to one.

"And you guys are going to build it, and I can come, and it will be after school is done?"

"Yes."

"Okay. Okay, yeah. And I could help. I mean, I can help a little. It's only an hour away from New Paltz and I do come home to visit my parents and stuff. But I just don't see like, how you're going to build it."

"Well," I declared grandly, sweepingly. "If the Indians could do it, we can do it."

"—Ha! Okay..."

I explained my philosophy of problem-solving:

"I mean that this first part was the really important part—like *agreeing* that we *are* going to do it. And now we agreed. We can iron out the details. I mean, we're not a bunch of dumb idiots. I think we can figure out how to do something that people figured out how to do in like, 5,000 B.C."

"Yeah I mean we went to college," Jared added. I pumped the lever on the keg. Mike speculated,

"We went to college. I don't know about you, but I didn't take any raft-building classes."

"I was going to take one at SUNY but it got cut along with the Classics program," I joked.

"Ha, ha, right. In this modern culture of ours all the great arts are dead. Latin, Greek tragedy, raft construction." Mike tilted his solo cup under the keg spigot as I continued to pump.

"You guys say some funny shit," Jared said. "How do you come up with this shit?"

"I donno," I said. Mike continued,

"But okay, let's say you get 'floaty shit' somehow, which I still don't really understand how you're going to do—"

"—I'll find a way—"

"—Okay so let's say you do. How long do you think it'll take to get to New York City?" Jared glanced at me for insight. I had no idea. "Okay, see? These are things that we should be thinking about." Mike drank from his foamy cup as Jared tilted his beneath the spigot, and my forearm began to ache from pumping.

"This is exactly why you are perfect for this trip, Mike. It's like a mission, you know? We each have parts and skills. I'm the idea guy and I'll put the thing together, you know, assume responsibility for making it. So I'll be the Captain."

"Of course," Mike said.

"And you're the guy with all the strategic knowledge, from your days as a Boy Scout and canoeing and stuff, and you know about New York City —"

"I do?"

"Better than I do."

"Boy Scout knowledge, huh?"

"Well you know about the tides, building things. The knowledge we'll need to plan the whole thing. So you're like the Admiral, in charge of orchestrating the whole campaign. And I'm the Captain, taking over once the mission starts and making sure the mission is accomplished."

"Admiral Michael. Ha! I like that. You know that means I out-rank you."

"While on land," I said.

"Okay."

"What am I?" Jared asked.

"Well you're First Mate."

"Sweet," he saluted us with his foamy beer. "What do I do?"

"Well you're second in command while on the boat, and you're in charge of all away missions. You know, like if we have to go to shore to get something, and so on."

"I'm down. I'll be in charge of making sure we have beer." Jared pumped so I could refill my plastic cup.

"The guy who's in charge of provisions on a ship is the *quartermaster*," Mike said.

"Yo I'm a *whole* master, not just a quarter," I said buffoonishly.

"I'm a master baiter," Jared added.

"Twice a day?"

"Yo like six times."

"Yeah, okay," said Mike. "So, again, how long do you think it's going to take us to get there?"

"Well, here we go. This is what I'm saying, let's think about it logically and figure out what the answer is. And we'll do the same with every problem that comes up, now that we know we're serious, and we'll accomplish what we want to do. So, okay, let's see. The tide goes out for twelve hours and comes in for twelve hours, right?"

"The tide is based on the moon —"

"No shit?"

"Yeah, on the pull of the moon's gravity on the ocean. It pulls the ocean up toward the moon on the side of the earth that's facing the moon. The closer you get to the ocean, the bigger the tides you get. But this happens *twice* a day—I'm not quite sure why. I mean that you have *two* low tides every day and *two* high tides every day."

"It's the same time every day, two times?" Jared asked.

"No, because it's based on the moon's rotation. So it changes every day."

"There must be a pattern to it, that we can figure out," I said.

"Yeah, or you could just go to a marina and get a tide chart," Mike said.

"What's that?"

"A schedule of the high tides and low tides that they publish for boaters, because it affects the depth of the river channel."

"See? Mike, you're full of useful information. It is an honor to serve under an Admiral like you."

"So how long will it take?" said Jared impatiently.

"Okay, well, let's say the tide comes in and goes out twice a day. That's four tides." Mike held four fingers up. "There are 24 hours in a day. So each tide lasts roughly six hours."

"So we launch the boat at the end of a high tide, and ride the tide until it's low tide, and then we drop an anchor so that we don't go backwards when the new tide comes back in. And we would like, chill and drink and shit for those six hours, and then untie our anchor or whatever when it's high tide again, and ride it out until low tide. So we're talking 12 hours of movement a day, and 12 hours of not going anywhere."

"Some of the hours when we're not going anywhere we can sleep, because we'll need to sleep," Jared said. "And then like, the other couple of hours, maybe we can explore the towns, go to shore and eat and stuff. I'd like to bring a fishing pole even though the Hudson is fucking dirty as fuck."

"Yeah I'd like to fish," said Mike, "but we can't eat it. In fact, I'm not even sure if you can swim in the Hudson. But anyway, so we have twelve hours of movement provided by the tide. And how fast would you say the water is moving?" Jared looked at me. I took a guess,

"I'd say, what, three miles an hour? On the treadmill three miles an hour is walking speed. I used to go for a walk to the river every March with my dad when it became spring, and we'd watch the icebergs float down. It seemed like it was going about a casual walking pace. I think walking pace is three miles an hour. Can you believe that Roman Legions on forced marches used to march eight miles an hour, for hours, with all of their equipment and armor?"

"Okay so let's say, conservatively, three miles an hour. Times twelve hours a day, is 36 miles a day. Now, New York City is like 150 miles from Albany, right?" Jared and I shrugged. "Yeah, it's 150 miles, at least by the Thruway. New Baltimore is closer, but the river isn't a straight line, it's all bendy and stuff, so let's just say we have to cover about 150 miles. By the way, what is the goal? The Battery at the tip of Manhattan? The very top of the island? That's where technically New York City begins. But the island is eight miles long, and it's going to be pretty busy with ships and shit down there."

"The goal is just to get to New York City," I said.

"Okay. Right at the top of New York City is where the George Washington Bridge is. Let's say our goal is the George Washington Bridge. So that's 150 miles, divided by 36 miles a day, is, shit—" Mike nodded and rubbed his chin, "—that's only like five days."

"Doable," Jared declared.

"I can do five days on the river," I said.

"Yeah," said Mike, slowly, looking up and to the left, into his brain, and folding his hands, then lightly punching his fist into his palm. "Yeah that's...I thought it would take like, at least ten days. Is this right?" His pupils shot upward and his hand returned to his chin, then he nodded and looked at me. "Yeah, the math is right. Five days. Huh. Wow. Well, that does seem pretty easy. Right? I mean, is that right?"

"It makes sense to me!" I said, taking advantage of Mike's movement. "So, five days on the river, and then we have a story we'll always remember."

"Yeah...yeah I guess you're right. I mean, what the hell, right? I'm getting done with college. Then, what, I'll get a job at some bullshit place and—let's be realistic—probably get a house, get married. This could be like, the last hurrah of being young and having a life."

"It'll be like the old days," Jared said. "I can get a week off work. I could *use* a week off work. All I do is like, work and shit now. It'd be mad fun and we could have a send-off party and invite our friends."

"If Cady and I are dating at that point, she could meet us in the city with beers when we arrive," I said. "She would get a big kick out of doing that."

"Okay, yeah, I'm down," Mike reaffirmed. Mike was like a heavy iron ball sometimes. It took a good amount of energy to get him moving, but once he gained momentum he was hard to stop. "I like this idea. I like the idea of telling the papers. *The News Herald* will definitely come. We'll get the first page. Imagine us, all dressed up and shit in pirate costumes. Yo, I say we go all-out for this. Why not call a bunch of businesses, all serious, and try and get donations and shit? 'We're protesting America's reliance on fossil fuels,' ha ha, that's great. It'll be like, 'Are they serious?' and the joke is on them! Ha ha ha!"

"Ha," I laughed cautiously. "It'll be fun. I think we could get maybe some materials donated, but I don't know about money donations."

"We could tell them we're accepting sponsorships!" Mike finished his beer and poured another. "Imagine we got like, *Huck Finn's Warehouse* and *Allstate Insurance* and *Lowes* and shit to sponsor us, and we floated down the river with mad like, logos and flags and shit?"

"Well..." I started to say.

"Yo," said Jared, "Maybe we could get a beer company to sponsor us. Then we could get mad free beer and drink for free on the trip."

"Yeah, but I don't think—" I started to say.

"We should try to get in all the local papers, and make it a big joke," said Mike. "Can you imagine if we call these local papers and shit, and then they all send out reporters. The reporters will be like, '*This* is my story?' Ha. Yo, when we get to New York, we should call up David Letterman and see if we can get on. He covers weirdo shit like that all time."

"Okay, but like, it shouldn't be *just* a joke," I said.

"Oh, come on," Mike argued. "How can it not be a joke?"

I stumbled articulating my feeling, that it was somehow not a joke. That it could not be both one last hurrah and also a farce. "I mean we're just doing something we wanna do. We can dress up or whatever, but..."

"I'm down for whatever," Jared said.

"Yeah," I said, "but like, we can't really say we're protesting America's reliance on fossil fuels, and then follow it up with just dressing up weirdly and trying to make reporters feel uncomfortable. I think, you know, there should be more of a point to it than that."

"Oh, come on," Mike sneered. "The whole thing is silly to begin with. It doesn't have to make sense."

"I donno. Let's agree that we're going to do this, and we'll iron out the details, say, over the next couple months, and figure out how we're gonna do it."

"Yeah, yeah, cool. I'll try and come up with some designs," Mike said. "We should all be on the lookout for like, wood that's on the side of the road and shit. Building materials."

"Great," I said. "I'll try and get some pallets, and if I see wood on the side of the road I'll get my dad's truck and throw it in. Then we just need floaty shit."

"Yo I got nothing to do all day at work besides watch DVDs and play Miniputt on addictinggames.com," Jared observed. He worked in a different branch of the same office where I was employed. "I can use the internet to find some local businesses and call them and ask for donations."

"Okay, well, it sounds like we have a plan, and that's the first step toward anything. Let's say we'll think about things over the holidays and maybe try to touch base in like, February. Maybe we could do some work on the thing during Spring Break."

"Yeah, and when is our target launch date?" Mike asked.

"How about June 1st? It'll be warm. We'll be done with school. Mike probably won't have like, a steady job yet."

We agreed. There was just enough of a silence that Jared felt obliged to add,

"This is gonna be great."

I changed the subject, then, so that the raft would not get tiresome.

Cady came up for the first time on the day after Thanksgiving, 2005. I met her at the bus station in New Paltz. She got off the bus dragging a suitcase and two dresses, wearing her pink and camo pants, a pair of big sunglasses, with a CD walkman and a set of headphones in her ears, with a colorful, light, loose-fitting top like Mary Kate Olsen would wear, her nine beaded necklaces and her sixteen bracelets jangling. On my right arm I wore the four beaded bracelets she'd given me. I wore them in a specific pattern and never took them off. I opened my arms for a hug as she dropped her bags to the gravel and jumped on me like a koala bear, wrapping her legs around my back, in front of all the other passengers. I blushed, smiled, and spun her around.

"It's so good to see you," I said.

"You too Dal."

She put her suitcase in the back of the car and hung her dresses from the hooks that fold out of the roof in the back seats of cars. She jumped into the front seat and put her feet on the dash.

"Don't forget your seatbelt," I said.

"Bah!"

"Nope, come on, we're not going anywhere until you put your seatbelt on."

"Boo you square. I never wear a seatbelt."

"Well, you should. Come on. If we got in an accident or something, it'd be my fault, and I couldn't forgive myself if something happened to you."

"Oh, fine." She clicked her seatbelt and we drove the hour back up the Thruway to New Baltimore, blasting oldies music and Jack Johnson. During the fast, syncopated, funky songs we sang together. During the mellow songs Cady looked out the window, to get her bearings.

We'd talked almost every night on the phone, sometimes for hours, sometimes just making silly noises and laughing, and we'd kissed and cuddled and slept next to each other. But we didn't talk about the future. Such conversations made Cady recoil.

I'd told Cady I needed a date for two important events that weekend.

The Friday after Thanksgiving was a day I looked forward to all year. The first year that college started, a coterie of my friends from high school had formed a group we called the *Symposium Society*. Each Friday after Thanksgiving thereafter, we held a Symposium dinner party. We'd meet at my friend Oliver's parent's house because his folks were always out of town that night. It was a nice brick two-story house on a hill in Ravena. It was our only annual opportunity to wear suits and dresses. Each of the 10 or 12 guests brought bottles of wine and a drinking goblet. On a white stone pedestal, about three feet high, we set a punchbowl for the wine. There was an after-dinner *'programme'* which proceeded in Oliver's parlor. Each guest recited an essay, sang a song, or lectured about a topic of their choice. At intermission we ate brownies. The presentations of the second act grew vaudevillian. Afterward, free reign was given to nostalgic reminisces, conversations on new and interesting political topics, and finally a dance party to tasteful music.

"Are these dresses okay?" Cady asked when we'd brought her bags inside my parent's house. "I hope they're alright. You said dressy, so I brought this gold one for tonight, and the purple one for tomorrow."

We hid the purple dress because my folks descended the stairs to meet Cady. She jumped and energetically shook their hand. I made us cocktails at the bar I'd retrofitted from a flea market. My dad asked Cady what she was studying in school.

"Oh, you know, I think there's like, a biology class. Umm, I forget what else. I donno, I'm not really good at school. I go to Nassau Community College."

My father smiled, charmed, relieved. I passed Highballs to Cady, my dad and mother.

"Have you ever been upstate before?" my father asked.

"Oh, yeah. To like, New Paltz and stuff. I go hiking there with my aunts and my step mom, Becky. They have a house in Vermont on Bromley Mountain. They call it *Ski Haus*. They're all nice. But, yeah, this is different. I donno. I never like…dated?…a guy who lived in the country before."

"Well, you and Dallas'll have to go to bed early so you can get up at dawn and milk the cows," my father said.

"No shit, you have cows?" Cady eyes darted to mine, then my mom's, then my dad's.

"Ha, I'm just joking," dad said. Cady pushed my father's chest.

"Aww, come on! Making fun of the city girl! Ha ha, I was like 'You have cows! Cool!' I'd help you milk them! Ha ha, I donno, I'm full of shit."

It was lame if you didn't bring a date to the symposium. Cady was excited, if a little nervous, to meet my friends. She'd asked what she should do for a project. I told her she didn't have to do one, but she said "I'm not gonna be the fucking loser who doesn't participate." She performed a solo rendition of "Circle of Life," from *Lion King*, dancing with severity while pretending to hit bongos with her palms, then waving her arms to show a circle. It was ridiculous and exactly appropriate. I think she won everybody's goodwill during a moment when I was the center of a conversation around the dinner table. As I spoke I turned toward Cady, but suddenly choked, coughed, and spewed red wine into her face. My fellow dinner guests gasped. Cady wiped the wine from her eyes, sipped from her goblet, and blew cabernet through pursed lips across my face. Everyone gasped again. Then she threw her arms in the air and laughed "blahaha!" and kissed me, and it was very entertaining for everyone. After carousing for hours we ascended the stairs and crashed cuddling together.

The next day my sister and I surprised my parents with a 25th anniversary party. They didn't expect it because their anniversary was in July, and it was now November. They thought they were attending a surprise birthday party for my mother's sister. When they walked through the door of the Knights of Columbus where their wedding reception had been, and all of their friends yelled "surprise!" my mother shushed them and said "Wait! It's just us!" It took her a minute to realize the party was in their honor. My parents, my sister Laura and her husband Rodney, and Cady and I sat at a head table.

"I can't believe how in love your parents are," Cady said during dinner. She looked grief-stricken.

"It's nice," I said. "Are you alright?"

"I've never been to a wedding," Cady said. "This is the closest thing. Everybody seems so happy and in love. I've never seen anything like it. It's like, is this real? People are really *actually* happy like this? What is this place?"

After dinner there was dancing to oldies music. Cady danced to every song. I danced to some, then got tired and mingled, and she kept dancing with anybody who would dance. When no one else was on the floor she danced alone spinning in circles.

"Honey, she sure likes to dance, doesn't she?" said my grandmother, smiling.

"It looks like that girl'll tire you out," my grandfather said.

When the celebration ended we returned to New Baltimore and crawled into bed.

"I've never had a night like this," Cady said, laying there in almost darkness, staring at the ceiling.

"I had a good time. Did you?"

She nodded, still sadly staring, with a tear in the corner of her eye.

III. The Slack Water That Follows Flood Tide

Movement is essential.

From a molecular to a cosmic level, movement is necessary for life.

That which does not move is inanimate. Not even dead. At least the dead were once alive. The inanimate are but parts or pieces of the living.

Planets orbit the sun, and the earth has seasons, because planets move.

The moon orbits the earth, and creates tides, and mixes up the sea and the land and the sun.

That which moves has energy. Electrons move. Chemical reactions occur because electrons move. We are made of chemicals, constantly reacting. *Thought* occurs because electrons move. We can think because our minds are made of chemicals, constantly reacting.

The earth spins beneath the air, mixing temperatures, dryness and humidity, causing electrochemical reactions above the land, which give us storms, like a snow globe shaken.

A neuron fires because the chemicals outside the neural wall are negatively charged, and the ions inside the wall are positively charged, and when the difference is great enough, electricity flows, and the chemicals reach equilibrium.

The earth spins, positively charged ions accumulate in clouds, negatively charged ions accumulate on earth, there is static in the air, moisture acts as a conduit, lightning strikes — a massive exchange of ions reaching equal electrical charges, like a neuron firing — and the product is ozone. Spinning causes storms which cause ozone, and ozone causes atmosphere, and life needs atmosphere. Thought and living bodies and the universe are aspects of one continuum.

Like a cadence, Cady expressed herself through movement. Her tonic was dancing, her home chord Long Island. There were variations on the theme: drinking and dancing in New Paltz or Vermont, hanging at *Ski Haus* with *Cluster*, her family's hippy friends, and snowboarding. But she resolved to Long Island, which she considered superior and her future. And always she had to dance, to express herself through that most physical of the arts.

In the winter, when we started exchanging each other's energy, we evened out, like ice cubes in a cup of coffee, averaging one another.

"You know how it is when you take a test," she'd prattled when we first began talking. "You write in like 'a' 'a' 'a' 'a' 'a' on the first page, go to the next page, write in like 'b' 'b' 'b' 'b' 'b'. And then get the hell out of there!" To sit in one place and consider was torture for her. But after the winter and spring of 2006, as we talked every night for hours, she said, "I'm starting to feel like I need to get serious about school and quit this Community College shit. I don't want to be a preschool aide forever. But I don't even know how to like, begin looking into school. I'm so fucking dumb. Can you help me?"

I didn't have to ask Cady to help *me*. She was like Adderall to my mind and Prozac to my mood. After years of living like a Dostoyevsky character, suddenly I didn't need to worry about companionship, romance, the war against loneliness. I began writing with resolve, and finishing stories. I submitted to literary magazines. At least once a month I traveled to New York and Long Island, sometimes to Cady's Vermont ski house, tasted new foods, and met new kinds of people. I was exposed to new kinds of music and family structures. I learned to predict Cady's emotional movements and counteract the blue notes.

It was winter cold and I was still poor and living with my parents, freezing in my hand-me-down wool blazer because I didn't own a winter coat. But for me Cady was precedent-breaking. If I could make a relationship with Cady work, anything seemed possible, because we were so different from one another in background, interests and dispositions. It was a challenge to date her, but it showed I could overcome challenges if I was dedicated, and that was a lesson I wanted to abstract. If I could succeed with Cady by putting my mind to it, I *could* be a writer if I put my mind to it, too. I *could* juggle school and work and family and a relationship. I *could* someday travel and get a job that I actually wanted, rather than some mind-numbing office bullshit.

If dating Cady was an ethereal satisfaction, rafting to New York City became the most tangible goal I could achieve, and therefore the easiest to picture and latch onto. It was just a matter of performing the requisite steps, and that meant moving, actually doing, and not just thinking. Unlike "getting published" it didn't require the goodwill of strangers, I thought, just my own effort. And unlike "a career" it was going to happen soon, in just a couple of months, like Mike and Jared and I had planned. What I started to call "the raft project" symbolized that with a can-do spirit and a little energy a man can accomplish anything. I wanted to prove that to Cady, who hadn't seen me succeed at anything. I wanted to prove it to my family who were suspicious of any of my plans that didn't involve getting a job immediately after college. I wanted to prove it to friends, who hadn't seen me do anything interesting since high school. Of course, the person I wanted to prove it to most was myself.

No one believed I would raft to Manhattan. People acted like floating to Manhattan from New Baltimore was impossible. As if it couldn't be done if Newton himself put his mind to it. It made me start to wonder if it was *me* particularly that people perceived as impotent.

"What do you know about building a raft?" My father mocked as he, mom, Mike and I sat around the dinner table. Mike was visiting during winter break from New Paltz. We dined on spaghetti with tuna balls, because it was a Friday during Lent.

"What's to know?" I said. "You take a bunch of wood, nail it together, and *voila*! I'm not building a suspension bridge over Niagara Falls, I'm building a raft."

"You better watch out for them barges," my mother warned. She held up her fork with spaghetti dangling down, shaking her head. "You're gonna get your ass run over out there."

"He's not going to do it," my father dismissed.

"I *am* going to do it!" I tossed my napkin on my plate. "I can't understand why everyone thinks this is so impossible!" My father rolled his eyes.

"Because, Dallas, you don't know anything about building things or rivers or boating. You think you can just *do* these things."

"Why can't I?" Dad shook his head and frowned.

"Oh, Christ. Fine, *Einstein*, go ahead."

I nodded, acknowledging the minor victory of having removed at least the explicit prohibition of my parents and cohabitants.

"Can I use some of that wood you've got rotting over the hill?"

"That's good wood!" my father exclaimed sarcastically. "I've been collecting that wood for years!" Over a hill behind their house my parent's had thrown pieces of paneling, pallets, a couple of cut-up and moldy sheets of plywood—anything the garbage man wouldn't take away—easy chairs, lawn mowers, wagons, rusted burning barrels and tires. In a century the stuff would make a discovery for an archeologist. "Fine, take it," Dad declared. "Now, question: where are you going to build this thing? Not here I hope."

Of course I wanted to build the raft at my parent's house, where I lived, and where the materials were. But I conceded for the moment, in order not to push my parent's patience.

"I don't know yet."

"Well, I don't want a bunch of garbage all over my yard you know. Build it at Mike's." Mike stiffened across the table,

"I don't think my parents would be okay with that."

"And Jared is going with you two idiots?" Dad continued, "I bet he'll be a big help. And, by the way, how are you planning on getting this thing in the water once it's built?"

"I have to get the thing built before I worry about getting it in the water," I said. "I don't want to get hung up on a part of the problem that's four months away, and not work on what I can get done now. You know, I think that the only thing we have to fear is fear itself. Some people look at a problem like this and ask 'why?' I like to look at a problem and ask, 'why not?'"

Mike and Dad rolled their eyes. My mother pretended she was putting on a long pair of boots.

"The shit's getting deep now!" she said, and the three of them laughed.

"Go ahead and laugh," I said as they continued laughing. "You'll see."

After dinner Mike and I went downstairs to play a game of *Forty-Five* on my dartboard. To win, you hit numbers that are divisible by five, and that divisor gives you the number of points, which you subtract from 45 down to zero. So hitting a twenty will give you four points, a fifteen will give you three, ten will give you two and a five will give you one point. Mike had beaten me 66 games to none since we started playing the previous July.

"I can't believe you still want to play this game," Mike said, *Bud Light* in hand. "I mean if I lost at something sixty-six times…Sixty-six times is a lot of times to lose. I mean, what's it like to lose so many times?"

"Okay, okay, just throw the darts," I said. "We'll see what happens after this match." Mike placed his toe behind a piece of masking tape on the brown carpet, aimed and threw. Bull's-eye.

"Okay. You can tell me what sixty-seven games feels like."

After Mike's three darts I stood with my toe at the line on the floor and held my arm perpendicular to the board.

"Or maybe you can tell me what one game feels like." I hit a double-twenty for eight points. Not a bad throw.

"Sweet comeback," Mike said. I threw another twenty.

"My one victory, when it comes, will be sweeter than your last sixty-six. If for no other reason than that it will be so unprecedented." I missed with my third dart, and Mike took my place in front of the board.

"I think that's something losers say," Mike threw another bull's-eye. "I think a sixty-six-to-one record is pretty fucking good."

"I donno," I said as Mike threw his second dart, hitting a twenty. "That one game is going to be like a blemish on a supermodel. It'll just eat at you and eat at you."

"It won't eat at me. And besides, it doesn't matter—" Mike threw his last dart and won the game. "It's sixty-seven to zero."

I occupied two rooms in my parent's basement, which I'd painted Hunter green and Brick red. The paint looked great when I was done and I'd gotten many compliments, even though my father, beforehand, had said, "What do you know about painting rooms?" The red room was at the bottom of some carpeted steps that led up to my parent's kitchen. That room served as my office and library. And the dartboard was there.

In the Green Room or drawing room, into which we now withdrew, were two couches, a cushioned rocking chair, an old phonograph from my grandmother which could play five-record stacks, and a bar which I'd bought at a flea market several years before, cleaned, and installed a light within.

"Easy, Einstein," my father had said when he'd seen the bar refinished.

I had two decanter sets atop the phonograph, one for red wine with long, delicate-stemmed, matching glasses, and a whiskey tumbler which I kept half-full of *Seagram's V.O.* It had matching crystal glasses. Into two of these I dropped four cubes of ice apiece, two shots of whiskey, and topped them off with ginger ale, producing two Highballs.

"You know, Winston Churchill and Franklin Roosevelt used to drink Highballs on yachts off Nova Scotia during WWII. It was said to be their favorite cocktail." I handed Mike his drink.

"No I didn't," he said. He sat on a couch while I strolled with my drink to the cushioned rocking chair. The halos of the lamps on the end-tables cast a mix of glow and shadow across the room. I folded my legs.

"My favorite story of Churchill is that old one about him being drunk at a party. As the evening wore on he apparently became visibly intoxicated. Some aristocratic woman waddled over to him and declared, 'Mister Churchill, you are drunk!' 'Yes Madam,' says Churchill in his old British accent, slurring slightly, 'and you are ugly! But *I* will be sober in the morning!'" I sipped and placed the glass on a coaster to my right. "Now, let us get down to business."

"Ah, the raft business," Mike sighed. "Seems like your parents are really supportive of the idea."

I brushed off the sarcasm.

"My parents ask me what do I know about building a raft and floating down the Hudson. Well, what do they know?"

"They know that you don't know."

"Pah! What does that mean? You know, I'm surprised, I really am surprised at the knee-jerk cynicism that people have when I tell them about this idea. Like it's the stupidest thing anyone has ever thought of doing."

"Well, it *is* pretty stupid, man." I placed my cocktail down without drinking.

"Why? What makes it stupid?"

"It's just like, pointless." I stood and paced in front of the phonograph.

"What does that mean? It's *pointless*? Does everything have a point? If it doesn't have a *point*, it's not worth doing?"

"Pretty much." I put my Highball on the phonograph and motioned toward the bar.

"Alright, okay. And what is the point, then, of fixing up this bar here, so that it looks good? What is the point of that? What is the point of drinking our drinks out of tumblers and matching glasses? Why not just drink them out of Solo cups? What is the point of cleaning up your house? Or reading poetry? Or painting a picture?" Mike folded his fingers,

"Well, the bar looks good, and so people come over here and they see your nice bar, and they say 'Wow, nice job Dallas,' and that's the point. And there isn't really a point to drinking out of matching glasses...most people don't care, you're just obsessive about that kinda shit. You clean your house so you don't look like a scumbag to other people, so that's the point there. And reading poetry is pretty much a bullshit waste of time, same with painting a picture, unless you're really good and can make money off it, but that's pretty unlikely." I shook my head,

"I think you're missing the point here."

"I don't think you've gotten to the point of making a point yet."

"My point is, why is it foolish—and I use that word because people act like you're a fool for proposing it—to want to do something out of the ordinary, just for the sake of doing it?" Mike nodded.

"It's not foolish. It's just…well…pointless. And if it's pointless it's a waste of time. So people are asking you, really, 'Why are you wasting your time on this?'" I grabbed my drink but put it back down immediately.

"But it's not a waste of time. Is having fun a waste of time? Is learning about the towns on the river—how far one town really is from another, what things look like—is that stuff a waste of time?" Mike shifted positions.

"Let me ask you this: are you still planning on wearing costumes and shit?"

"I'm glad you brought that up." I drank from my Highball. "I'm probably going to just wear what I wear whenever I go on a big adventure: my linen adventurer's jacket and my fedora. But I don't think we need to get crazy and silly and dress as characters in costumes and stuff. I feel like that'll just make us look immature in the papers." Mike's eyebrows arched.

"Yeah…about that. You're going to call the papers? You think they'll give a shit about three assholes floating down the river?"

"Actually, I think the local papers *will* be interested in the story. I think the front page article in *The News Herald* this week was about a woman whose ceiling collapsed because of the snow. Last week it was about an abnormally large pot-hole in 9W. One week the headline on the cover was 'Pet Goat Assaulted.' Hell, I think we stand a good chance of making the front page!"

"Well, I doubt it. I think they'll ignore us totally. But we'll see."

"You'll see. I guarantee we get at least local press. We'll do it, man."

"You're not gonna do it," she said. I frowned.

"Cay, I told you: when I say I'm going to do a thing, I do it. A man only has one thing, and that's his word. If he doesn't have that, he's worthless. At the end of the day, he's got nothing of value to base any of his claims on. You know, I think Shakespeare said it best in Polonius' speech to Laertes: 'This above all: to thine own self be true, and it must follow, as the night the day, thou canst not then be false to any man.'"

"Okay Socrates," Cady teased. "You keep telling yourself that. But I'll believe it when I see it."

"You'll be believing it when you're seeing it on June first," I spluttered.

I couldn't find a single person who believed I was actually going to do what I said.

"You'll get sucked into a jetty," a girl in English Theory class said, when I told my study group about the idea. "When the water rushes past the supports of bridges it causes whirlpools and you'll get sucked in."

"I used to live on the river," said a kid with a wispy goatee and pimples. "Those barges come up and you never see 'em. You'll get get chopped into pieces by the propellers."

"Eunice Gallagher from Children with Special Needs says there's currents by West Point that'll slam you into rocks," my mother warned me at dinner. "She and her husband's got a boat and she said the current by the city is so strong they had to call the Coast Guard to tow 'em to shore. And she was in a power boat! Honestly Dallas, I think it's too dangerous."

Even my boss was skeptical, and she was always supportive of my creative avocations.

"I have no doubt that you will build the thing," Maureen said one afternoon. She'd gotten two flatbeds of logs delivered to her property and we were cutting, splitting and stacking them. She wanted to sell the wood by the cord the following fall, even though she made about nine hundred thousand dollars a year from the offices she ran. "But what will you do if you start to sink in the middle of the river?"

"Get wet," I said. "But I mean the idea is to make the thing seaworthy."

"And Jared is going with you?" a chainsaw idled on a stump by her foot.

"Yup."

"Are you sure he can go without his hair gel for that long?"

When I came back to Jared's house after parties, the parade, and more parties that St. Patrick's day — the traditional start of spring in Albany — I was greeted with laughter at the door. It was two in the morning and four or five friends were sitting on couches finishing off the beers as I came in. Someone threw me a can of *Keystone*.

"I was just telling these guys about your plans to build a raft," laughed Nick, Jared's roommate. I got the feeling he'd been deriding me just prior to my arrival.

"Yo. You know the river has tides, right?" That was Andrew Wilsey. He was a year older, an engineer at his family's architecture firm.

"Of course I know the Hudson has tides," I said. To parry the interrogatory missiles, I joked, "What do you take me for, some kind of amateur?"

"Yes!" they laughed. I waved them off from the foyer.

"You nay-sayers, you just want to say 'nay' to everything. Well, I'll show you what can be done." I opened my beer and cheersed them.

"You won't make it past Kingston," Andrew declared. The crowd turned in his direction and nodded.

"Why not?" Assuredly, Andrew answered,

"At Kingston the tides overpower the current, and if you don't have power you get stuck there." The crowd murmured that Andrew was right. With affected confidence, I concluded,

"Well, we'll see about that when we get there."

"What are you gonna do with the thing when you get down to the city?" Andrew asked.

"We're going to set it on fire," I said. Laughter crested across the couches.

"Ha ha, oh yeah? You'll set it on fire, huh?"

"Yeah, you know, we'll say some terrorists stole it and burned it as a symbol of American freedom." Laughter. "Gimme another beer!" Someone handed me a cold *Keystone* can. I played the politics of distraction. "Yum, Keystone! My favorite!" I chugged the beer in a series of gulps to stall the conversation.

"Okay," said some kid on the couch I didn't know. "I put a lot of stock in what *this* guy says."

"Now listen!" I wiped my face with my arm. "When Dallas Trombley says he's going to do something, he does it."

"Okay Dallas," Andrew dismissed.

"No, I'm serious." I declared.

"Okay," said Nick to the crowd, laughing and talking from the bottom of his throat, sarcastically. "I'll believe it when I see it."

"Well you'll believe it on June mother fucking first!"

"No way," Nick declared.

"Way."

"No way, dude. Not a chance."

"Look, I am fucking serious!" I slammed my beer on the coffee table. I noted a change in my friends' expressions. "Listen—if I don't float on a raft down the river with Jared and Mike…you can all call me the biggest asshole in Albany."

"We might have to call you that anyway," Nick laughed.

"No dude, I'm serious," I said. "I will do this."

"Okay okay," said Nick. "I'll believe it when I see it."

There is a lesson that I would like to go back and teach to my 21-year-old self. The lesson is called "the point of no return."

At the end of *Back to the Future III*, Doc explains to Marty, once the locomotive pushing the time machine passes the windmill, it will have gained so much kinetic energy, so much momentum, that it cannot be stopped before it reaches the chasm with the not-yet-completed bridge. Therefore, once the train passes the windmill, they must accelerate to 88 mph and actuate the flux capacitor in order to travel fourth dimensionally to a time when the bridge will be completed, or else they will go careening off the cliff.

It is possible to take a step, and put yourself on a path, and then you must see the endeavor through to completion, because the cost of going back is too high. The string of confrontations with my parents, Cady, and especially in front of a dozen friends, was the point of no return as far as I was concerned.

I met my friend Brett in New Baltimore one evening in early April. After months of cold we were happy to don short sleeves. My boss had given me two premium cigars so we decided to stroll along the surf-smoothed stone beach behind the colonial houses by the river. Dusk was just descending as we ambled and chatted along the grey and brown cobble, climbing over tree-limbs, strolling and discussing the upcoming summer.

"Hey look at this thing," Brett bent toward a piece of smoothed white glass in the shape of an old make-up cream container. He handed it to me. I rubbed my fingers around it. It felt like silk. "We should keep this and use it as an ashtray," he said. A few paces later he picked up a petrified rock, but when he lifted it, we saw it was an old wooden doorknob, also smoothed by the waves over years. "I guess I'll throw this one away."

"I'll take it." Brett placed it in my hand. The wood was gnarled, marbled. I slid it in my pocket.

Something about the water at dusk, with no cell service, was peaceful, natural, like the obligations of daily existence were off, in the future. "We ought to pick up a bunch of things we find around — just old stuff that looks interesting — and keep it all in order to remind us of being out here on this day, and how it felt."

After an hour we arrived at a riverfront restaurant which had just turned on white Christmas lights in the trees and wrapped around its patio railings. I found the lights cloying, unnecessary, since my pupils had dilated on their own. We walked out on an empty dock that extended a third of the way into the river.

I kicked off my sneakers. The warm air was refreshing to my ankles. We sat with our bare feet off the end of the dock, sucking in the sweet, peaty smoke from our cigars, and exhaled.

The water reflected the darkening blue sky, where stars were appearing amid fading blankets of orange and cyan. Behind us on the riverbank, dark-green-black blocks of land rose from the water, with New England style homes with miniature square window lights shining like ceramic Christmas town-houses.

As we looked around in silence, we perceived new sounds: the quiet undulations of the waves against the cobbled shore; the first high notes of crickets chirping; the long, low croak of bullfrogs. Up the river and down, fog had begun to coalesce. Floating buoys flashed red and green.

"Boy, it sure is nice out here," Brett said. Indeed, though we'd lived by the river our whole lives, we'd never really noticed how calming yet invigorating just *being there* was. I pointed my toe and felt the water. It was warmer than I expected.

I stretched out my arms and puffed my cigar. Maureen had taught me that you should only puff a good cigar about once a minute, and the tip should never glow. It's not a cigarette, which you smoke to distract yourself. Nor should you ash a good cigar—a measure of its quality is how long the ash will stay on the tip before falling off. Smoking a cigar should be a mindful activity.

"I'm going to build a raft this summer and float down the Hudson," I declared suddenly. "Look at where we are. I'm not crazy to want to be here!" I considered the mockery I'd endured "I'm going to teach those nay-sayers not to say 'nay' so much."

Brett's cigar was down to its nubbin so he let it drop into the river. It bobbed away like a piece of driftwood. "I never thought about the meaning of that word before. *Nay-sayers.* They're people who say *nay*," he observed.

"There's a lot of words like that. Words that, if you really consider them, have a pretty exact meaning you never realized."

We could have been Huck Finn and Tom Sawyer on that dock, or Sal Paradise and Dean Moriarty. We were free from everything for as long as we sat under what had become a fresh, American, night sky, full now of sparkling stars and warm, southern breezes.

But I started thinking. Involuntarily, I drew my cell phone from my pocket before remembering I had no service by the river. Then like the fog encroaching on all sides, I feared my parents or my boss or Cady were trying to reach me, and since they could not, they'd be angry because I'd been unavailable. Now I expected that as soon as I returned from the river, someone would yell at me. Now, too, I expected to hear the footsteps of the restaurant's owner behind us as he yelled to get off the dock. The world was suddenly small, and owned by other people, at least on the land.

IV. Rotten Wood and Floaty Shit

My friend Oliver worked for Tenuis Van Slyke after leaving The New School for Jazz and Contemporary Music in New York City. After his freshman year, Oliver worked at Van Slyke's warehouse in an old brick building in Albany's former industrial district.

Tenuis Van Slyke lived in the town of Coeymans about five miles upriver of my parent's house in New Baltimore. He'd profited by $400,000 by selling a parcel of undeveloped land to the City of Albany, so that Albany could build a garbage dump among the flora and fauna of Coeymans. This chagrined the nearby homeowners, who put aside their differences to form a coalition opposed to a dump within town limits. The coalition secured an injunction against the dump's construction. But the injunction took effect after Albany contracted to pay Tenuis Van Slyke $100,000 a year for his land, which Albany was obligated to pay while it appealed. Thus Mr. Van Slyke received a substantial annual income above the proceeds of his warehouse business, while the dump was never built.

"It pays the bills," Oliver said about his job, which was rather cheeky because he didn't have many bills, seeing as he lived with his parents and didn't have student loans or a mortgage.

Oliver and I had been friends since the days when I had a plastic badge and solicited other elementary schoolers to be part of my "police force" at recess, of which I was Chief. We played with his massive Lego collection in middle school. In high school he and I wrote and recorded such original songs as "Screw You", "Paranoid Schizo (With a Side of Bipolar Disorder)", and "Urinary Tract Infection." None became hits. He provided piano accompaniment for some live performances at various venues of my parodies "Blue Cheese" and "Girlfriend State of Mind." Oliver hosted the *Symposium Society* each year at his parent's house.

Since leaving music school in New York City, Oliver had been living with his parents next to *Joey's Pizza and Pasta* in Ravena. One day while driving to work a van crossed into his lane and totaled his car so that his driver's seat was the only non-mangled portion of the whole vehicle. After that, if you didn't initiate a rendezvous with Oliver he would cocoon-up and disappear for months. So I made a standing appointment with him every Sunday. We went to *Paul's Pizza* in Coxsackie and goggled at the waitress.

"I can't wait until I'm 21 so I can ask a girl to get a drink," I'd said when we were sophomores. "Easy. 'Want to get a drink?' Then we go get one. This waitress here—what am I supposed to do, ask her to go to the malt-shop?"

"She probably has a boyfriend," Oliver observed.

"Don't crush my dreams, man."

At *Paul's* we began an outline of a story which centered on two friends who met at a pizza joint once a week and had a crush on the waitress. It was not my most original piece. Thematically it was notable because the point was to contrast two categories of people, *thinkers* and *doers*. Oliver, who once commented that he "would rather not try at something than try and fail," personified the first category, while I had not-infrequently been criticized for impulsiveness.

The waitress in the story thought both characters were assholes.

Anyhow it was this Oliver who now drove me to the rural estate of Tenuis Van Slyke.

The Van Slyke property was situated on the west bank of the Hudson River, upon a wooded vista, approximately ten miles south of the Port of Albany as the crow flies, or five miles north of New Baltimore. We turned off state route 144 onto a gravel drive which cut into the forest. We passed through an iron gate between brick pillars, guarded by two stone staring lions.

"Jesus Christ, who lives here? Bill Gates?"

Oliver laughed. "I guess the birdseed business pays well."

After a quarter-mile of trees, with shadows flickering through the branches and leaves overhead, the road turned sharply and we emerged atop a sunshined slope. We gazed over a rolling expanse which cascaded to the river. The sun and the blue sky reflected off the river water. Nearer, an old man on a Kubota tractor rolled noisily down the gravel road toward a three-story stone house complete with a solarium, a wraparound porch and five chimneys. I half-expected Scarlet O'Hara to emerge on the veranda in a hoopskirt. We continued to drive toward the house until we rolled up behind the tractor and followed it as it crunched along at two miles an hour oblivious to our presence.

"Honk the horn," I suggested.

"He'll have a heart attack," Oliver said. "He's a hundred and ninety years old."

When the old man stopped the tractor I saw that Oliver was exaggerating by perhaps fifteen years. Like a wax figure in slow motion, Mr. Van Slyke brought one leg onto the foot-stand of the tractor, then moved an arm to the handle bar, then slowly brought around the other leg, and so on, until after perhaps three minutes he succeeded in dismounting. Only then did he look up and see the blue F-150 parked right behind him. He started back.

"Who's that!" he shouted. Through the rolled-down window Oliver shouted his name.

"Who?"

"Oliver! We came to get those barrels!"

The old man shook his head and shuffled toward the house.

"Jesus Christ," I complained as we stepped from the truck. After a few minutes the old man came back with keys in his hand and a dour expression on his face.

"We'll go down to the yacht club," he barked. "I'm sure they got barrels down there. I don't have pull there like I use ta."

We followed Mr. Van Slyke south on 144 and took a left at a waterfall on the Coeymans Creek. We drove down a treacherous unpaved road past a stone house where the homeowners had found the skull of a woman from the 1800s in a wall. We kept going down past swampland to an unimpressive pavilion that was the Coeymans Yacht Club. There was a hand-painted sign over the door which announced that it was the yacht club, but it reminded me of the picture from the cover of "Bearenstein Bears: No Girls Allowed" when Brother Bear paints his "Boys Club" sign with backward letters in sloppy script. There were about a dozen boats up on vice-jacks, a pile of docks, two piles of blue and white 55-gallon drums, a half-dozen pickup trucks, a crane and some kind of machine that looked like it was left over from the Spanish-American War.

We stopped the truck and I ran to the drums. Oliver followed and thirdly, Mr. Van Slyke.

"Can we take these?" I asked.

"We gotta find someone's got a boat here. I used to have a boat here but I don't anymore. Keep it behind my garage nowadays. I keep tellin ya they don't like me here. Well, I don't need a yacht club anyway."

"Okay," I said.

So we looked around for somebody with authority. The yacht club was not a friendly place to an outsider searching for a favor. The men taking covers off their boats or repairing their engines shot us suspicious looks, or ignored us. Curled upper lips; stone faces—yuck. I felt like a tramp wandering into a gala of aristocrats, or middling types with pretentions to aristocracy, which is viler. Anyhow, Oliver and I broke off and looked at the old machinery, then the driftwood in the river breezing by. After a few minutes we saw Mr. Van Slyke in conversation with a man by the pavilion. So we wandered back.

No sooner were we in earshot than the middle-aged man shouted,

"Now, what is it you tryna do?" When we'd stepped within talking range, for I did not want to shout, I responded,

"We want to build a raft to float downriver to Manhattan."

"Manhattan!" The man roared, as though this was the punchline to a great joke. "Ha ha! No, seriously, what are you tryna do?"

"We want to build a raft which floats on barrels and float from Coeymans to Manhattan," I repeated.

"Manhattan!" he roared again. I was waiting for him to slap his knee. Then he said, "Wait wait, Hank! Come here and listen to this!" I frowned at Oliver, who grinned widely beneath his blonde beard, and even Tenuis Van Slyke smiled for the first time. Meanwhile Hank put down his wrench and the guy I was just speaking with caught his breath to say, "Hey kid, tell Hank what you just said."

"I'm looking for six barrels if you've got any lying around."

"What for?" Hank asked.

"Yeah yeah, tell him what for!" said the first guy. I hesitated.

"To build a raft. To float to Manhattan."

"Manhattan?" Hank shouted but didn't laugh. In fact, he scowled nastily. "You'll never make it. No way. That's stupid. You'll die. You know when the barges go by they make six-foot waves. They'll wash right over you and you'll capsize."

"Nonetheless I'd like to give it a shot," I said.

"You know the river's got tides, dontcha?"

"Yes, sir."

"Well, frankly I think it's a dumb idea, period. Why would you want to do something like that?"

"For the adventure of it."

Hank seemed to find me despicable. But after some persistence his laughing friend told us there were a few old barrels in the woods up the hill from the pavilion that we could take. Hank gave him a jeering look and they went back to fixing their boats. Oliver and I hiked up the hill into the brush and burdocks. We found ten barrels amongst the rotting leaves. Some were sunk six inches into the muck. When Oliver and I lifted one, black putrid liquid poured on Oliver's jeans.

Tenuis Van Slyke watched us load a barrel into the back of Oliver's truck and then took off without bidding us farewell. Clouds were massing overhead. We could tell a storm was coming. Tiny sprinkles announced its arrival. As we loaded the barrels in the truck we saw they were in a sorry state. We heard liquid splashing inside some of them. Others had big dents in their sides. We tied ropes around them and drove them back to Oliver's house, where we planned to build the raft.

At Oliver's we mulled throwing the barrels into his swimming pool to test their soundness but concluded it would be too messy, so we lined them up in his parent's driveway and called it a day.

"This was a *barrel* of fun," Oliver quipped as I stepped into my car.

"I think this trip will be as easy as shooting fish in a *barrel*," I replied.

"More fun than a *barrel* of monkeys," Oliver added.

"Yes; but right now we've *barrel*-ly begun building."

"Well, we'll just have to *barrel* away until it's complete."

Next we had to gather wood. By now our launch date was less than a month away. May first—the date we'd set to finish the raft, in order to give us a month of testing—had come and gone with only a half-dozen barrels in Oliver's driveway.

Mike was just returning from his final semester at New Paltz, I was working at my boss's house picking weeds and finishing finals, and Jared was working full time at our boss' insurance office. When I'd gotten together with either Jared or Mike that spring—never both at the same time—we'd talk about our raft plans and label that "progress." But it wasn't progress, it was talk.

On my way back and forth to work and school I noted places where pallets were placed outside, but I never picked them up. I figured I would do it all in a single day, after school was over, when I had somebody to help me.

Then I had a big setback with school. At the time I had no motivation to do work which I didn't like, and that included work in courses required for my major. I was taking an upper level course in English Theory, and I just couldn't bring myself to read the feminist authors who described writing as a sexual assault, because it involves using a phallic-shaped pen spewing ink onto the blank womblike page, *blah blah*. I started putting off the work and then I fell behind, and then the idea of showing up without the work made me anxious, so I didn't show up, and then I failed the class. I'd started college a semester ahead, thanks to Advanced Placement courses in high school. Each fall term I took between 18 and 21 credits and managed straight A's. Then in the spring semesters I'd get Cs, Ds, Ws (for withdrawing too late) and Fs. Thanks to my bipolar transcript and failing my recent class, I now had too few credits to graduate, and instead of finishing a semester early as I'd once planned, I had to spend an extra semester in college.

And now, instead of our raft trip being a final hurrah as we bid goodbye to school attendance and all that, it was just another obligation I had to fulfill over the course of the summer, along with working and saving money and visiting Cady and helping out around my parent's house. Instead of a triumph commemorating conquering childhood, the raft was just another challenge to overcome, and it was getting harder to explain to people what the point was.

I really wanted to show Cady some progress when she came up two weeks before the launch. It was a mid-May weekend, bright and shiny and full of blue skies and spring air. Jared drove down from Albany. We planned to spend the day gathering supplies and beginning building. He, Cady and I found a box of nails in the aluminum cabinet in my parent's basement left over from when they built their house in 1981. We put these in the back of Al, the decaying white F-150 with the crumpled fender. Then we went "over the hill" and found a couple of pieces of rotting plywood and some "texture-one-eleven" wood siding and threw that in the bed of the truck too. We raided my grandfather's work shed and found various lengths of two-by-fours. We threw these in the bed of the truck. Then we drove the stuff up to Oliver's parent's house. He came outside grinning beneath his bushy blonde beard and mustache. He chuckled as he peered into the bed of the truck.

"So — these are the materials, huh?"

"Yes sir!" I said. "Nothing but the best for this project!" Cady rolled her eyes. She bent down and scratched Oliver's dog, making *ruff* sounds and getting it excited so it jumped up. Then she affected a child's pitch and asked,

"Who's a good puppy?" Oliver continued his inspection.

"Two pieces of — is this plywood? Cut in half. Hmm. A 2x4 that's been cut in half...and — oh, some paneling. And how are you going to make this into a raft?"

"Hey man, you're the carpenter," I said. (In his spare time Oliver built cabinets and guitars.)

"Well, I'm not Jesus so you better get some more wood."

"Fuck, man," Jared groaned. He and Oliver shook hands.

"How'd you get roped into this project?" Oliver asked with his ironic smile.

"Just wanted an adventure, you know," Jared replied, scratching his neck.

Cady threw Sadie the dog a stick but Sadie just looked at her without understanding.

"Do you guys have a name for the raft?" Cady asked.

"*The U.S.S. Crab Legs*," I said. Cady and Oliver laughed incredulously. "Me and Jared were at the Chinese buffet. We go there about once a week—the one up on Western Ave across from Crossgates Mall—"

"What's the name of it?" Oliver asked.

"*Chinese Buffet*," Jared laughed. "Mad original."

"—Anyhow it's the best Chinese buffet around. It's got all the traditional favorites plus crab legs, peel and eat shrimp, muscles...what else Jared?"

"Chicken wing."

"Yeah chicken wing, human chicken as I like to call it—"

"—Dallas goes there so much the waiter pulls out the chair for him and says 'I get you woot beew wight away.'"

"—Haha, yeah. Well, me and Jared ate so many crab legs one time our plates were just full of the shells, and there was a bridge of exoskeletons connecting our plates. We ate so many they stopped bringing out more. So sitting there stuffed Jared picked up a claw and was like 'We should call the raft the U.S.S. Crab Legs," and I thought, 'Well, why not?'"

"This boat is never going to get built," Cady said.

"I second that," said Oliver. "You guys have two weeks to get this thing ready. A.K.A. this weekend and next weekend and you set sail the weekend after that."

"Relax man," I said. "Help me unload this wood. I know where there are at least twenty pallets we can get for free. We'll bring them back here and build the raft outta those." With that promise in mind, Jared, Cady and I got into the truck.

On my way to my boss's house to pick weeds from her flagstones I'd passed a house a dozen times that had whole heaps of pallets outside with a "free" sign, but I never stopped to pick them up because I was always in my car not my truck. They sat there for two weeks and nobody took them. When we got to the house on this day they were all gone.

"Fuck dude!" Jared lamented. "Where are we gonna get stuff now?"

I did not have an answer to that question.

A few days later on my way to Albany I passed a house where the inhabitants had torn down a dilapidated wooden fence and thrown the posts into a pile by the road. These gray, almost paper-like posts — together with three rotting pallets I'd found buried under leaves in my parent's back yard, would provide the balance of the wood to build the raft platform. In his first physical act in support of our endeavor, Mike drove to the house and loaded the posts into his station wagon. He met me at Oliver's later that afternoon while Oliver was working at the warehouse and Jared was at the office. Mike pulled into the driveway, got out and looked at the pile of wood and barrels. He did not say hello. Rather, he began pacing with a look on his face like he'd swallowed something putrid.

"Hey man!" I said.

"Hi." Mike tapped his foot.

"What's up," I said.

"Nothing." Mike looked at the wood, then at the trees and the sky and then back at me, while kicking at the pavement.

"What's the matter," I asked impatiently. Of course normally Mike would greet me with an enthusiastic salutation; we would shake hands, make a joke, and engage in small talk.

"Dude, we can't do this." A flat declaration a week before departure. I jerked my head.

"What do you mean we can't do it?"

"I donno man," Mike audibly exhaled. "What, are we just gonna float down the river?"

"That has been the plan all along! Mike, we've been planning this trip for ten months. The whole time the plan has been to float down the river."

"Okay but look at this pile of shit. There's no way we can get a raft built *and* shipped in a week. We're just going to have to cancel or at least postpone."

It was a scorching day. The sun beat down and beaded drops on our foreheads. The cicadas rattled and went silent again.

"Mike," I gestured enthusiastically, "we'll spend today getting this thing built. We'll attach the barrels and ship it this week." I smacked his arm, "Come on man, all we gotta do now is build it."

But Mike was immutable.

"And then how are we gonna get it to the water? And how are we gonna steer it? Let's face it man, we didn't do any work and this was a stupid idea to begin with." I threw my hammer onto the wood pile.

"*We* didn't do any work? *I* did, man! *I've* gotten the barrels; *I* got Oliver to let us build it at his house, *I* found rope, wood and nails. *I've* Google-Earthed the whole trip along the river and every time I've seen either you or Jared I've asked you, 'Hey, still planning on doing the trip, right?' 'Right.' 'Good because June first is coming up.' But not until a week before the trip do you guys think of lending any sort of hand."

"Dude I was in New Paltz. What was I supposed to do? I told you I couldn't help with the building until this week. Now it's too late."

I thoroughly believed that if Mike, Oliver, Jared and I worked for a day putting the pieces of wood together and tying on the barrels, we'd be ready to ship the boat to the river, and I also thoroughly believed that if Mike didn't pitch in enthusiastically, we wouldn't get anywhere. We needed his help physically, and also when it came to practical problem solving.

"I told a lot of people about this. Now it's *my* name associated with this project. Whole rooms of people laughed in my face and told me I'd never make it, that we wouldn't even try and that we were full of shit telling them we were going to try even to build it. Now you're saying we ought to prove these people right. These are a bunch of nay-saying old hags with nothing better to do than shoot down other people's enthusiasm."

"Maybe they were right," Mike said.

For a nanosecond I wanted to say, "Fuck it, then," and let Jared and Mike bear the guilt for killing the project through inaction and complaint. But that's how children reason, and I wasn't about to scuttle what was becoming solely *my* project just to spite Mike and Jared.

"Alright man," I took one step backward. "Look. There's no use in us two getting mad at each other because of a project we're supposed to be doing as friends. Now I really believe that if me and you work on this thing all afternoon—and Oliver and Jared help tonight—we can turn these pieces of wood into a box and strap the barrels underneath. That's all we need to do. Then we can worry about moving the thing to the river. We'll find a way to deal with that problem when we get to that step. But we *can* get this thing built, we *will* get this thing built, we *will* ship it to the river, we *will* be in the paper—the *News Herald* called me yesterday to make an appointment to take pictures—and we will float down the God-damned river to New York City!"

"The *News Herald* called?" Mike smirked.

"Yes!" I cried. "They're coming to take our pictures when we launch. So are about twenty-five of our friends and family, who're all planning to come when we launch. That's why I'm saying we can't just give up on the project now. We'd be worse than laughing stocks. We'd be liars and people would think we either pulled their leg making a joke on them, or were too stupid to build a raft."

"You told your parents?" Mike asked. I wanted to say *You were there when I told them*, but I thought better of it.

"Of course I told my parents. I'm floating down the Hudson on a raft; I'm going to be gone for ten days. Of course I told my parents! Haven't you told yours?"

"I kind of mentioned it back on February break. They didn't sound thrilled. They thought it would be dangerous…" We said nothing for a moment. The sound of a diesel truck accelerating at a green light at the bottom of Oliver's driveway echoed up the hill. "Alright well look," Mike said. "What is your plan for building this thing?" He followed me over to the pile of wood, at the top of Oliver's driveway, where the driveway became the back yard, in front of a garage, on top of blacktop. I took off my button-down shirt because the combination of the sun in the cloudless sky and the blacktop turned the immediate area—our workspace—into a solar fryer. I flipped a pallet upside-down in the driveway.

"We take these pallets, and we put them together into a square. The middle we reinforce with the two-by-four." I picked this off the pile and dropped it on the blacktop. "Then we take all those fence posts you just picked up and nail them all over the pallets to connect them. Then we take the couple of pieces of flat wood we have and nail them to the top as a deck. The whole thing will sit on top of the barrels which will be attached with industrial-strength zip ties usually used to attach air conditioners to the sides of buildings. *Voila*: raft."

Mike looked down at the pallet. Then he took another pallet off the pile. Together we laid the pallets in a 12x12foot square on the driveway.

"Okay," Mike said, "so now you're saying we take the fence pieces and use them to connect the pallets together?"

"Yeah."

"Hmm. Okay…And we'll cut the two-by-four to reinforce the center where it's weak?"

"Yup."

"Okay. Yeah. I think we ought to cut the two-by-four into diagonal pieces to reinforce the corners of the center frame. That might give it a little flex and let it take some of those six-foot waves."

"Now you're thinking!"

"Haha, six-foot waves. What an idiot that guy was that said that to you. Have you ever been on the river and saw a wave come that was taller than you?"

"No. Fuck that guy."

"Haha yeah. Yeah—okay. Yeah! I think we can build this, right? A couple of diagonal two by fours…the plywood ought to reinforce everything. Yeah we can build this today."

"Easy as falling off a log."

"Okay well what do you got to cut with? A circular saw?"

"Hand saw," I said. "And I got a miter box. But we gotta drive to my parents' to get it. Let's get that and we can eat lunch at my parents' along the way."

"Okay man I'm in," Mike said. When we were in my truck he said, "Sorry about being a nay-sayer before."

When we were eating potato chips for lunch at my parents' house the phone rang.

"Hello. Is this Dallas Trombley?" A female voice asked.

I figured it was a bill collector so I said "This is he" flatly. I stood in the kitchen. Mike stood in the adjacent parlor looking out the window.

"Hi Mr. Trombley my name is Ashley Clay and I am calling from the *Ravena Ledger*—it's the new newspaper that just got started last year—"

"Oh, yes!" I said loudly and slowly to get Mike's attention. "I know that *news-pa-per*. How are you Ms. Clay?"

"Umm, I was wondering if I could ask you a few questions regarding your raft project." I made waving motions with my arms until Mike looked at me.

"Sure, I'd be glad to answer any *questions about the raft*!" I put my palm over the receiver as we both grinned shit-eating grins. I suppose we only thought we'd make the *News Herald*, not two newspapers, so we were a little star-struck. We were happy to get our picture printed, but now a story too? The reporter began asking her questions as though reading from cue cards. She verified basic information about our names and ages and the date of our launch. "We prefer to go by Captain Dallas Trombley, Admiral Peterman-Glenis and First Mate Jared Ableman." I put my hand over the phone as we laughed through our noses.

"What is your raft composed of?" Ms. Clay asked.

"Well, we wanted to use only *recycled* materials," I said. Mike whispered *You mean garbage?* "So we, you know, salvaged some plywood from my parents' back yard, reclaimed some fence posts and pallets, and we're just going to nail it all together. The folks at the Coeymans Yacht Club were nice enough to donate us barrels. Otherwise I'd have had to steal my mother's Tupperware for floatation."

No laughter from Ms. Clay, who was all business.

"How long do you anticipate it will take you to reach Manhattan?"

"Well, Admiral Peterman-Glenis and I have calculated the tides. We assume that the tide moves at maybe three miles an hour. We'll go out with the tide for six hours — or eighteen miles — tie up while the tide comes back in, and go out again with the tide when it goes back out. So that's thirty-six miles a day. We ought to be there in five days."

"Where do you plan to sleep?"

"We'll pull off at the marinas we pass along the way. Otherwise we'll bring sleeping bags and sleep on the raft."

Mike stood in front of me as I talked through the phone, nodding as I answered. Now she asked,

"Is there any reason you are doing this project?" So I responded,

"Yes — to protest America's reliance on fossil fuels!" and clasped my palm over the phone as Mike and I snorted laughing.

We starting building.

Mike and I took slices of dead trees and fused them together using spikes of metal. As the summer sun bronzed our backs we hammered home the nails. We wiped the sweat from our foreheads with the backs of our hands as our forearms hardened. We broke pieces; we cut pieces; pieces splinted and we had to yank them off and use new pieces. Soon we turned the pallets into a wobbly frame. We kept hammering.

Jared came and saw and hammered with us. Oliver came and saw and said we should have used screws, and then he hammered with us. We used the fence posts to make the frame rigid, by reinforcing the perimeter, especially the joints where the pallets joined. We hammered plywood pieces of various shapes and sizes, sometimes overlapping on the top of the pallets, which sat at different heights relative to one another, and therefore provided an uneven surface to attach to. We hammered all day, until the evening came and the mosquitoes bit us. Then we stood up and saw we were almost finished, so we made plans to finish nailing everything together over the next few days.

(The U.S.S. Crab Legs under construction in Oliver's parent's driveway. In the background are some of the barrels collected from the Coeymans Yacht Club.)

We finished assembling the platform on May 31st, the very afternoon before our launch.

"Now it's built," Mike said. "And we are leaving tomorrow. Now how are we going to get it to the river?" I quoted the poster from Mrs. Cushman's math classroom in high school,

"The best angle to approach a problem is the try angle."

The problem was that it was three o'clock in the afternoon and if we failed to get the platform, which measured twelve-feet by twelve-feet, down the hill, through the Main Street of town, down the steep hills of Ravena which descend into Coeymans, to the river *that* night, we'd have to postpone the trip. We needed the morning of the next day to put the barrels under the platform, to shop for food, pack, and meet reporters. So we had to get the thing to the river that evening.

The first idea I proposed was to try to lift one end of the platform so we could back a truck underneath, propping the underside of the platform on the top of the bed of the truck. Once it was propped on the tailgate, I thought we could lift up the back of the platform and slide it onto the bed of the truck.

"You can't do that," Oliver warned, "because a truck bed is only eight-feet by six-feet. It'll hang off the sides three feet, and off the back four. And how will you tie it to the truck?"

"Anything over eight-feet wide and you need to get a special permit to transport it on the road," Mike added. By now Oliver's parents had arrived home from work, and they suggested we call a towing company for a flatbed.

"Special permit *splecial* permit," I said. "Come on, let's try lifting one end."

So two of us bent and grabbed each corner of the front of the wooden square and lifted, but we could only raise the end two-feet off the ground. The platform was heavy, but also very flexible, so that raising one end only made the center bend like a giant slice of semi-melted cheese. Lifting the front by two feet did nothing to raise the middle off the ground.

Now, it happened that Oliver's parents were rebuilding the walkway behind their pool, so they had a pile of bricks stacked next to the driveway. I proposed we lift the front of the platform high enough to slide three bricks stacked on top of one another beneath each corner. Then we had to rest. Then two of us lifted while the other two placed another brick onto the stack, and one beneath the middle of the platform, where it still bent to touch the ground. By that method we got the front of the platform lifted three feet high, and the middle about six inches off the ground. By now an hour had passed. Oliver said,

"I don't think you're going to be able to transport this whole thing in one piece. You might have to cut it in half."

I ignored his suggestion because it was impossible. We had nailed the platform together every which-way and we'd never be able to cut it or recombine it. And three of us were certainly not going to float down the river on a 6x12 foot block. Instead I grabbed a nearby 4x4 and a metal drum, and these we placed under the front to raise it to three-and-a-half feet off the ground. We backed up the truck and saw we had to raise the front of the platform twice as high. We gathered more bricks, now placing them further back and thereby lifted the front to four feet.

(The day before launch. Moving the raft platform Plan A: balancing it on a pickup truck. Jared stands at left; I am on the right.)

At that point we were hit by a sudden summer storm and got soaked trying to work through it. When the storm passed we were no further along but it was early evening and we were wet and the mosquitoes started biting.

"I'll throw in fifty bucks for a flatbed," Mike said.

"Damn, I will too I guess," Jared said. So we called three towing companies. Only one answered and the person said he had to get authorization from the owner, who wouldn't be in until the morning. If they didn't get the go-ahead from the boss we'd be up a creek — or rather, up a hill from the river. We were at a dead end, stuck in Oliver's driveway, like driftwood beached at high tide.

Then Jared remembered that Andrew Wilsey's father had a trailer, so he took off in his car to go get him. In half an hour Jared returned in his father's truck with Wilsey and his father's trailer. The trailer was a small metal cage about big enough to transport a lawn tractor. It had a metal railing that required us to raise the front of the platform — what we started to refer to as the *bow* — another foot higher, and that was the damnedest last foot. We pulled and pushed and clenched and slammed but we couldn't get the trailer under that

12x12 slice of wood. We got splinters and mosquito bites, and we got angry.

"Look," Oliver said, "you're just going to have to cut the thing in half!"

"With what?" I said, "A chainsaw?"

"Yes!"

"You going to let me use your chainsaw? You going to cut through nails with it?" Mike stepped in.

"I think Oliver's right Dallas. I mean, face reality. We're not going tomorrow." I threw my hands up in frustration.

"But wait," said Andrew, who had come equipped with strapping and chains and wore a big pair of fireman's overalls. "We're like an inch beneath the top of the trailer. What if I take this post and stand on the back of the trailer, and use it to leverage-up the front of the raft as someone backs up the truck. Jared, when I get it lifted, you back up and get the trailer underneath."

Wouldn't you know it worked, and we got six-inches of the platform set on the back of the trailer. Then we went through all the motions again to raise the back of the platform higher: stacking the bricks, then the bigger objects underneath, until it was the same height as the front. Then four of us lifted the front a couple inches while Jared backed the trailer as far as it would go, just a little back from the middle of the platform.

Voila! The heavy platform balanced on the trailer like a spinning top that was losing momentum, overflowing on all sides and constantly threatening to spill. It began raining again as Andrew strapped and roped the thing onto the trailer. These straps hardly provided more stability.

(After nearly four hours, the platform is loaded on the trailer.
Here Jared (left) and I (center) have donned ponchos. At right
Andrew Wilsey straps the platform to his father's [much smaller]
trailer.)

Now we faced the greater challenge of transporting the hulk through town to the river. As we inched down the driveway — Jared in the driver's seat of his dad's truck, me in the passenger's, Andrew and Mike ahead and behind with flashers — we knew our chances of getting to the river unmolested were slim. As we came to the bottom of the drive, glancing back frequently to make sure the raft hadn't slipped off the trailer, suddenly the skies opened and dropped such a volume of water that the street flooded with an inch of runoff. Across the street the road onto which we slowly rolled became a sheet of water descending as a shallow lake dimpled by a million falling droplets. Rather than a bad omen, the storm cleared the streets of traffic so that even at our snail's pace of five miles an hour we were able to tow the trailer the mile from Oliver's house to Coeymans Landing right down the yellow line on Main Street. We never came close to swiping anything, and no cars passed us.

Nonetheless at the very bottom of the hill in the gravel parking lot a stone's throw from the river, after we'd parked and were unloading the barrels from the bed of the truck in the dark and the rain, we were startled by a bright spotlight and saw an SUV police car coming toward us. I jumped from the bed of the truck and walked toward the cruiser. The spotlight blinded me.

"What's going on down here?" asked a figure behind the spotlight. I walked closer hoping hard he wouldn't make us bring the platform back to Oliver's, or threaten to tow it away. But then the officer said, "Oh, hi Dallas," and turned the spotlight onto the raft. The officer was the father of a friend of mine. "What is it that you've got there?" he asked. Still standing in the rain I explained,

"Well, that's a raft we built and we're setting sail from here tomorrow. Tom Tucker is coming from the *News Herald* tomorrow morning for a picture."

"No kidding," said Officer Cunningham from his cruiser. "Well, how long are you going to keep it here, just overnight?"

"Yes sir," I said. "Tomorrow morning we're coming down at ten a.m. to attach the barrels and then we'll put it in the water." The officer leaned out of the window and squinted at the raft. He looked around at the parking lot, which was otherwise vacant.

"Okay," he said to my extreme relief. "Well, just keep it over there so it's out of the way, alright?"

"Definitely, thanks." He drove away. I felt good now that I could say I had informed the police of what I was doing, and I had their permission. We finished unloading the barrels and, our work done, we went to our homes for the night around eleven p.m.

V. Something to Float On

Mike took a Civil Service exam the morning of June 1st, 2006. So he wasn't available to help Jared and I get the raft ready for launch that morning. Jared and I met at the river at 10 a.m.

"Man, not feelin' you getting' your mad-early piece on," he grumbled.

We stood outside our cars, next to the trailer with the platform tied on top, next to the stacked plastic blue barrels, on the gravel on that dewy Thursday morning. The sky undulated gray and white. A stringent breeze whisked across the lot. I scratched my chest; Jared scratched his groin; we yawned and looked out at the river. The water was brown and choppy. We looked at one another and laughed.

"Well, here we are," I said.

"It's really something now."

"It's really something now," I amplified.

We laughed a little more and noted the choppy waves.

"Well…" Jared said, "How the fuck are we gonna get this shit in the water?"

"I thought about this. Mike is gonna see if he can get plastic industrial zip-ties. The kind you can get for air conditioners…or so I've heard. We'll use those to attach the barrels to the underside of the wood platform."

"When is he getting here again?"

"He hopes around 12:30 or 1."

"Geeze. Cutting this shit close aren't we?"

"In the meantime I have some rope in the back of my car. I say we back the trailer up into the water with the platform on it, and we put the barrels in the water before we back the trailer up. We can then try and lift up the back of the platform, which will be hanging off the trailer over the water, and rest it on top of the barrels. We can tie those on with ropes, and then that part of it will float and we can put the other barrels on as we pull the platform off the trailer, floating."

"You'll have to show me. But yo let's get started, I have to have my dad's truck back by 3 p.m. sharp."

We walked to the boat launch. Jared backed up the truck with the wobbly wooden platform on the trailer. He had to back up and go forward two or three times to get lined up with the ramp. Then I stood at the bottom of the ramp and he backed the truck until I was up to my knees in the water and the back of the platform was touching the waves. Then he put on the e-brake and came back to look.

"Help me pull the raft off the trailer a little," I said.

"Dude. I gotta get in the water?" With an exasperated sigh he doffed his sneakers and socks and waded to the bottom of his red basketball shorts. He looked kind of silly with gel-spiked hair at 10 a.m. in the Hudson River.

After we were both in the water we realized the platform was still tied to the trailer, so we got out again to untie it. The night before we'd tied the knots so tight that we couldn't untie them now. After pulling with my hands and teeth I opened the trunk of my car, retrieved a hacksaw and cut the ropes. Then we got in the water and each grabbed a corner of the platform. We bent and prepared to lift. On the count of three we grunted and nearly pulled our backs out. But the platform didn't budge.

"Damn man, did this thing get heavier overnight?"

"It certainly seems like it. Maybe it absorbed the rain." We tried lifting one corner a couple of inches. This was possible. So we decided to use the same method we used the night before in order to get the platform on the trailer. We lifted the platform together, jammed a piece of wood beneath it to prop it up, then lifted again and stuck another piece of wood on top of that, until we'd raised the platform high enough to float a barrel beneath the end that was hanging off the trailer. We'd brought a couple of 2x4 pieces as well as a wooden end-table my parents had thrown "over the hill" a couple of years before. So we grabbed these and brought them back. We lifted the platform, slid the rotting wooden end table under for support, and put the platform down — and it smashed the end table.

"Fuck dude!" Jared cried.

"Yeah," I said as I examined a gash I'd just gotten from a rusty nail. "This isn't working."

By that time it was about eleven thirty and we'd made no progress getting the floatation under the boat. Next we tried lifting the platform from another corner, but had no more success there. Then I had the idea of pushing a barrel underwater and letting it float up beneath the platform. So I waded into the water up to my hips and tried pushing down a barrel to submerge it. But instead of sinking the barrel, I floated. When I got out of the water with my pants clinging to my legs I saw a raised square in my pocket and realized I'd submerged and ruined my cell phone.

Besides the monetary value, the loss of my phone posed problems for me and for the trip. First, Mike could no longer reach us, because he didn't have Jared's number. Second, both reporters had my cell number and were planning to call me to rendezvous. Third, most of my friends and family planned to call me to find out if the launch was still happening that evening. And last, June 3rd would be my six-month anniversary with Cady and I was trumping that occasion to go on the rafting trip. Now I couldn't even call to remind her that I noted the significance of the date.

Nonetheless the most important thing was to get the platform on top of the barrels and after an hour and a half we were no further along. At least the weather had improved. A *Bic*-pen blue sky had appeared from behind the clouds and the afternoon sun began evaporating the puddles left by the previous evening's storm.

We must've looked like a couple of morons trying to get that thing in the water — me in my brown slacks and canvas "adventurer's jacket" and Jared with his spiked hair and baggy basketball shorts, both of us thoroughly drenched and heaving at the platform which wouldn't budge.

As we toiled in vain a huge town dump truck pulled into a parking spot beside the boat launch. It was a diesel job like a convoy truck. It came to a stop on top of the boulders that formed the west bank of the river. Inside the truck sat two town workers in orange shirts who began to eat sandwiches and watch us. Now with their glare burning us we began to really get frustrated. The tide had receded and Jared had to back his truck up to get the back of the platform close to the water again.

"Dude what a fucking day for Mike to take a test," Jared grumbled. "We could sure use another hand here." We decided to give a fifth or sixth attempt at heaving the platform but it was no use. "Fuck dude! I gotta have this truck back in two hours!"

I tried getting on top of the trailer and jumping up and down. Jared tried standing alongside and pushing the platform and slipped and fell face-first into the water. I knocked a barrel into the river by accident and had to swim after it.

Then we heard two doors slam and looked toward the top of the launch. The two town workers stood beside their dump truck. These guys were as much a sight to us as we were to them. Two burly, bristly men — as big compared to us as their truck was compared to my Chrysler. They stood there with steel-toed boots, paint and concrete speckled jeans, and identical short sleeved hot-orange shirts that read "Town of Coeymans: Wayne" and "Jerry." As we stood in the water up to our knees with our clothes clinging we looked up and awaited their derision. Wayne chomped the end of a sandwich while Jerry wiped crumbs from his beard with the back of his paw. Both wore the visage of a master craftsman who watches an apprentice ruin a time-consuming project.

"What the hell are you trying to do?" Wayne bellowed with a voice like a megaphone.

"We're trying to get this wooden thing on top of these barrels so we can tie them on," I said.

"What the hell for?" Jerry boomed.

"We built a raft. We're trying to float to Manhattan."

"Manhattan!" Wayne roared. "You mean like down in New York City?" Jared rolled his eyes,

"Yeah, that one."

"No shit," said Wayne to Jerry.

"Ain't that far?" Jerry shouted.

"A hundred and forty-four miles," I said. Wayne roared,

"And you're gonna go on *that*?"

"That's the plan," I said. Then looking at Jared I motioned to the platform. "Come on, let's both try lifting near the front of the trailer." So we got out of the water and bent down trying to lift at the front corner with no luck. It was well after noon and we were sweating. Jerry and Wayne, meanwhile, walked to the other side of the boat launch and watched us from a different angle.

"How long you think it'll take you?" Jerry asked.

"Five days," I grunted while trying to push.

"Five days! Phew!"

"What is this, some kind of a college project?" Wayne shouted. Jared chuckled and looked toward me for a response.

"Yes," I lied. I figured that would be easier than explaining the whole thing.

"Well wowee," said Jerry. "Geeze I wish I was in college so I could do this kind of stuff all day."

"Yeah," I said.

Now the two oxen made their way to the dock in the middle of the boat launch. On the dock they towered over us. While Wayne and Jerry stood there, an old man with a bag of crusts feeding ducks came over to stand and watch. A moment later two kids on beat-up bikes stood pointing at us and giggling to each other on the shore.

"How you plannin' on takin' a shit?" Jerry inquired.

"We'll stop off at marinas and parks along the way," I said.

"You gonna do that every time you take a piss, too?"

"Nah," Wayne admonished Jerry. "They can piss right in the river, right?"

"That's right," I said.

"Well geeze this is some project," Jerry said, and then he paused. "Say, you want some help getting that wooden thing off the trailer?"

"Yes!" Jared and I shouted at once.

Wouldn't you know it? Those two gorilla men in their orange shirts jumped down to the launch ramp and work-boots and all walked right into the river up to their knees. Without even rolling up their jeans. Even with their help we had a hard time getting the platform to dislodge. Jerry's pants kept falling down. When he groaned and lifted, his ass cheeks hung like two hams at the bottom of his shirt. On Wayne's forehead sweat drops beaded.

"Say, what are you fellas doing?" asked the old man with the bread crusts after a while.

"It's O.K. it's a college project," Jerry said.

Finally, with the help of those two good-hearted strangers we got the platform off the trailer and onto the barrels, and I began tying them in place. We thanked the two men vociferously.

"Hey it was nothin. No problem," Jerry said. They took turns crushing our hands in handshakes before getting back in their truck because their lunch break was over. As they drove away they honked their horn and wished us good luck. Jared and I swam under the barrels and tied them tentatively with clothesline. We planned to affix them more permanently when Mike arrived with the industrial zip ties. When we were done we tied the platform to the dock and beheld our work. There was no mistaking it then. We had built a raft.

Mike showed up just as Jared was leaving to bring the trailer back to Andrew Wilsey's.

"Well, whataya think?" I said to him. Mike was speechless. "Hey, were you able to get the zip ties?"

"Oh, no," Mike gazed at the raft. "I tried a couple different places and nobody knew what I was talking about." We walked onto the dock to get a close-up look at the boat. "I can't believe you guys got it together," he said. It was quite a sight: a multilayered hodgepodge of split flat paneling and plywood straddling six blue plastic barrels. The white rope I'd used to tie the barrels hung like *Silly String*. "Oh man, why didn't you put the barrels into two rows instead of every which way? Now there's gonna be all kinds of drag."

"Well," I said as I plucked a sliver from my palm, "getting them on wasn't exactly a cakewalk."

"Yeah but they would've cut through the water easier."

"Since we'll be moving the same speed as the river I don't think it's a problem. Well, here we are! Behold! *Ecce*! It's really something now!"

We still had to gather our provisions. I left Mike with the raft and scrambled to *Family Dollar* for supplies. I bought five cans of vegetable beef soup—one for lunch each day—a jar of peanut butter and some mixed nuts for breakfast and snacks, and a thirty pack of *Coors Original*. I figured we'd eat dinner at marina restaurants. I bought two *Styrofoam* coolers and ice and some lanterns and lantern oil. I brought all that back to the river and Mike helped me load it on the raft. I helped him load his duffle bag and sleeping bag, and we carried on a broken wooden filing cabinet I'd brought from over the hill at my parent's house.

"Why the fuck are we bringing this cabinet?" Mike complained.

"For effect. You know, it's like a strongbox."

"The door doesn't shut, the lock doesn't work, and we have nothing of value to put inside it."

"That's why I said 'for effect' and 'it's *like*' a strongbox.'"

"Jesus Christ."

We loaded the remaining unused fence posts, the life jackets everyone insisted we had to bring, one canoe paddle which belonged to Mike, a tarp, some garbage bags, a box of nails, a hammer, and a charcoal barbeque that had been in the trunk of my car for a year. There was such a pile of junk in the middle of the deck that there was hardly any room for us to stand. And Jared and I hadn't loaded our personal gear yet. Our launch time was T minus two hours.

"Do you think you could try and straighten this up while I run home, get my stuff and come back?" I asked.

"Sure *El Capitan*." I smiled.

"Thank you Admiral Peterman-Glenis." We saluted one another before I jumped into my car.

At my house my parents were just getting home from work. I put a change of clothes in a duffle bag and scarfed down a quick meal with them. Then I donned my "adventurer's outfit"—a wide-brimmed leather hat, a canvas jacket with buttons and pockets at the breasts and hips and belt loops at the waist and shoulders that reminded me of epaulettes, a pair of brown slacks, a canteen filled with water, and a knife on a lanyard on my belt. I wore a pair of binoculars around my neck and put a pen and tide chart in my breast pocket. I think I looked the part of an adventurous explorer. When I'd buttoned my lapel I jumped back into Mindy, my car, and blasted

Sink the Bismarck as I drove back toward my rendezvous with destiny.

June 1st, 2006 was a Thursday. I felt the shaky nervousness I used to get before Drama Club productions in high school.

June 1st, 2006 is a sticky label, like a barcode, affixed to a specific period of time consisting of 86,400 seconds and falling chronologically between other units of equal duration, of which we have divided the endless river of time. The label itself is meaningless, like an empty file folder, until it is filled with content, stuff, significance.

June 1st, 2006 was not the date of the Pearl Harbor attacks. It was not the day that the Soviet Union invaded Czechoslovakia, that the markets crashed in Indonesia, or that Darius crossed the Hellespont into Greece. It is not a day that will be recorded in history books because it did not alter history—that is, affect the course of many people's lives in some notable way.

Maybe Mike and Linda LaFollete were married on June 1st, 2006. Maybe Anton Rasolov was stabbed in an Estonian village. It is a day thousands will call their birthday, until they die.

Every person, the day before the end of this great chemical reaction of existence, could look at a list of the dates they have lived through, and with a yellow highlighter, color the most significant. Depressed people expect to see a white sheet. But anyone who keeps a journal knows it is quite the opposite—nearly every day can be highlighted for one reason or another. Maybe people who keep journals tend to lead interesting lives. Or maybe journaling helps people understand how each day changes the next along a continuum. Regardless, I kept a journal and for 10 months I'd looked forward to one particular date: June 1st, 2006. And now the river of time caught me up with my imagination.

I parked Mindy and emerged onto the gravel by the riverbank. There was the *U.S.S. Crab Legs*, floating silently. Mike had run up Old Glory, the big American flag he'd hung in his apartment in New Paltz. It was a beautiful summer evening. The wind was picking up and stretching out the red, white and blue, which unfurled upon a fence post. Mike had also hung about a dozen smaller flags, waving in the wind.

Done up in my leather fedora and canteen I strutted down to the dock. Mike stood on the raft talking to a cute brunette. His posture was tense.

"You're really wearing that outfit?" Mike said when he saw me.

"Of course!" I said. "It's an adventure."

"Where's Jared?"

"He ought to be here soon." I turned to the brunette and said hello.

"Hi," she said, extending her hand. She stood exceedingly erect. "I'm Ashley Clay from the *Ravena Ledger*. I was just asking Mr. Peterman-Glenis a few questions about your project. Would you mind if I—"

"—Sure, ask away!" I'd never seen such a stiff reporter. She held a spiral notebook with a bunch of handwritten questions with spaces between each one so she could write the answers down.

"I'm going to load the rest of my stuff while you're here," Mike said as he went off to his car. When he was out of earshot the reporter said quietly,

"Mike said I shouldn't publish an article on this."

"What?" I thought I'd misheard her.

"He said it isn't newsworthy and it's a big joke."

"Really?"

"So I want to know if, like—are you really planning on going to Manhattan?"

For a moment I didn't know what to say. The reporter stood with pen poised.

"Look, Mike is really enthusiastic sometimes. I think we get each other going when it comes to planning what he likes to call 'a dog and pony show.' But that's not what this is. This is a real attempt to make Manhattan."

"Do you think Mike feels that way?"

"The *Ravena Ledger* asks the tough questions," I joked. She smiled.

"Will he be okay with us publishing the story?"

"Definitely," I said. "And so will this guy—" I waved to Jared who was walking down the dock with a case of *Keystone Lights*.

"Whatup," he said.

"Miss Clay, this is Jared Ableman, the First Mate of the *U.S.S. Crab Legs*."

"Hi."

"How did you come up with that name for the boat?" She asked.

"We love crab legs," Jared and I said.

"Jinx."

Mike returned to the dock with a duffle bag and a 30-pack of *Poland Spring* water.

"What's that shit?" said Jared, pointing.

"Water," said Mike.

"I thought that wasn't allowed," Jared said. "I thought we were only supposed to drink beer."

"That's all I brought," I pointed to my *Coors Original.*

"Nothing but beer for five days?" Mike said incredulously. "Don't you think we'll get a little dehydrated?"

"There's water in the beer," I stated.

"Yeah, weak dude," Jared added. Mike put the water onboard.

"Well, Miss Clay, this is the crew of the *U.S.S. Crab Legs*!" The reporter asked if we were still planning to launch at six, and I said "Yes! Six on the dot!"

"Actually Dallas," Mike interjected, "You might want to take a look at that tide chart again. I don't know where you're seeing that high tide is at six today." So I retrieved the tide chart from my pocket. It contained columns listing geographic locations and, in the rows beneath the location headings, the days of the month and the times of the day at which the high and low tides would occur. There was no listing for Coeymans, our launch site, so I had looked at the high tide times for Schodak, which is upriver, and Catskill, which is downriver, and averaged them. But I'd looked at the wrong date when I calculated that high tide would be at 6. In reality, I now saw that high tide would be at 8 p.m. Before that point the flood tide would be making the water flow north—the wrong direction.

"Admiral Peterman-Glenis illustrates the importance of checks and balances aboard a naval vessel," I said. "Our launch time shall be at oh-eight-hundred on the dot."

"Twenty hundred," Mike corrected.

"Exactly."

We posed for a picture and the reporter left.

As we made ready our craft our friends and family started showing up. I expected a half-dozen people, but as folks trickled in the group swelled to five times that number. They walked down to the dock to get a good look at the raft. As they looked on we got our belongings in order. We erected a fence post at each corner so we could string a tarp over our heads, because the sky was turning gray and the wind was picking up. We only had one paddle, so we decided to construct two more out of 2x4s and pieces of plywood we had on hand. The crowd was sarcastic.

"I hope you got health insurance!" my dad's pal Muck remarked. My father kept repeating,

"Behold: The Ark!" and "Okay, let's see this paddle you're building. Okay Einstein—here's the expert raft builder," and such other things to make the crowd laugh.

I put a 2x4 on the dock and a narrow piece of plywood on top of it, in order to make a paddle. Then I nailed the plywood to the 2x4 with three nails. I didn't realize that the nails had gone straight through the 2x4 and nailed the paddle to the dock. Everyone laughed when I tried to pick up the paddle and it wouldn't budge. But I shrugged that off, used shorter nails, and then we had a homemade paddle.

Oliver arrived with his parents. His mother said that when we couldn't get a flatbed the day before, she'd thought our trip was over. My sister and brother-in-law taped the scene with a camcorder. Some of my friends from high school, the ones I kept in contact with who'd heard about the project, showed up. Several of my extended family members and Mike's immediate family were there, as well as Andrew Wilsey and his family, Tom Tucker from the *News Herald*, some other acquaintances, and a group of strangers who happened to be at the river at the time.

As the sky grew ominously gray my mother said,

"Oh Dallas you aren't going to leave if the weather gets bad are you?" to which I replied,

"Whether snow or rain or sleet or hail..." and there was the familiar chorus of "I hope you brought lifejackets."

As it got to be six the crowd grumbled, "When are you taking off?" and when I said, "Twenty hundred" they cried, "What will we do 'til then?" So I pointed to the bar in the local marina a hundred yards away and shouted "Drink!" and no one protested.

(June 1st, 2006, the U.S.S. Crab Legs in Coeymans. Mike (left) samples champagne as I treat with the crowd of family and friends. Behind Mike is a cement block which served as our anchor. Note the flags furling northward because of the wind blowing from the south. The south wind was a significant obstacle to overcome.)

I led the 30 or so of us into *Yanni's Too* bar and restaurant [formerly the *Muddy Rudder*]. Through the windows it was obvious a storm was building, yet we were in a merry mood. We occupied the bar and took it over. All of our friends and family were wishing us luck and congratulations and a *bon voyage*. It was heartwarming to see family and friends from different cliques mingling and laughing together. My friend Morgan bought Mike, Jared and I a round of *Blue Moons*. They tasted great after the hot sticky day. Oliver handed me a notebook inside a *Ziploc* bag.

"This is for a Captain's Log," he smiled through his blonde beard. I thanked him for all his help getting the barrels and letting us build the boat in his driveway. At the bar I wrote the first entry:

Captain's Log
1 June, 2006. 19:15
At Yanni's Too. Drinking Blue Moons. Preparing for launch. So many friends and family. Floating.

My parents bought us crew members a round and we all said Cheers! Then the skies opened up. Some celestial cistern overflowed so violently that the drops hitting the side of the building sounded like tacks dropped on a tile floor.

"Our shit is gonna get soaked!" Mike exclaimed.

We told everyone to sit tight and ran outside in order to put a tarp over the raft. Cold rain cascaded from up in an anvil-shaped thundercloud. We got soaked to our skin as we put up the tarp, which did little to protect our bags from the slanting rain. It rained so hard it ran in rivulets down our cheeks and foreheads into our eyes as we tried to cover our stuff.

"Our bags are gonna get drenched!" Mike shouted.

"We'll have to dry them later! Right now *we're* getting drenched!" We sprinted back to the bar and schlepped through the door, our shoes squishing and dripping puddles onto the floor inside. The crowd gasped. We might as well have taken showers in our clothes. The bartender threw us a towel to wipe our faces. For another hour we drank as the rain relentlessly fell outside.

Summer storms come quick and fast and often fizzle out. By a quarter after eight the rain had slowed to a drizzle and the crowd was anxious to see us off. So we took one last departing shot and made our way to the dock. Jared, Mike and I stood aboard the *Crab Legs*, a foot above the murky brown water. Our friends and family crowded onto the dock, huddling under each other's umbrellas. Their breaths made little clouds of steam. The sky was dark gray as the sun sank somewhere behind a cover of cumulonimbuses.

"Speech, speech!" someone yelled. It seemed appropriate. So I shouted above the chatter,

"Friends, Ravenians, countrymen, lend me your ears!" Mike had been sipping from a bottle of cheap champagne, which he now handed to me. "First! Three libations to Poseidon!" I poured three offerings into the river.

"Gimme that!" Mike snatched the bottle.

"That's alcohol abuse," shouted my father's friend Muck from the peanut gallery. We polished off the bottle and I handed it to my mother to complete the christening ceremony.

"Sandra Trombley will now christen the *U.S.S. Crab Legs*!"

My mother brought the bottle down on the deck of the raft. It didn't break. The crowd was silent. She brought it down again, and again it didn't break. The wet plywood absorbed the impact.

"Can I try?" Mike asked. He then brought the bottle down with the same result.

"Must be a defective bottle," said my father.

Jared, never one for formalities, said,

"Alright, you wanna get the fuck outta here?" and we agreed. Amongst cheers we untied the *Crab Legs* and pushed off. We floated in slack water and went nowhere. I realized then that the current does not instantaneously accelerate when the tide changes; rather, there is a period of slack water with no current whatsoever. So, it was up to us to paddle until the current picked up. We stood on the raft and dug our paddles in, millimetering downstream. After a full minute of paddling, we still could've stepped from the raft to the dock.

"Wow, watch them go!" shouted my father.

"You guys better move faster than *that*," I heard Nick the naysayer exclaim.

"At this rate they'll make it to New York…by Christmas!" Muck chimed.

To be completely fair, the onlookers laughed and said such things largely out of anxiety, rather than derision, because here we were, doing what we said we were going to do, and nobody on the dock would've wanted to spend the evening onboard our raft—cold, wet and dark. To rid themselves of that anxious feeling while standing with people they hardly knew, uncomfortable and squished together, they made jokes. Now I understand that. But at the time it was exceedingly agitating.

"Okay you wanna man-up and paddle hard until we get around that peninsula down there?" Jared suggested. We dug hard and deep into the water and achieved some movement. After forty-five minutes we'd reached a peninsula, beyond which we'd be out of sight from the marina. By now it was almost dark, and still drizzling. As I looked back I was touched to see our friends and family still standing on that dock—now little figurines—in the rain watching us, so many of them standing there that the dock was nearly submerged. Then, continuing to paddle as hard and as frequently as our wet limbs and our cob-job paddles allowed, we crawled past the peninsula. The rocks jutting from the western bank obstructed our view of our waving friends. It was just the three of us then, on black water beneath a black sky. Our adventure had finally begun.

VI. Rattlesnake Island

We put our paddles down and scrambled to make a shelter, tripping over straps and *Styrofoam* coolers, losing *Koozies* and cans to the wind.

"Quick, grab the tarp—let's try to make a lean to!" Mike shouted. Our tarp couldn't keep the rain from driving in diagonally. We tied twine around the tops of the fence posts and the corners of the tarp. Water ran down our faces.

When we'd made a small triangle to huddle under, we sat and got our asses wet on the spongy particleboard deck. By the time the rain calmed to a drizzle again we were tired and shivering. To warm ourselves and to feel like we were doing something, we took turns paddling, one person with a paddle on one side, another with a homemade paddle on the other, and for a while, the third person using the other homemade paddle at the middle of the front like he was piloting a gondola. But the cob-job paddles were impractically heavy, and soon snapped. So one of us sat on a cooler in the middle of the raft while the other two sat Indian-style on either side and paddled, one with a real paddle and one with a flat piece of wood. We decided to rotate one position to the right every five minutes. We did that for half an hour.

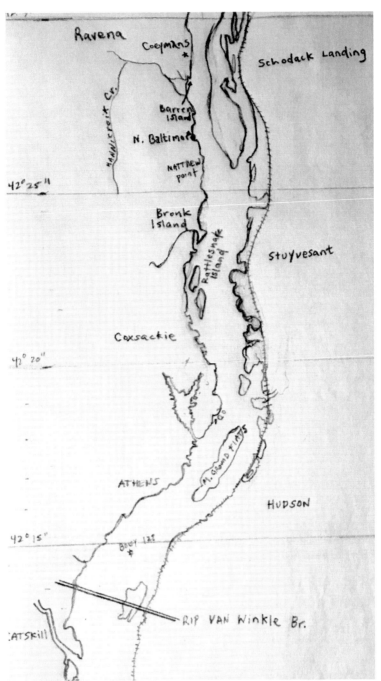

"Dude I didn't know this was gonna be a fucking relay," Jared complained.

"Yeah let's stop rowing and see how fast the tide takes us," Mike suggested. I agreed. My shoulders and arms burned. It was about as dark as gray can be without becoming black. Fog hovered over the bistre water. The foliage on the river bank seemed to crawl backward as one creeping mass.

"If you look at the trees against the clouds you can kind of see how fast we're moving," Jared pointed out. Mike quipped,

"You mean how *slow* we're moving?"

"Well, we got all night," said Jared, twisting onto his hands and knees. "Who wants a *Keystone*?"

"I'll take a *Coors*," I said. Mike took the cover off the plastic cooler and threw us each a beer.

"Cheers," he said ironically. We drank and looked in front of us, our eyes fixed on a single green, blinking light silently alternating on and off downstream. Indistinguishable grey-black mass surrounded us. "It's really something now."

It was one of those moments, like on a second or third date, when there is silence but it is O.K.

"Maybe I should light a lantern?" Mike asked after a while. Since it was dark it seemed like a good idea. I lifted a long-stemmed lighter for him to see while he poured lantern oil into an aluminum dollar store lamp. I'd brought three lamps but one got smashed in the storm. In the darkness Mike poured the lamp oil on himself and the deck. "Don't get that lighter too close."

He got the lamp lit and adjusted the wick so we had some light. Shadows flickered across our faces and the deck and transformed the raft into a little illuminated island in a sphere of darkness and haze. The lamplight felt warm. The rain seemed to slow, then it stopped. Calmer now than when we'd launched, we arranged the deck so we could sit on the life jackets and rest our backs against the coolers and duffle bags. After the storm passed the clouds dissipated into smaller and smaller wisps, and soon above us within the sphere of blackness an array of stars appeared. Only where the stars stopped did we deduce that the sky ended and the tree line began. The darkness, the whole scene, felt otherworldly, peaceful, vacuous, spiritual. Essentially, it felt *new*. Yet maybe the closest sensation was *deja vu*.

"Wow. This is beautiful," Jared spoke.

We had only a vague idea of our location—a couple of miles downstream. With no city lights and no moon, each star shone like a glowing pinprick in a black satin sheet shielding a celestial spotlight. After a silence, Mike pointed upward.

"There's the big dipper."

"Which one?" Jared asked.

"Those three bright ones above that tree, to the right of Polaris."

"Polaris?" Jared repeated.

"It's the last star on the handle of the big dipper."

"Oh, I see it now!"

Cricket chirps emanated from either shore. The chirps to our left were a little delayed reaching our ears because we were closer to the western shore as we floated facing south. When fireflies glowed they were like terrestrial stars among the black foliage. A mile downstream a green buoy blinked. It sent a long, reflecting trail onto the black water.

"How do you know so much about stars?" Jared asked Mike.

"Oh, I don't know," Mike said, thoughtfully trying to remember. "I guess through Boy Scouts or just a general sense of interest. Huh."

"I used to love looking at stars," I said, leaning on a paddle on the right side of the raft. "I used to go up on top of the hill by my grandparent's house. I'd argue that the top of that hill is the second-highest point in New Baltimore, behind the one that's marked "highest" on the map at the Conservancy trailhead. Anyway I used to love to go up there because you could see 150 degrees of sky, above the trees. I used to be able to find Sirius, and then the Big Dipper, and based on the Big Dipper's bottom two stars, find the Little Dipper, which was halfway between Sirius and the Big Dipper, if you turned left."

"Didn't you used to have a map of that tacked to your bedroom ceiling in middle school? With yarn and *Post-it* notes?" Mike chuckled.

"Yeah. I remember being up there one night when it was dark like it is tonight, with no moon I mean, and all of a sudden I saw this black mass on the ground coming toward me slowly up the hill. I thought it was a cat. But as it came closer I saw a white stripe down its back and I knew it was a skunk."

"Haha! What did you do?" Jared asked.

"I fucking stood there stiff as a board afraid it would see me move and get scared and spray me."

"What happened?"

"The thing waddled up to me—it waddles like a penguin—and doesn't the thing walk right between my legs and even push his head against the inside of my leg like a cat would."

"Holy shit dude what did you do?"

"Well, let's just say I still had to wash my pants because of the smell. But seriously the thing just went through and disappeared into the woods behind me. I went inside after that; I'd had enough star gazing."

"Dude that's crazy." Mike pointed to the buoy down-stream.

"Let's see how long it takes us to get to that buoy. What would you say it is, a half mile away?"

"I guess," I said, "I don't really have a good idea of distances."

"Jared, would you say it's about a half mile away?" Mike asked.

"Dude I have no idea. Yeah—no—it looks like about a half mile."

"Okay well I'm going to guess that it'll take us fifteen minutes to get to that buoy. What do you say?"

"Twelve minutes," Jared shot back. "What about you D.T.?"

"I think it will take us eight minutes," I said.

"Eight minutes?" Mike said. "No way. More like twenty."

"We'll see…" I said. I looked at the waterproof watch my brother-in-law had lent me for the trip. "It's 10:06 now. We'll note the time when we pass alongside."

"What's the winner get?" asked Jared.

"I donno, what?"

Jared declared, "The loser has to chug a beer and the second closest has to chug a half, deal?"

Said Mike, "It looks like we're heading in the general direction of that buoy. Maybe we ought to take a couple of paddles on the left side so we don't get too close."

We each paddled ten times on the left side of the raft so that we faced about twenty degrees to the right, or west, of the buoy.

"That's one really nice thing about living in the country is being able to see the stars," said Mike when we rested after paddling. "I remember I had some friends up from New Paltz who came from the city—out to my parent's house, and at night they couldn't believe how many stars there were. They never saw so many because they'd never been away from light pollution at night. They were just amazed."

"Dude imagine there was no such thing as stars?" said Jared.

"What do you mean?"

"Like, imagine there were no stars and at night everything was just dark."

"Like, no lights at all or just no celestial lights?" Mike asked.

"No lights at all."

"Well," I interjected, "if there was no such thing as celestial lights, does that mean there is no such thing as the moon? Because if so, there's a good chance we would never even exist."

"Why? Without the *moon*?" Jared scoffed.

"Because it makes the tides. I found this out researching for this trip. I mean I always knew the moon was responsible for the tides, but I really learned *why*. The gravity of the moon pulls back on Earth. It has an unnoticeable effect on solids, but on the oceans it literally pulls them away from the earth. The fuller the moon the stronger the pull—and the earth itself continues to spin as the water is lifted, which is what pulls the tide up into the bays and rivers and causes high tide."

"Yeah the moon makes a bulge on the earth if you were to look at the oceans from space," Mike added. We were jarred from our discussion when Jared pointed toward the buoy.

"We seem to be facing right at that thing again."

"Maybe there's a current and it's actually going to the left of the buoy?" Mike hypothesized.

"Maybe," I said. "Maybe we ought to paddle on the right side of the raft and pass the buoy on the left side instead?"

"Okay."

To make it quicker two of us sat on one side and paddled together, until we were facing the far shore and would now pass inside the buoy, closer to the east shore.

I'd never really gotten a close look at a buoy. As it crept within nighttime visual range I could see it was essentially a large green bulb bolted atop a short steel tower, which itself was welded atop a big steel sphere, which must have been hollow, because it floated. The buoy must have been connected to the river bottom by means of a chain of significant size, which allowed the buoy to rise and fall with the tide and also anchored it in place during storms of wind, rain and ice.

"The buoys mark the inside of the channel," Mike reminded us.

"Okay what does that exactly mean," said Jared as though asking a question he'd harbored for some time.

"If you're going down the river one way you want to keep the green buoys on your left, the red ones on your right, in order to stay inside the channel."

"Because the channel is a certain depth so big ships don't bottom out," I added.

"How deep?"

Mike and I shrugged.

"Well which ones should we keep on our left going downriver?" Jared asked.

"Not sure," said Mike. "But jeeze we're really moving right toward that buoy."

It was true. The buoy seemed to grow in size at a quicker rate now than a few moments before. Now we noticed the green light bobbing back and forth, and distinguished that the steel structure was painted green, and that the sphere on which it floated had dimples from collisions. It seemed to stand as tall as a man in the water ahead of us.

"I can't tell what side we're going to pass it on. Can you, Captain?"

"No. We seem to be heading directly toward it. Let's each sit on one side of the raft with a paddle and when we get close and we can tell which side we're going to pass it on, we'll paddle on the side closer to it."

"If we need to we can push the buoy away with the paddle," said Mike. So we took our positions and watched the buoy approach. Jared sat on the left and Mike on the right of the deck. I took up a position in the middle of the front.

"A couple of paddles on the left," I said, and Jared dug into the water twice.

"We seem to be going at a pretty good clip now," Mike observed. "Well, it's 10:16 and I bet we'll pass that in less than a minute. It's been ten minutes so if it was a half mile away when we made our bet then we're going like two and a half miles an hour."

"Jared—can you give about five paddles on your side?" I interjected. "Two and a half miles is good. If we each paddle so that we move relative to the water at point-five miles an hour we'll go at three miles an hour and get there in five days. Damn, Jared, we need like fifteen rows on your side."

"Damn dude."

Now we could really see that the buoy was almost fifteen feet tall, and made of welded steel, and connected to a steel sphere the size of a car, splashing in the middle of the oily depths. The shore now seemed very far away. With some urgency, Mike arose.

"I think we'd better all paddle on Jared's side or we're going to hit that thing."

So Mike and Jared paddled hard until we faced the eastern shore instead of downstream. Then they caught their breath.

"Good job guys," I commended them.

But the current seemed to pick up, and almost immediately the side of the raft where Jared and Mike sat seemed pulled toward the buoy.

"Quick—hand me a paddle and I'll point us south," I urged. I put a few paddles in and got our unofficial bow pointing downstream again. But I must've paddled too many times because we found ourselves pointed right at the buoy again, and picking up speed. It rose up out of the water to such a size that we feared the effects of a collision. Still we seemed to move more quickly.

"Guys you—"

"Yeah, paddle on this side!" Now the raft pointed away from the buoy, we'd pass. No—we were going to hit—Mike and Jared paddled again. The buoy was an industrial, cement and steel, permanent fixture anchored by iron chains and we were a nailed-together piece of driftwood on fragile plastic barrels—in the middle of the river on a moonless night, far from shore.

"We're going to hit that thing," Mike said matter-of-factly. The realization settled and we stopped paddling. In the middle of the river it became silent except for the schlep of waves. Then Mike said "Hold on!" and the vessel lurched violently. For a second we could make out the marks left by every piece of driftwood, every dropping from a bird, on buoy number 173. Slowly our stern gravitated toward the western shore, then shifted downstream and became the bow, as we sat still looking at the buoy now shrinking backward into the night. After a minute Mike mused, "I don't think we could've hit that buoy if we tried. We actually steered ourselves into it."

The buoy receded, like a dream-thing, slowly and quietly into the blackness.

"So…how many minutes?" Jared asked.

"Oh, let me see—" I looked at my watch, "—eleven. Looks like Jared wins."

"Sweet! Who has to chug a whole one, who has to chug a half?"

"Mike's a whole; I'm half." I said. As Mike climbed over to the cooler I looked downstream at a red blinking light. "I hope this doesn't happen at every buoy."

The middle of the river at night is dark and quiet and rhythmic. The chords of crickets and the swish of waves grew subtle as our clothes on our skin. It was a novel experience, such little external stimulation while awake.

We were careful to stay outside the channel, near the western shore, after misjudging some lights downstream for stars. We were puzzled as we watched these stars closest to the horizon rise, over minutes, until we realized they were the lights of a container ship chugging upstream. As the ship passed we sensed the mammoth hull moving. We heard the motor humming inside its great steel chest. Then we heard gurgling water as the man-sized propellers chopped through. In the dark the ship displaced a hump of water which radiated outward. We held onto the deck, afraid our gear would bounce around. But thanks to the flexibility of our boat—the same characteristic that'd made the platform so difficult to load onto the trailer, because it flopped like melted cheese—we simply rode the contour of the wave and perceived a gentle rise, a gentle fall, and then the sensation that we'd returned to our original orientation and height.

"Ha! Six foot waves my ass!" I shouted triumphantly. "Take that, Hank from *the Coeymans Yacht Club*!"

Later we drifted into a field of lily pads and littoral grass. We felt that we had slowed. Mike held a lantern over the water. The surface was covered in leaves the shape of painter's pallets. In the dark, where human eyes see light but have a hard time distinguishing colors, the water and leaves appeared as though covered in oil. Between the leaves grass-like reeds emerged from the water's surface.

"Are those lily pads?" asked Mike. "We're just outside the channel. It must get shallow really quick at this spot. And it must be really shallow here at low tide." As we floated on we started to feel and almost hear the stem grass and pads brushing the bottoms of the barrels.

"Is that shit slowing us down?" Jared asked.

"It can't be doing us good," Mike said. "You wanna all paddle until we get out of these weeds?"

"Fuck; fine." Jared said.

It wasn't easy getting out of the grass. For one thing the raft wasn't easy to steer. We could paddle on one side and thereby point the "bow" in a certain direction, but the best we could do to move forward faster than the water was for two people to paddle, one on either side. Even then we were heavy and the barrels faced every which-way, plowing the water instead of slicing through it the way a boat hull does. We felt like mules dragging the boat forward. We had to reach deep into the water and pull back with great effort, each "paddle" taking a long time to complete. Our shoulders and arms burned.

"Maybe this is low tide?" Mike speculated.

"It can't be, it's only 12:30," I said. "This tide doesn't get over until 2:00. So we still have an hour and a half left." As I said this our faces became illuminated in white light. We jerked our hands to our faces. "Who the hell is that?"

"Fuck is it the police?" Mike shouted. "Put away the beer."

The light died. But we heard the gurgle of a motor grow louder and saw small green, red and white lights moving in our direction from the ether. Then the hull of a small motorboat with four figures inside.

"Woah look at that!" we heard a female voice. Then the spotlight came on again, but it pointed in front of us so that it didn't hurt our eyes.

"Sorry for blinding you," a male shouted. As the boat got closer we made out four adults in raincoats and caps, with nets and poles in their hands, and lifejackets around their necks. They stopped their boat alongside.

"Wow you guys are rafters?" said a thirty-something guy with a bristly beard. With pride that the guy understood what we were doing, and seemed interested, I affirmed,

"Yes sir!" A woman with a camo cap leaned forward.

"You guys okay? Where'd you come from?"

"We left from Coeymans," I said.

"Wow that's like six miles. When'd you leave?"

"Tonight at 8:30," said Mike.

"In the storm?"

"Yeah."

"That must've been crazy! You got a motor on that thing?"

"Nope," I said. "We're just driftin'.'"

A couple of them asked at once, "Where you gonna go?" and "How far you going?"

"To Manhattan." I said.

"Hahaha!" They laughed. "How long you got?"

"Five days we think, but we'll keep going till we make it."

"Wow," said the guy with the beard. He reminded me of my friend's older brother's friend, who had money and education and talked to me just a little patronizingly. A guy who was nice, who you wanted respect from, but who came from a higher class, and therefore held a modicum of authority. "I don't know about five days…" he said.

They asked numerous questions about the raft, our plans, equipment and food. Finally, Mike asked what they were doing and who they were.

"We're from En Con. There're bird houses and fish cages in the littoral waters back there." I looked down and noticed we were clear of the grass and drifting downstream again. "We were saying to ourselves, *What kind of boat is that? Do you recognize that light pattern?*" The women laughed. Eventually they said, "Well, we better get to work. We have to check all the cages and see if any of the tagged fish made it back." They wished us luck and started their motor. It sounded like a chainsaw after the lull of the night quiet. As they motored away we heard one of the women say, "Wasn't that crazy?" and a guy say "I'd do it too if I was eighteen."

"We're not eighteen," Mike grumbled to Jared and I.

At the time it made a difference.

An hour later our eyes were swollen and heavy. More and more our conversations enveloped meditative silences. We leaned back and watched, now and then putting a paddle in to steer. The shoreline slowly ceased sliding backward. The stars remained longer in the patches where there were no branches, black on black. The flood tide was growing closer.

We decided to make a last effort for the night. We paddled toward a light we saw peeking from the trees on the western shore ahead. The rest of the shoreline on both sides of the river was impenetrable with brush down to the waterline. We paddled — casually now, not with the unsustainable effort we'd expended earlier — toward the light. It grew larger as the minutes passed. In a while we saw a lighter black mass juxtaposed against the darker black shoreline. A few minutes later we saw that an island protected a natural harbor on the western bank. As we approached the island and passed inside close to the shore we saw a patio set and a wooden sign illuminated indistinctly by starlight. As the minutes turned to dozens of minutes we paddled rhythmically, hypnotically. I closed my eyes to rest them as I paddled. Soon two more small lights appeared a short distance from the first, again, visible through holes in the trees. As we got closer we squinted to make out white patches along the shore. Only as we crept closer did we distinguish that they were pleasure boats, then buildings, and a long dock.

"What marina is this?" Mike whispered. No one knew.

"Dude I'm just glad I'm gonna be able to shut my eyes," said Jared. We paddled toward the dock and grasped it.

"Can we keep this thing here?" Mike whispered as we tiptoed onto the dock. "What if somebody comes?"

"I donno, man," I said. I was making up the plan as we went along. We tied the raft to the dock's cleats. We decided to scout the area for a bathroom and a place to sleep. It was hard to see in the darkness, but we grabbed our sleeping bags and duffle bags and crept up the dock. Once on land, Jared whispered,

"I know this place. This is where Kelly's family has their boat. This is *Hager's Harbor* or some shit."

"In Coxsackie?"

"Yeah."

We crossed a gravel lot toward a square metal building.

"Is this place twenty-four hours?" Mike asked.

"Nah it's a boat club. People come and go to use their boat, use the clubhouse. It doesn't look like anyone's here," Jared replied.

"Do they lock the door to the pavilion?" Mike asked.

"I donno man I don't own the place. Probably not. Let's try it. They might even have some free beer." Mike turned the doorknob on the steel-framed building and the door clicked open.

"I don't want to be ripping people off," I whispered. "It's nice enough just to be able to sleep under a roof in case it rains." We sidled inside.

"It's okay," Jared whispered, "it's stuff on tap so they'll never know." We made a search of the place for a bathroom, which there was, which was lucky. Then Jared gave us a tour of the facility. "This is the kitchen." He turned on a fluorescent light that pierced our eyes.

"Turn that off man!" Mike shouted.

Jared flicked the switch and continued the tour. "Here is an empty keg. Here is a room with a bunch of picnic tables. Tour complete."

We dropped our bags and blankets and rolled a jazz cigarette by flashlight. It was celebratory. We'd wanted to smoke it on the raft but it'd been too windy and dark to roll one. Mike lit it and passed it to me.

"Here's to proving those nay-sayers wrong," I said.

Jared took a puff and passed out for the night. He lay on his back on a sleeping bag on the cement floor, half beneath a picnic table. Mike and I sat Indian-style. After Mike turned off the flashlight the only thing visible was the glowing red dot on the cigarette as we passed it and philosophized.

"Well, here we are," Mike said with a chuckle.

"A great place to be," I said.

"Coxsackie?" Mike laughed.

"Just here in general." The smoke danced out of Mike's mouth as our pupils adjusted to the darkness again.

"Well, I can't argue with that," he said.

"I suppose the problem comes when you wish *here* was someplace else," I mused.

"If we're in Coxsackie that's, what? Eight miles downstream?"

"I don't know."

"And we were on the water five hours? Jeeze that's bad. What is that, like one-and-a-half miles an hour? A tiny bit more?"

"Slow but steady. Like the tortoise," I said.

"Yeah but jeeze, eight miles a tide—that equals sixteen miles a day. It's what, about a hundred and fifty miles to New York City? That's going to take ten days," Mike emphasized.

"If that's what it takes…" I said.

"Yeah…" Fatigue overtook us like the fog earlier in the evening. It'd been a long, surprising, challenging day, all things considered. After all, that morning I'd stood with Jared on the dock at Coeymans Marina, wondering how we would affix the barrels to the platform. Who knew where we would be the next day? Mike seemed to come to some conclusion in his head, for he asserted suddenly, "No but I'm totally in. This is great. I can't believe all the people who came to see us off. And the newspapers." He nodded and passed the cigarette. I agreed and noted that the scene did not seem real.

"It almost feels like today is yesterday and I'm dreaming about tomorrow. As though the present hasn't happened yet but I'm experiencing it as a premonition." We were now fully reclined on our sleeping bags beneath the picnic tables.

"I bet you a part of that is because we planned this trip for so long that it doesn't seem possible that we could be living it," Mike said. "And part of it is because you're stoned."

"I believe you are right on both accounts, Admiral," I said as I closed my eyes.

"Thank you, Captain."

I was asleep by the time my lashes intermingled.

VII. That Sinking Feeling

Captain's Log
2 June, 2006. 09:27 Hours

Awoke this morning to the sound of a Miller Lite truck delivering beer. Took a while to get up, but snuck out to the dock for a getaway. Untied and made a break for it, evading capture.

But we did not move thanks to slack water. Even as we paddled we seemed to move backward. It was seven a.m. and the sun had just risen. We sat still a quarter-hour. After a while the beer delivery man—whose tee shirt was threadbare and too small—noticed us. He stood on shore, hands on hips, staring at us like zoo animals. We were groggy, having slept on cement for four hours, but we paddled just to be out of his stare.

In the cloudy morning light, we saw the end of the island that created the marina harbor a half-mile downstream. Before we reached the open water a man in a kayak paddled up to us. He had a salt and pepper beard and a camera with a lens like a wide-mouthed telescope. The side of his kayak read *Kayak Guy*. He told us he traveled up and down rivers and streams across the United States, taking pictures of what he saw. But he lived in New York. He snapped our picture and told us we could see it at *kayakguy.com*. He grew concerned when we told him we were trying to make it to Manhattan.

"That'll take you six months," he said. "A piece of driftwood takes six months to float from Albany to Manhattan on the tides."

"A piece of driftwood doesn't tie up when the tide comes in," I pointed out.

"Even so, you won't make it on *that*. I hope you have life jackets." Annoyed with his nay-saying attitude we bid him good morning and he bid us good luck.

Around 8:00 we ate our breakfast—chunky peanut butter, a can of beer, and some uncooked beef and barley soup I opened with my knife. We passed the town of Athens a few minutes later. We hoped to make Catskill, about five miles farther downriver, by the end of the tide.

The sound of a beer can opening, *schleck*, and a moment later, three of us saying *ahhh*! The morning birds chatting. The sound of a breeze nudging us gently from behind. We smelled morning dew.

We untied the tarp from the fence posts and rigged a square sail to make use of the wind. It filled with air as soon as we spread it across the back two posts. We gained a little speed. Athens, a colonial town with a riverfront park and square brick buildings, faded behind us. It was overcast and damp as we drifted past a shoreline made of stone boulders.

We sat, two of us with a paddle on the port and starboard sides, just to steer. The wind and the current did the work.

"This morning when we were taking off, the tides must not have changed yet," Mike observed.

"According to the tide chart it was time to change," I noted.

(Rattlesnake Island in Coxsackie, eight miles south of Coeymans, June 2nd, 2006. This picture was taken by Kayak Guy. He was unimpressed with the U.S.S. Crab Legs. Note the front barrels have taken on water.)

"Well, we were actually moving backwards. Maybe it takes a while to get going."

We had a 'map' of the marinas along the river. It was an elementary thing from a boating magazine with cartoonish pictures of the establishments along the way, printed primarily for the benefit of riverfront restaurants. It had some information on the tides as well as scant historical anecdotes, which Mike read aloud to us.

"This is great," Jared said. "I want to learn as much river shit as possible on this trip."

Along the shore the boulders grew into small cliff faces. Sprouts of trees and little waterfalls bubbled from the crevices where the rocks split.

"Well, we seem to be moving at a pretty good clip now, Captain. We're definitely going three miles per hour. I say this calls for a jazz cigarette!"

"I second that!"

"I third it," said Jared.

As Mike broke out the necessary supplies we felt the sunlight strike our faces and hands. The clouds were breaking up. We now sat smack in the middle of a beautiful Friday morning. The sun started drying the puddles on the deck, sucking the moisture from our sandals and clothes. It grew warm enough to sit in shirt sleeves and bare feet—and then the sun really felt good on our skin. By the time Mike was done rolling, the clouds were a gray mass moving upstream and out of our minds, leaving bright blue overhead. Mike sat Indian-style and lit the cigarette. We passed it around, drank our beer, let the sun hit us in the face, and took everything in.

"Man," said Jared, "Cheers." We cheersed; he sighed with pleasure. "This is the life guys. I'm sitting here in this beautiful weather, looking at these mad beautiful waterfalls and cliffs, drinking a beer and smoking with you guys. I tell you what—I couldn't pick another place I'd rather be. I don't have a single thing that's on my mind worrying me."

"Same here," Mike said. "I was a little nervous at first, but fuck it. This is beautiful. I don't have a single worry either."

I considered that.

"I feel almost exactly the same except I have one thing causing me anxiety," I said.

"What?"

"Just—well, Cady."

"Booo."

"No I mean it. I love being here and I wouldn't exchange it for the world. But tomorrow is Cady and my six-month anniversary and I dropped my phone in the water and—she's mad cool about this kind of stuff—but it's on my mind because I feel bad. I picture her being lonely and that sucks."

"You can call her from my phone," Jared said.

"Thanks man. It is a pleasure to be out here with you guys. This really at some point turned into a mission for me. Living it is surreal."

"Here's to living the dream," said Jared. "It's really something now!"

We cheersed, exhaled, leaned back on the palms of our hands, stretched, and looked around.

"So...anybody have an idea where we are?" Jared asked after a while.

"I'll get the map," Mike said. But the map had only major landmarks on it, and made only a minimal effort to reproduce the contours of the coast line. All we could make out—with our eyes looking downriver—was that we were approaching some kind of bend a couple of miles downstream. I held up my binoculars and distinguished that there was some kind of landmass jutting out into the river a ways ahead where the river bent. But we couldn't decide if it was an island in the middle of the water or a peninsula protruding from the western shore. I thought it was an island and advocated staying close to shore in order to keep a straight trajectory. It would be the safest, fastest, and easiest route. Mike thought the landmass was a peninsula producing a deep bay where it connected to the shore downstream. If so we needed to paddle to the other side of the river in order to avoid getting trapped in the bay. Mike's plan meant we'd have to paddle across the channel and across the river, which would be very difficult against the current. We started to argue over what to do and I was tempted to throw out the *I'm the captain* card when Jared asked if we could tell which way to go based on the buoys. Sheepishly, we said, "Yes, of course."

Now it became a simple matter of determining on which side of the landmass the buoys were stationed. As we were trying to judge where the buoys were, we noticed that whenever we stepped on the front, right side of the boat our weight pushed that corner of the raft underwater. That didn't happen when we stepped on any other part of the raft.

"Is the barrel under that corner taking on water?" Mike asked.

"I don't know. I don't think so." I said. The thought made my stomach sink. "Just don't stand on that corner."

"It wasn't doing that last night, was it?"

"I don't know," I frowned. "I can't tell what side these fucking buoys are going on, can you?" I handed Mike the binoculars.

"It looks like they go on both sides."

"Can they do that?" Jared asked.

"I donno. I think it means the channel is on both sides?" Jared sat down.

"Sounds good to me. Less paddling." Mike looked downstream at the landmass, and then at the starboard bow of the boat. He looked concerned.

We took a wait-and-see approach. We paddled to the center of the river just inside the channel, so that when we determined if the landmass was an island or a peninsula we could go on either side of it. I wondered if this was how Henry Hudson explored the river, tentative and nervous about every decision to move just a few degrees to port or starboard.

"We really need a map," Mike grumbled.

"'Do what you can with what you have where you are,'" I said. "Teddy Roosevelt used to say that."

We crept closer and saw the landmass was an island, so we stuck close to the western shore where we'd been floating all along. It was around one in the afternoon and Jared made a bed out of a sleeping bag and a life jacket and went to sleep. Mike and I kept steering. The afternoon grew humid and overcast as we drifted past fields of underwater grasslands sprouting through the shallows. Now and then we'd pass a big fancy house with gables, French doors, and expansive verandas and patios. I told Mike a joke I'd heard on *Golden Girls*.

"What's Irish and stays out all night?"

"What?

"Patty O'Furniture."

"That's terrible."

At the other end of the island was a brick lighthouse in the middle of the water. On the east bank we saw the City of Hudson hospital rising from the tree line with buildings I didn't recognize. Farther, titanic steel towers straddled the river with high-voltage power cables strewn across. Beneath them were marshlands on either side of the river channel. In the distance through the haze we could barely distinguish the *Rip Van Wrinkle Bridge* which connects Catskill to Hudson. Our goal for the tide was to pass beneath that bridge. We estimated it would take two hours from our current position. Jared was now awake and I figured I'd take a catnap. So I laid out on the sleeping bag at the back of the boat.

"—Yeah. Hey Captain I think you better wake up," I heard Mike say. Half awake, I was startled by the blast of a fog horn. I sat up and rubbed my eyes. "Actually Dallas we need you, like *now*." I focused on a barge coming toward us from downstream. *Burrrrrrr!* It bellowed. I jumped up to help Jared and Mike paddle.

"All on Jared's side!" we paddled quickly.

The barge was six stories tall. A giant metal basin which steered slowly and could not stop. The barge was pushed by a tugboat. It was filled with thousands of tons of gravel or cement. It bore down on us a half mile ahead.

"How'd we end up in the channel?" I shouted.

We paddled hard and fast to get outside the buoys into shallow water.

"We're not going anywhere!" Mike shouted.

The steam horn bellowed again.

"Oh, fuck dude!" Jared pointed behind us. There was a tanker coming from upstream. We were in the channel at exactly the place where a barge and a tanker would pass one another in about three minutes.

"Paddle!" I shouted.

As the tanker pressed us from behind we paddled franticly to get the raft outside the channel. We grabbed the two paddles and even used our hands to get the raft out of the way of the maritime machines now casting their shadows over us. But we couldn't even inch out of the way.

Seldom have I been as frightened for my physical safety as I was in that moment. We considered jumping overboard, but we stayed on. As the tanker passed the barge, it came within two dozen feet of us. We tilted our heads straight up watching it pass. Its sheer enormity was creepy—its rusted hull with depth measurements painted on. Its engines boiled the water as it droned past. We stood silent, mouths agape, until its stern finally slid by. It read *Andrea Maria; Stockholm*.

A moment later a seismic wave sent our port side up, then then diving down into a trough. That wasn't so bad, but when the ripples from the barge mingled with wake from the tanker, boiling white crests banged us to our knees on the deck. It sent us spinning and rocking, as though the air in the river was bubbling out. When the vessels had passed and the waves subsided, we crouched on all-fours with our hearts racing.

"Jesus Christ…" I spoke. After another moment Mike said,

"We've got even bigger problems," and pointed to the front starboard bow, which was below water. I looked at the back starboard corner. That was almost under water too. Our barrels were leaking. We were sinking.

There was little time to think. We were just inside the channel. If we stayed where we were our raft would sink 30-feet deep. So we tried to paddle to the western shore. But as soon as we got outside the channel our barrels hit mud and we bottomed out. It was low tide and the water outside the channel was shallow enough for birds to walk on. Then instead of sinking we were stuck.

"What are we going to do? We're going to lose all our shit!" Mike exclaimed. "Our bags, our coolers, our food our sleeping bags our clothes! It's a long way to the shore. I don't think we can swim that if we're just on a sandbar or something and the water gets over our head between here and shore."

He was right. We couldn't paddle to the western shore because it was too shallow. We couldn't try to paddle across the channel to the eastern shore because we might sink in the channel trying to get there. We couldn't even stay bottomed out in the middle of the river just outside the channel, because when the tide came back in we wouldn't rise with it. I pointed downstream.

"Look, there's a buoy." A quarter-mile ahead, it was a steel structure built atop a tiny island of rocks. "Let's get back into the deep water and paddle for that."

It was the only choice. We pushed off the sandbar. Now the water was nearly level with the deck, waves lapping the corners of the platform. As we paddled it was like trying to pilot a cast-iron bathtub. Meanwhile darker clouds moved in, the wind started slapping up the water, and it began to sprinkle. It took us fifteen minutes of continuous effort to reach the pile of boulders with the twenty-foot tower and buoy on top. We hit the rocks, I jumped off with a rope and tied us to the tower. The raft was going down. We formed a bucket brigade and conveyed our supplies onto the slippery, sharp rocks. We made a pile of ripped tarps, plastic bags, broken coolers, food wrappers, soaked sleeping bags and backpacks, shards of wood, cracked glass lanterns, cans and lifejackets. We slipped and cut our palms and knees on the mud-covered rocks. Then we climbed to the top and leaned our backs against a concrete cube that formed the base of the buoy tower, which was covered with green layers of seagull shit. It smelled like a pack of wet dogs. Stunned by the suddenness of events, we gazed over our supplies, the mucky rocks and water now washing over the particleboard deck.

"Well, there goes that dream," Mike muttered. And of course Jared chimed in,

"It's really something now."

What a terrible, sinking feeling. *I should have taken Cady on a vacation instead of doing a stupid raft trip,* I thought.

For better or for worse I couldn't indulge in self-pity yet, because I was too afraid of the trouble and cost of being marooned. First Jared called our friend Dusty to see if he might be able to tow our raft to shore using his parent's boat or his jet ski. But he was out of town. So we stood and had a beer. We couldn't call a salvage company. I had almost no money. For two hours we ate gummy bears and drank beer and tried to think of a way off our rocky island in the middle of the Hudson. A few pleasure boats went by and wondered what three idiots were doing on a tiny rock in the middle of the river beneath buoy 128.

The raft was floating but an inch above the water without any weight on it. If we escaped and the platform broke loose from the buoy and a speedboat hit it, it could kill somebody. We could-

(On buoy 128 just north of Catskill and Hudson, in the middle of the river, the wreck of the U.S.S. Crab Legs.)

("There goes that dream," said Mike. Jared (left) and I ponder.)

not afford to pay to have the thing towed away. So we tried to sink it. We'd brought a hammer and a knife. We tried to pry the deck apart and to stab the barrels. It was sad to destroy something we'd spent so much time creating. Anyhow, we couldn't pierce the plastic and we'd nailed the boards together with so many redundant nails that we couldn't tear it apart. Even if we ripped the barrels off somehow, then we'd have put a bunch of barrels in the river for boats to hit, and the wood platform might not sink all the way. So we tried throwing rocks on top of it. But the rocks were mostly boulders we couldn't budge. We ended with an even more smashed-up deck with a pile of muddy rocks on top still barely floating. And the tide was rising. As it rose it forced us up the rocks. Since the island was only the size of an office cubicle there was little room to move. The waves began slapping our bags and carrying away our food wrappers and empty beer cans. Finally, we knew we had to do what we dreaded: call the cops. Mike did the dishonors. Since there was no such thing as a smart phone we couldn't look up the number for the local police, so he dialed 911 and asked to be transferred to the City of Hudson police department.

"Hello? Hi…umm, is there a maritime unit? We've been in a…we're kind of stranded in the middle of the river. Yes everyone is fine. Um…Okay. 225-1413. Okay." He closed his phone. "They're going to call us back."

"The police are gonna call us back?"

"That's what they said."

A half-hour later Mike's phone rang.

"Hello? Yes. My name is Mike. We're at buoy 128. A *make*? No. Umm…tan, I guess? Or brown? Well it's more like a raft. Yes, homemade. Okay, bye." He closed his phone. "They're sending a river unit."

"Great," Jared rolled his eyes.

We were really afraid of getting in trouble. Our only interactions with police up to that point were when we'd been pulled over or when cops busted-up parties for underage drinking. We were conditioned to think of police the way mice think of cats. We weren't exactly sure everything was on the up and up with our raft expedition. We hid the cannabis in a duffle-bag. The phone rang again.

"Hello? Yes this is Mike. What? No everyone is fine. No, no, no one is bleeding." Mike made a surprised face. "What? We don't need an ambulance. No no, no one is in the water. Yes we're warm. Okay, okay, thanks." *Click.* "Jesus Christ they have an ambulance standing by in Hudson."

From downstream a patrol boat motored up, complete with flashing blue lights and two officers in uniform. A moment later from the opposite direction a bigger patrol boat sped toward us, this one with three policemen aboard.

"Here comes the cavalry," I said.

The police tend to increase the tension in such situations. We just wanted to get off the pile of rocks with our stuff, but here came these two police boats with flashing lights yelling to us asking if we needed medical attention, pushing off the rocks with big poles to avoid grounding out and throwing us florescent life jackets and yelling "Put these on!" Always yelling.

They 'rescued us' by grabbing us and putting us into one of the boats. They said it was too dangerous for us to retrieve our own belongings, so they slipped on the same muddy rocks we'd been slipping on for three hours and conveyed our bags into their boat. As the tide continued to rise we watched helplessly as it overturned our Styrofoam coolers and sent a silver stream of *Coors* cans bobbing downriver. I doffed my hat at that sorrowful sight. When they'd stowed our essentials they got back aboard and revved up the throttle. They radioed to shore to send the ambulance home. As we chugged away from buoy 128 we saw the smashed raft with broken Styrofoam and rocks and trash juxtaposed against the leaden afternoon sky. In the distance was the *Rip Van Wrinkle Bridge*. That was the last we ever saw of the *U.S.S. Crab Legs*.

Looking at all the garbage, Mike commented,

"So much for saving the environment with this trip."

The police took each of our names, ages, addresses and telephone numbers and ran our information. But they ended up being pretty nice. They told us we made them each about a hundred and fifty bucks because they were getting overtime at double pay. They laughed at us and called us ridiculous and at that point how could I argue with them? When I asked what would happen to the raft they said they would tow it someplace and burn it. So all that time, work and boasting was for nothing. The police dropped us at a park in Hudson and helped us unload our stuff. There Mike called his father. We waited another hour in the drizzle for him to pick us up in their family minivan.

The ride home was silent. I leaned my head against the window and watched it rain. Mr. Glenis dropped me off at my parent's house, which was empty and dark, because my parents were at work. By then I'd been wet for six hours. I was cold.

Looking back, that sinking feeling marked "the end of what we know now as innocence[7]" for me. It was the end of my childhood.

At my parent's house I ran bath water. As it filled the tub I made a whiskey and ginger ale by the light of the fading sky through the kitchen window. Soon I would have to tell Cady that she was dating a guy who was full of shit. I shook the glass to hear the ice cubes clink. I lifted it up, to watch the world get distorted through its curvature. I took a drink—it was a strong one. Through the pane I watched the "long day's journey into night."

---

[7] The quote is from "Hailstorm," a 1965 poem by Twyla Hansen.

VIII. Moods, M*A*S*H, and a Theory of Decision-Making

In the summer of 2006 I was 21 years old and putting off worrying about the rest of my life in favor of exploring the possibilities.

I worked for a 58-year-old woman who was also exploring her possibilities, who had steady expendable income. Like me, Maureen was a Cancer: moody, sensitive, ebulliently orbiting an anxious nucleus. Like me she'd been an English Major at the State University of New York. She'd spent a summer in Massachusetts shucking clams before deciding she wanted to be wealthy. She sold insurance in a department store before renting her own office, which ballooned to three offices. She'd recently built a house on 35 acres of woodland about 45 minutes northwest of New Baltimore at the base of Thatcher State Park. She'd transferred me from her office to be her landscaping assistant.

"I'd like you to help me make my woods immaculate," she stated as she guided me around her property. "I want to be able to walk through the woods and not see any sticks and shit lying around. You know? Like, I want you to go around and pick up shit like this," she lifted a branch from the leaf-covered ground.

"Got it, boss," I said.

"Great. I mean, don't waste your time picking up shit like this," she said, picking up a branch that was one millimeter smaller than the first. "Got it?"

"Got it."

She was speculating on ways to make money outside of her insurance business. She attended car auctions and sold a few cars from her house. Then she bought an ice cream shop and I worked as her sole employee selling scoops in Rensselaer across from the train station parking lot. But the shop closed two months later, after Maureen refused to enter the place or refill the stock, because she said it gave her anxiety. I helped her to cut, split, stack and deliver firewood from her property.

I spent many hours musing about life and exchanging anecdotes with Maureen as we worked around her property or engaged in speculative endeavors. Often I felt she paid me for my company as well as my labor. I admired her unorthodox life, figuring that if I was going to ascend the socioeconomic ladder I'd have to do something novel too. And I think she saw something of herself at 21, in me at 21, and wondered what my path would be. She had no children; I wanted to mimic her trajectory; we enjoyed sharing epiphanies and life lessons.

But lately she'd started dating a new woman who convinced her that she was wasting money (which she was). She spent a lot of time with her girlfriend out of town, and meanwhile her girlfriend prepared lists of things for me to do while they were away. The tasks became less grand — like our previous efforts to build a creek and fountain on the side of a hill in view of her living room, or to turn the woods into a kind of scenic park — and grew redundant and irksome. Now I was charged with picking weeds from between the flagstones of her walkways and around her pool, while bees swarmed me in the July sun. Payment transitioned from a weekly salary to an hourly rate. I gradually stopped showing up until I informed her that I wouldn't be showing up anymore, and she wished me luck finding work elsewhere. I lost both an income-stream and the daily affirmation that there were unorthodox paths to success.

Although the year before I thought I'd be permanently finished with school, in the summer of 2006 I knew I'd have to take yet another semester in the fall.

In the summer of 2006 I still lived in the basement of my parent's house, broke, static, in a town where no one my age lived, my friends having all moved and created lives for themselves in Albany or New York City.

The only signifier of progress whatsoever since the previous summer was that I now had a girlfriend. But like taffy the longer it stretched, it was strained and getting more so. To see Cady required an hour drive to the New Paltz bus station; a three- to five-hour Greyhound bus ride to the Port Authority, depending on the traffic; a seven-block walk to Penn Station; and finally an hour ride on the Long Island Railroad's Babylon Line. At first it was exotic, adventurous, full of new smells and sensations for both of us, novel, hip, Kerouac-style. But things that require a lot of effort become trying. I am sure she began to compare her relationship with her boyfriend (me) to those of her girlfriends living nearby, whose boyfriends took them out, while I was seldom around.

And of course in the summer of 2006 I'd just failed to build a raft and float to New York City, as I'd claimed that I would. It was a public failure, witnessed by my closest friends and reported in the local newspapers. Instead of re-affirming the can-do spirit, I'd shown that it's better for one's reputation not to try anything unusual.

The idea of a "mood" is a unique concept in American culture. We base a lot of our ideas about the nature of existence on things that Socrates, Plato and Aristotle said 2,300 or so years ago. These philosophers strictly distinguished between "the body" and "the mind" (or, as they described it, "the soul"), like two antagonists battling for control of a person.[8] This is one of the main tenants of the permutations of the Judeo-Christian religions, which have dominated discussion on the topic of existentialism over the course of American history. We are so conditioned to think of "the body" and "the mind" as two different entities that we retain almost no words to describe their interplay; and if you have no word for a thing, you have a very hard time describing it or picturing it, even if you understand it instinctively.

The idea of a "mood" gets at the cumulative interplay between the mind and the body like no other word in the English language. A mood is not merely a mental state, nor is it only a feeling. It is all of the thoughts and feelings that a person is experiencing wrapped up together and aggregated. Seldom do we feel simply "bored" or simply "happy," but we feel *excited*, which is to say we are happy [a general euphoric feeling] and we are anticipating some positive outcome [a mental calculation]; or we feel *ennui*, which is to say we feel bored and anxious [we sense surplus energy in our body] and realize we have no occupation or avocation with which to use it [a mental assessment]. "Mood" as an idea gets at the sum of one's thoughts and emotions.

Since a mood is the aggregate of *all* impressions, both mental and physical, at a certain time, in a specific person, the mood of a specific person can be changed by adjusting *either* the mental *or* the physical impressions. A person who feels *morose* can improve their mood by thinking happy thoughts [an improvement to mental impressions] or by taking a pill which adjusts neurotransmitters [an improvement to physical conditions]. It is easy to imagine changing some person's mood from *relaxed* to *anxious* either by telling that person that their closest friends and family have just been killed [a mood change affected through mental processes] or by injecting them with adrenaline [a mood change affected through physical processes]. Whatever happens to bodies and minds after death, at least while alive, these things are linked, and our "experience" is a combination of impressions from both parts.

---

[8] In *Phaedrus*, Socrates famously described the body and the soul as two horses guiding a flying chariot through the sky. The body with its mortal passions wants to dive toward earth while the soul with its heavenly pursuits wants to ascend. The chariot is pulled in both directions. Plato, *Phaedrus*, S.P. 247-250.

Moods, being based partially on the physical and partially on the mental, are often based on a string of recent experiences, and they last for a while. That part of a mood that is based on the physical is relatively short-lived. One is tickled, one laughs, one discharges the laugh, one feels the hilarity in one's body dissipate, and one returns to normal, unlikely to be affected emotionally for any significant duration due to the experience. But if one fails an important test, discovers that one's partner is unfaithful, that a friend or relative has perished — these mental realizations repeat and replay in one's consciousness and affect one's mood for a long time. If we catch our fingernail on something, we jump and curse in agony, but we are not depressed. But some existential injuries which cause no physical trauma can degrade our mood for weeks, months, or years. These experiences affect the lenses through which we view the world. We come to perceive differently, to calculate differently, to assume negative outcomes. We start to note unhappy news and write-off spontaneous good fortune as so many anomalies or flukes. A mood is an aggregate thing not only because it contains components of the mental and the physical rolled up in one impression, but because the mental components are themselves cumulative and based on many impressions over time. Thus one can become happy or unhappy because one great or terrible thing occurred, or because many small occurrences accumulated, each a little fortunate or unfortunate.

Benjamin Franklin noted, "Human felicity is produced not so much by great pieces of good fortune which seldom happen, as by little advantages that occur every day."[9]

Yet I'd have retorted in the summer of 2006 that human *un*happiness is produced by an endless string of little *dis*advantages that occur every day. You can't always be working and planning and looking forward to *some* nebulous time in the future when you *hope* that things *might begin* to improve. You need feedback along the way. Moods naturally disintegrate, like elements undergoing radioactive decay. Eventually, they become poisonous. Things, including moods, fall apart when they have nothing to keep them together.

The day after the raft sank, as I bumped along inside a crowded Greyhound bus on my way to the Port Authority, I jotted notes in my "Captain's Log" about ways to improve our design. Surely, with more planning, using lessons from our recent debacle, the next raft would succeed.

---

[9] Humes, J., *The Wit and Wisdom of Benjamin Franklin (A Treasury of Quotations, Anecdotes, and Observations)*, Beckon Books, Nashville, P. 34.

My handwriting bounced with the potholes in the Thruway:

The problem is that we went off half-cocked the first time. Nobody helped. We built it at the last minute. If we can just not *sink... Maybe we could get a section of dock donated to us, and then we'd know it won't sink, and then that's the main problem, solved.*

We learned:

- *you cannot see barges and tankers at night until they're on top of you, so you must stay out of the channel at night;*
- *'slack water' lasts a couple of hours, so we do not get six hours of 'ebb tides' when we can ride on the water. It takes a while to build up speed. Instead of 12 hours of propulsion over two tides each day, the water gives us something like 8 hours of propulsion over two tides each day;*
- *the river is often shallow right outside the channel;*
- *tide charts only list the high and low tides at big towns every dozen or so miles, and the high and low tides differ significantly in the different towns, based on each location's proximity to the ocean. Mistakes are easy;*
- *more time must be devoted to building the boat, and it should be able to be shipped fairly easily to the water;*
- *a trailer will need to be procured;*
- *a good map of the river will need to be procured, not some touristy thing;*
- *the barrels should be affixed in a line for minimal drag, and some means of propulsion should be added to the boat besides paddles...Could a bicycle-powered paddlewheel be possible? (talk to Oliver Cross).*

I looked at the list and thought, "We *did* learn a lot on this trip." And now I had the beginning of a plan for a new boat, which I pictured while trapped in the gridlocked Greyhound as it tried to enter the Lincoln Tunnel. I looked forward to my new plan, to getting back to New Baltimore, to talking to Oliver and Jared and Mike, and getting things moving again. *This was just a setback,* I thought, glancing at the list in my notebook, feeling my mood improve. *Yes,* I will *do this thing. It will just take a little more work and determination!* I smiled and would've texted Mike and Jared, but my phone didn't have that capability in June of 2006. And it had drowned in the Hudson River two days before, and I couldn't afford a new one.

Two days later it was still raining as I got ready for the trip home. Cady kissed me on the Massapequa Park train platform. I could see in her eyes the emotional frustration: the feeling that we kept working ourselves up only to leave each other the next day. It made the highs harder to achieve and the lows harder to bear.

The train brought me through the filthy rail yards, into the black tunnel of Penn Station where the car lights always flickered off. Then a seven-block walk through filthy New York streets in the rain—past the shish kabob stand and two porn stores and the statue of Ralph Kramden I always said "Hi Ralph" to. Then a cramped and stuffy Port Authority bus ride up to New Paltz. Then an hour drive back to New Baltimore and the only thing I had to look forward to there, which was raft building.

At *The Boathouse* restaurant at Shady Harbor in New Baltimore, I spoke to the proprietor, Charlie, and he pointed me to a pile of docks and foam that I could have for free. So I drove home and asked my dad if I could use his truck to move the dock to our backyard sometime that week.

"Oh Jesus Christ you're gonna try that *again*?" Dad dropped an armful of firewood into a trailer connected to the lawn tractor.

"Yes. I'm sure that if we'd have just stayed on for 10 days as planned, we'd have made it to the *George Washington Bridge*. In one tide we made nine miles. If we made that on each tide we'd make 18 miles a day. 150 divided by 18 is less than 10." Dad wasn't listening. He stacked five chunks of wood on his left arm.

"Yes Dallas but you think you're gonna get somebody to go with you?"

"Jared and Mike," I replied. Dad stopped throwing wood into the trailer, holding a piece mid-toss and looking at me for the first time in the conversation.

"They agreed to go with you?"

"Well, I haven't verified it with them yet but either way I need to get the dock from the river up here." He returned to tossing wood.

"And what are you gonna do if you get it up here and Mike and Jared don't want to go? What are you gonna do then? Leave the dock in the yard?"

"Mike and Jared will want to go—I know those guys—and even if they didn't I still think it could be done."

"No."

"No what?"

"You can't take the raft down the river alone."

"I'll get someone else to go with me. If you let me borrow the truck and bring the dock here I'll show you."

"Fine," Dad said. "Try not to make a mess."

In the meantime, I needed help moving the dock from the river to my parent's house. I decided to take a walk one night after work with Jared, from his apartment in the middle of Albany to *The Pump Station*, a restaurant by the river clear across town.

Jared had had apartments in the "College Ghetto" since his sophomore year at St. Rose. The latest was in a more residential, less broken-window district than his previous places on Yates and Morris Streets. Now he lived with Nick the Naysayer and a rotating third man in the bottom floor of a two-family on Park Ave.

On his porch, Jared greeted me with an enthusiastic "Whatup dude" and invited me inside. He still had to finger on his *Axe* hair gel and spray himself with *Abercrombie and Fitch* cologne. He told me to play some sweet new songs he'd found from his Mp3 player, like Cake's version of *I will Survive* and Pinback's *Fortress*. I moved a pizza box so there was room on the couch, and sat and listened until Jared was ready.

The main utility of Jared's neighborhood was that it was in walking distance to the college bars, which we passed as we strolled to the river. We passed The Partridge Pub, Sadie Klutz, Madison's Pizza and Bogies before we hit Quail Street, the dividing line between upper and lower Albany. These bars thrived when I was in school because they catered to the 18, 19, and 20 crowd. After operating for decades they were raided and turned into vacant buildings.

"It's mad weak that they shut these places down," Jared observed. Our theory was that the police had been on the take for years to keep the college bars open, but a new D.A. had raided them and prosecuted offenders. "Where're people supposed to drink then? Their house? That's mad stupid. People should be able to get together. I feel like big house parties are worse for like, noise and underage drinking and drugs and even rapes and shit."

I agreed and added that in bars, at least there is the social pressure to behave because you're sharing public space with strangers. In bars, novice drinkers share space with people a decade older, who are relatively successful and low-key, and therefore serve as behavior models. And it was hard to see how a string of vacant buildings was an improvement over a line of thriving businesses, especially since shuttering the businesses only drove the activity from above to below ground.

We followed Madison Avenue east, downtown, until we got to Washington Park, which we cut across, past the park lake and the dog park, to arrive at State Street. Now we tread unfamiliar territory. At State Street the buildings abutted, and rose three- to five-stories high, of brick or brownstone with sandstone stoops spreading like hardened lava onto sidewalks twice as wide as in Jared's neighborhood. We marveled at the Gilded Age architecture and wondered how much it cost to live in one of the brick apartments. They were the nicest city apartments we'd seen.

"Maybe $1,200 for a two bedroom?" I guessed.

"Dude that's totally doable. I'd live down here if I had a real adult job. That's $600 a month per person, so like $5,200 per year. That's why I feel like if I had a job that paid like $40,000 I'd be happy. I don't think I'd need more than that. It's like twice what I made last year. But if I had to work a lot more for like $10,000 more a year so I'd make $50,000, I feel like it wouldn't be worth it, to give up your going-out-time and road trips and shit."

We descended State Street past the New York State Capitol, to our left—the grandest statehouse of the late 1800s—and Empire Plaza on our right—a post-modern stone and steel expanse which rises from the city like machines in *Empire Strikes Back*. Jared asked me to tell him what I knew about the plaza and whether I liked it.

"I like it because it draws people to Albany and gives them something to visualize," I said, "but I also think it's kind of ugly. The story I heard is that Nelson Rockefeller built it after being embarrassed walking through the neighborhood with the Queen of Holland. Holland sends us thousands of tulips every year for the Tulip Fest, because we used to be a Dutch colony. The Governor's Mansion is across the way, on Eagle Street. So anyway the queen or somebody was visiting and Rockefeller was walking with her from the mansion up to Washington Park for the festival, and he was embarrassed by the neighborhood that used to be here—you know, working class Italians and Irish and such riffraff. So he decided it all should be torn down so that Albany could have structures worthy of being the capitol city of the Empire State. And like the leader of an empire, it seems he was able to force the huge project through even though it displaced thousands of people.

"Dude that shit is interesting," Jared said. "I feel like so much cool shit happened in Albany and nobody knows about it."

I agreed.

We continued down the hill until State Street met Broadway. Here the skyline is dominated by what looks like a white stone castle, with two wings protruding from a 13-story central tower and three turrets topped with green copper pyramids.

"What's on top way up on the tower there, a ship?" Jared asked. I told him it was an 8-foot weather vane depicting Henry Hudson's sloop, the *Half Moon*. He said he thought that was a funny thing to put on top of the SUNY Administration Building.

"But it wasn't built as the SUNY admin building," I said. "It was originally the Delaware and Hudson station. Trollies came down State and made a loop at the bottom of Broadway; trains travelled in four directions out from here, and steamboats docked along its piers, because the land back of the station used to be the riverbank. I got a picture in my old Albany book."

"Man," Jared shook his head, "All that shit happened here, and now it's like a ghost town. I feel like this is the deadest part of the city." Indeed, it was 6:30 p.m. and we were the only pedestrians on the street on downtown Broadway. "What's the deal with that anyway? I feel like the river is the coolest thing about Albany—even Ravena and Coeymans—and nobody uses it. Why?" This was the first time I ever thought about that question.

"I think because nobody can get to it. I mean like in Albany, how do you even get to the river? Through a building, or across a highway? Every place you go there's a fence then railroad tracks and a three-lane freeway. And if you get past that stuff, what do you do when you get to the river? If there's no park or dock or way to drive there, you can't kayak or picnic. So instead we drink in midtown. Or, that's what *we* did. 20-years-olds now will have to drink in their houses I guess. And then adults will say they're lazy because they never go outside."

"Maybe instead of fossil fuels we should've protested all these ugly stupid fucking bridges and fences and shit that cut off the river from Albany." We turned left, north, onto Broadway. "So what about the raft anyway? It sucks it sank. Have you been thinking about it?"

"Actually, I've been thinking about another trip." Surprisingly, Jared said,

"Dude I'm glad you brought it up I've been thinking the same thing. If we can just *not* sink—dude I'm down to just get on there and stay on till we arrive, no matter how long it takes."

I stopped mid-stride to shake his hand. "Sweet dude! I got a dock donated to us so I know it'll float. I'm gonna need a little help moving it. I've got some other ideas too. This is great."

"Just call me and I'll be there."

That was one crew member down. The next day I drove to Mike's parent's house. He was living back out on Indian Fields Road now that he'd finished college. He immediately dismissed the idea.

"Absolutely not, no way. You're really thinking about trying that *again*?"

"Yes I'm serious. All we need is barrels that don't sink."

"Nah man, I don't want to be a part of that project—I just can't focus on that right now. And honestly, I don't want to. This was an embarrassment." He added perfunctorily, "Sorry."

Fine, I thought, *I'll do it without him.* So Mike was out.

The most important thing is to identify the first step and then take it, I thought. But how does a novice know what the first step is? In my case I decided it didn't matter. I didn't have a full crew or know how to construct a shelter and a rudimentary propulsion system. But at least I could get the dock to my house. That would start things moving. So I rounded up Jared, our friend Jon and Nick the Naysayer. I borrowed my dad's leaking-gas, crumbling truck and a trailer from my uncle Dave, and we drove to the river.

There I met Charlie, the owner of Shady Harbor, and his two sons. They were large guys with Brooklyn accents and tough-guy demeanors. The sons were about my age and good-natured. I said I was working on a college project and alluded to press coverage. They were new owners and, either out of a desire to generate local publicity or to get junk off their property, they said I could take anything that was down a certain path through the woods for free. Charlie led us to the side of the cove where the gravel gave way to grass and weeds. A path the width of a cart cut through the woods. Then Charlie left us alone.

Down this path we wandered through a veritable maritime machine museum. There were trucks on either side that seemed specially made for some purpose I could only guess. There was what looked like a rusted fire engine with a brown crusty crane arm diagonally falling from the bed in back, resting in the weeds. The wheels were overgrown with grass. Further along the path was a rusted tractor with a curved chassis like something out of the 1950s. There were axles and wheels without vehicles atop them, with cattails growing through their steering columns. As we walked further the grass grew taller and thicker, so that we had to step high rather than leisurely stroll. Now we were almost in a forest. To our left were triangular boat jacks—pyramid-shaped metal frames, through the middle of which ran a bolt and a wing nut. By twisting the wing nut one could raise the height of the bolt relative to the base of the jack, and provide a platform to hold a boat. Then finally there were piles of cyan-colored foam and two docks stacked together.

"And how the fuck are we gonna get this dock outta here?" Jared asked.

"We'll use my truck," I said.

"Dude the path back here is like two-feet wide. Maybe they have a crane or something we could use?"

"I don't want to disturb these people who're trying to run a business," I said. "I'll just back my trailer up here and we'll throw the dock on."

I followed the path back to the parking lot and started the truck. It came to life with the sound of jelly beans bouncing in a coffee can. The opening to the path was close to a hydraulic boat launch, so I had to make a 15-point turn to get the trailer aligned. I couldn't get the trailer aligned with the path to back up, and I saw Charlie's sons looking at me wondering if I knew what I was doing. So I turned around and drove in truck-first.

"You got the trailer in here but now how are we going to get it out?" Jared asked.

"Let's worry about that when the time comes," I said. "Meanwhile let's just get this thing on the trailer." We walked over to the two docks, one stacked on the other. Both had seen better days. The wood planks were rotting, with holes eaten through. Around the perimeter of the top dock a fire hose had been accordioned-up and nailed to one side as a fender, but the hose had fallen off and lay like a snake with nails jutting out, squiggling into the leaves and grass.

"This dock looks good," I said. The four of us tried to lift but it was too heavy. Next we tried all four of us lifting one side and a barrel fell out of the bottom and rolled a couple of feet away. "Put that in the truck," I said. A black organic ooze stuck to the bottom of the dock; when we lifted it smelled like fecal muck. Out flew gnats and small flies. The dock left an impression on the ground where slugs, earwigs and pill-bugs crawled.

"Dude this is fucking gross," Jared complained.

"Now hold on — we'll have this thing loaded in two shakes of a lamb's tail. I'll get the trailer backed up closer. We'll get one corner of the dock on and then push it up."

But no matter how I maneuvered the truck I couldn't get the trailer lined up in front of the dock, so eventually the four of us just grabbed and lifted the trailer into position. Then we each grabbed a corner of the dock and succeeded in pushing it on. In doing so Jared cut his palm on the nails sticking out of the fire hose. Then we tied the dock to the trailer using very un-seamanlike *ex-under-and-pull* knots and tried to back the trailer out. We got stuck for half an hour before we turned around after executing another 25-point turn. Then Jared said,

"Hey, you think we could use a couple of these boat jacks?" And I said,

"Yeah, throw four of them in the bed of the truck. And some of that blue foam too," and then we drove out of the path past the decaying machines, bumping over sticks and logs, and high-tailed it up the hill out of Shady Harbor because we weren't sure we were allowed to take the jacks (but we needed them to lift the dock in order to work on its underside). We towed the dock up two miles of country hill to my parent's house, where Jared and the others were checking their watches and grumbling about the places they had to be. I managed to get them to help me take the dock off the trailer and lay it in my parent's yard, and then they took off. That was the last time Jared or any of them saw the second raft.

Aside from making the new raft safer, the most important innovation was the new propulsion system. Dick Brooks, my fourth grade teacher and a local historian, had told me about the winners of the previous year's *Wacky Raft Race*, which was a five-mile river race between Athens and Catskill. Annually, entrants competed for booby prizes on homemade crafts. Mr. Brooks told me the previous year's victors, a group of local firemen, had built a bicycle-powered paddlewheel. So I asked Oliver, who was an amateur carpenter, to help me design one. He came to measure the dock and asked me to show him the bikes I planned to use. We retrieved two second-hand bicycles with flat tires from my parent's basement, unbolted the back wheels and laid them in the grass. Then we found a length of metal pipe behind my grandfather's shed to use as an axel. I watched Oliver and nodded. I figured my function was to play the enthusiastic assistant. Oliver said he knew a guy who might weld the bike gears to the pipe axel. "Okay," I said, not really understanding. So Oliver left with the wheels and the metal pipe and I put *the means of propulsion* on the back burner of my brain. There was a lot of other work to do in the meantime. Three weeks had gone by since the end of the last voyage and all I had was a dock lying in the grass. I wanted to launch on August 1st so that I could get the trip done before the fall semester started. That gave me five weeks to get it built, shipped, and find another crewmember.

My friend Jess, who had just finished her BA in opera singing from Ithaca College, came to New Baltimore and helped me sew Venetian-blind-like covers for the outside of the cabin. We made each "sheet" by sewing plastic drop cloths to old bed sheets I stole from my mother's linen closet. The cotton sheets would keep the plastic from ripping, while the plastic drop cloths would be waterproof. These would eventually cover the frame of the cabin, the way old airplane wings were made of cloth stretched over balsa wood.

When I couldn't find anyone to help me work on the raft I tried to keep Cady happy. She had just gotten accepted to Cortland College, would be moving off Long Island, and she was thinking about life changes. I didn't want to fall into the category of things she planned to change.

I needed money to see Cady and provision the new raft.

My friend Pritesh's parents owned a number of motels and laundromats in the area, and for a few months he'd been asking me to bartend at the new place his parent's bought, the *21B Rest Area* just off the New York State Thruway in New Baltimore. It was a truck stop with a weigh station and motel rooms. Most of the truckers slept in their trucks in the parking lot. The place sported a little diner and a bar with two pool tables, a dartboard and a jukebox. There was also a bathroom with epithets and invitations for young men (and presumably women) to suck the truckers' cocks at such and such a time, if they were so inclined. So this is where I began working Mondays through Thursdays from 4 p.m. to eleven for five dollars an hour, plus tips.

I was a little intimidated at first, for although I'd taken a bartending class I'd only worked a single day at a resort bar when I was 18. My clientele at the truck stop were not resort types. They drove big rigs twelve or more hours a day and stopped at specific places out of habit. They had very particular mannerisms and didn't like anything out of the ordinary, including a new face behind the bar.

I acted the way I thought a bartender should act, based on the ones I admired from movies. I wore black pants, a white button-up shirt, and a black apron around my waist. I made sure always to have an ordering pad, pen and straws handy. I kept a white wash towel in my back pocket. I brought a CD player with me and each afternoon as I set up and each night as I broke down the bar and cleared out the well and ran hot water down the tap and counted the dollars and coins I played Tommy Dorsey, Billie Holiday and Frank Sinatra: "*It's Quarter to three; there's no one in the place...except you and me...*" It got me into the mood and character of a bartender. I always found it easier to do something if I pretended to be a character who was good at doing it.

The patrons were interesting.

"They oughta just nuke those fuckers," said Jack, the old time owner-operator who carefully considered his meal, chewed every bite slowly, and always tipped exactly three dollars.

"If I were the leader of this country, I'd send a Tomahawk missile into their little launch pad," said Dave, the middle-aged guy with the goatee. He brought the fingers of his hands together and then gestured with his arms and grunted to simulate an explosion. Dave came in Mondays and Wednesdays, always drank *Bud* bottles and unscrewed the bulb in the lampshade above his barstool. "You can just keep 'em coming unless I tell ya to stop," he said, pointing to his empty red bottle. "You don't gotta ask me every time."

Whenever a patron said something to the bartender, the customers looked at him (me) to see what reaction I'd have—if the patron was critical, whether I was offended or combative; if the patron made an off-color joke, whether I was a common guy or pretentious; if the patron asked a personal question, they tried to gauge whether I was easy to talk to or standoffish.

"You got it boss," I said. I opened another *Bud*, placed it in front of Dave and took away his empty bottle.

I never said more than necessary. Talking can signal nervousness. Instead I cleaned the glasses, dusted the bottles on the shelves, wiped down the bar top, or took an inventory of the bottles in the cooler. It would've been easy to sit and watch T.V. with the two or three truckers who congregated there. Instead I tried to *live* my character—to *be* a good bartender, to keep the patrons happy and the bar making money. Then I felt good about what I was doing.

It was delicate, being the intermediary between the truckers and the management. The owners, my friends' parents, were Hindus who'd never owned a bar and didn't drink or eat meat. The patrons were a rabble of Americentric xenophobes who hated liberalism and political correctness.

"Whata they pay ya in here, *rubles*?" The guy with a glass eye used to say (mistaking *rubles*, the currency of Russia, for *rupees*, the currency of India). He and two young guys were doing work on the shoulders of the Thruway and came in Tuesday and Wednesday nights. The guy used to come in sober and drink bottles of *Bud Light*. He'd drink and do shots until he started to complain about the price of the beer (three dollars) and that the place was owned and run by non-whites. "That's the problem with this fucking country," he'd shout and spew. "We got Mexicans in the fuckin' kitchen; camel-jockeys own the joint—you know gas is three fuckin' dollars a gallon because they got the oil and they got us by the balls with it. You know how much it takes to fill my tank?"

"I don't understand why we don't just carpet bomb fuckin' Iraq," interjected the stocky guy with the tattoos who drove a Harley, not a truck, but came to the truck stop because he liked the ambience. "Listen: fly over the desert with bombs, or fuckin' nuke the place. All the sand'll turn to glass. Then you can see the weapons of mass destruction buried underground. It's so simple it's stupid."

"Ah, this fucking country and the liberals arte draggin' it to hell in and hand-basket," the one-eyed guy trailed off. Often he got so drunk he'd pass out on his stool and leak water out of his glass eye socket down his cheek. He'd stoop bent-backed until his young co-workers brought him off to his room.

That was the rough side of them. The side that wanted to watch Bill O'Reilly and warned that "If we let North Korea launch their 'experimental fucking satellite,' which everybody in the world knows is a goddamn missile—and we don't do shit, then we'll be watchin' 'em launch missiles again and again, this time with A-bombs on 'em flying over New York City!"

But there was another side to the patrons, a side that came out when they talked about their sons and daughters or their home town. In his spare time Dave built custom birdhouses you could take apart level by level, and Jim was saving money to buy a house so the courts would look more favorably on his custody rights. I couldn't help but feel that maybe the patrons dressed and spoke the way they thought truck stop patrons should dress and speak, just as I was taking my cues about bartending from images of barkeeps in old-time movies.

*M*A*S*H*, of all things, brought everybody together. The *Hallmark Channel* played *MASH* episodes in a two-hour block every weekday from five to seven p.m. The truckers and I might've been in the middle of a discussion about moonshine or women masturbating while driving, when those four guitar chords of *Suicide is Painless* (the *MASH* theme song) interrupted us, followed by the sound of choppers. As that melancholy melody picked up, the conversations quieted and eyes drifted to the T.V. screen. To me it was a nostalgic song because my grandfather used to watch the show and I'd hear the theme as I went to sleep as a kid. To the men of the road, I don't know why they were so entertained by it. Perhaps they respected the situations in which the doctor-soldiers found themselves, for in that show there seems to be no rest for the nerves of the "4077" doctors and nurses, continually bombed and mined and going crazy longing to get home with all their arms and legs. The truckers even nodded at the liberal bent of the show. They laughed in the episode where Hawkeye gives a blood transfusion from a black man to a white racist, who is then outraged. Over the episode the doctors gradually pigment the racist's skin until he thinks he's turning black. At the end they explain that the man who invented blood transfusions died because he was in a car accident and needed blood, but the nearest hospital refused to admit him — because he was black. Mostly I think the truckers quieted down to watch *MASH* because it reminded them of a home life — they ate their meal and watched T.V. with familiar faces nearby — and everyone needs that sometimes. At eight o'clock I'd put on a baseball game and the place would turn back into a truckers' bar.

I'd call Cady at one in the morning when I got home, and we'd talk about our day. She'd usually be asleep because she worked full time as a daycare assistant from 7:30 to 3:30. Sometimes we'd only chat for a few minutes because she was very tired. Nonetheless it was always the highlight of my day. It was the one pretty thing I encountered each evening among a procession of lowbrow conversations, aging relatives, stagnant plans and isolation. We'd say "goodnight girl," and "goodnight boy," and sometimes it'd be hard to get off the phone because each of us wanted the other to know how much we really wanted to see and touch the other. Then she would hang up, and I'd pour myself a Highball and type on AIM until the early morning, when I'd watch reruns of *MASH* on the *Hallmark Channel*.

Working nights meant I had days free to construct the raft, which I named the *U.S.S. Crab Legs 2.0*. But no one else in my social circle had days free. Jared still worked for Maureen's insurance office 9-5; by the time he was done with work I was bartending, and he lacked the drive and vision to come to my parents' to work on the raft alone. Mike had softened his position and had begun asking about the raft, with the air of a parent who inquiries into a child's hobby, smirking, but not going so far as to conclude that it would fail. He digested my oratory on the new raft's improvements and offered suggestions to strengthen the cabin and allow room the walk around its perimeter. His interest grew, but Mike had started working at the State Comptroller's Office in Albany two weeks after our first raft sank. So he couldn't help me construct the new boat. And Oliver worked at the warehouse during the day. So I did what I could to get the boat ready during my days off, alone.

I formed a theory of labor working on that boat in the hot sun, sweating and getting nibbled by bugs. I'd always thought of *labor*—I mean work-performed—as a function of simple addition, like a word problem in middle school math class. If it took me two hours to paint a fence, then it should take me *and one other person* one hour to paint the same fence, right? But to screw one cabin wall joist to the deck took me, alone, ten or fifteen minutes. I had to hold the board perpendicular to the deck, brace it with my foot, hold a screw in one hand and the drill in the other, and everything fell if I shifted my weight. With *one other person* the same task would've taken sixty seconds. One afternoon, after skipping lunch and sweating in the July afternoon, I spent twenty minutes trying to screw one board to another, only to split the board down the middle when the screw turned in. I cursed and threw the board across the yard before stomping inside and vowing to give up construction until someone gave me a hand. I realized that simple tasks take a lot of time *when only one person is working*, because it is awkward to hold everything in place. One additional laborer would divide the amount of time it took to build the raft not in half, but by a factor of 20 or 30. A second person does nothing more than hold a board in place, but their presence drastically diminishes the first person's effort by allowing for quick repetition through basic job specialization. And they make the work more tolerable by providing moral support. So as I threw boards across the lawn that July, I cursed not just the lumber and nails, but the fact that every task took eons because I couldn't find another person for something so simple as holding a board.

At the time, too, I knew nothing whatsoever about carpentry. My father owned a hammer and a Philips-head screwdriver and that was the extent of his tool collection. My grandfather had many tools in his basement, but they were all in a mess on his worktable, most of them were rusted, and I had no idea what they were used for. I borrowed his circular saw and it screeched like a tortured cat and burned more than it cut through lumber. I borrowed his drill which weighed 25 pounds and had a chuck-key for replacing the bits. Between the lack of good tools, the lack of company, and my own inexperience, I accomplished very little between mid-June and mid-July. Soon there were only two weeks before I'd told everyone I would make another launch, and all I had was a dock on stilts with some vertical boards sticking up, half-painted, in my parent's yard.

Then Jared informed me that he wouldn't be allowed to take more time off of work that summer, because someone else in the office had been fired. That left me with no crew either.

What was I to do in a situation like that? What would you do? If this was a "choose your own adventure" book, the following options might be given:

Choice A: Wait to do any more building until you find a crew to go with you. Turn to page xx. (On page xx it would likely read: "Two weeks have passed, and although you found someone to go with you, the boat was not constructed. You fail to set sail.")

Choice B: Give up and admit defeat. Turn to page xxi. (On page xxi the text would read: "Your character ends up the butt of jokes to everyone you know, and you have a rotting dock in your backyard to remind you of it every day. You fail.")

Choice C: Keep working as much as you can, by yourself, in the hopes that the work will not be wasted effort, in the hope that you find one or more persons to help you within two weeks. Turn to page xxii. (Page xxii is the rest of this book.)

People tend to choose whatever course requires the least risk. That includes the risk of losing money, time, or reputation. Most of the people I talked to, my friends and my parents especially, thought the "right" course would be either to give up, or, (knowing I wanted to complete my trip and put the endeavor behind me) to wait until I found a crew — until I could share the risk — *and only then* to work on the boat.

The rational course, supported by the kind of "if -> then" logic one can't ignore, supported continued work, if for no other reason than that IF I did no more work on the raft THEN no one would join me. Of course, the contrapositive was *not* true. It was not the case that IF I did more work THEN I would have a crew. But there was a *chance* if I took the latter approach, and it was the *only* chance.

IX. Up and Down

It's easy to overbook yourself. To plan things, one on top of the other, forgetting the things you cannot do while you're doing other things. In mid-July, 2006, I had two weeks to complete my raft. But I'd planned to spend ten days with Cady in Vermont and Upstate New York, months before. I couldn't skip out—spending the time together had been my suggestion. Cady was already intimating that "this raft trip of yours" was impairing our relationship, since it took a lot of my time and money and annoyed her as a repetitive topic of conversation. Most importantly, she was relying on me to drive her from her family's Vermont "Ski Haus" to her college orientation in Cortland five hours away. I'd volunteered, and I was looking forward to it. But it came at a most inopportune time.

"We never spend this much time together," Cady said on the phone from Massapequa. "What if we end up hating each other?"

"What if we end up becoming inseparable?"

"I'm afraid of that, too."

First I had to drive to Bromley Mountain, just outside of Manchester, Vermont, to meet Cady at a "Cluster" party at their Ski Haus. It was to be a big hippy drinking dance party. I was to arrive on July 15th, the day before my 22nd birthday. We'd party all night and the next day we'd drive back to New Baltimore. Then two days later I'd drive Cady to Cortland for her orientation. Then, finally, I'd drive her to Trumansburg, Upstate New York, where we'd meet up again with Cluster at the *Grassroots* music festival they attended every year. Cluster would drive her back to Long Island, and I'd go home for three days of crash raft-building before my launch.

Very excited I hopped into Mindy my Chrysler Cirrus and sped off for Vermont two hours north and east of New Baltimore. I popped in a summer CD I'd made especially for our adventure, which had Cream, Billy Preston and *Honky Cat* by Elton John. I loved driving as long as I had good music and I could roll the windows down. That hot July afternoon I had the speakers blasting and the sweet smell of farm fields and freedom blowing all around me. But half an hour after leaving my parent's house, I smelt something like rotting fish. I'd sniffed the smell the last few times I drove Mindy. But this time it grew pungent and when I turned down the music I heard a sound like corn popping.

That's new, I thought.

I'd also noticed a new light on the display near the engine temperature gauge. It was in the shape of a little glowing *tilde*. Who knew what that meant?

As I continued to drive the smell and the bubbling increased, so I thought it prudent to pull over. When I turned off the engine the bubbling kept up, so I popped the hood. There I saw the fluid in some tank boiling away, and the smell of fish was from a piece of plastic melting. So I sat in my car for ten minutes until the bubbling died down.

I bet this is what an overheating engine is like, I thought. I was still an hour and a half from Manchester, and I really wanted to see Cady, so I got back in the car. I turned the music off and drove with the heater on to draw off the engine heat—boiling myself in the process—and stopped whenever the engine temperature made the coolant boil and smell skanky. That plan worked until I got to the highway north of Albany, where one crosses the Hudson toward Vermont, when I was unable to stop when the boiling began. I piloted a bubbling Mindy into the first gas station on the east side of the river, and popped the hood. A smoky effluvium arose from the engine.

"Wow that sucks buddy," said a man walking past, and then a teen on a tricked-out bike said,

"Wow you're fucked."

"I am *not* fucked," I declared from the sidewalk outside the store, "This car will be up and running in ten minutes. She just needs to cool off a little."

"Okay dude," said the teen, who turned to his friend and said, "That guy is fucked."

I left the hood up and went into the gas station. To the mustachioed man at the counter, I inquired,

"Hey man, got any suggestions for an overheating engine?" Looking up from his newspaper, he said,

"Don't drive it. Let it cool down."

"How long?"

"At least an hour. You can try putting a pint of oil in it after it cools off but use a glove opening it up or you'll burn the shit out of your arm. That you out front with the steam coming out?"

"Yeah."

"How far you got to get?"

"Vermont."

"Haha, yeah. Are you serious?"

"Yes. Bromley Mountain, near Manchester."

"I'm saying, you better nudge that thing to the nearest garage. It ain't makin' it to Vermont."

"That's a 1995 Chrysler Cirrus," I smiled.

I walked out feeling somewhat-delightedly spiteful. By now I identified with situations that made other people despair of ideas. Feeling that my future was likely to include a perpetual string of setbacks, I told myself that I was particularly adept at working through them, because I didn't let challenges that frustrated most people get in *my* way. Spite was a good motivator. "Where's your engine oil?"

After the bubbling stopped and I'd put two pints of fresh oil in the engine I called Cady. (I'd re-activated my first phone, from 2002, to replace the one that drowned in the river). Cady sounded upset.

"See? I told you something like this would happen. You're not coming. Something like this always happens it's like Fate preventing us from getting to spend time together." I responded slowly, logically,

"I don't believe in Fate. This is a temporary setback. I am regrouping and will be there after an hour's delay."

"Larry says you can't come with an overheated engine. He says it won't make it and you'll have to go home." Larry was a grey-haired, middle-aged deadhead with a hair tail and yellow teeth who hung around Cluster. A miserable man himself, he got his jollies from sabotaging my relationship with Cady whenever possible, because misery loves company, I suppose.

"Tell Larry he can go…mind his own business."

"Dal stop it he's just trying to help."

"As helpful as it is having *Larry* tell you that I'm not coming, I'm going to help *myself* by waiting forty more minutes, then carefully driving to Bromley Mountain, stopping when I need to, and arriving there this evening as agreed. Okay?"

"Okay," Cady sighed. "I'm just saying, Larry knows about cars and that kind of stuff."

"See you then baby."

"Bye."

Just like that a mood can change. It is wretched the way that happens. My car sitting there steaming didn't bother me. I wasn't bothered that Cady was unsympathetic. But the thought of Cady valuing the words of some creepy old jerk over mine made my blood boil like my engine coolant. Now I drove to *Ski Haus* filled not with pleasant expectancy, but with malignant questions about the strength of our relationship and a poisonous ill-will.

Cluster was the self-adopted moniker of Cady's step-mother's family and friends. They thought of themselves as hippies. Music was their religion—they played it always, traveled to shows frequently, and loved to get drunk and dance. They dismissed other lifestyles.

I had fun with Cluster and enjoyed their novel conversation, new music, and hospitality. They reminded me of my acquaintances with bachelor's degrees in the arts who were therefore politically apathetic, hedonistic and cynical. But at 22, I felt that "adults" should be beyond the stage where, well, where most of my friends were at that point. Adults, I thought, should either have a family or be focused on great exploits. I guess I was jealous of Cady's infatuation with *Cluster's* lifestyle, and they were probably jealous that I was trying to get Cady on a different life course, to experience new things, so that she didn't end up with nothing to base her happiness on but her looks after college was over.

Cady loved the liberal culture and for three years had foregone college to pursue a life of drinking and dancing, idolizing Cluster like they were Dalai Lamas with the secrets to eternal happiness. That's probably what attracted her to me. But after knowing Cady for almost a year I was starting to get annoyed with what I saw as Cluster's deleterious effect on her and their air of superiority.

These thoughts brewed in my mind as Mindy and I climbed Bromley Mountain bubbling away, like the Little Engine That Could. I pulled in last behind a dozen Subarus in the gravel outside *Ski Haus*.

"Hi *Dally*!" A voice shouted as I stepped from the car. It was Larry, standing with a coterie of cigarette smokers on the front porch of the cabin. He spoke with feigned familiarity, using that demeaning nickname, "Dally," that no one had called me since kindergarten. "Glad you made it."

Ski Haus was a black A-frame silhouetted against the orange of the dying day sky. I said hello and walked past the people on the porch, nodding to each, carrying a thirty pack of *Sam Adams* and a bag of clothes and toiletries. I was greeted by sincerer salutations as I walked through the screen door into the mud room, a landing decorated with candy-cane colored wall-paper. It smelled of mildew. This hallway opened into a large room with a gas fireplace and a bow-window and porch overlooking the trees of Bromley Mountain, down into a valley. At one end of the room a dozen people stood and sat on couches and tables drinking beer or wine in front of the fireplace. This room smelled like hamburgers and grill lighter fluid.

Reggae music played from wooden stereo speakers wired to a cassette player. To the left beneath a dusty iron chandelier was a sixteen-foot table made from a solid slice of stained maple, where partygoers played drinking games. There was only room to stand as I walked in. Yet with all those people around I felt emphatically lonely. As Francis Bacon said, *a crowd is not company, and faces are but a gallery of pictures.*

"Hi Dowas," I heard a mousey voice. I looked down and saw Cady's little sister, Julia, standing up to my hip, holding a unicorn doll. That made me smile. Then I heard my name called from this corner and that, and a small group formed around me, asking all at once about my car and the unsuccessful raft trip. I tried to look past them to spot Cady — excitement is hardest to bear the seconds before the realization of a desire. Then, like a scene in a movie, the crowd parted a little and Cady was standing across the room, wearing a red floral-print summer dress with a halo around her and a beer in her hand, with a sad-happy smile looking at me. The conversations blurred into the background music. We walked toward one another silently, awkwardly, like cats. Then we hugged, and the second our skin touched some impulse clicked on, and we hugged so tight it felt our bones might break. We couldn't hide our smiles, and we whispered to each other "Thank God, it's so good to see you." Such were our feelings then, two people who felt, maybe, more than other people feel. Suddenly all of the problems and frustrations of the past month disappeared.

We settled into our selves and into each other. We drank and lay around together. We warmed in the glow of symbiotic affection.

As the night wore on the music grew louder, funkier. Cluster kept costumes in a chest upstairs for dance parties. People donned vaudevillian outfits. Cady wore a jester hat while I grabbed a bunny costume with flopping ears. We danced to the wooden speakers blasting Kirsty McCall, Lucinda Williams and Van Morrison with other costumed characters.

When I rested from dancing (Cady never would), acquaintances and strangers asked about the raft trip, and whether I'd try again. I explained that I had another raft almost ready to go but for the life of me I couldn't find a crew.

"I'll do it," said a brown-haired man with a bushy beard sitting at the maple table. We'd been introduced just a few hours before. His name was Steve. He was in his mid-thirties. He was walking the Appalachian Trail from Maine to Georgia. He stopped by *Ski Haus* with his trail-mate, Joe, twenty-three, because he knew some Cluster folks and it presented an opportunity to unwind after walking and camping for the last 40 days in a row.

"I'm serious," I told him. "I really need a crew."

"I'm serious too," Steve said sternly. "And so is Joe. We were listening to you tell the story earlier and we think it's great." Joe, blonde and bearded, nodded and smiled. Joe looked about a year older than me. "When are you leaving?"

"August first."

"Fifteen days. Let's see…" From his pocket Steve retrieved a map. Clearing the table in front of him of wine glasses and ashtrays, he spread it out. Nine or ten people watched and listened to us talk. They pressed in to look at the map and hear us better. "We can walk up to eighteen miles a day, or as little as ten if it's rough terrain," Steve explained. "Looks like there's a steep slope and then it's pretty flat going. So let's say, what Joe? –Ten to fifteen miles a day on average?"

"We can walk that easy," said Joe. He had a pink scar preventing his beard from growing in spots on his chin and cheek.

"Fifteen miles, hmm." Steve made some mental calculations, then from his pocket he removed a twig with black pencil marks denoting miles according to the scale of the map. He moved this twig along the map starting at Bromley Mountain and following the path of the trail. "That places us around Salisbury Connecticut two days before your launch. If you drive and pick us up at the trailhead at Salisbury Connecticut in the afternoon on July 30th, we'll meet you and go on your trip."

The group of listeners laughed and rubbed their faces.

"Excellent!" I exclaimed. "Do you have a phone or something? So I can call before I set out to pick you up?"

"No phone. We shake hands on the Appalachian Trail and that's that."

"That's how I operate," I said.

"Okay. We'll be there. Don't *not* come, because we're adjusting our schedule just for you."

"Salisbury, Connecticut; July 30th. What time?"

"Let's say three o'clock."

"3 o'clock. You're on." We shook hands as observers chuckled and clapped. Cady was dancing and didn't notice.

Memories are organic recordings of seconds-long sensory data. Memories are not stories. They lack duration. We can recall a day, an event, something that happened over time, but we really only recall a series of pictures and impressions strung together.

Dreams are the same way. I've never seen an accurate dream sequence in a movie. In movies, dreams are too complete, too coherent, too full of detail and movement. In a real dream we see an object, maybe only a part of an object, while the background is sketchy and vague. Then we see another object, perhaps totally unrelated to the first. Our minds, which love to organize objects into recognizable wholes or patterns — into a *gestalt* — fill the blanks between these images, and when we wake, we feel we experienced a story or moved from place to place, when really we just saw, heard or felt discrete sensations in succession.

Memories, like dream images, are discrete. Particular memories establish points where the mind stops and muses. At those points memories may be elaborated and developed. The rest of the stuff between the points is fuzz that lacked significance. I remember the week with Cady like a photo album of mind pictures.

The next morning I turned twenty-two. Cady gave me a silver pocket-watch with a back made of glass so you could see the gears interacting. I have a memory-image of that pocket-watch sitting in my car's cup holder on dried-coffee-covered pennies.

Down the mountain we nursed Mindy, driving in neutral to avoid overheating the engine. But at the bottom of the mountain was a twenty-mile stretch of flat road to Bennington. By the time we got to Bennington the car was bubbling and popping, so we steamed into a flea market barn in the country just outside of town. We parked in the shade of a big tree to cool off. It was about 95 degrees and we were hungry. An old woman at the flea market told us we could eat at a place called *Kay's Diner* a mile or so down route 7.

"It's named after me; it's my diner," Cady joked. So we started walking down the macadam road with no sidewalks or shoulders under the blue country sky. We held hands. I gave Cady piggy-back rides. Once we almost toppled into a grass ditch, laughing.

Kay's Diner was a quaint little pie and sandwich shop on the first level of someone's two-story ranch. Ten circular tables squeezed into the room. The smell of boiling soups and the red and white checkered table cloths reminded me of eating lunch at my grandmother's house ten or fifteen years earlier. A young blonde waitress sauntered to our table. She had a tongue ring and ignored Cady while we ordered, but she smiled and joked with me. Cady got a jealous, then relaxed. We ate ham sandwiches and a slice of pie, then walked back along the road to the car. There are snapshots in my mental photo album of a farmhouse along the highway where a dozen colorful pinwheels spun; of the cobble-stone floor at Kay's Diner; of Cady's face after we ordered pie.

The next picture is of Cady and I lying on a towel in the parking lot of a *Sunoco* gas station, ten miles down the road, waiting for the engine to cool again. We lay behind the building, beside a blue dumpster. Cady rolled her shirt up and laid back to tan her belly as I ate a strawberry *Charleston Chew*.

"I'm sorry you're spending your birthday in a gas station parking lot," she said. She picked up the little notebook I carried and wrote:

7/16/06
@ Sunoco
Happy Birthday Dallas
+ What a happy birthday it is.
   Mindy is real sick.
      We are doing
         everything
            we can.

I wrote in small characters precisely atop each line. Cady wrote in large, curvy letters, fitting but a dozen words per page.

After *Sunoco* we rolled in neutral down a big hill, before the car gave up altogether outside a firehouse in Brunswick, New York. We called my parents. Now I see Cady and I drinking sodas and playing Ping Pong in the firemen's recreation room. Now I have a picture of my parents showing up with two jugs of water. We put the water in the radiator and she started again. So Cady and I nursed Mindy home while my parent's followed. They took us out for surf and turf for my birthday, at *Red's Restaurant* in Coxsackie, which has a neon lobster sign on a road enveloped by farm fields. I have a picture of Cady's face on a pillow an inch away that night.

"This was the best birthday I've ever had," I said.

Cady was nervous because Cortland College was 122 miles west, but my car was dying. At the garage the mechanic told me the water pump was busted, but if I continually filled the radiator with water I could probably get by. So with a couple jugs of water in the trunk we set out.

Cortland is in the Finger Lakes region of New York State. To get there from Albany you spend most of the trip sailing along route I-88—a long highway transecting farm fields and foliage, climbing up and descending down hills. It was another beautiful sky day, and we had the windows rolled down.

"Wow look!" Cady suddenly exclaimed, "What are those?" She pointed to a field of freshly harvested hay rolls.

"That's hay," I said. "They've just cut it up and they'll go out in a truck and get it soon with pitchforks."

"That's crazy! That still exists?"

"Of course hay still exists, silly." Cady sat back and gazed out the window.

"Upstate is funny. And then what — it just goes to a barn?" I smiled, taking my eyes off the road to look at her for a second.

"Well, horses eat it, other animals eat it too."

"Is that the stuff they put on new lawns?"

"To cover the grass seed, yeah. I'm not sure why they do that." Cady looked out the window intently, like a puppy.

"It's beautiful up here," she said. After an hour or so we pulled off the highway and put more water in the radiator. Then we began following the meandering, rural roads that *Mapquest* told us was the route to Cortland. We passed through Coventry and Greene (est. 1792, according to the blue historical marker) and Cady marveled, "These towns look like 1950's movies!"

Her face grew concerned as we neared Cortland and there were no large buildings. Route 11 took us past manure-smelling farms and dilapidated sheds. Across from the "Welcome to Cortland" sign was a dairy with rusting tractors and a milk tank painted to look like a giant cow. Cady's expression turned painful.

"This is where I'm going to school?"

Cady was challenged by institutional education. She was not stupid. But she thought she was unintelligent and that was all that mattered according to her philosophy. Reflexively she would say "I can't do this" or "I'm just not smart enough," and that would overpower and prevent her from learning anything from that point forward. She didn't know where to start a lot of things. There comes a point where one finds oneself so far lost that one begins *intentionally* to do badly, out of spite.

But Cady was proud and, if she cared, she had an enviable work ethic. So despite poor grades in community college she applied to Cortland and New Paltz to pursue her goal of working with kids. New Paltz sent her a rejection letter. Cortland put her on a waiting list.

"It sucks. I know I'm not going to get in," she'd said one night as we chatted on the phone. "I'm just too dumb and I have too many bad grades." But her friends encouraged her to write a follow-up letter, and she did. She told the Cortland admissions staff that she knew she had bad grades, but listed all the reasons she was focused and determined now. "At least now if I get rejected, I won't feel any guilt at not trying hard enough," she said. "That feels good."

Cady was accepted. She signed the forms, paid the deposit, cried filling out the FAFSA because she didn't understand it—we finished it together—and now she was on her way to orientation, ready to spend three years living in a town she'd never visited, living in a dorm with kids three years younger than her. That all hit her when she saw that painted metal cow milk tank.

We parked at the college in the late afternoon, during that time when nostalgia sets in. We left our bags in the car and explored the pretty campus. It was quaint in the way Kay's Diner was quaint: it seemed anachronistic in form and baring. We let ourselves into the old brick buildings where darkened hallways led us to schoolhouse style classrooms with wooden desks and green chalkboards. It was quiet like being in an elementary school after hours, like you'd expect, echoic. Cady seemed unsure.

We booked a room at *The Imperial Motel* for forty bucks and took off on foot to have dinner and discover the town. We made one wrong turn and found ourselves among boarded buildings. A black cat ran in front of us.

"Here kitty kitty," I said.

Screeched a scraggly old woman from behind a curtain in one of the shadowy houses, "No here kitty kitty!"

We giggled, "Fuck this street!" and ran off.

The trouble started when we had our first drink at *Hairy Tony's* bar. First, there was a good-looking bartendress so Cady got annoyed. Later we went to another bar and some towny guys hit on Cady—she was loud and ball-busting as she returned their conversation, which they took for flirting; I told her that sort of thing encourages more flirtation—she told me to mind my own business. Drinks, jealousy, more drinking. We got more annoyed at one another and drank more. We got drunk and fell into our hotel room and had sex smelling like booze.

In bed afterwards we both lay thinking. How is it that you can argue and fight one minute, and make love the next? In my mind I pictured Cady the Queen of Fun going away to school for the first time, getting drunk and spending the night with some frat guy with spiky hair who didn't care about her. Relationships as a general rule don't survive college. Cady coughed all night. She was sick from staying up at *Ski Haus* and smoking cigarettes with Larry.

"You need to take better care of yourself," I admonished after a couple of restless hours. That ignited the powder keg.

"Who the fuck do you think you are, telling me I need to take care of myself? You think you're my dad or something."

"If I thought I was your dad I'd be out drinking till 4 a.m."

"You think you know everything. What the fuck am I even doing with you?"

"Good question."

...And so on. If things were going well our emotions verged on euphoric. But if things went badly our energy discharged in an ugly direction.

Neither of us slept. The next morning Cady went to her orientation and couldn't keep her eyes open. Overwhelmed by paperwork, unpreparedness and fatigue, she got yelled at by a college functionary for not paying attention. I slept in my car until three in the afternoon, when Cady came to the parking lot, slammed the door and started crying.

"I hate my life I'm never going to make it in college. Fuck all this!" she threw her folder, cascading papers, and kicked the dashboard, ripping off her toenail and bleeding. "Fuck my toenail I don't care!" She screamed, then looked at me sitting silently in the driver's seat. "Dallas...I can't do this! This isn't me...I'm scared!"

Cady crying melted my practiced aloofness. I gave her a long hug and she soaked my shoulder. She looked exhausted and sick. We reclined the seats and held hands, looking at the ceiling of my car...wondering.

I put a gallon of water in the radiator and drove us to Trumansburg, an hour away, for the *Grassroots* music festival Cady had been looking forward to. As we drove there we held our relationship together the way you move a put-together puzzle from one table to another — very carefully because of the obvious cracks.

At *Grassroots* we met up with Cluster. Larry greeted me with his demeaning "Hi Dally" and I had a hard time holding my tongue. We met up with Cady's high school girl friend and Cady accused me of being secretly in love with her, because some ex-boyfriend of Cady's had been infatuated with her, and I grew more and more annoyed with the childishness of her behavior and the debauchery of the crowd. And meanwhile I was wasting time out there when I had less than a week to get the raft built back home. Larry and Cady went off to dance together all day while I sat around smoking and drinking with her step aunts. It poured. There was water in the bottom of the tent when we slept on a deflating air mattress. I couldn't wait to leave and Cady couldn't wait to see me go. Our sourness hung in the air as a counterweight to the smell of reefer and wet grass, as her family looked on us with distaste for dragging down their mood. Cady walked me to my car and we gave each other a perfunctory hug. She watched silently as I put water in the radiator. Then I drove away and we both wished we'd said a dozen things we'd kept inside. It was a long, lonely, loss of a ride back to New Baltimore. That is the end of one memory-album in my mind, and there is no picture. Just a piece of black deconstruction paper.

X. Building

Steve and Josh sat on the side of the road. Between them a sign read "Appalachian Trailhead." In the grass was a six-pack of *Bud Light* tall boys. Josh was eating homemade trail mix from a *Ziploc*. They grinned through their beards as I pulled Mindy onto the grass.

"Captain!" Steve shouted as they rose to their feet. "I was getting nervous."

"I told you I'd be here," I smiled. We shook hands. Steve and Josh smelled like pubescent boys after gym class in June. It almost choked me. We loaded their belongings—only what they could carry on their backs—and slunk into the car. Steve took the front seat. I'd rigged the CD player so a track started as soon as I turned the key: a few chimes, then a violin, then the Doobie Brothers singing *Well...I built me a raft and she's ready for floatin'*...

"Haha! Nice," my new comrades cheered.

We headed back through Salisbury, Connecticut, a settlement of shops and houses just across the border from New York. As I drove out of town the streets turned to *country roads*, those long, sun-shined expanses of grey that cut through corn fields, dotted with red barns and farm tractors.

"There a reason you have the heat blasting when it's 90 degrees out, Dallas?" Steve asked.

"Yes. My engine overheats. But a girl I dated in high school had the same problem with her car and her dad told her that blasting the heat draws the air past the engine into the car."

"Does it work?"

"It delays the inevitable." Steve gazed out the window.

"That's all you can ever do."

After three minutes all signs of town life disappeared. We drove through field after field.

"So, how's the trail going? You guys walk it all together?"

"Not all of it together," said Josh from the back. He looked out the window like he was seeing a nice memory out there.

"We walk at different speeds," Steve explained. "Some days I wanna just get where I'm going. Other days I'll take a rest and we'll end up at the same rest spot. But we planned ahead to be here today and here we are. You mind if I smoke a cigarette?"

"No, man," we rounded a sharp curve. "I never pictured a trail-hiking person smoking cigarettes."

"I smoke them infrequently. They're not any worse for you than anything else if you only smoke 'em once in a while." Steve's tone was mildly defensive. He unzipped his backpack and pulled out a *Ziploc* bag with a pack of *Camels* inside. From the same bag he retrieved a pack of matches. The smoke blew backward out the window.

"I smoke them now and again myself," I said. "Mostly when I'm drinking or when I'm depressed."

"Want one now?"

"Yes." *Friend of the Devil* began playing as I lit the cigarette and exhaled. With the sun shining and the green grass and the good music and two new adventurers in my company I felt relieved all of a sudden. I exhaled. I slumped a little and put my left foot up on the seat as I drove, half-Indian-style. It occurred to me that these two men in my car met me, as promised, and now I was about to achieve what I'd worked so hard on for months. "Thanks for coming, guys."

"Thanks for the adventure," Steve said. He leaned back a little too, and now when he looked at me his face was amused.

"You know, I think it's great, man," Josh shouted from the back—over the wind rushing past the open windows and the heat blasting and the music playing. He leaned forward so we could hear him better. "You know, I'm walking the Appalachian Trail 'cause I want to just...see everything I can and just see where the adventure takes me. Like, I never thought I'd be getting in a car and driving to wherever your town is, like south of Albany, and taking a raft on the Hudson River to New York City. I mean, this is amazing! I hope I have little side trips like this all the way down."

"Thank you! Thank you!" I shouted over my shoulder. "I'm glad somebody understands! Like, why *not* do shit like this? You learn a lot, you meet people. It's better than sitting at home and watching fucking *Laguna Beach* or whatever. Yet everybody looks at you like *you're* nuts!"

"It took me until I was thirty-five to realize what you guys are knowing at twenty-two or however old you are. How old are you?" Steve inquired.

"Twenty-two ten days ago," I said.

"I'll be twenty-three in two months," Josh said.

"Right so you guys are ahead of the curve. Don't let 'em tell you what you gotta do. It gets you nowhere." Steve frowned and took a drag of his cigarette.

"I hear you there, man," I said. "I'm pretty much going to lose my job the day we take off for this trip."

"Why?"

"I told them I had to take two weeks off, but there's only one other bartender besides me and she only works two nights a week, but a) it's not my fault they pay $5 an hour and you only earn $30 in tips over a seven-hour shift and the liquor is never stocked; and b) I can't *not* go on this raft trip it's been built up so much…I can't not go now. I need to get it over with so I can focus on new shit, you know?"

"Good for you," Steve nodded. "I was a manager at the accounting branch of a construction firm—" [Cady had told me he was raking in $80,000 a year.] "—and I just looked around one day and thought, 'I'm thirty-five. I've worked sixty hours a week for the last five years. What do I have to show for it?' I was starting to get grey hairs. Well, here I am now. And you know what? Every morning I wake up to a beautiful picture of nature; I'm doing something. It's hard, but it's so much better than spending all my energy working for someone else."

"Where is the raft right now?" Josh asked.

"At my parent's house in New Baltimore, a little south of Albany."

"So we're actually headed north-west right now," he observed. "And we're going to sleep at your parent's tonight and tomorrow night as we get it to the river and all ready?"

"Right."

"I'm interested to see this thing in person," Steve said. "I think it needs to be big enough for all of us to sprawl out. And definitely needs a good shelter. We don't want to be out during a thunderstorm. We have to make sure that our stuff stays dry. If you get your equipment wet on the Trail you're screwed."

"Well, it sort of is what it is," I warned. "You'll have to see it in person to really get the idea."

"I'm just saying," Steve continued, "we need to have a plan. We need to have everything we need right where we need it to be. We don't want to be in the middle of the river and need something in an emergency and not know where to find it. We should have a deck of cards. We should have—"

"—I've got a list of everything and you really need to see it before you can plan for it," I said. "This trip is not going to be a really cozy experience. Our shit is probably going to get wet—although I've built a venetian-blind sort of system to keep most of the rain out and also function as a sail—but we're not going to be able to spread hammocks out and stuff like that."

"I think we'll be able to," Steve said.

"If you can find a way to do it I'm all for it," I said.

"I will. Don't worry I have a lot of ideas about how we can improve this boat. *With us* with you, we'll get to New York City."

I had conflicting thoughts about his last sentence.

We pulled into my parent's driveway.

"This is what we're taking to New York?" Steve's expression soured as he surveyed the dock with the match-stick-looking frame shelter. I'd painted an old piece of plywood white with red letters spelling the words *U.S.S. Crab Legs 2.0.* "This is going to need a lot of work."

"If the Indians could do it," I said from behind him, leaning against Mindy with my arms akimbo.

"The Indians had dugout canoes and a system of alliances up and down the river to supply them with food and potable water," Steve declared.

"I'm not sure the Indians made trips that far," Josh added.

"Well anyway I've got two friends coming tomorrow to help finish this up, complete the shelter on top, attach the paddle-wheel..."

"And that's the trailer we're using to get the dock to the river?" Steve pointed to the trailer I'd borrowed from my uncle Dave. "That's too small."

"I used it to get the thing up here," I said.

"Well," Steve demurred, "let's talk about the plan over dinner. Can we put our equipment inside and get washed up? I haven't had a shower in two weeks."

Steve and Josh laid their camping mats on the carpet floor in my office in the basement. Like *Maniac Magee* they refused softer accommodations. They perused the newspaper clippings I'd preserved from the first raft and laughed when they saw the pictures.

"It's hard to believe that that thing in the yard is an improvement over anything, but I'd say it looks like you've actually come a long way," Steve jibed.

They took turns showering, to my parent's relief, because they smelled awful. Both men had red, almost scabby rashes around their waists where their pants chafed as they sweated and climbed and ambulated eighteen miles a day.

"Look at their beards!" my mother whispered to my father and I during a private moment. "And God, how they stink! Well, they seem nice though and it's a good idea you found them because it worries me so much to think about you going down the river alone."

"Yes mom."

"Don't yes mom me."

"Yes mom."

"Good."

"I can't believe you got these guys to agree to go with you," my dad said.

"Well, what else are they doin', right?"

"Exactly."

We went to *Yanni's Too*, where we'd drank before our first launch, for a dinner of wings and beer. Since they were "on a thirty-six hundred calorie schedule" they ate 24 wings apiece. I struggled to eat ten.

"That'll change when we start on the raft," Steve explained. "You'll find that you burn through your calories much faster when you're constantly going, like we'll be on the boat. Somebody needs to be paddling all the time, to give us that extra two, three miles an hour that we need."

On the one hand, I was encouraged to hear Steve offer ideas to bring about my objective. But at the same time I felt I'd obtained a measure of wisdom by experiencing the first endeavor. That wisdom allowed me to listen patiently while Steve pontificated. But it was annoying, as it always is, to hear someone make pronouncements when they don't know what they're talking about. And there was another thing, too. This boat trip, it was *my* project. I wanted help with it, but I was reluctant to have it hijacked and turned into Steve's.

I listened to his suggestions, trying not to correct him too much. He was in shape; he was sort of fanatical about meeting goals. It didn't seem necessary to correct him about things he would learn in the near future by himself. I decided my job over the next two weeks would be to sit there and offer practical advice and, if necessary, *orders*, to keep us out of harm's way and moving on schedule to New York. Whether I liked it or not, I needed Steve's help.

"So you're the captain, Dallas," Steve said as he tossed a wing bone into a wooden bowl full of wing bones. "So what does that make us?"

I could tell that question had significance by the way Steve leaned back in his stool with a look on his face like an expert asking a protégé for his opinion for the first time. It was a look that said *I already know the answer and I'm testing you.*

"Well, on the last trip Mike was Admiral and in charge of the overall campaign. I was the Captain and in charge of the raft when it was in the water. Jared was Commander—you know, in charge of special missions to shore."

"Interesting," Steve said, smiling. "Admiral. I like the sound of that."

"You can be the Admiral, and I'll be the Commander," Josh chimed in.

"Admirable Admiral. I like that," Steve grinned. Never one to let alliteration slip by unnoticed, I smiled too.

"It does have a nice ring to it: Steve, the Admirable Admiral."

"What can mine be?" said Josh. "Like, the *Ca*...the *Clo*...what sounds like *Commander*?"

"Nothing works with 'Commander.'" Steve said, then repeated, "Admirable Admiral. I like the sound of that." He tapped his hand on the bar, gulped his *Sam Adams*, and seemed to relax for the first time since I'd picked them up in Connecticut.

Steve was in the center. The conversation pivoted around him. He asked the questions. He seemed to have an answer for each one, waiting to be proffered as a correction to my answer.

In a way Steve made the trip seem *real*, like it was about to happen. His observations were the views of the raft from outside of my locus of associations. His dismissiveness was both frustrating and humiliating, yet he brought the closest thing to an objective viewpoint I could find. I mean here was a man who, unlike the nay-sayers I'd previously formed my arguments against, was an adventurer who'd given up everything for a perambulatory tour across the Appalachians. Rather than telling cynical people why the trip was possible, now I was defending my role as creative leader against someone who wanted to take over after most of the work was done, and ride to victory like a *deus ex machina*. Thoughts like these entered my mind as we conversed, and distracted me. So I was a little surprised when Steve changed the subject to ask,

"So what's it like dating Cady?" He pushed his empty pint glass toward the bartender. "I'll have another."

"Make it two, I've got this round," I said. The bartender placed our glasses down. Rock music played as we took freedom-drinking draughts and rubbed foam from our mouths with the backs of our hands. A cute waitress took away our bone baskets and washed the counter with a blue rag. "Dating Cady is good...excellent." Steve looked at me with one eyebrow raised higher than the other. "I mean in certain ways, of course," I added quickly. "Like, it's weird...the first time I saw her I wanted to do everything with her and I ended up sending her a postcard from Albany and we didn't date until six months later after talking on the phone for hours every night and shit." Steve and Josh nodded, so I went on. "It's great in some ways. Like to me, I think she's so fucking hot...I've never *not* lost interest in a girl after a couple of months. After a couple of months, that's when my relationships tend to crash and burn. Or, not really...they usually have so little fuel left that they crash and break apart like a *Lego* airplane. But with Cady, I feel like I can't keep my hands off her. And it's not just looks. There's also something about her that is almost like, emotionally perverse in a way that's really...engaging."

"What do you mean?" Steve asked.

"It's almost as though she and me are on two sides of a teeter-totter, and whatever I do on my side emotionally has the opposite effect on her emotions on the other side."

"Wow dude, sweet analogy," Josh laughed. "Are you stoned all of a sudden?"

"I understand exactly what he means," Steve said. "Believe me, it can be emotionally exhausting. I was married for twelve years before I got betrayed in the worst possible way." Josh and I stopped smiling, expecting Steve to elaborate. "But for you, hey, you seem good together. She seems fun. I hope it lasts, man."

"Thank you, as do I," I said, realizing possibly for the first time that I felt used-up and anxious. "We fight often, now," I added. "And it's intense fighting." I frowned inwardly and said in a low voice, "I'm always the one to apologize, just to get past the argument, even though I really feel I'm right."

"Yeah," said Steve, "that happens."

"Hey!" I shouted, "What do a walrus and a *Ziploc* bag have in common?"

"What?"

"They both like a tight seal!" We all laughed. "And speaking of seals, I gotta go break mine." We laughed less, and Steve patted my shoulder as I jumped off the barstool. In the bathroom I knew I was starting to get drunk because I caught myself mechanically repeating parts of the recent conversation aloud. That was always a dead giveaway.

Jess Gadani stopped down and helped Josh and Steve and I the next day. I'd known Jess for years, since our days in Drama Club together, and I'd visited her several times in Ithaca when she was getting her opera singing degree. We finished sewing the bed sheets to the plastic drop cloths for use as covering on the raft. Then we hot-glued lengths of half-inch by one-inch boards to the bottom of each sheet, so that we could roll them up and down. Meanwhile Steve and

Josh raised the raft higher using the boat jacks I'd commandeered from Shady Harbor and stuffed blue foam in the spaces between the plastic barrels so that the boat would present a more streamlined shape to the water, like two pontoons. For tools we used the antiquated things we found in my grandfather's basement: the drill you needed the chuck key to tighten, a hammer with only one prong on the crow-bar end, a measuring "tape" that consisted of eight wooden rulers that swiveled out to make an eight-foot rule, and a collection of screws that Grandpa kept in recycled glass jars and medicine vials. That evening—the night before our launch—Mike came down after work. I met him in the driveway. As we walked toward the dock, he asked how we planned to get the boat to the water.

"We'll use my uncle's trailer," I said.

"That's a step up from last time. Does the trailer have lights?"

"Hell yeah this is high class fucking shit man."

Mike gestured toward the work that Steve and Josh were doing under the boat.

"Looks like you got two pontoons this time. Ought to cut through the water a little better."

"That's right."

"And what are these?" Mike pointed at the blinds Jess and I had made, which were rolled up on the frame on top of the dock.

"Let me show you." I jumped aboard and unrolled the blinds. In total there were seven lengths of sheet. I rolled two down on each side, one down at the front and back, and one I unrolled lengthwise on the top of the cabin frame. When all of the sheets were extended I had a cloth-covered cabin, not unlike a square wigwam made of sticks and covered in animal hides. These sheets, scrolled down, could be tied to the deck to keep them from blowing in the wind.

"Oh, I see it," Mike said. "I get it now—that should help protect you from the rain."

"Exactly. This trip will be a breeze, man. See—last time was practice. We had to go through a trial to learn a couple of things we never could've predicted until we tried. And now that we learned those things, all we've got to do is float. You sure you don't want to come, man?"

"I have to work," Mike lamented. "I just started at the Comptrollers, I can't take two weeks off after being there six weeks."

Steve and Josh had been under the dock. They were cutting into strips the fire hose which had been nailed to the dock. They used the strips of hose to cradle the blue foam under the dock and hold it in place. Now Steve crawled out and announced triumphantly,

"Pontoons done, Cap'n!" I turned,

"Thanks. This is really great. I really appreciate all the help."

"Yeah," said Steve with a smirk. "No more amateur stuff. You've got a couple of serious guys helping you now. You should have called us for your last raft!"

"Thanks again."

"Yeah, you know, when you're walking the Appalachian Trail you learn you can't go unprepared. You've gotta cross every T and dot every I, or you might as well get off the path."

"Yeah. Steve, this is Mike. He was one of the people who went on the first raft with me." Mike and Steve shook hands. Steve continued,

"Ah, the first Admiral. You were my predecessor." Mike chuckled.

"So you're the Admiral on this trip? Good luck!"

"Well, it's not luck. I'm happy to help out your pal Dallas. So, you're the one who said this was a stupid idea?" Mike's head jerked and tilted a little to the side. He looked at me, then Steve, then back at me, and forced a laugh.

"Well, I didn't say it was stupid." Steve was not coy.

"Uh, that's not what the newspaper article said. What did you say, 'It went horribly' and 'I didn't think we were going to make it there and we didn't?'" Steve looked at me while pointing a thumb at Mike, "Some help you had on your last trip."

"Well, okay, come on," Mike said more assertively. "I mean, the thing was a piece of shit. It had barrels that didn't hold water. It was a joke."

Steve was unrelenting.

"Well, from what I read, it sounds like Dallas did all the work, and you just laughed at it, and then said it was stupid in the newspaper."

Mike looked at me as if to ask, *Is this guy serious?*

"Well, Mike was in school down in New Paltz, so he couldn't really help to build the thing," I said. "And it was my idea, really." Steve fired back like a prosecuting attorney,

"Your idea that he jumped on to get in the paper, and then he made you look like a fool in the paper."

"Yo, what the fuck?" Mike replied.

"Yeah, let's all chill out a little," I said. "You know, Mike did what he could, and it was really my project, and he and my other friend Jared who went with me, they didn't know really how serious I was."

"Okay Cap'n," Steve said, "if that's how you wanna play it, okay. So, Mike, what are you doing now?"

"What am I *doing*?"

"Yeah. I mean, why don't you join us on our trip? We launch tomorrow."

"I know you launch tomorrow. I have a job I have to go to." Mike softened his tone as he turned to face me. "You know, honestly, I wouldn't mind joining you guys for a couple of days, like, maybe Saturday and Sunday morning."

I smiled and nodded; Steve cocked one eyebrow.

"How would you get on and off the raft? We're not planning on stopping once we start," he said.

"I have a canoe," Mike looked at me to remind me that Steve's opinion was irrelevant because, as I'd just said, it was my project.

"You know, it'd be a big help to have a canoe on this trip," I reasoned. "The raft itself isn't so easy to move around. But if we had a canoe, we could go ashore a lot easier. We could even paddle ahead of the raft if we knew there was a town or something, get supplies, and then bring them back to the raft. That way we wouldn't have to stop." Steve nodded,

"That would be a good contribution. Could we borrow the canoe for the whole trip?" Mike back-peddled.

"Well it's my parent's canoe. You know, I'm not sure if it's okay."

"Bah!" Steve waved him off with a hand gesture.

"Well, I mean, yeah, I think it'd be okay. I'd have to ask. As long as you promise to bring it back and don't damage it. It's not mine, it's my parent's."

"Don't worry we're not going to get you in trouble with your parents," said Steve. "Dallas, you know how to canoe?"

"Eh, Mike took me out once and gave me a lesson. I wouldn't say I've really perfected my technique."

"I can paddle a canoe," Josh said as he climbed out from under the dock.

"There, see? Problem solved," said Steve. "Now we have a taxi so we can get stuff from the shore."

"I don't know," Mike said.

"Oh come on, man!" Steve exclaimed. "It's a fucking canoe. We really need it. Dallas is your friend. Lend him the canoe. You're not going to get in trouble. Jesus Christ."

"Okay, okay, Jesus," Mike said. Steve stood nodding. Mike stood with a clenched jaw, tapping his foot.

The sound of crushed pebbles announced the arrival of a red station wagon in the driveway. It was Oliver. He emerged from his car with a shit-eating grin and sauntered to the boat before gesturing grandly and proclaiming, "It's really something now!" We shook hands.

"It's really something now!" I repeated. "Oliver this is Steve and Josh. Steve and Josh, this is Oliver. Also, Josh, Mike; Mike, Josh."

"Hi Oliver."

"Hi Steve."

"Hi Oliver."

"Hi Josh. Hey Mike."

"Hey."

"Mike nice to meet you. Josh."

"Hi Josh."

"Hiiiii!" Jess sang-shouted from the house. "When did everybody get here?" She spoke these words the way she spoke all of her words, in dramatic fashion, as though the arrival of Mike and Oliver were akin to news that some *coup d'etat* had occurred and we were all living under Russian rule now, or something. "Oliver!" she exclaimed, descending the porch steps, "give me a kiss. Mike: how are you? Tell me everything."

"I like Jess," Steve said to me as my three old friends broke into conversation.

We lifted the paddlewheel from the back of Oliver's station wagon. It didn't look as I'd pictured. What I'd wanted was essentially a pole that went through a small wooden drum, like the kind cables get wrapped around, with bicycle sprockets welded to either side. Instead Oliver had built two heavy crosses out of 2x4s, attached them together with four more 2x4s, so that the thing was six-feet long, and created four paddles by screwing 1/2-inch plywood to the four crosswise boards. A cross-section would have looked like a "plus" sign, the four paddles each beginning at the circumference and continuing to a common point in the middle of the circle, with nowhere for the water to run out. Instead of running the metal pipe straight through the center of the wheel, extending a little wider than the paddles, Oliver had screwed a circular floor flange to either side of the wheel, and screwed in two-foot-long pipes, one on each side, that had the bike sprockets welded on. It was much longer and heavier than I'd pictured, and without the pipe running through the center as an axle, the stress from turning the wheel would fall on the screws that attached the floor flanges to the sides. But I could hardly complain, seeing as how Oliver had voluntarily done all the work himself without so much as a sketch from me. And anyway we were launching in 24 hours so criticism would serve no purpose.

To attach the paddlewheel to the raft we screwed 2x4s to the deck extending off the stern. Perpendicular to these we screwed two more, shorter 2x4s extending toward the water. We cut circular holes through these extensions and through the holes we slid the pipes with the bike sprockets. Then, with everything in place we screwed the pipes via the floor flanges to the either side of the paddlewheel, which was now suspended. We could spin the paddlewheel by hand.

"You know, if this was a real boat, and we were doing things right," Oliver said, "we probably should've put something inside the pipe mounts, to lessen the friction between the paddle-wheel pipes and the wood that holds it up."

"Like, pipe couplings with ball bearings or something," Mike said. "If the wood gets wet it might swell and pinch those pipes and make it hard to turn the wheel." Oliver laughed,

"You'd find yourself in a *pinch* if that happens."

"Hopefully that's not how things *turn* out," I added.

"I guess *wheel* just have to wait and see," said Oliver.

"Oh you boys!" Jess exclaimed. "Come on, I want to see how this thing works with the bikes hooked up!"

So we grabbed the two bikes that we'd taken the back wheels off of and placed them on top of the dock. We slid the bike chain, still attached to one of the bikes, around the teeth of the sprocket on the left side of the paddlewheel. Then we moved the bike forward until the chain was taut. It took us more than an hour to mount one of the bikes straight and sturdy enough. Then I climbed up on the raft and sat on the bike. When I peddled it turned the paddle-wheel via the bicycle chain.

"Now we've got it!" I shouted.

It was dusk and although we hadn't mounted the other bicycle we started to load the dock onto the trailer. I backed the trailer between the boat jacks and we lowered the dock onto it. Compared to what we'd had to go through to get the first raft on a trailer, this was so easy that Oliver, Mike and I laughed out loud. Mike and Steve argued over which kind of knot to use to tie the boat to the trailer. Then I started up ole *Al*, my dad's rusted white F150 with the leaking gas tank and crumbled fender, and we inched forward down my parent's driveway. Jess drove in front of us and Mike brought up the rear as we pulled onto New Baltimore Road, then onto State Route 144, going five miles an hour, the paddlewheel bouncing with each bump. A mile further and we crossed into

Coeymans and Albany County, took a right down a hill and pulled into the gravel parking lot where we'd kept the first raft overnight two months before. Then I backed the trailer down the boat launch, my parent's joining us now, and the *U.S.S. Crab Legs 2.0* was floated. We dispensed with the ceremony of breaking champagne over the bow because no one was around to share in the excitement.

We untied the raft from the trailer. We were happy that it floated, but our good fortune was short-lived. When we tried to peddle the bicycle, the chain slipped off the paddlewheel sprocket, rendering it useless. When putting it together in my yard, we had no idea what height to mount the wheel. We guessed at a height where it'd be half-submerged, right through its diameter, when in the water. But now, it seemed, the buoyancy of the wood, and the flexibility of the 2x4 frame, caused the paddlewheel to float upward as far as the 2x4 frame would bend. It was only a couple inches of displacement, but the increased height of the wheel relative to the deck meant that the bike chain slacked and fell off the sprocket. This deflated everyone's hopes.

"Well, let's not get depressed over that," I tried to pep. "Tomorrow, either before or after we launch, we can mount the bike farther forward so the chain gets taut again. Or we can glue circular plastic tops like the kind that come on *Country Crock* to the sprockets to keep the chain from falling off, like a chain guard."

Standing and using two canoe paddles we paddled the dock, very slowly, along a concrete pier by the boat launch. At the end of the pier the town park became woods where the land met the river. We tied the raft there, more or less out of sight, where we could get to it easily the next morning, when we planned to continue finishing the thing before launching that night. Then we went to *Yanni's* again.

"That was an inauspicious launch," Steve said when we got our beers.

"Is that what you were expecting to happen?" Josh asked. I sighed and looked around the room at all of the people drinking and talking. They all seemed so happy. I wondered how they spent their time.

"Yes that was what I expected," I said. "I expected to put the paddlewheel in the water and have it *not* work."

"Yeah that paddlewheel's not gonna work," the Admirable Admiral declared.

"We've got tomorrow to work on it," I said. I downed half a pint.

"We've got a lot to do tomorrow," Steve continued. "We've got to shop for all our supplies, pack the boat, finish putting on those blind-things, make an anchor. I think we oughta ditch the paddle-wheel."

That wheel was my main innovation this time around.

"We will get it done," I said. On the other side of the bar a young waitress snuck up behind a muscly guy in a tight-fitted shirt. She wrapped her arms around his chest and biceps. He turned around and saw her and they laughed and kissed. I flipped open my phone and thought, *what is Cady doing right now*? I imagined her stewing because we'd barely talked in two days and things were on the rocks. Or maybe she was all dressed up and out getting plastered, in order to illustrate that she didn't care that we hadn't talked. I wondered how a night like that would end.

"So...I leave tomorrow."

"...Are you going to be able to call me on your trip?"

"I want to but I'll only have one charge on my cell phone."

"...So I'll sit here wondering what's going on. When do you think you'll get to New York City?"

"I'm not sure. I think ten days."

"And you got the time off work?"

"No, you know I didn't get the time off. I'm just not showing up."

"That's responsible."

"I told them I needed it off."

"But if *I* show up late for work because I'm a little hung over, *I'm* not serious and *I'm* an asshole."

"I never said that. I think pursuing a goal one has had for a year is a little different than coming in late because you got drunk the night before."

"Of course...If Dallas Trombley does it, it's okay! Anybody else, fuck 'em! And it's ten months, not a year, to be accurate."

"This is not the conversation I wanted to have before this trip."

"..."

"...I was hoping to leave things a little sweet since I know we won't be able to talk for a couple of days."

"So you're not planning to call me for a couple of days?"

"I don't know I'm just guessing."

"Before you didn't know, but you just said it'd be a couple of days, so you do know."

"I don't know. Cady, I'm just trying to be honest."

"Me too. I just want to know if you're planning to call certain nights so I know not to go out and get blackout drunk and leave my phone at home on those nights."

"That's so fucking annoying. I can't tell you I'll be able to call on *x* day at *x* time for the next two weeks after calling you every day for a year—"

"—Ten months."

"—Ten months...I can't schedule that, so you're going to go out and get obliterated and leave your phone home, intentionally, so that if I *do* call there's no chance that I'll reach you. That's great. What is that, payback for doing something I've told you I was going to do since the third time we ever saw each other?"

"I think it's fair. If you're out having a vacation with other people unreachable I should be able to have a vacation too."

"Okay, you win! I admit it, I lose. I feel worse thinking about you going out getting intentionally and unconsciously drunk than you'll feel thinking about me floating with two smelly bearded men on a ninety-square-foot block in the middle of the river. You win! I care more than you do. Cady always wins!"

"No, this is about you and your stupid raft projects, not me. I shouldn't say stupid. It's not stupid. It's not stupid—God, that's what I love about you. That you won't stop doing what you want to do—but where does Cady fit in? I've had to call your fucking friends to get in touch with you because your phone is ruined. We chat for ten minutes. We see each other every other weekend. Now you're going to lose your job...for the raft! Do I get to be a part of your life? Or am I always going to be second on your list?"

"Do we have to have this conversation tonight? It's two a.m. I'm leaving tom...today. I have a million things to do, I'm a little stressed out."

"Sure, fuck it. Enjoy your trip."

"Cady—"

"No, seriously, enjoy it, call me when you can or want to."

"Cady I want to it's just—"

"Goodnight."

"Seriously—"

"---" *Click.*

"Cady? Cady...Hello?...Well, that conversation fucking sucked."

XI. Down....River

It was hot and sticky on the morning of August 1st, 2006. The sky was overcast. I woke up feeling I'd lived the same experience before — with the raft, with Cady — and there were few indications that this time would be better than the last.

I called Cady. She didn't answer.

I woke Steve and Josh off the basement carpet. They took long showers and talked about how good they felt after having spent so many days walking the Appalachian Trail and how this little trip of mine would be a good vacation.

We drove to *Family Dollar* for our supplies. Since I had less than fifty dollars to my name my plan was to steal a bag of oyster crackers and some cans of vegetable soup from my parent's pantry. But the Admirable Admiral admonished me.

"You need serious carbs," he said, throwing bags of marked-down candy into his cart. "On the Appalachian Trail we burn 4,000 calories a day, and you need to replace those calories." He set a big can of *Dinty Moore* beef stew in his cart. "You're going to need some quick sugars. You need to get candy."

"I'm not a candy fan," I said. "I prefer meats, cheeses, breads. The kind of shit they'd eat in Ancient Rome."

"Dallas you're going to need 50% more calories than you normally ingest," Steve corrected. "What are you, 130 pounds?"

"140," I said. "And I'll be fine. I've got my stuff packed already."

"Suit yourself," said Steve. "But Josh and I have been doing this for four months now. We know what we're talking about, right Josh?"

"Right, Admiral."

"You've been rafting for four months?" I asked.

"Walking the Appalachian Trail," Steve said.

"Oh that's right, I forgot."

I drove the crew and our provisions to Coeymans Landing. We parked in the gravel lot and walked to the pier where we'd tied up the boat. The water was choppy and brown-grey. A weak breeze blew up from the south making cat's paws on the river's surface. We formed a bucket brigade to convey our bags and groceries from the car to the dock. The reporter who wrote her questions in a notebook called and said she was on her way. She took a picture of us while she stood on the pier. That is the only surviving picture of the *Crab*

Leg's 2.0. It shows Josh, standing shirtless, with a big beard, on the bow of the boat, his hand holding one of the 2x4 crossbeams that made the frame of the cabin. I'm standing in the middle with a black tee shirt and an old pair of soccer shorts. Steve holds a 2x4 in one hand and a water bottle in another, with a gray cap, a set of sunglasses and a beard. He wears a pair of cargo paints and *Ugs.*

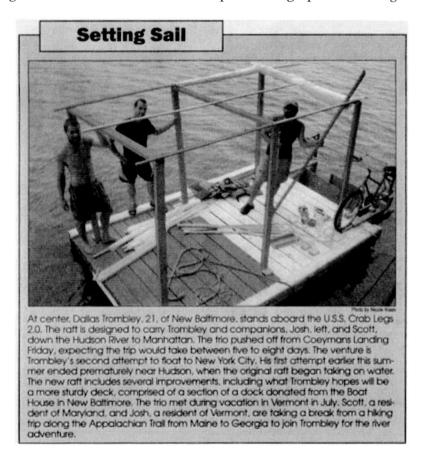

Setting Sail

At center, Dallas Trombley, 21, of New Baltimore, stands aboard the U.S.S. Crab Legs 2.0. The raft is designed to carry Trombley and companions. Josh, left, and Scott, down the Hudson River to Manhattan. The trio pushed off from Coeymans Landing Friday, expecting the trip would take between five to eight days. The venture is Trombley's second attempt to float to New York City. His first attempt earlier this summer ended prematurely near Hudson, when the original raft began taking on water. The new raft includes several improvements, including what Trombley hopes will be a more sturdy deck, comprised of a section of a dock donated from the Boat House in New Baltimore. The trio met during vacation in Vermont in July. Scott, a resident of Maryland, and Josh, a resident of Vermont, are taking a break from a hiking trip along the Appalachian Trail from Maine to Georgia to join Trombley for the river adventure.

We brought my grandfather's drill and a fifty-foot extension cord to the river. We tried to move the bike forward to increase the tension on the chain. This took a little more than an hour to accomplish, because we had to unscrew everything from the original mount and then move the bike and mount it again in a more awkward position. With the bike remounted we tried to peddle the paddlewheel once more, but again the chain kept slipping off. We tried to mount the other bicycle, using a rusty handsaw to cut boards, but after a while we realized that time was slipping away and we still had to load more provisions, go home to get our sleeping bags and oars and lights and make an anchor. We spent the afternoon doing these things and soon it was three hours before high tide, which would occur at 8:07 p.m. on August 1st, 2006. We went to my parent's house and ate spaghetti.

Back at the river we tried to get the paddlewheel working. Josh jumped in the water and held onto the frame of the wheel to test if weighing it down increased the tension on the bike chain. It didn't seem to do so, and in the process Josh lost a *Ziploc* bag with his wallet and phone somewhere in the river. We spent some time looking for that, and finally Josh found it beneath the waves after diving under water and opening his eyes four or five times. Then Mike showed up with his canoe and provisions. We loaded these on the boat and tied the canoe by a nylon rope from the back. I asked him to look at the mechanics of the paddlewheel. We were able to increase the tension on the chain if both Mike and Josh stood on the frame, one on either side, using their weight to push it down. Now the chain grabbed the sprockets on the wheel well enough. But although it'd been easy to turn the paddlewheel the night before, suspended in the air from the back of the boat in my yard, it was a different matter when it was half submerged in the water. Oliver arrived just in time to see Mike and Josh standing back there, me peddling, moving the boat through the water at about a half-mile an hour on a test-run. Then the screws on the flanges that attached the sprocket-pipes ripped out of the wood. The paddlewheel sagged off balance, three quarters of the left side submerged, the chain dangling. So we threw a rope to Oliver who pulled us ashore. Disappointed beyond description, I ripped the two bikes and the paddlewheel off the raft and threw them into the woods. With them I threw my hope for tolerably easy progress, and entered again the realm of uncertainty.

Jess arrived and we went to *Yanni's* for a couple of beers. Mike and I were happy that it wasn't raining like when we launched the first *Crab Legs*. Around eight we walked to the boat launch and Steve, Josh, Mike and I got aboard. Dusk was descending. We had four paddles, enough for everyone this time. So we bid my folks and Jess and Oliver and the one or two pedestrians who happened to be watching us *adieu*. Steve and I sat at the front corners of the boat, Josh and Mike at the back. We reached deep and with legitimate paddles and sound, aligned barrels we were able to paddle from the dock three times faster than on the previous attempt. Still, three times the rate of the previous raft was only about a mile and a half an hour with the tide just beginning to help us. After a half-hour we rounded the little peninsula just south of Coeymans where we were out of sight of those who saw us off. So the second raft trip had begun.

Last time we rounded the first peninsula we were scrambling to make a shelter. At least this time it was still light: though later in the season, there were fewer clouds to obfuscate the descending sun.

Onboard, I looked at where I was. I wore my beige linen adventurer's jacket with its four buttoned pockets and straps with buttons on the shoulders. In the pockets I buttoned my wallet and cell phone and the tide chart of the river, so I wouldn't lose them. I still hadn't managed to procure a good map. Around my waist I donned a thick green belt which held a canteen of potable water. From a lanyard on my belt hung a plastic sheath with my knife. I wore a leather fedora. I felt like I looked like an adventurer.

"This is too slow," the Admirable Admiral announced. "What should we do, Captain?"

"We could smoke one of these," Mike offered, holding up a cigar. I smiled.

"Let's focus on making progress," Steve said. Mike glowered. I suggested,

"Why don't we each grab a paddle and sit at once corner of the boat and try to paddle for fifteen minutes. Then we can rest. We should do that for fifteen minutes each hour."

"Dude, I don't want to paddle," Mike said in a low voice, to me.

"It's only for fifteen minutes," I said.

"Yeah but this trip is not about paddling constantly —"

" — Mike," Steve cut in, "This isn't even your trip, is it? Come on, it's fifteen minutes *buddy*."

I grabbed a paddle and sat in a collapsible camping chair on the right at the back of the boat. Mike sat reluctantly at the left, also in the back, with a very unhappy look on his face. We paddled to the Admiral's count.

When we were kids — even, just a few years ago when we were in high school — Mike was a fountain of ideas and energy. He returned the ball harder than I served it to him. That was the energy I expected — no — *depended* on, when we decided to pursue the raft thing in the first place. Now it was a struggle just to get him to paddle. And Steve — I'd looked forward to his cheerful help. Instead he was barking orders and agitating Mike, precisely the wrong tactic if we wanted Mike's help over the next two days.

"Can we put the radio on or something," Mike implored.

Josh retrieved the black boom box we'd brought from my parent's cellar and extended the silver antenna. It ran off of six C batteries. Josh adjusted a dial to tune to a Rock station from Albany.

The chords at the beginning of *Stairway to Heaven* emerged from static.

"Alright!" Steve shouted, "Keep this on!"

Music is that strange property of some vibrations which changes the constitution of our minds and can at times actuate our bodies through an ephemeral medium. As we paddled in synchronization to the commencement of each four-beat measure, the solo guitar played tentative, slow, arpeggio notes, and centered us, so that we looked around and said in our minds, *Remember, here I am, this is new, but it is real, do not forget.*

Now recorders added accompaniment, holding whole notes in harmony, issuing an eerie Native American ambiance as we floated between darkened banks once alive with Algonquians and Mahicans. Glancing ashore we could almost see their campfires as Robert Plant began in falsetto voice to sound a story which seemed to hurt him to sing. I looked down and saw my paddle ripple the water and break the dying sky's reflection into a series of glimmering swirls. Each sweep of the paddle bubbled like swimming fish. The lyrics seemed to mimic the scene ashore, the passing of the waters beneath the overhanging oaks and maples:

> *In a tree by a brook; there's a songbird who sings;*
> *sometimes all of our thoughts are misleading.*

I looked around at our dock, glowing as it was with soft oil light, and paddled without speaking. The moon was a white plate suspended in orange-black, amid the thick smell of summer and muddy river water. The backs of Steve and Josh, the profiles of their faces, reflected the undulating lantern light. Mike appeared in shadow from my perspective.

Now the guitar played eight beats per measure and we rowed twice as fast, which was still but a moderate pace, but leisurely no longer. And the singer sang,

> *Oh it makes me wonder...*

Because the music's tempo quickened, I paddled faster; because my body moved faster, I thought faster.

Who, really, are these people on this boat with me? Here was Josh—*what did he do for a living? Who was he? Why was he walking thousands of miles?*

> *It makes me wonder...*

And Steve... I thought. As he paddled his gaze was fixed downriver as though on a distant object, like something was down there that would salve some wound.

And it makes me wonder, the singer repeated.

And then there was Mike, paddling as though to paddle violated our contract of friendship. In my camping chair I reached deep down and scooped at the water.

A little more than four minutes in, the song began cresting toward crescendo. Then a drum dropped. Percussion stimulates action, movement. We paddled faster and harder now to keep up with the rhythm.

"That's the ticket!" I said. Steve turned back and smiled. Mike shot a morbid look.

> *Yes there are two paths you can go by, but in the long run;*
> *there's still time to change the road you're on.*

The tempo picked up again as the narrator reminded us that, *It makes me wonder...*

Wonder about what? I pushed a shovelful of water backwards. It hurt my shoulders and arms but it felt good to think we were moving. If we moved fast enough, maybe finally I would get someplace. I reached down and pulled back the water with all my strength, sending the opposite corner of the boat, where Steve sat, pointing toward the channel and forcing him to paddle harder to keep us pointed straight. He turned his head, nodded, and tacitly took the challenge. He dug at the water and forced the bow back, pitching the bow toward the western shore, pointing us straight again. To the rhythm of the music we paddled with a lot of effort, equaling each other out, our trajectory straight and our momentum forward.

After six minutes the song suddenly jolted and paused. Then it shed its cerebral bent and became a power rock song.

Now we paddled atop ascending electric guitars and pounding drums.

"Turn it up!" I shouted. Josh leaned back and dialed up the volume on the black boom box. I was sweating now. We paddled and wondered how long our arms and shoulders could stand it. The song and the night and my mind became a continuum, one leading into another and back again. I forgot anyone else was around me. I just pictured a spot in the darkness ahead and paddled with shaking hands to scoop the water back, like the boat was sinking and the only hope was to bail as fast as possible.

As the vocals screeched back into the song, Steve shouted, "Row, Mike, row," because Josh and I were paddling so hard that we turned the boat toward their side.

"I am!" Mike shouted back.

Syncopated jamming guitars and banging drums caused a cacophony of competing exertion as Mike gritted his teeth and dug at the water, not out of camaraderie and common interest, but to beat me by turning the boat toward my side of the river. I redoubled my effort, bending from my folding chair way down to the water and pulling back with all my strength. As the song climaxed I focused every ounce of energy on each stroke, grasping, fighting the water, nature, punching and grabbing at the water to win. *I will row harder!* I thought. *I will row deeper and faster!* I was manic and explosive and bursting and then the world turned upside down...and I was wet.

I found myself suddenly surrounded by something warm, thick, opaque. It was dark and darker above me, a little lighter below. I was weightless and suspended and there was nothing to hear. A sensation like dreaming, disorientation, the thought: *Where am I?* An orangish light below my feet. Then it hit me: *I'm underwater!* I kicked with heavy sneakered feet but I couldn't tell which way to swim or how deep I was submerged or what weird river things were around me. It all happened in a second, but I felt my camping chair sinking, so I swam in the other direction. Just as my head broke above the waves I heard a splash and saw Josh swimming toward me.

"I'm alright!" I shouted.

"What happened?" Mike and Steve shouted, bent over the side of the boat, which now floated south with a little momentum.

I still had my shoes on, and my jacket and fedora, which was attached by a drawstring to my chin, and my canteen, so Josh assisted me in swimming to the boat. I pulled myself up onto the deck, right-leg first, then the left, sending streams of water between the planks. Josh climbed up behind me.

"I guess I got a little too into that song," I said as I removed a sneaker and poured it out. I held my binoculars up to my eyes and saw nothing but condensation.

"The Captain is enthusiastic," Steve said.

"That's what we get for paddling," Mike spat. "It doesn't get us anywhere. It just uses up our energy."

Now I was cold and wet. I threw my fedora onto the deck and started emptying my pockets. A soaked tide chart—*check!* A soaked wallet—*check!* Then I felt a different kind of sinking feeling as I reached into my right breast pocket and pulled out my cell phone. It was fried. There went my promise to call Cady a couple of times over the course of the trip, because neither Steve nor Josh had a cell phone I could borrow. There was no telling when I would talk to her, but I knew she'd be mad whenever it was, and she'd cite my failure to call as another sign that fate didn't want us to be together. I pulled my socks off and wrung the water out.

"Hey Mike," I said, schlepping one of the socks onto the deck. "How 'bout that cigar you were talking about before?"

As embarrassing as it was for me—the supposed leader of our troupe—to fall into the water like an ass, perhaps it was exactly what we needed at that moment. We needed a little levity to level the field between us. I'd accidentally illustrated both that I was as enthusiastic as ever, and that I was fallible.

"I think I went a little *overboard*, paddling back there," I joked. The incident made the other men pity me a little, and that diminished any resentment that they felt for being shanghaied along on a project that was hardly destined to succeed. Josh, nobody felt any animosity toward him. He was a pleasant guy who seemed to be enjoying himself as Steve, Mike and I argued cattily over stupid things. Now Mike was rolling a cigar, and that was a nice contribution we'd all enjoy. Steve was pretty secure now in his position as the wise older guy whose lead we ought to follow. So he came off his high horse a little, too, and relaxed.

As Mike rolled the cigar, sitting Indian style, on the top of a cooler, Josh grabbed us each a beer from another cooler, and Steve arranged the remaining chairs and life jackets into cushions so we could sit in a semi-circle talking and looking out at the water. Josh tuned the boom box to a station playing jazz music. Trumpet notes echoed off our little oil-lit boat, struck the trees on the shore, and refracted back to us. It was a clear night, full of stars, and windless. We knew we were passing New Baltimore because we saw Shady Harbor Marina, where I'd procured the dock, on the western shore, and below that, a halogen street light by a gazebo I knew was Cornell Park. To our left, on the eastern shore, a red buoy blinked silently. Mike looked at his watch.

"So, it's almost ten thirty," he observed. "We left Coeymans at what, eight fifteen? New Baltimore is pretty much exactly two miles south of Coeymans. So that means that all things considered, including paddling, we're moving at a little less than one mile per hour."

"That's not very fast," Josh noted. Recent events confirmed Mike's basic point, that the trip was hard and slow-going and a lot could go wrong. Now with Josh also attesting that we were moving at a snail's pace, Mike became a measure more optimistic.

"It's actually not so bad considering we've only had slack water so far. Now that we're getting to the middle of the tide, that ought to move us along. Maybe a good idea would be to paddle at the beginning and end of the tide, when the current isn't doing anything, and conserve your energy in the four or so hours in the middle of the tide when the water is moving you."

Mike lit the cigar and we started to pass it around. It was a nice night. We opened more beers. Josh wondered aloud when the next time would be that we'd pass a store to resupply. Steve joked that we ought to be pirates and commandeer our supplies from other ships.

"That reminds me of the pirate who walked into the bar with an old-timey ship's wheel sticking out of his pants," I said. "The bartender was like, 'Is that a steering wheel sticking out of your pants?' And the pirate said, 'Arrr, it's drivin' me nuts!"

Everybody had a good laugh.

"You've got a lotta jokes, huh Dallas?" Steve said.

"Well, I guess."

"I can't remember all those jokes. I forget 'em too quick."

"I'm—I don't want to say *blessed*—I'm *lucky* to have a good memory for those sorts of things."

"Tell another one," Josh said.

"What kind?"

"I donno, just any one."

"You have to say something to trigger some thought that the joke is associated with—I'm not a searchable encyclopedia."

"How about one with an animal," Josh suggested. "I feel like animals always make a joke more funny."

"Okay," I agreed. "Ready? So this man, he goes to the brick store to buy some bricks. He goes up to the guy at the counter and he says, 'Hey man, I need a hundred bricks delivered to my house tomorrow morning."

"Okay," Steve and Josh nodded. Mike smirked, because he knew the punchline. I continued,

"Okay so the guy repeats, 'Listen, clerk, I want exactly one hundred bricks delivered to my house tomorrow. Not ninety-nine; not one hundred and one, exactly one hundred bricks, you got it?' 'Yeah dude I understand,' the clerk says. So the guy goes home, watches T.V., drinks a six-pack and goes to sleep. The next morning, he wakes up because he hears a dump truck backing up and he looks out the window and sees workers unloading the bricks. He runs down the stairs and counts them, one, two, three, four...and how many bricks does he have?" I smiled widely.

Josh and Steve looked confused.

"A hundred?" Josh offered.

"No, ninety-nine!"

Mike and I erupted in laughter.

"I don't get it," Josh said.

"Me either," Steve frowned. "Why ninety-nine?"

"He's got *ninety-nine* bricks!" I emphasized.

"So what? Explain the joke," Steve said.

"What's to explain," Mike and I kept laughing. When Josh and Steve shook their heads I said, "Okay okay, hold on, I'll tell you another one."

"No, explain this joke to me," Steve insisted.

"Wait I got another one," I said.

"No! I want to understand this joke first," Steve repeated.

"Eh it's okay, I forgot that joke didn't even have an animal in it," I said. "So this man gets on a train—"

"—Wait a minute," Steve interrupted, but I ignored him. Now there was tension in the air as he frowned, Mike chuckled, and Josh looked confused.

"—This man gets on a train, okay? And he's smoking a big fat cigar. He sits down across from this well-dressed lady with diamonds and pearls and shit, who has a little dog that keeps yapping. The woman says to the man, 'Put out that cigar, it's disgusting and obnoxious!' The man says 'Shut that bitch dog of yours up, it's aggravating everybody in this car!' 'Get rid of that cigar!' the woman yells, 'Silence that dog!' says the man. The argument escalates until the woman grabs the man's cigar right out of his mouth and throws it out the window. The man grabs the barking dog and throws *it* out the window! At the next stop the passengers look back and they see the dog running up the railroad tracks after the train, and what does it have in its mouth?"

"The cigar!" Steve shouted.

"No! The brick from the last joke!"

Mike and Josh laughed, while Steve sat cross-armed and stone faced. After we continued laughing for some time, he grinned and conceded,

"That joke only works if you get someone like me to insist on explaining the punch line of the first joke."

"Yes," I said.

Hours passed as we floated slowly downstream. The moon rose and the sky became a lighter shade of black, so that we could distinguish where the tree line began, like two black walls of uneven height on either side of the river. Now and again we floated past a house with a floodlight on or a window where a T.V. screen cast a blue hue against an interior wall. But mostly there was nothing to see, and indeed, were it not for the movement of a plane high up in the sky like a sluggish shooting star, we'd have thought we were the only people in the world, floating in black limbo, alone.

It felt good to pass the buoy we'd crashed into two months before. To Mike and I it was amusing to recite what we'd experienced on our previous trip in June. We paddled when two or more of us had enthusiasm. Otherwise we talked, napped, or zoned out into our thoughts. It was not unpleasant except for the rift between Mike and Steve and the anxiety that I felt about Cady expecting a call that wouldn't come. Thoughts about emails and cell phones don't jive with rafting through nature in some places untouched since the recession of the last ice age.

"You've got to get over that feeling that it's the end of the world if you don't talk to her for one night," Steve said to me as he lit a cigarette and the crickets chirped. Mike and Josh were napping. Steve's features glowed orange as he ignited his stogie, then became white again as only the moon reflected down. We'd let the lanterns burn out.

"I don't know how *not* to feel it," I confessed. "I met Cady a year ago and our relationship has been about the only thing that's...do you mind if I bum one of those off you?"

"Sure Cap'n." Steve retrieved a pack of smokes from his breast pocket and held it out. "I thought you didn't smoke."

"I don't," I said. I lit it. It made me dizzy. "The other night you asked how things were going with Cady. I said great, I'd love to get married. Then I called her that night—I guess it was last night, wow—and we got in a fight and almost broke up, except I wouldn't let it die, so after an hour of convincing her that I care, we're still together." I let out a puff of smoke and tossed Steve his cigarette pack. "And that's how it goes, every week, almost every day, like a big emotional roller coaster that I didn't know I was getting on. And I don't want to get off. But I'm sick from all the ups and downs and why can't we just ride the Lazy River?"

"You shouldn't smoke just because I'm smoking," Steve said.

"I'm not."

"But you wouldn't be smoking if I didn't have cigarettes."

"Right now, no."

"Right," Steve sighed. After a while he continued, "But don't take me as an example of relationships. Sometimes they work, I guess. In my case no way. Never happy unless I—I don't even know. It didn't matter what I did. It's not worth giving up all of this."

We looked around our makeshift boat, scattered with empty beer cans. Mike croaked a loud, asphyxiated snore.

"What could be better than this?" I gestured around.

We laughed, then only the crickets chirped. We smoked another cigarette.

As we approached one thirty in the morning we could make out Rattlesnake Island in the distance. That, I learned, was the name of the island with the cove where we'd spent the night inside the yacht club two months before. Now, since we had an hour of tide left, (that was how we'd begun to refer to "an hour before low tide occurred"), Mike and I advocated floating farther than the island to maximize our progress. Steve said that we were barely making any progress, so we should tie up and sleep instead of passing the club. As Josh and Mike listened, Steve and I argued over the prudence of making progress as long as we had the opportunity, versus resting.

"We learned that lesson on the first boat," I declared. "Since it's really our only propulsion, we ought to stay on as long as the tide is moving us south at all."

But Josh threw in with Steve so that, in the end, annoyed as I watched suds and sticks continue to float downstream, we tied up our raft. Restless and irritated, I suggested to Mike that we smoke another cigar.

"Nah let's just go to sleep," he said curtly.

So they went to sleep and I sat on the dock, watching the tide go out.

XII. Setbacks

It was hard to get the others going at high tide the next morning. When Mike slept deeply he was downright un-wakeable. Steve rolled away from me and muttered "We need to get our rest to have the energy to row. We'll row into the next tide to make up time." It aggravated me because he knew it was impossible to paddle into the tide. So I waited. When the others woke they cooked cans of food on a small butane stove they carried on the Appalachian Trail, and ate breakfast. Then, a third of the tide gone, we finally untied and pushed out.

Like two months before, it took us half an hour to paddle the quarter mile out from behind Rattlesnake Island. Later I learned that the current close to shore can flow opposite to the current in the channel, depending on the shape of the riverbank over a mile or so up and down the river. The night before, when the tide was changing to a flood tide, and the current was flowing up the river, the current inside Rattlesnake Island had been flowing downstream. But now, as the main current was flowing downriver according to my tide chart, the current was flowing upstream in the cove. So not only did we miss out on a half-mile or mile of progress the night before because we tied up too soon, but now, the next morning, we had to fight the current, rather than float with it, for half a mile. The little mutiny on the previous night had cost us several miles. Paddling out of the cove that morning, I wondered how many miles we would lose each tide by being undetermined, and how many days that cumulative-lost-mileage would add to the trip.

Mike was in a sour mood. I was too, but I hid it while he showed it. Maybe my days in school theatre made me a better actor. More likely Mike felt no reason to affect cheerfulness on a trip where Steve had demoted him from Admiral to appendix. A short time after we paddled past Rattlesnake Island Mike said he was taking a nap. Possibly to sprawl his legs and have quiet, but more likely to get away from us, he laid his sleeping bag in the bottom of his canoe and slept there, towed thirty feet behind the raft. Steve mischievously let out the tow line until the canoe floated fifty feet back, and then untied the line and set Mike adrift. Thinking that I'd better keep up relations with Steve, with whom I'd be sharing a tiny space for the next ten days, than Mike, who was getting off the next day, I watched Steve pull his practical joke, even though I figured Mike would be pretty peeved, and possibly even hurt. About fifteen minutes later Mike woke up, floating about a hundred feet back, with no paddle.

Steve laughed as Mike was forced to use his hands to get to us, gesticulating and frowning severely.

"What the fuck guys? I go to sleep and wake up in the middle of the river, a hundred feet away?" Mike shouted as he tied his canoe back up.

"Oh, come on, it was a joke," Steve laughed.

"Some fucking joke, man. I didn't even have a paddle. I'm floating in the middle of the fucking channel. What if a barge came, and I'm sleeping?"

"Oh, we would have yelled to you."

"Wow, thanks, and then what? I'd use my hands to *try* and paddle out of danger?"

"Bahh," Steve scoffed, "you weren't that far away. We didn't realize you didn't have a paddle." I knew that was a lie, because all four of our paddles were sitting in the middle of the deck. But I didn't point it out. I was sick of arguments.

In the early afternoon we approached Athens, on the west bank of the Hudson, which was about ten miles south of Coeymans, our departure point the day before. We were making slower progress than the first raft. Since we were low on beer and out of ice, Steve decided someone should go to shore to resupply. The tide was starting to slack, but we had perhaps an hour of movement left.

"If two people take the canoe and paddle down to Athens, two others can stay onboard and we can keep the raft going. Then the two canoers can canoe down to meet us. I doubt we'll get very far past Athens so it shouldn't be a long canoe ride," I suggested. "Mike should obviously take the canoe, because it's his and he has the most experience. Maybe Josh should go with?"

"I'll go with," Steve volunteered. "I'll buy the beer and ice this round. I gotta get smokes anyway, and maybe Mike can show me a thing or two about canoeing, and we can get to know each other better, right *bud*?"

So Steve and Mike paddled for shore while Josh and I stayed on the raft. We floated just past Athens, and then a National Weather Service Wind Advisory interrupted the songs playing from the boom box. We paddled to the eastern shore and waited there, because the tide had begun to come back upstream. We played Crazy Eights and organized the provisions. After two hours we wondered where Steve and Mike were. Dusk descended and still they hadn't returned. I tried using my binoculars to look back upstream, but they were filled with condensation. So we sat and waited some more. The dusk grew darker and we lit our lanterns. Then finally we saw a silver cylinder moving over the water in the distance. It was the canoe. But only Steve was inside. When he finally reached us he threw us a rope and we tied him up.

"Man, what the hell is up with your friend Mike?" Steve said as he stood in the canoe.

"What do you mean? What happened?" I asked nervously. Steve handed us three plastic bags with ice, beer and sandwiches.

"We got to shore and we're looking for supplies," Steve said as he stepped aboard. "And he's like 'I think I'm gonna call my parents and go home.' Okay. Whatever. Then he's like, 'That's my canoe so I gotta take it with me.' And I'm like, 'Man, what? I need it.' And he mumbles 'Well it's not my canoe, it's my parent's, you know, it's theirs so they'll put it on top of their car and take it with them when they pick me up.' I said, 'Mike, hello? I need the canoe to get back to the raft.' 'Oh yeah,' he says like he just thought about it, 'I donno...' I'm like 'There's nothing to know. I don't have a phone. Dallas' phone is dead, I don't live in this state, I need the canoe to get back to the boat. What the hell else am I going to do?'" Steve adopted a sissy voice to mimic Mike. "'Well, my parents could give you a ride to Dallas' parents' house,' he says, 'or maybe somebody could give you a ride out to the raft.' I'm like 'Go back to your parent's house or whatever. I'm taking the canoe.' He got all pissy and mad at me. I'm like, 'what the fuck?' I told him he'd get the canoe when we're done with the trip. But Jesus, talk about not caring what happens to anybody as long as he gets picked up by his parents. Bah—we don't need him."

I wished I had a working cell phone, so I could hear Mike's side of the story.

By the time Steve returned it was dark and two hours past high tide, according to our tide chart. We got buzzed on *Busch Lights* and drifted down paddling when we felt like it. Even with three men we couldn't move the dock more than a quarter-mile an hour, and we couldn't paddle continuously, so it was up to the tide to move us. After a couple of hours we saw the lights of the *Rip Van Winkle Bridge* downstream, which connects Catskill to the City of Hudson. It was still too far to make out the vehicles driving on top of it. Around eleven thirty we floated ever so slowly past Buoy 128, where Mike, Jared and I had marooned ourselves at the end of the first trip. We drank to the fact that we had made it farther than two months before, although, in my mind, I noted that it took us half a day longer to get there. We floated less than a mile farther that night, the *Rip Van Winkle Bridge* still but an illuminated line in the distance. Then it was slack water again and Steve and Josh didn't want to paddle. So we paddled toward shore and slept as best we could in a field of lily-pads onboard the raft.

The next day, our third day aboard, was Sunday. According to the tide chart, high tide was at 7:47 in Catskill, a couple of miles downstream. If we wanted to make the most of the day, we'd have gotten going about an hour before that and paddled through the slack water at the end of the flood tide. I set my waterproof watch for 6:45. It was just before sunrise when my alarm went off. I tried to stir my raft mates awake, but they kept sleeping. So I set my alarm for eight o'clock and went back to sleep. At 8 I tried to wake them again.

"It's Sunday, the day of rest," Steve said tongue-in-cheek, without opening his eyes.

"Come on. We have to get going now. It's high tide," I said.

"It's slack water. We'll sleep for another hour and a half and take off when the tide gets moving."

So we sat there. Around eight thirty my comrades woke up and started moving.

"Time to go!" I said cheerfully. But Steve merely rubbed his eyes and said,

"Eh, it's not moving yet." They leisurely stretched, opened soup cans, lit their small gas burner, ate their breakfast, took pisses off the side of the boat. Finally, around nine, a fifth of the way through the tide, we took up paddling positions and extricated ourselves from the lily-pads that held us in place. "We'll pass under that bridge by ten o'clock," Steve announced.

"I don't think so. It's still about three miles away," I noted.

We passed beneath high voltage lines strewn above the river. They had red balls so planes would see them. The bridge grew larger. Soon we could see little boxes moving left and right on top of it. Over the course of another hour the boxes became distinguishable as cars and trucks. It was after noon by the time we reached the bridge, and we were running out of tide. Nonetheless we agreed to make passing-beneath-the-bridge the goal for the tide, and started paddling, hugging the western shore. Finally, we passed beneath the steel framework. It rested upon huge cement pillars. The bridge made us feel tiny, looking up through the metal, hearing the cars and trucks rumbling overhead. As we passed close to the cement pillars we seemed to move quickly, but it was only because of proximity. It took about nine minutes to enter and emerge from the shadow of the bridge—a distance of only forty feet or so. Then, completely out of tide but having achieved this tangible accomplishment, we pointed the bow toward the western bank and paddled to shore. The tide was over and we spent the afternoon in the untamed foliage of the river bank about a mile above Catskill. We'd travelled only three miles that tide. I couldn't help but extrapolate that at that rate it would take us twenty-one-and-a-half more days to reach Manhattan from our current position.

That Sunday night was the last enjoyable evening. We pushed off around seven p.m. A light breeze blew behind us, so we rolled down the bed-sheet-drop-cloth-sail at the stern and got a little push. We passed Catskill at twilight. Catskill is situated on a peninsula with a bay to the north and the Catskill Creek to the south of it. Three bulbous oil tanks reflected the pink setting sun. A small restaurant, and a public park sat in the shadows of the Catskill Mountains, which rose as orange and red giants above the trees on the western shore. We felt ourselves gain speed as the creek waters entered the river. As it grew dark we tuned in to NPR, which was playing *Marion MacPartland's Piano Jazz*—an octogenarian who'd toured with the Benny Goodman Orchestra and now played duets with up-and-coming jazz artists. The night was clear. The wind died. Fire flies made a million imitations of the blinking buoys. Steve had a little "one-hitter," as he called the cylinder made to look like a cigarette that he packed a tiny amount of pot inside of. We smoked and drank beers, taking turns giving toasts.

"Over the teeth, past the gums, look out liver, here it comes!" Josh said. We gulped.

"Here's to my enemy's enemies!" Steve said. We drank. I recorded the toasts in my journal. I'd brought a copy of *The Dharma Bums* by Kerouac. Josh and Steve asked me to read a chapter aloud to pass the time, so I read to them by lamplight. We listened to more jazz. I noted "Guy Davis * Watch Over Me" so I'd remember to download the song to my PC when I got home. It was picturesque on the river that night, which made me awfully melancholy.

Ask Cady for a picture and a note I can carry around and read when I am lonely, I wrote while the others dozed. Forgetting my frustration from the previous day, I observed, *I just realized the incredible amount of pleasure I get just from being around Cady. I need to tell her about this when I get back...I'm sad because everything is warm and breezy and beautiful and bright but she's not here so it all feels like wasted time.*

We spent the night tied to the western shore again, with no idea where we were or how far we'd gone. I wondered if Mike would have known, had he still been aboard.

By Monday morning it was obvious that we wouldn't reach Manhattan five days after our launch, as had been my projected best-case scenario before we set out. We were already on day four and we were, we guessed, about 15 miles south of Coeymans, and 125 miles north of New York City.

One of Cady's step-aunts was having a surprise 40th birthday party on Long Island 11 days later. It was going to be a big Cluster get together. Steve, Josh and I planned to attend. When we'd set sail I thought we'd have more than enough time to get to New York, where Cady would pick me up and I'd spend a week or so with her on Long Island before the party. Now Josh, Steve and I wondered if we'd make it to New York by then.

"Well, we'll go as far as we can go by then," Steve said, "And then we'll get off wherever we are. It'll still have been an adventure."

I nodded, fantasizing about being off the raft. But at the same time in my heart I felt cheated, because the whole point of the trip was to get to Manhattan, not to float around lackadaisically. In my pseudo-conscience I thought, *if we're not going to make it to New York anyway, why should we spend the next 11 days on the river, wasting time?* I shook my head, still hoping that if we paddled over the next few days, the wind might blow from the north and push us, or something, and we still might make it.

So we put our paddles in again, Steve and Josh having one objective—a mere good time—me clutching to the idea that if we expended as much effort as humanly possible, we still had a chance.

Nature soon thwarted that notion of mine. Just at the time when the tide ought to have been strongest, and we'd paddled to the middle of the river so the current would push us, a breeze blew from the south and stopped us dead. We paddled to try and break through the breeze, but it did us no good, even with the tide helping us. For the raft sat but a few inches in the water, while the great majority of the boat rose above it, pushed by the wind. In a battle between the tide and the wind, I now learned that the wind won. We paddled until our shoulders grew sore, to no effect. In fact, taking our bearings against a particular tree on the western shore, it appeared that we were moving backward! We paddled harder, but it was futile. All we did was waste our energy. Extremely annoyed—just at the cusp of losing my temper—I gritted my teeth and suggested we go to shore, so that at least we didn't lose ground. Since we were right in the middle of the channel, we decided to row to the eastern shore, because there was a little mud beach. It took thirty minutes of hard paddling to get to the beach, where I jumped off and kicked at the sand. If we'd made any progress at all, we'd have had to measure it in feet rather than miles. And now the tide was going out, leaving us behind, and the damn wind wouldn't let us move.

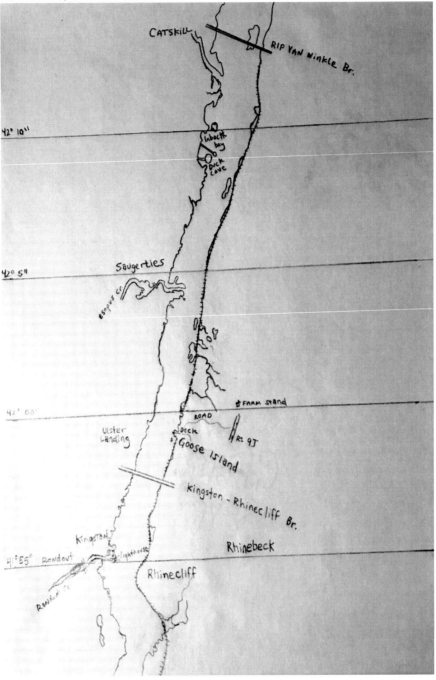

On shore we made a fire and drank the rest of our beer, which was warm now, because all of our ice had melted. And we ate the second-to-last can of beef stew. We played cards and took naps, waiting for the wind to change.

At first it seemed lucky: as the high tide crept up and it became slack water, the wind died away. It was four-thirty in the afternoon but it looked later because the sky was overcast. We felt the moisture in the air as we pushed off. The tide started moving us and for the first time that day we saw the shore float backward. I stood and clapped.

The sky grew darker as gusts of wind blew from different directions. Then the wind died and it was calm. We floated, slowly, downriver. Then the wind gusted again, this time from over the trees on the western bank, and kept blowing. Pleasure boats sped by in the channel, all headed downstream.

Sooty haze appeared over the tree line to the west downstream. Then the clouds in the western sky cast darker shadows over the shore. Heavy clouds rolled over.

A 30-foot *Bayliner* with a red stripe passed to our left, its bow pointed diagonally skyward. Fifty yards ahead its bow dropped as it reduced speed. It turned and motored toward us, piloted by a man in his mid-fifties. He wore a baseball cap, a set of sunglasses and a lifejacket. When he was in earshot, he turned his motor off, and shouted,

"Hey! Are you guys alright? You know a storm is comin', right?"

"Excuse me, sir!" Steve yelled. "Could you tell us how close we are to the nearest marina?" The question surprised the man.

"Oh, I suppose either up in Catskill, or down in Saugerties. Where're you comin' from?"

"Coeymans!" I yelled.

"Wow, holy cow! You guys came all the way from Coeymans on that? How long did that take you?"

"Four days so far!"

"Wow!" We had to yell because the wind was rushing past the trees, jangling our lanterns, blowing our drop-cloths, turning the papers of the magazine that had the tide chart on the deck, making waves on the water and pitching our boats up and down and sideways. "Well, you fellas got a place to take cover or something? The storm is comin' and there's no way you're makin' it to Catskill or Saugerties."

"Where do you think we should go?" Steve yelled. The man looked up at the clouds. There were only a couple of other boats on the water now, and they were disappearing downstream. The man looked at his own boat and back at us.

"Jeeze, I donno, fellas. There's no way I could tow you that far." I felt cold sprinkles on my arms and face.

"Do you think you could tow us up around the next little bend, so that we can tie up along the shore there?"

The man agreed. He tied a thick white rope to a cleat on the back of his boat and threw us the line. We tied this to the cleats on the bow of our dock. The man throttled his motor up to about five miles an hour. It sent the stern of his boat into the water, and we started moving forward. It was a new sensation, almost like we were on a theme park ride. I wished we could have a motor boat tow us for fifty miles. Then we'd be back on schedule. After a clap of thunder, the man increased his speed. For some reason this dragged the front of our boat into the water at a shallow angle. When the man increased his speed further, so that we trolled along at seven or eight miles an hour, the front of our boat pitched so low that waves splashed over the deck. The water was choppy; after riding up a wave our bow plowed into the trough of the next one. We scrambled to grab our bags, coolers and chairs, because the water crashed over the front of the boat and splashed all the way back. Josh tapped me on the shoulder and pointed toward the whitewater we were making behind us. Our deck of cards and a magazine were floating away.

"The tide chart!" Josh shouted over the waves and wind. It was the last useful thing that I'd based our success upon bringing, following in the path of Mike, my phone, and the paddlewheel. I really had nothing now to suggest I had any more experience than Steve and Josh.

The man trolled his boat close to the eastern shore and slowed. He shouted that the water was getting shallow, so he could tow us no farther. By then the rain drops were falling frequently, and any moment the sky might open up. We thanked the man vocally and with clasped hands, wondering what we'd have done if we'd gotten caught in the middle of the river in a windstorm, unable to paddle. He sped off, and we unrolled the venetian-blind-style cloth and plastic sheets that were tied at the top of the overhead framework. We clasped these to the deck, unrolled a sheet to cover the roof, and unrolled the front and back coverings, creating a square room covered in plastic and bed sheets, which we sat inside of after throwing a rope around a tree that stuck out from the shore. A few minutes later the sky opened up. Thunder boomed as wind turned the starboard sheets of our linen cabin concave. We huddled inside for about twenty-five minutes, but we were almost perfectly dry.

What an improvement that piece of engineering represented over our previous raft's leaking tarp suspended from fence posts.

When the storm was over we rolled up half the sheets and witnessed a pink and golden sunset, which showed the more spectacularly because it was reflected in the surface of the water, which now rested like glass. We paddled to the center of the river and travelled another three miles as the sky grew black and star-studded.

"Well, that does it for following the tides," Steve remarked off-handedly as he reached into a cooler and passed around the last three beers. "From now on I think we have to run this thing more Appalachian Trail style."

"What do you mean 'that does it for the tides'?" I said.

"I mean we lost the tide chart—it didn't seem like it was very good at predicting the tides anyway. We could never figure out where we were and what time to start moving. So from now on we do this more like we do on the Trail. None of this getting up in the middle of the night stuff, when we need to be getting valuable sleep to recharge—"

"—umm—"

"From now on, we get up at a reasonable time when we've rested well, we eat a good breakfast, and we go out and do as much as we can do, paddling when we need to, but also, like, relaxing and just enjoying ourselves, because this is a vacation for Josh and me, and we should be having beers and keeping up our caloric intake, and maybe at night having a bonfire and roasting marshmallows, who cares what the tide is doing."

"Okay, I mean, that stuff sounds fun. And I don't want to say that that idea is *lazy*. But I think the point of this mission is to get to New York City, and I think fooling around should come second. Like, if the tide is moving, we should be on the water."

"That's not a good way to get things done, burning yourself out," Steve said. "No, if we're going to be able to keep going for ten days we can't go on like this. We need beer and ice. We need more food. We should stop at a marina the next time we have a chance and have a solid meal with lots of carbs and proteins."

I rubbed my forehead and eyes.

"Okay—look. I want to get to New York City. We've only been making like six miles a day, and that's because we've been missing half the tides. If we stop whenever we want to and ignore the tides, we're not going to go anywhere."

"Okay, look," Steve said. "I want to go to New York City too. We know it's your goal. We want to help you. But you know, it may not be realistic at this point. So here's what we do, we compromise. Like, during the night we ignore the tide, and we get a good night's sleep. And during the day, any way we can make progress, we do it."

"We can't paddle against the tide, even during the day."

"I'm not saying paddle against the tide the whole time. Look, there's got to be a better way than what we're doing. Like sailing. I bet you I can turn this thing into a sailboat. All you've got to do is keep one set of sheets down, and that's your main sail. We have a rudder that works. There's no reason we can't sail this, right Josh?"

"Well, I donno. I did some sailing in Oregon growing up, but that was in a sailboat."

"But this has basically the same elements," Steve. "You've got the sail. These sheets ought to catch the wind. You've got the rudder and a tiller."

"It does have all of these things," Josh said.

"And you can sail into the wind, can't you?"

"Just about."

"So there you go, Cap'n. Think smarter not harder. All we've got to do is turn this thing into a sailboat and the problem's solved. See? This is why the Admirable Admiral is here."

"Hey, if you can get this thing so that the wind moves us downstream, and we don't have to do anything but sit here and drink beers, I'm fine with that. All I'm saying is, if it doesn't work, we still ought to take advantage of the tide whenever we can, even if it's at 2 o'clock in the morning. There's no reason you two can't sleep while I stay up and pilot us."

"That's too dangerous, just one guy up at night. What if you fall asleep?"

"I'm not going to fall asleep. I'll drink coffee all night. I don't care. I like being up at night and I'll enjoy the idea that we're moving and making progress."

"You'll see," Steve said. "Once we get this thing rigged up for sailing, we'll probably get—what would you say, Josh? Like ten or fifteen miles per hour. Then we do like that for ten hours a couple of days and that's like 45 miles a day, 90 miles. We're there four days from now."

"You know, I'm not going to be a spoil-sport here or try to stop you out of spite. If you can make that happen, I'll call you admirable for the rest of my life."

Steve extended his hand and I shook it. Then he set about examining the sheets and frame, and started turning the dock into a sailboat.

Evening came and morning followed, as God said in the first chapter of His book: The fourth day.

The morning of the fifth day, Tuesday, brought neither cloud nor wind. The previous afternoon's storm had zapped the moisture from the air. The sun hung above us now, a fiery sphere unobstructed. Its rays reflected off the water. For the first time we were forced to smear sun screen on our skin.

Barges, tankers, and especially pleasure boats passed at a slower rate now that it was midweek. When a boat with three young people motored alongside and asked what we were doing, we were grateful for the company. They gave us a six-pack, two sandwiches and a joint after we explained that we were out of beer and low on food.

By early afternoon we had to roll down our canvass cover because the sun was so hot and the air so stagnant. The weather man on the local radio station said that a heat wave was beginning in the Hudson Valley that would comprise four consecutive days of more than 100-degree temperatures, so a heat advisory had been issued by the National Weather Service. Horse flies, which we hadn't encountered before, began biting. To cool off we jumped in the water and swam alongside the boat.

To pass time and feel like we were doing something, we brainstormed ways to move the boat faster than the tide. We tried tying a rope from the boat around our waists and swimming to pull the raft like dolphins. This was unsuccessful. Josh and I jumped in the water and pushed at the back of the boat with our hands while kicking with our feet. This had no discernable effect, either. To distract ourselves from hunger and boredom, we ran and jumped as far off the boat as possible, seeing who could jump farthest. Steve and Josh gave me a diving lesson, but I couldn't seem to force my head into the water before my feet. It was mildly entertaining to swim under the boat and come up in the shade between the barrels, with the underside of the deck boards above us. Steve said we should hide under there and wait for a boat to pull alongside and for the people to come aboard. Then we could swim under their boat and come up on the other side, quickly climb up, and speed away with their motor and their food and beer. Then we could get to New York City. I noted that we'd get caught because our names were in the newspaper with pictures of us standing on the raft, and it'd be pretty easy for the cops to piece together who the boat thieves were. Steve grew agitated, as though he'd been seriously considering the idea.

In the early afternoon we rounded a bend in the river and saw a tiny line that was the *Kingston-Rhinecliff Bridge* miles downstream. Our stomachs were grumbling. The sight of the bridge motivated us to paddle, because we thought that if we could reach it, maybe we'd find some civilization to buy food. But after an hour the little line that was the bridge seemed to have grown no closer.

A light breeze began blowing upriver from downstream and westward, which Steve and Josh welcomed because it cooled us a little, and afforded an opportunity to try their hand at sailing. They secured the sheets on the right side of the cabin frame, so that they faced parallel to our lengthwise axis, like a mainsail on a sailboat. Steve stood at the back of the boat, holding a makeshift tiller in his hand. He pointed the rudder forty-five degrees toward the eastern river bank, so our bow faced directly into the breeze. We looked toward the shore and wondered if we were going any faster. The same trees, the same rocks, sat on shore for a while. Steve and Josh tried turning the boat to face the other shore, and orienting the rudder in the opposite direction, but this had no effect at all. We simply sat in the water, going nowhere. Whatever the physics of "tacking" and "trimming" that Steve continuously lectured, they didn't seem to apply to a raft with bedsheets and plastic drop cloths for sails. So after a while trying to sail we gave up the idea that we could make effortless progress.

We were only a mile or so downstream from where we'd started that day, and we weren't even sure where that was. We were in the middle of a stretch of river with no towns or houses. Josh suggested that perhaps he could get in the canoe and tie the back of it to the the raft, and maybe by paddling the canoe he could tow us. He tried, paddling leisurely at first and then digging into the water, but this, too, had no effect. The canoe merely lurched forward when he paddled, the tow rope became taut, then the canoe sprang backward. It was a series of starts and stops that failed to achieve any momentum. So Josh came back aboard and we waited for something to happen.

Since the southerly breeze (that is, the breeze which blows up the river) was getting stronger we decided to paddle ourselves close to the eastern shore. South of us a tree-covered peninsula jutted into the river and broke the wind. Close to the shore, perhaps in one of those areas where the current flows in a different direction than the main current, we seemed to gain a little speed. Then again, it may just have been that things that are close seem to move faster than things that are farther away. As it grew to midafternoon and the sun pressed down, we saw mansions emerge from the tree line on the east bank. Then the tree line became a manicured yard with small buildings designed like Greek temples, with stone columns supporting triangular marble roofs, open to the air from four sides. We wondered who lived in such affluence. Then the shore grew tangled in trees and jungle again. Finally, around three in the afternoon we spotted a small, rocky, tree-covered island ahead of us, and opposite this island, on shore, there was an aluminum ramp angling down to a metal dock. At the top of the ramp was a tiny gravel parking area, but no sign to indicate what the place was. Since we were famished, Steve suggested that someone explore what was up the road from the dock. Maybe we could find some place to buy provisions if a town was within a couple of miles. Josh volunteered to lead the mission in his role as Commander. I agreed to come along, hoping to find a phone so I could call Cady. So Josh and I got into the canoe and paddled toward the dock, while Steve stayed aboard the raft and said he'd ride it to the island a half mile downstream and land there. The idea was that after we'd bought some provisions we'd canoe to the island and have a feast.

On shore Josh and I tied the canoe to the dock and walked up a little path to a country road that had no markings.

"Should we go right, or left?" Josh asked. I had no idea. I crossed my arms in front of my chest like the Scarecrow in the *Wizard of Oz*.

"Maybe we should go both ways." So we took off in opposite directions to see if we could see anything from a little distance. But we only saw more road cutting through more woods. So I doubled back and joined Josh walking north.

After about three-quarters of a mile we came to an intersection with another unmarked macadam road and had to make another decision. We could keep walking north, parallel to the river, or take a road that cut through the woods up a steep incline. We were sweating in the afternoon sun, but we decided to climb the hill because we figured civilization would be farther from the river, and maybe we'd find a highway up the hill. Hot and tired, we didn't talk much. We just climbed, watching our sneakers fall one after another up the asphalt hill. After a mile or so we came to another intersection by an abandoned farmhouse with a crumbling rock wall. We said we'd stick out our thumbs to try to hitch a ride if any cars passed. None did. We walked, and it was like walking through some place where a war had killed off all the people, and then the trees and vines had grown back up, so that only the road and abandoned houses suggested that civilization had once been on Earth. The cicadas sounded their cymbals like a thousand rattlesnakes. Now and then we swatted flies and saw grasshoppers flitting across our path.

Finally we came to the side of a highway with a sign that said "9G" in black letters on a white shield. Another sign, this one green with white letters, stated that "Hyde Park" was a dozen miles to the right, and "Red Hook" was one mile to the left. Since Red Hook was closer, and presumably important enough to warrant a road sign, we took a left and walked along the shoulder of the highway. We ascended a little hill, and at the top we saw an intersection with a street light and a farm stand a hundred yards away. We were hoping to see a *McDonalds* or a diner, where we could rest, eat, gain strength and figure out where to buy groceries, but the 15-year-old girl at the farm stand said that there was nothing like that in walking distance. A man with salt and pepper hair was buying fruit, and we asked him if there was a grocery store nearby. He said that there was a *Walmart* "or some such box store" in some town we'd never heard of, and told us we could get there by taking a right out of the farm stand, then a left at the next intersection, and walking up another hill and following a road. So we left the farm stand and found the road and starting walking up another big hill, not really understanding how far this grocery store was. We walked uphill and kept walking and started asking ourselves how long we ought to walk. We said that we'd climb to the top of the hill and then see what we could see from there. After about twenty minutes we reached the top and we could see behind and in front of us a long ways. In front of us the asphalt continued like a line into infinity, down the other side of the hill, before bending to the right and disappearing into the trees a significant distance away. There was no sign of any business whatsoever as far as we could see. So we figured our only choice was to turn around and walk back to the farm stand. Back at the stand there was little to buy. They sold no prepared foods, nothing in cans, not even any bread. We bought some green beans, a cucumber, a peach, three apples, some goat cheese and several ears of corn. Then we carried these items in plastic bags back down the shoulder of the highway, back down the road that led past the abandoned farmhouse, back down the unmarked country road to the path to the dock by the river, sweating and snacking on raw green beans. We loaded our stuff into the canoe and pushed off toward the island downstream where we were supposed to meet Steve.

We saw smoke rising as we approached the island. Paddling around the inside of the island, near the shore, we saw the raft tied in a little shale bay, next to a blue kayak. We secured the canoe and followed a path. It brought us to Steve, who'd started a fire and cooked the last can of beef stew, and a ten-year-old kid with long brown hair who'd seen us floating and came out to meet us. After Steve had described our circumstances to the boy, he'd kayaked home and grabbed some candy and chips. Steve tossed Josh and I a *Snickers* and two *Airheads*, which we gobbled up. We described our disappointing scavenge ashore and showed him the meagre supplies we'd brought back. Then we roasted three ears of corn to eat with the beef stew and raw beans and goat cheese, keeping an ear, some beans, and an apple apiece for our dinner. Then the kid said he had to get back home because it was time for supper, and we napped on the shale island, lulled by digestion and the afternoon heat.

That evening we looked downriver at the *Kingston-Rhinecliff Bridge*, about four miles downstream. It might take us all night, even a whole day to raft there at the rate we'd been going. We decided the best plan was for Josh and I, the youngest guys, to canoe ahead those four miles to Kingston, up a creek to the middle of the city, to buy food. Then we'd canoe back out to the Hudson and meet Steve, who would've rafted downstream in the meantime. Hopefully we wouldn't have to canoe back upriver very far, because Steve would make it to Kingston while we were resupplying. In order to avoid becoming ships passing in the night, if Steve reached Rhinecliff — the shore opposite Kingston — before we returned, he was to pull off and wait for us. We had no way to communicate with each other except by planning to be in the same area later that night.

Josh and I took off about an hour and a half before sunset. Josh took the back of the canoe, where the more experienced person sits, in order to steer. I sat in the front and provided auxiliary power. It felt like we were in a rocket ship, moving three miles an hour in the canoe, after having been on the raft for five days. After fifteen minutes the raft was a little white-and-red square getting smaller behind us.

Since we were going south and west, in order to cross the river, we paddled into the setting August sun. The waves reflected orange light like flickers of liquid flame. I wondered if I had the strength to paddle the four miles to the bridge, for the most I'd ever paddled was a mile up and down the river with Mike the previous spring. It was hard to row in sync, and therefore the canoe kept zig-zagging. So I started singing *Row, row, row your boat, gently down the stream; Merrily merrily merrily merrily, life is but a dream!* We naturally paddled to the rhythm and straightened our trajectory. It also distracted us from the monotony and hunger. Since we had four miles to go, I sang all the verses to *Bye Bye Miss American Pie* and *The Weight* ("Take a load off, Annie"). Josh joined for the choruses and it was actually fun. We kept on like that for a dozen or so songs and after a little more than an hour we were gliding under the steel superstructure of the *Kingston-Rhinecliff Bridge*. I'd never driven over the bridge. I knew Kingston was about 40 minutes south of New Baltimore by driving on the Thruway. I knew that my grandmother was from Kingston because of the stories she used to tell when I was a kid. That was all I knew of Kingston.

The sun was a glowing half circle semi-obstructed by the shore trees now. Ahead, a brick lighthouse rose from the water about 100 yards offshore. As we paddled closer we saw that the lighthouse was connected to the shore by a causeway. So we paddled around the outside of the lighthouse, and agreed that it'd be an awesome job to be a lighthouse person, whatever he was called, sitting in the lighthouse all day, doing whatever the lighthouse person does.

The lighthouse marked the opening to the Rondout Creek. I remembered the name from my grandmother's stories. It was wide and navigable. It had lights marking a channel inside of it. As we passed the lighthouse small boats motored out of the creek or up, so we figured there must be at least a boat club or something up there. So we paddled up.

The sun had sunk completely now, though ambient light hung in the atmosphere, fading quickly. It smelled like a field of grass. We heard the crickets chirping as we paddled slowly up the creek, cattails to our right, the wrecked remains of an old wooden pier collapsed into the water to our left. The oranges and yellows disappeared from the sky, turning to a spectrum of blues near the horizon, fading to black above us. We paddled past an old-time ship graveyard, close enough to touch the hulls. The ships looked like first-generation iron-clads. Weirdly shaped, some with hulls of wood with dried planks missing here and there, granting glimpses inside of some cargo-hold that had been sealed up for a hundred years. Bats darted overhead. Atop some of the rusted hulks were bird nests and plants growing. One ship had once supported a metal crane, but it'd collapsed, so that it lay across its deck and another ship. The rivets protruded like metal boils. It was creepy to see those boats, some half-submerged and resting on the creek bottom, rusting away there, at dusk.

"My grandmother's sister drowned in this creek when she was four or five years old," I told Josh. I'd suddenly remembered the story my grandmother used to tell, of how her sister and her playmate had wandered off together. Suddenly it felt unhealthy to be in that water.

By the time we got a little upstream and found a place where we could tie up it was totally dark. We tied the canoe to an empty dock and jumped a chain-link fence into an empty parking lot. We walked across the lot and jumped an iron fence, crossed a set of railroad tracks, and found ourselves in another empty parking lot, beneath a bridge which supported a highway overpass eighty feet above our heads. We strolled across the parking lot beneath a single buzzing streetlight and then we were at the bottom of a hill where cars were parked and several restaurants were set up to serve dinner on their patios.

A sign said that we were in Rondout. It seemed like a really nice place. Like a mini version of Greenwich Village, I thought at the time, having never been to little affluent places in upstate New York and therefore having only my few road trips to NYC as a reference. At the bottom of the hill a large, white three-story building full of rectangular windows, each made of a dozen smaller rectangles, stood like a refurbished warehouse or factory, separating a little village center from the creek. Behind this building, at the bottom of a steep hill, was a street with several fancy restaurants with their doors open to let the summer evening air in. Music poured from the bars inside. I would've loved to spend the night in one of those places. The street was cobbled stone and the restaurants had iron tables with ruby colored cloth napkins and menus spread out, and — what made me think the places were really high class — glass bottles of spring-water with elongated stems.

We knew we couldn't eat at any of those places, because we were dressed in rafting clothes we'd been wearing for five days straight, and we were unshaven and smelly. So we started hoofing it up the hill. These were the days before smart-phones, so we had to interact with the human beings we passed, who looked at us like we were a couple of convicts, in order to find out where we could get supplies. A young couple directed us to a *Stewarts* up the hill, past a graveyard, through some ghetto streets, about a mile distant. When we got to the convenient store I called Cady from a pay phone that cost a dollar because it was long distance, and left her a voicemail when she didn't answer. Then we bought a case of beer, six cellophane-wrapped submarine sandwiches, cans of soup, hot dogs, chips, cards, dice, orange crackers with peanut butter and cheese between them, and some big bags of mixed candy. Then we had nine bags of stuff to carry. We cut through the graveyard and I found a stick that I balanced on my shoulder with two bags hanging from the front and two in back of me. Josh and I took turns carrying the 24-pack of beer. We stopped every block to rest. Finally we made it back to the bottom of the hill, under the overpass, over the railroad tracks. We passed the plastic bags inside the poles of the iron fence and jumped over, crossed the abandoned lot, jumped the chain-link fence, and loaded our stuff into the canoe, sighing in relief having accomplished our mission. Then we remembered that we'd seen a Mexican bar and grille on *our* side of the tracks, just a block away from the canoe.

"You know, there's not a chance in hell that Steve has floated to Kingston yet," I said. "We probably have some time to kill."

"You're right," Josh said. "And there's that Mexican place there. I bet they have margaritas."

"I bet they have all kinds of shit."

"Should we have a drink? You know, give Steve some time to float down to us? Otherwise we're gonna have to row further to meet him."

"Yeah. We'll be responsible. We'll only have one."

So we went to the Mexican place and had two pints of *Blue Moon*, a bottle of *Tecate*, three salt-rimmed margaritas, and a shot of well tequila apiece. Then we strolled back to the canoe laughing and singing "*La Bamba*" and "*La Cookaracha--cha cha cha!*"

"Ha ha, *cha cha cha*!"

"*Cha cha cha cha cha cha cha*!"

"*Cha cha cha.*"

We paddled down the creek back to the Hudson. We crossed the channel and searched the other side of the river shore to see if Steve was there with the raft, which he was not. So we started paddling back upstream. We paddled back under the *Kingston-Rhinecliff Bridge*, and kept paddling. It was a drag now, our buzz wearing off, having to do work.

"Do you think it's possible that Steve made it past Kingston and was making great progress and either couldn't pull off, or kept going because he thought it would be a waste to pull off, because he was making progress?" Josh asked.

"Man, I don't think so. We haven't made four miles in a tide yet this trip. It's fucking discouraging as fuck."

"You're disappointed in the trip, huh?"

"Well, jeeze man, I don't wanna be Debbie Downer. I'm really glad you and Steve came and agreed to help me. But the whole point of this for me is to get to New York, you know? That's the point. That's what I said I was doing it for. To me fun is like, coincidental.

This is a mission for me. All these fucking assholes who say I'm so dumb I can't float a boat to New York—Cady and I are falling apart because of this thing. I just want it done. I don't want to float around for five fucking weeks. I just want to get there and be done with it so I can repair me and Cady. I just want to like, to lay with her all day and look at her and not care about anything else."

"I'm envious of you. I've never had that. I've always been traveling around, trying to find it," Josh said.

"Had what?" I said. "A relationship on the rocks? That's sinking as fast as my last raft?"

"Nah like, being in love."

"Well...that's a good thing?"

"I think so."

"Yeah. Well it's a good thing for dressing up and going to parties where you need a date and shit. But the other person has to be in love with you too. Otherwise it's like when two people are trying to push a car that won't start up a hill, and one person doesn't try, so that the other person has to do all the work...and that sucks, to do all the work."

"Is that what it's like with Cady?"

"Sometimes. I donno. I'm sure I'm not the easiest guy to date. I'm always fucking broke. I'm sure she looks at her friends who all date fucking professional firemen and stockbrokers with money, and thinks *Why am I with this scumbag?* I guess that's part of why I want to win this trip—to get there. To show that I can do something, you know? Like, I don't have a trust fund...I don't know a mother fuckin' guy I can call who can get me a job at a firm. Sorry. But you know, maybe there's more to life than fucking going to some job you hate so you can buy the clothes you need to say that you're a guy to date. Wow, sorry man, I got off on a tangent there. Must have been that one *Tecate* we had."

"I didn't get the impression Cady was like that," Josh said. "When I was talking to her at the ski house she seemed mad cool."

"That's 'cause she's attracted to guys like you more than she is to guys like me; so she was saying what she thought you wanted to hear, or hearing from you, the traveler, what she wanted."

"Oh, man...I didn't mean to cause any problems by talking to your girl..."

"Dude people can talk to other people. It's not like you guys crawled off into a coat closet to fuck, did you?"

"Ha ha, no."

"She's going to college in three weeks. If I don't trust her at *Ski Haus* while I'm there with her..." I trailed off.

"You think you'll have a hard time when she goes?"

"I don't know." We were only a mile or so from the island we'd departed from three and a half hours earlier, and Steve was nowhere to be seen. "What about you? You got a girl someplace?"

"Ha — far from it man. I had a girl once, about two years and seven months ago. We were 19, high school girlfriend and boyfriend, who kept dating in college. We moved in together. I thought maybe she was the one. Then she started cheating on me with a kid she met at the underage bar at the end of the block from our apartment. I saw them out one night. His name was Tanner. What a pussy name."

"Man that's like, the awfullest thing I can imagine. Honestly, I'd rather lose an ear or something, than have that happen to me. It's like, you trust somebody and then, all of a sudden, it's a lie. And you've been the asshole the whole time, saying *I love you*, to some fucking bitch who knew it was a lie."

"You'd rather lose an ear, huh?"

"Yeah. It's awful."

"How 'bout a tooth?"

"Nah. An ear you can grow your hair to cover up. A tooth — if you lose that, you go down a whole level in socio-economic status."

"Haha, that's true." We were getting close to the island we'd departed from, and still no Steve in sight. We figured we'd see the lights from the oil lamps on the raft by now. "Do you think we somehow passed him and didn't notice?" Josh asked.

"Man, I don't see how that could happen. We're not Ray Charles and Helen Keller."

We paddled to the island and got nervous because we still saw no trace of Steve at the place where he was when we left. We circumnavigated the island and on the opposite, or north, shore we saw two dim lights in the distance, even farther north, at the dock by the road which Josh and I had taken to the farm stand earlier that day. We canoed to the dock and saw it was Steve, who'd tied the raft to the dock. We asked him why he hadn't gone *down* river.

"Because as soon as I tried to take off at high tide, the fucking breeze blew me back, Cap'n. I could barely control the thing alone. It took all I could do to paddle the boat to this dock, so that I didn't keep getting blown *way* back upstream."

So, the tide nearly over, we unloaded our supplies, ate and drank. We slept in sleeping bags on the pitching metal dock. That day we'd made a total of two miles between the two tides. That included the three or four miles Josh and I had walked trying to get food that afternoon, the nine miles we'd paddled down to Kingston and back, the two miles we'd walked around Kingston with groceries, and the negative .4 miles that the raft had blown backwards with Steve onboard.

XIII. Nowhere Men

On Wednesday, the sixth day, we woke with aching backs, having slept shallowly on the aluminum dock that pitched all night. It was oppressively hot even with the wind blowing hard from the south. We didn't need to untie the raft to see that we couldn't float with the tide. We just let the rope out and the raft moved swiftly backward. So we sat all morning on the dock, in shorts and tee-shirts baking in the sun, having to swat the horseflies that kept landing on our exposed skin. If we failed to swat them they bit and left painful, itchy welts. So we passed the afternoon napping, now and then eating, now and then playing a game of cards and drinking beer.

In the evening the wind was still blowing relentlessly from the south. We tried untying the raft and all paddling together to get to the little island where we'd camped the afternoon before. When we paddled as hard as we could, we inched forward, but after several minutes we still hadn't even cleared the end of the dock. We stopped and were pushed back. I jumped off the raft and tied us to the dock again.

"Son of a fucking bitch!" I shouted.

"Calm down," said the Admirable Admiral.

"Calm down? Calm down! We've been stuck in the same place for more than a day! No...a day ago we were a *farther* downstream! We've made *negative* progress. At this rate we'll be in New York in *negative* 60 days!"

"Look, okay, we're not going to make it to New York," Steve said. "But we can still have fun while we're out here."

"Have fun? What fun? This is fun to you? Sitting on a fucking dock doing nothing?"

"Hey, Captain, it's your adventure."

"It's a bullshit fucking adventure. It sucks. With this wind...we can never get downstream with this wind. We could actually take off and get back to Coeymans in like a day with this wind. We ought to be going back upstream. Then we could actually get someplace."

"Do you think so? Maybe we oughta do that. Maybe we can't make it to New York, okay. But we could make it back to where we started from, and then we can unload everything. You can keep your raft. We can say 'Hey, we tried, but look, the weather was so bad that we actually covered 15 miles in the wrong direction.'"

This had a certain face-saving appeal. Maybe if people saw just how quickly we moved backward, I could show that it wasn't a lack of determination on my part, but terrible luck, which caused us not to succeed. Plus if we went back, we'd be home in a day or so, we wouldn't have to find something to do with the boat and our supplies when we got to New York, and I could spend the rest of the week with Cady. So we decided to spend the night on the dock again, and if in the morning the wind was still blowing upstream, we'd say to hell with it and float back to Coeymans. That was our plan on Wednesday, the sixth day. We spent the night on the same dock we'd slept on the night before.

On Thursday it was hotter still, once more we'd barely slept, and we were again running low on provisions. Now the wind was blowing from the southwest rather than the south. So we figured we'd push off and test where the wind took us. We untied from the dock and started paddling toward the center of the river. We expected to move back quickly. Instead, somehow, we just sat there going nowhere, neither forward nor backward. We paddled hard, and could barely creep closer to either shore, but we couldn't make distinguishable progress up or down the river. On the east bank the same metal dock sat to our left. Ahead of us the *Kingston-Rhinecliff Bridge* straddled the river, getting neither larger nor smaller. On the western shore was the same municipal beach with the same lifeguard stand, which we descried if we squinted.

Out of food and beer again we started losing patience. Why were we not moving backward, at least? I declared that I'd be damned if we spent another six days trying to float backward, only to make it back just a little ways, so that we'd spent twelve times longer on the water this time around, and only reached the same location. No, New York was our goal again. But paddle as we tried, we could not beat the wind. So we spent all morning trying to go south ending up nowhere. Finally we decided to paddle across the river to land at the municipal beach. At least there might be people to talk to and maybe a place to buy food and sodas. So we paddled again and landed at the southern end of the beach in the middle of the afternoon. We ran a rope from the raft to a tree. Then we walked along the shore up the beach to try and learn where we were.

The beach was saturated with horseflies. I thought at first we'd landed in a cloud of them swarming a dead fish or something. But a dozen paces up the beach they buzzed just as densely. Every few of steps I felt little touches on the back of my neck behind my ear, on the back of my calf, on the top of my pinky-toe, and if I didn't swat them instantly, a sting that itched and burned so that I shouted out loud. Steve and Josh suffered just as badly. We put our bags, cards, beer, books and cooler by a picnic table in a shady area and walked up the beach to where the people were. We kept our feet in our sockless sneakers, because there were rocks and sharp driftwood sticks, and because of the incessant flies. But the sand got inside and chafed our ankles and the cords of our Achilles. So as we walked we bent every few seconds to swat or scratch. They swarmed a little less as we walked past the few families using the developed section of the beach. We arrived in front of the lifeguard's chair, which was old and unpainted and cracking. The lifeguard was girl about 16 or 17 wearing a white shirt with no sleeves with a red plus sign, a whistle, a red hat, and shorts. She wore a towel over her legs and feet to protect them from the sun and horseflies, which must've been a continuous and constant annoyance. We stood eye-level with her feet.

"Hi," Steve said. "We're from that red and white raft you might've seen land just downstream a few minutes ago."

"Hi."

"Ah—. Is it okay if we leave our boat there for a little while and use your beach?"

"Yeah, it's a public beach. What're you guys doin'?"

"Well, we're just...we've built that boat down there and we're seeing how far we can get."

"I seen you guys all day yesterday and today. I couldn't tell if it was a boat or what. I was like, what *is* that? So it's a raft? What does that mean?"

"We're doing it without using any fossil fuels," I said. "To show that it can be done."

"Oh. So...you guys like, sleep on that thing?"

"Yeah, we've been on it for six days. We came from Coeymans."

"Where's that?"

"Upstream about, maybe 18 miles."

"Catskill?"

"No, Coeymans."

"Huh. Is that by Albany?"

"Closer to Albany than to here."

"Wow. Six days? That's crazy. So what are you doing *here*?"

"We couldn't go downriver because of the wind," Steve said. "So we came over here. Do you guys have like a hot dog stand or candy stand or something?"

"No, I wish. There's nothing here but the beach and the picnic tables and the bathrooms."

"Hmm. Do you know if there's a store of some kind within walking distance?"

"Oh wow. No. I mean, how far is walking distance?"

"Like a mile or," Steve looked at Josh and I, "two miles?" We nodded yes, what the hell.

"Jeeze I don't know. I mean this is like, *Ulster Landing*. There's nothing here. It's like the middle of the woods. The closest place where there's like, a store is like a ten-minute drive."

Our postures portrayed profound disappointment.

"Not even like a gas station or, God, even like, a place that might have a vending machine or something?" Steve asked.

"Man, I donno. Maybe. You should ask somebody else, but I don't think there's anything for like, ten miles or something." We thanked her for the information and said we'd be back to sit on the beach and she wished us luck.

We sat around the picnic table where we'd set our stuff. We tried to play cards to pass the time but the wind kept blowing them over. I found a dead fish and threw it a downwind as a ploy to draw off the flies but there were so many that they just formed a black cloud around the fish and also kept masticating us. Finally, we decided to sit in the water up to our necks just so the flies couldn't get us. They were like some biblical pestilence. We'd accrued red itchy bumps everywhere our skin was exposed, so our flesh affected the texture of cobblestone. At least the water kept them off and cooled the welts. Yet now we were trapped in the water like soldiers in a fox hole under continuous fire. After a while Steve got up and said he was taking a walk up the road through the woods to see what he could see. Josh and I sat in the water looking across the choppy waves at the silver square that was the dock where we'd spent the last two days. After a while I said to Josh,

"Are you having fun yet?"

"Ha." I felt a fly land on my hair and shoed it off.

"This is not how I pictured this trip."

"Yeah. You thought we'd be in New York by now."

"Or someplace close."

"Well...at least we did *something*."

"Yeah. But it's not *enough*."

"Maybe it never is," Josh offered. "What's *enough*? Maybe the lesson is that nothing is ever enough, right?"

"No. Thank you for trying to lift my spirits. But *enough* would've been New York City, and we're not even close." I stood up out of the water. "I'm going to call Cady from the pay phone by the john."

"Dallas?"
"How'd you know?"
"The area code."
"How are you?"
"My uncle died Monday. The funeral was yesterday. I wanted you to be there but you weren't."
"Oh, I'm so sorry. I tried to call but I got your voicemail."
"Yeah, sorry I didn't answer. I have like, a life, and sometimes there're these times when I'm not waiting right next to my phone in case you get a chance to call from a phone that's not yours because you don't have one. I guess I should've called back the gas station or wherever you called from and asked them to go find you so we could talk like girlfriends sometimes do with their boyfriends."
"My trip is going terribly. Thanks for asking."
"Oh yeah, I'm sorry, I should've asked, because I have nothing going on. God, I just told you my uncle died and you didn't even say I'm sorry. What the fuck is that? Do you care at all about me? Or am I just like, something for you to think about after Steve and Josh and 'the raft'?"
"I'm sorry Cady. You're right. I feel horribly. I want this trip to be over so I can see you."
"No it's cool, you should do this more often."
"Cady—"
"You should build like, ten rafts. We'd see each other all the time. It'd be cool."
"I want to see you as soon as possible."
"Build another one. We'll see each other when we're forty. I'll be like 'Hey! I remember that guy!'"
"I'm sorry. Look, we're not going to make it to New York. I just want it to be over. It's like day after day of torture. Mike left. I'm starting to hate Steve. There's no food or beer. We can't get anyplace. It's a failure."
"That sucks."
"*Please deposit twenty-five cents.*"
"Shit, hold on a second...Okay, sorry, I had to put a quarter in."
"...."
"Cady I can't stand this. I'm done adventuring. I just want to be with you as soon as possible."
"Now that you're done rafting."

"I've been thinking about you the whole time."

"But you didn't call."

"You don't know what it's like out here. You can't just pull over and call. There is nothing around."

"Most boyfriends call their girlfriends."

"I had planned to call but my phone got wet."

"Of course it did. And now we're talking about you. I just got back from a depressing funeral, but let's talk about the raft some more!"

"I'm sorry about your uncle."

"What's the raft made out of?"

"I wish I could've been there when you were sad, Cady."

"What's the raft look like? Is it painted?"

"Please, I don't want to fight."

"What does it float on, barrels? Is it brown?"

"Cady —"

"No it's cool I love talking about the raft. I wish it was all we talked about. Oh wait, I'm so stupid, it is! How could I forget that? Duh!"

"You know, why is it that Mike, Steve, Josh, Jared, all these people can enjoy themselves for a few days of peace without worrying about anything, but me, I can't go a day without talking to you, or it's the end and everything falls apart? I feel like you expect it to be my job to hold everything together, like I can't even look away or everything will fly apart. It's like, give me a break! I'm having a horrible experience. My reputation is shot. I have absolutely nothing to look forward to except being broke and alone and looking like a fool, and when I need a little comfort, no! I can't talk to my girlfriend! In fact, she just makes me feel anxious all the time!"

"It must be me. I'm such a selfish bitch. What an asshole. Too bad I can't be more like Dallas Trombley. Then I'd be perfect."

I walked back to the picnic table fuming from the hundred-degree weather and the conversation.

"The trip is over," I said.

"What?" Steve exclaimed, "Already?"

"Already? Already!" I shouted. "It's been seven days! We've gone less than twenty miles! In the last three days we've gone less than two miles. What the hell are we doing?" I slapped my calf. "Fucking flies!"

"But I just got a twelve-pack of beer," Steve pointed to the cooler. "I found a guy who gave me a ride to a gas station and back. Here Cap'n, have one and calm down."

"I don't want a fucking beer, Steve. I want this whole experience to be over, because it sucks ass. It's an embarrassment. I've done nothing but waste my time and yours. I wish I never had the idea to build a raft."

"Oh, come on. It's been fun."

"No, it has not."

"You haven't been having fun, Cap'n?"

"No! Maybe a few times. But mostly I've hated it, Steve. I don't know you guys. I don't know why you're spending six months walking around. I'm not trying just to waste time, okay? I want to get someplace. And we're not getting anyplace together, are we?" Steve seemed wounded.

"Well, if that's how you feel..."

"Look, I'm grateful for you guys to have joined me. I couldn't have done it without you. But it's over."

"I mean, Josh and I...we're having fun. It seems to be you that's bothered and annoyed. We're fine to, you know, keep on keepin' on, seeing where we get over the next couple of days."

"It would be pointless."

"Well, it's your decision, Captain."

"It's over."

I would like to say that the decision was cathartic, but it was not. When something is cathartic, one realizes that a thing has cost them too much, and they stop what they are doing, and experience a burst of energy and enjoy fantasying about the new and interesting things they will do with their newfound resources and liberty. But I felt no relief, no burst of energy, and being done meant nothing more than that I'd failed again. The only thing I had to look forward to was rest and being alone. And even that seemed like a distant experience, because first I had to figure out how to get home.

As often happens when one experiences a personal, financial and social crisis, the only people I could call were my parents to get us out of there. So I called them from the pay phone. They were very pissy because they hadn't heard from me for a week and now I was asking them to pick me up in some place they'd never heard of. They said *fine*, and told me to give them directions. I said I didn't have directions, that I only knew the place was called Ulster Landing beach. They said I should get directions from someone there. So I hung up and went around to strangers asking if they could give me directions from, say, Kingston, to the beach. Then I called my parents back and gave them the pieces of directions I'd culled from the strangers, which were not very helpful. So I suggested they go online and type in "Ulster Landing" on *Mapquest* and they said "I don't know how to do that." So I suggested they call my aunt Dot, who'd made an effort to keep up with modern technology, and ask her to search *Mapquest*, and they said *"fine"* and that my "ass better be ready to go" as soon as they showed up because it was "a work night" and they didn't want to be "taking care of my shit all night." Then Steve, Josh and I made trips from the raft and back and piled our belongings in the parking lot. We pulled the raft onto the shore and tied it up. About three hours later my parents arrived very angry because they'd driven around unable to find the place. We loaded our things into the back of their Jeep Grand Cherokee. Then they became more aggravated still when I said we had to put the canoe on the top of the Jeep, because they were afraid it would scratch their paint job and they'd never driven with a canoe obstructing the view out the windshield and they were afraid it'd blow off and cause an accident. Us three rafters crammed into the back seat as my parents rolled down the windows because we smelled like body odor and river water. The ride was silent except that my father said "I think that's enough rafting," my mother said "I hope you're not planning to try again" and I assured them "I'm not." We got home after dark and threw our provisions in the yard as my parents complained that their Jeep was going to smell in the morning on their ride to work. I slept upstairs in a bed for the first time in seven days. Steve and Josh slept in the basement. I'm sure they discussed my character before they went to sleep. Then the next day I drove them to Salisbury Connecticut, stopping periodically to fill my radiator with water, and they went back to walking the Appalachian Trail.

Book II: September, 2006-April, 2007. The Badlands

"If it had not been for my years in North Dakota...I never would have become President of the United States." Teddy Roosevelt[10]

I. Vacuum

At the time, college was a *prerequisite* of Facebook and Facebook was a *perquisite* of college. Only students from a limited number of universities had access to the site, which required a school email address to sign in. Facebook began as a way to orchestrate group presentations. The webpage was invariably white with blue trim, and most users uploaded fewer than a dozen photos. There were no status updates or links posted on endless wall scrolls. Instead it was something of a personal networking encyclopedia, like a modern permutation of Tappan's Mercantile Agency of 1841, or a predecessor of LinkedIn. It had an air of exclusivity; people were careful to construct clauses correctly.

Quickly it transitioned from a professional and academic to a social site. Students posted pictures of parties and such scandalous situations, because only other college students whom they'd accepted as friends could see them. Within two years a second generation ushered in a new era of cultural existence, which has evolved and devolved simultaneously into the post-post-modern world of today.

Just before school started, Cady friended me—she hadn't had access to Facebook while at Nassau Community College. Her profile image was a photo she'd sent me affectionately a year before: a "selfie" as it would be called later, smiling in her bedroom in her parent's house. Then just a few days after school started, we broke up. Her photo changed to a picture of Cady dancing on a table with a forty-ounce bottle of *Olde English* raised over her head, and sixteen bracelets jangling on her arm, as a crowd of 18-year-old girls and jock guys raged and leered. If a picture speaks a thousand words, the heading of this one read, "I'm young, single, and I party!"

---

[10] Morris, E., *The Rise of Theodore Roosevelt*, Coward, McCann and Geoghegan, Inc., New York, 1979, p. 374.

"A piece of driftwood will take six months to float to New York City," Kayak Guy told us three months before.

"But a piece of driftwood is not *trying* to get to New York City," I'd pompously pointed out to the man more than twice my age.

Trying was the key, I'd thought, so full of optimism, three months earlier. Just *to try* was the main obstacle, the first step that everyone else was too scared or lazy to take. Like Oliver, most would rather not *try* than try and fail. Therefore they failed before they ever started. But me, I was different. *Trying* would be my penchant, my unique capability. That would be enough. I would try, *ergo*, I'd succeed. Now, in the fall, reality inserted itself into my calculations. It said,

"Trying is not enough."

Trying was necessary, but not sufficient. I considered the simple lesson for weeks, driving to school and home, sitting in the bathtub after reading textbooks. I thought about it as I poured myself a Highball in the basement of my parent's house.

It meant that something else was needed: *means*, perhaps, or *expertise*.

Means and expertise are not character traits the way *willingness-to-try* or *the can-do spirit* is. Therefore my *character*, which was the only thing I could control, I thought, was not sufficient for succeeding in rafts or relationships or any other task.

In other words, I did not carry around the key to success in the cockles of my heart. I still had a lot to learn.

I had to plug the holes I'd smashed into the hull of my life before I could think of getting anywhere.

If I can just get done with college, I thought, pacing in my basement.

I'll devote myself obsessively to finishing school, and then I'll have a free schedule, and I'll devote myself obsessively to making money, and with money I'll have the ability to go out with my friends and repair things there, and maybe I'll meet a nice girl then.

But that plan was flawed, because my car needed gas to run, and it needed to be fixed by a mechanic, and those things cost money which I didn't have.

I will devote myself obsessively to making money, I thought instead. *Then I'll be able to fix my car and pay my bills and I'll then be able to focus on school without distraction.*

But that plan was flawed, because school had already started and I had to spend thirty or so hours a week driving there, attending class, reading and writing papers.

It turned out that really I was like "most people" who I'd disparaged for not knowing where to start. So I drank alone in the basement for a couple of nights as my affairs sank toward the bottom. Then, with creditors calling and threatening to sever my service (I'd borrowed my cousin's old flip phone) I worked myself full of spite and declared,

Alright, I will do both! I will work wherever I can, making as much money as I can, and I will go to school, and I will do things around the house to get the place ready for winter, and I will go out with my friends, and I will write, and I will observe my family obligations, and I will do everything I need to do, and I will do more than most people dream about doing, and I will not tire, I will work harder!

I called Maureen, my old boss, and Adam, a former teacher who owned an apartment building, and I started splitting and stacking wood for Maureen and raking leaves and painting for Adam, whenever there was daylight and I wasn't in class. At night I'd return from class to take a three-hour bath while reading textbooks, descend the stairs to read more, and then I'd smoke and have a cocktail and write until three or four in the morning, and get up the next day to do it again. After a month I ran myself ragged.

By October I was a third of the way through my final semester. One morning I descended into the cement block basement. I turned on my PC and opened several Word documents related to a midterm on *Deconstructionism* I had to write. The cordless phone beeped. It was my parent's mechanic, who had examined my car. He launched into a litany of problems with the vehicle.

"There's just nothing we can do at this point," he summed up gruffly. "You'd need a brand new engine and the parts are going to cost a lot more than the car is worth."

"It's dead?" I said. "Shit. Boy this is bad news." As I held the phone in my hand I opened my *Hotmail* account. There was an email about a short story submission I'd sent three months earlier. I couldn't wait to get off the phone and see if I'd finally been accepted for publication. Simultaneously I considered the price of purchasing a new car. That would be impossible, since I'd owed my bank money for several weeks. "Man," I said, "is there any way I can get, I don't know, a recycled engine from somewhere or something?"

"You mean like a junk yard?"

"Yeah, I guess." I clicked on the email about the story submission. There was another link to a feedback web-page.

"You could try. But really I mean the car is dead, it isn't worth it."

Suddenly the computer monitor turned black.

"What?" I hit some buttons. The screen stayed black.

"I said it's not worth it—"

"Okay yeah. I'll call you back let me think about what to do." I hung up the phone. I pressed all the normal buttons on my computer, pulled out and re-plugged cords, reset power adapters, all to no avail. I looked at the wall and saw a big octopus of wires with power strips full of extension cords leading to other wires. I smelled burning plastic.

My car and my computer were both dead.

Normally I would've thrown something across the room. But I didn't feel all that angry. I felt more like, logically, of course my car and my computer would die on the same day. It hadn't happened yet, and it was problematic, so it was bound to occur.

"Of course, of course," I repeated in maudlin fashion as I stood and paced the room. "It would be far too easy for you to finish your final semester of college with the aid of a computer, with which to research and type required papers, and a car, with which you could actually commute the twenty miles to class. No no…that would be too easy. Something more challenging for Dallas Trombley!" My stomach sank as I realized that hundreds of hours of writing expired with the silicone capacitors in my hard drive.

I went to the liquor cabinet feeling particularly victimized. Up until that year I figured that good things and bad things happened in a basically balanced way. You find a dollar on the sidewalk, a few weeks later you lose a few bucks in the dryer. But I'd experienced a string of setbacks with no compensating good-fortune, and any attempt to abstract a system of karma seemed like wishful thinking.

"Hello old friend," I joked to the bottle of *Dewar's*. In a rocks glass I dropped three ice cubes and a four-count of scotch. Then I dripped a little water from the kitchen sink and stirred it around with the handle of a spoon. I placed it on the counter to let it age. It was 11:34 in the morning.

"So, I think it's time I got an apartment in Albany," I said to my mom and dad that night at dinner.

"Oh, now don't be stupid," my father chastised. "You live here for free, why would you want to get an apartment. Sandra, hand me the salt." My father coated his Salisbury steak.

"I need to get to class. And I'm going to have to be at school like all day, since I'm going to have to use the computers there. I have sixty pages of papers to do in the next six weeks."

"Where would you even live?" My mother asked. "I could never live in a city where everybody just tries to rob and kill you all the time. No thanks."

"It's a little different…"

"Don't be silly," my father said. "Your grandfather has a car he never uses. Just use his until you get a new one. You know, at some point you're going to have to get a real job so you can save up money so you can get a new car."

"Maybe I won't get a new car—" my father rolled his eyes "—I'd rather spend my money on an apartment and take the bus to college for one last semester." I was too annoyed to chew my steak.

"Yeah okay. You know, you always make these plans, without any appreciation for the expenses that go with it. You know, you're going to need health insurance after December. How are you going to pay for that with an apartment?"

"I donno Dad I haven't gotten that far yet. I'm still thinking about the fact that I have to graduate in the first place."

"You always rush. Honestly, why would you ever move out of here? You've got it made. I lived at home until I was thirty years old, when your mother and I got married." I got up from the table, walked to the fridge and popped open a *Coors Original*.

"When you were my age, Dad, your friends lived in the same town. Everybody went out to the *Halfway House Tavern* or someplace, or had parties at Frangella Beach, and drove home. No one lives here anymore. No one my age. If I want to see anybody I have to go to Albany. And there's no drinking and driving these days, like when you were a kid, so I have to sleep up there."

"I keep telling you to have friends down and you never do. How come you never invite anyone down here? Your mother and I won't be in the way." I poured my beer into a tall glass. Dad paused, changed directions. "I think you have a problem."

"Okay Dad, I have a problem."

"Well… you finish a six-pack every night. When I was a kid we drank, but not to get drunk. I mean sometimes it happened, but we didn't set out to get drunk."

"Times change, pop," I said and sipped. "A) the fact that the drinking age is 21 means that until that point kids steal their parent's booze, because it's the only way they can get it, then chug it in a field or an abandoned warehouse to see what it's like to have what they're not allowed to have…and they get used to drinking like that and form the habit of getting drunk, because of a Big Brother drinking age. B)…gimme a break man."

"I'm just saying…I don't think you could go a week without drinking if you wanted to."

"A week! I could go a week without drinking if I wanted to."

"Are you going to?"

"No. I don't want to."

"See?"

"I don't see anything. Jesus Christ. I'm going downstairs." My mother said,

"Well, this is a nice dinner we're having."

"Sorry to ruin it." I pushed in my chair. On the way to the basement I stopped by the fridge and grabbed a brew for the descent.

I started borrowing my grandfather's mint green Mercury Sable to commute to college from New Baltimore. I returned cans, cleaned my grandmother's house once a week, and painted my professor's stoop to pay for gas.

Two weeks later I drove to SUNY on a rainy morning. I parked in the student lot and walked ten minutes through the rain in my hand-me-down wool blazer to the Lecture Halls at the center of campus. My socks were soaked because my sneakers had holes in the soles. During the class I felt my phone buzz, saw a number I didn't recognize, and hit a button to send it to voicemail, figuring it was a creditor. Then after class I listened to the message as I walked back to my grandfather's car:

Hello Mr. Trombley, this is Tim Reilly from the Hudson Valley Writer's Guild. I was calling to tell you that we received a copy of your story "Flowers and Cigarettes" for our Local Writers/Local Actors performance series at RPI, and we'd love to perform the story. We think it provides a great perspective on an off-beat subject and…well, give us a call back if you'd still like to have your piece performed.

I stood in the rain for a second, then jumped and shouted "Yes!" Somebody actually wanted to publish something I had written! This was the first piece of good news I'd received in months. I smiled as I pictured the book deals rolling in. "Yes yes yes!" I pounded my fist into my palm, "Finally!"

When I started the car *Get Back* by The Beatles was playing. I turned the volume up full blast and rolled down the window. I didn't mind the sprinkles coming in. Immediately I thought about who I'd call to tell the good news. I shifted the car into drive and sped out of the parking lot, merging onto the highway, thinking a hundred things. Man, what a good feeling. Like: validation. I shouted the lyrics, *"Get back Loretta! Yo momma's waiting for ya! Wearin her high heeled shoes. And a looooow neck sweata. Get back home Loretta!"* I banged the drumbeat on the steering wheel. I couldn't wait to tell Jared and my parents. I'd finally accomplished something. I felt like I had *value*. I felt…the wheels of my grandfather's car losing traction as I drove around an onramp. Then I felt the car spin around twice, plow into the guardrail at the front, spin around again, and plow into the guardrail with the rear. Grandpa's car — ten years old — was totaled.

* * *

Some people enter your life and change it through changing you. They surprise you with new insights, different forms of humor, innovative methods they employ to overcome challenges. Sometimes you meet such a person and fall into conversations with them, looking forward to the next time you'll talk. You realize you face similar problems, and want to achieve similar goals. You start unconsciously to mimic their mannerisms and seek their counsel. The person becomes your *friend*. Even a kind of mentor. It was like that for me, in 2006, with Morgan Watson.

Morgan Watson was a year older me, so that made him 23 in 2006. He went to my high school and shared the same social circle as Jared, a grade above me. He'd completed his Bachelor's degree fifteen months before, and had since been working for a New York State agency in Rensselaer, just across the river from Albany. He commuted each day from his parent's house in South Bethlehem, which was between New Baltimore and Albany.

Morgan was six inches taller than me, with curly unkempt locks layered atop a pale English complexion. I'd been acquainted with him for years, since I mingled within the group of people from our high school that Jared invited to house parties whenever we were in Albany. But we were by no means close, Morgan and I. Morgan was competitive at Beer Pong and had a knack for employing the perfect word or phrase to make a point, and that was about all I knew of him. At parties I sometimes avoided him because I thought he misunderstood me as a buffoon. I did often act buffoonish then, using self-deprecation to make friends. But when I turned off the *buffone* (as the Italians call it) I wanted to be taken seriously, and Morgan seemed not to realize it was an act.

Then one day we were at a party at Jared's where everybody was drinking boxed wine. I sat on the floor next to Morgan, who was watching a couple of other guys play a racing game on *Nintendo 64*. I held up my glass of blush and emulated a priest at a Catholic mass.

"Through himmmmmm, with himmmmm, in himmmmm," I drew out each word absurdly. "In the unity-and-glory-of-the-holy-spirittttttttt, for the praise-and-glory-of-his-nameeeeeeeeee, forever and evvv errrrrrrrrrrrrrr." The *Nintendo* players looked at me and shook their heads, but Morgan nearly spit up his wine.

"Ha ha, that shit is ridiculous," he laughed. "I take it you had to go to Catholic Church too?"

"Every Saturday or Sunday for sixteen years, until I got confirmed," I said. "Did you?"

"Dude, I had to go to Catholic school until eighth grade. My parents still make me go to mass. I feel like I'm still getting over the guilt and shit that they teach you."

"Yeah but the songs are great. I mean they've got that one, *Amen*, that goes 'Ah-ha-men, ah-ha-mehen, ah-ha-ha-ha-mennnn.' Really moving shit. And the *Lamb of God*, I'm surprised that's not on the Top Forty."

"Ha ha yeah the songs are so old and boring. I'm glad somebody else had to go through that. Well, not glad for your suffering but nobody else in our group understands what it was like. I think Jared said he's been to church *once*."

"The guilt really is all they have," I said. "They have to layer it on to get you to go every week and hand them money."

"Well, sure. It's not like people go based on the logic of the arguments. The church has to make them feel bad if they don't, like they're going to burn in hell."

"Yeah, but do you think fear of hell is why people go? I feel like it's more of a guilt associated with making your parents and grandparents unhappy than a fear of like, eternal torture or something."

"Ha, maybe you're right. Like, I go because I don't want to get into the argument with my parents. But the catholic guilt permeates everything. Like, I feel like it even made dating weird in college. At first I was like 'I should not want to be thinking about fooling around with girls unless we're going to get married or something.' Meanwhile sluts are getting drunk and fucking all the frat boys. Finally I realized like, the point of *not* hooking up with a girl is because you don't want her to get pregnant and you don't want to catch an STD. But if you're into each other and exercise a little caution, you should hook up with her and it's the best feeling ever. Why should we feel guilty about it?"

I appreciated that Morgan had a similar upbringing and reached similar conclusions. More, I appreciated that he didn't merely agree with whatever I said. He thought about it for a moment—it was almost uncomfortable as he paused—and then answered with a considered opinion. It was casual but it also felt *productive*.

A few days after I crashed my grandfather's car Morgan sent me a message on AOL Instant Messenger (I'd found my parent's PC from 1996 so at least I could use AIM and type papers). Morgan said he wanted to get an apartment in Albany, because after four years of living with people his age in college out of state, he felt he was reverting to childhood living back at his parent's. I said I was surprised he would want to live with me, and did he not find me silly and annoying?

"No way dude I think you're money," he assured me. "We both like records and Big Band music, we both like to read and drink and go out. We're both single and trying to find girls. I think the little adventures and weird shit you do is interesting. Plus we always have good conversations."

I thought those were really nice things to say, so we started looking for an apartment in Albany the next day.

Morgan and I moved into an apartment above a bike shop called "The Downtube" on Madison Avenue near Lark Street in Albany. Lark Street was known as "The Village in the City." We thought our budget would require us to live in a tiny place in the "student ghetto" uptown. But we found the Downtube within our price range in the coveted "Center Square" neighborhood in Albany, between Washington Park and the trendy bars and restaurants that graduate students and young professionals frequented. The second-floor apartment was cheap and dirty, with white walls with mint-green trim and a pink, painted chair rail. It had a drop-ceiling that was stained yellow by years of cigarette smoke and was missing several tiles. It had cabinets without doors, a leaky sink, a hole in the floor and grime everywhere. It smelled like an attic that hadn't been ventilated in a generation. Still, it was better than living at home, and the landlord said he'd reimburse us for materials we bought and used to fix the place. So we figured we'd expend our labor to improve the apartment which was only affordable because it was derelict. The landlord would raise the rent after we moved out, and Morgan and I would get to live in the best part of town. It was a win for everybody.

If you are greater than twenty years old and living at home, move out right away. Move out move out move out. Do not save up money. Do not weigh the benefits of *x and living at home* versus *being independent without x*. Just enfranchise yourself, shed excess anxiety, remember you are free, and leave. When you live with your parents you are not a person, but a dependent. This is the terrible fortune of the very disabled, the very old and the immature.

"I want to write a book called *The Quarter Life Crisis*," Morgan said one evening as we stood covered in paint and dust in our new dining room. "It would have advice for kids who are like 22 to 25, have finished college and then are trying to figure out what the fuck to do with their lives, like all of our friends. Chapter One should be about moving out. Or maybe not moving back in."

"Moving back in with your parents is like getting castrated." I applied a paint roller to a wall.

"Let me get a look at what you're doing 'cause I want to learn the technique," Morgan said. Morgan wanted to learn everything. I showed him:

"Paint a square about three feet by three feet at a time. Make a big 'W' then go back over the square with vertical strokes. Finish it off with horizontal strokes, and as the paint settles it'll blend into a solid sheet. If you finish with vertical strokes you'll see lines."

"You're good at painting walls. Yeah buddy, this place is going to look money when it's done. It *is* like being castrated when you move back home. That's a good analogy. After living at college? *Chhh.* My mom is like 'Morgan, now, how late will you be out tonight? Will you be back by eleven? Don't forget you have to work tomorrow morning.' It's like, are you serious? At eleven o'clock I'm probably gonna be a *Sadie's* drinking my fifth shot, trying to find some girl to hook up with. It's like a different world living home, and you go from having all this freedom to being a high school kid again, leaving notes and shit about where you're going and when you'll be back. Another brewski?"

"I'd love one. This wall is just about done." Morgan returned to the living room with two dusty bottles of *Honey Brown Ale*, and a slice of pizza.

"Cheers, buddy. That wall looks good. A little progress all the time and this place'll look great."

"Slow but steady, like the tortoise," I agreed.

The apartment looked like a bombed-out building with one painted wall.

A person's mental health will atrophy without human connections. Babies raised in orphanages in *fin de siècle* Europe, who were fed but never caressed, often expired.[11] Adolescent outcasts turn antisocial, machine gun schools, and blow their brains out. We need human connections. The lonely worker goes postal. The lonely executive ODs. The lonely artist is prevented from ODing by pecuniary paucity, but he dies of malnutrition or alcoholism, or maybe he steps in front of a train. The value one places on one's life is a direct function of one's perceived human connections, or lack of them.

"I'd like to meet a girl that cooks," Morgan said one night as he seared a veggie burger and I drank a beer in the kitchen. The cabinet doors sat in a pile on the floor. "What girl cooks these days? Have you ever dated a girl that cooked?"

"No. I love to have dinner parties too. But I always end up doing the cooking, showing the girl how to cook stuff. Lindsay never cooked anything. I had to teach Cady how to cut with a knife properly." Morgan stood with his back to me, facing the crackling stove.

"What does a guy get out of a relationship these days, except for getting laid? Girls don't cook. Girls don't clean. The guy pays for everything. Sweet deal. It's like, the girl just expects to be complimented all the time and every now and then she throws the guy a bone and fucks him. Or I should've said, he throws her a bon*er*."

"Oh, snap."

"But it's really bizarre. This idea that a man should adore the girl he's with and worship her all the time. I can't even *respect* the girls I meet at the bar, and where else are you gonna meet girls?" Morgan pressed his burger into the pan, sending up a cloud of smoke. "At least in the 50's you'd have a partnership in a *couple*. Now the girl wants to be adored even though she does none of the sweet things she used to do. Girls act like the only function they perform is to look pretty. And that's supposed to be liberating for them?"

"It's liberating in the sense that it's easiest. There're meathead guys who'll buy them shit all the time just for looking pretty and

---

[11] The term is *maternal deprivation*. I believe that infants require touch because it serves as evolutionary feedback that the organism (the child) will be sup-ported. It is a natural misery-mitigating mechanism: if the child is going to die of exposure or neglect, better for it to be a short existence than a long one. If no one is touching the child when it is neediest, when it hasn't developed the use of its limbs, better for its body to shut down. It's like infant-suicide caused by social-ostracism signified by lack of contact.

fucking. And they live in a messy apartment, watch MTV, and eat *Ramen Noodles*, because neither of them clean or cook. And that's the new American Dream. Don't think too much, Morgan. It's bad for your health."

"Changing tasks is as good as resting your mind," Morgan mused one evening as we kneeled on all fours sanding the floor by the baseboards. "I read that someplace. It seems pretty true. Like, maybe you wouldn't think that we'd have the energy to work on this apartment at night after having already gone to work or school for eight hours. But this is totally different work than sitting in front of a computer adjusting the fields in spreadsheets and shit. This is physical work. And besides, I'm working with a buddy, drinking a beer, instead of in a state office full of bureaucrat zombies."

I put my hands on my lower back and stretched, covered in dust particles. Then I considered what Morgan said and jumped to the most extreme extrapolation, as I tended to do, spewing my thoughts in a jumble to Morgan, who was the only person I talked to about such things.

"Changing your task *is* better than taking a rest. It's better because you don't do anything while you're taking a rest, but you do do things while you're working on a task. I wonder if it would be possible to continue changing tasks all the time, and never resting. Maybe I could do that. That's how I should live my life. Like, eight a.m. to ten a.m., practice learning piano. Then from ten to eleven, jog. Then from eleven to one read philosophy. Make lunch one to two. From two to three read history or physics. From three to four read some other subject, and so on, changing tasks every hour, stimulating one part of my brain and letting the other part rest, and then stimulating the part that was just resting and let the other part that was just working rest. Think of how much work you could get done!"

Morgan raised an eyebrow. "Ha, well, I think you'd need a regular rest at some point. You can't just always work or you'll get burned out. By the way, it's eight o'clock, time for a beer and a rest."

The apartment had a bow window that looked out over Madison Avenue. We sat in the window and watched the people and the cars pass by. There was a one-way street that began in front of our apartment and continued several blocks into the distance, ending with the green copper spire of a Presbyterian church where Martin Van Buren's wife is buried. Morgan said it was important to plan one task per night and not stop until we finished it, nor do any more than what we'd planned, lest our work on the apartment interfere with my coursework and his career work. So we'd cooked a *Price Chopper* pizza and now we popped open a couple *J. W. Dundee's* variety pack beers.

"People worry too much about getting burned out," I said. "It can get unpleasant, but so what? I think people ought to jump head-first into projects like fixing up this apartment, and then when they're in the middle of it, they'll get it done. No sense in pussy-footing around saying 'This is going to be too hard, I better make sure I have mini vacations scheduled exactly every few increments of time, *wahhh wahhh*.' Just start a thing and you'll be in it and then you'll get it done."

"Okay DT. And what happens when you have a lot of projects that you jumped into, and they're all competing for your time and energy?"

"Well, then, you work harder," I declared.

"Don't you think there's a point where you're working as hard as you can and you can't work any harder?"

"Bah, that's just laziness."

"Ha! Okay. So right now, when you're in school and you have that to worry about, and you owe me and Jared and Mike five hundred bucks apiece, so you have that to worry about, and you have next month's rent and utility bills and cell phone bills to worry about, and your writing to worry about, and meeting girls...it's just laziness that you haven't finished up any of those things?"

"No, *Morgan*. I am *in the process* of finishing up those things, because I'm working hard on them every day, one after another."

"Yeah but look at your lifestyle. I mean, look at the apartment, right? Half crumbling. Look at the state of your finances. Your health. Look at what you eat every day. Beer and three *Price Chopper* pizzas a day."

"They're healthy!"

"No they're not."

"They have all the food groups. Look, they've got bread, cheese, meat, sauce which is like a vegetable..."

"Having all the food groups doesn't make something healthy, DT. Especially when you put the pizza on the radiator to keep it warm as you sand spackle off the wall. Honestly, it amazes me that you're not sick all the time, the way you eat and drink. You're pretty much the most unhealthy person I know."

"Hey, you know, sometimes you have to put things on the back burner. You think I like eating *Price Chopper* pizzas every day? I'd rather be eating steaks and chops, but you want me to pay you back, don't you? And pay for next month's rent, right? And you're glad I moved in here, right? And you want the place to get fixed up, so you appreciate that I work on fixing it up when you're at work, right? So, that's just how life is. I had to move in here because I need to finish school and I don't have a car. And that means I have to work more in order to pay for the place, I don't have a choice. And I don't have a choice about going to school. So I can't turn those obligations off. But then, what am I supposed to do when I'm done with those things? Come home and live in a shit hole? Sleep on spackle dust, walk across a floor covered in nails and particle board shavings? Bring a girl back to a place like that? No. It's got to get fixed up, and the sooner the better, and the only way to fix it up is to work at it after all the other work is done. And you know what? When it's done, then we'll be really happy we jumped into it and worked harder."

Morgan smirked and drank from his beer bottle.

"And yet, nothing is ever done, is it?"

"What do you mean?"

"Well, when is this apartment going to be done? After the walls are painted? Or after the floor is re-sanded? There's enough shit to do here that we could work on it for a year. And your writing...you do it often, I think it's great, but when is that done? You're trying to learn piano now. How about your raft projects? Where do you fit in working and meeting girls? Don't you see? You keep jumping into these projects—head-first, like you said—and giving yourself more things to do, and then it's hard to finish them because you have so many. Slow but steady wins, man. I'm telling you."

It might seem like I was losing my mind, but in retrospect, I was discovering it. Morgan hadn't moved in yet, though he stopped at the apartment for a couple of hours each night. Our lease began on November 1st but the landlord let me live there from October 15th. My domicile was a pull-out couch on a floor covered in plaster and dried paint flecks in the living room. I slept at the apartment in order to catch the uptown bus to get to classes. Then I'd come back and work on fixing the place, alone.

One afternoon I painted a portion of a wall, then felt an urge to check my "away message". I got off the ladder and sort of just asked myself what I was doing. There was no away message to check, because the apartment didn't have internet. I wondered why was I compelled to check a machine I knew wasn't there. At least until Morgan moved in I decided not to get internet in the apartment.

I turned my phone off and put it in a kitchen drawer. It was unexpectedly peaceful.

Basically I considered my new routine. A routine constitutes a large portion of one's identity. I had no regularly-scheduled job, no romantic connections, no car to go anyplace. Inside my apartment were no people, television or internet. There were only a couple of textbooks, a microwave, frozen pizzas, and the routine of painting and thinking.

The paint is flecking off the wall, I noticed as I stood in the kitchen. I leaned close to examine the texture. *The paint must be latex*, I thought as I touched it with my finger. *Yes. Only latex paint would chip, because oil paint would be absorbed into the wood, but latex forms a layer on top.* Did I know that only latex paint can chip, or did I just deduce that for the first time?

As I painted I realized I thought about paint flecks because I *could* think about them, because I wasn't constantly pushing ideas *out* of my consciousness in order to re-focus on AIM messages. I decided I wouldn't install any computer games if I got a new computer, either. They took too much of my attention away from thinking about things like paint flecks.

I started to have day-long conversations with myself as I worked. *Thoughts…you have them all the time, and they disappear*, I mused. *If you think about the same thought, dwell on it, it becomes a* meditation. *When meditating, you ignore distractions. You <u>focus</u> on what is happening <u>in your mind</u> by <u>ignoring</u> what is happening in the <u>outside</u> world. If you completely ignore the outside world and completely focus on the activities of your mind…in that case you are…super-meditating?... oh, dreaming!*

I experienced an *aha*! moment. It's called an *epiphany*, and it describes the sensation you feel when you learn something for the first time. When you put together previously-unrelated pieces of information and see a way they *are* related, you *sense* that you learned something. You discover a *relationship*; that relationship or *connection* is a new *thought*; the epiphany is the pleasurable *feeling* associated with the realization. That's why we say "That's funny, I never knew…" It's not really funny, but the euphoric feeling is the evolutionary reward we receive for learning. We've learned to stimulate the sensation through *jokes*, which are a succession of statements which we anticipate a relationship between.

Around day three or four in the apartment I decided to make it a life goal to free myself from habit-forming distractions like AIM messages and video games. By avoiding such wastes of time I secured for myself four or five extra hours a day.

One of my first epiphanies was that the mind is programmed — it *wants* — to evaluate the world, find relationships between objects and concepts, and remember them. It is its *function*. Then epiphanies become the units on which new epiphanies are founded:

Deep-thinking is inversely-related to the presence of external stimuli; or, the absence of stimuli is necessary for thinking and sleep and dreaming. This explains why loud sounds or shaking a person — significant external stimuli — "wakes them up." But what has changed when one "wakes" versus when one "sleeps?" Just that a portion of "the mind" that had been running one program no longer performs that function.

I realized that if the mind can *either* sleep, *or* be awake, *or* check AIM, *or* think about paint flecks, then it must be limited in some way. If it was unlimited there'd be no such thing as a distraction.

I wrote on a scrap of paper: *"Limited attention: a result of finite mental energy or capacity?"* I wrote other questions on other scraps. The questions and the epiphanies had no immediate relevance or practicality. Yet I felt that thinking in this fashion was a better use of my time than chatting on AIM or checking *Myspace* pages.

Morgan was right that a change of task was like a rest — maybe not as good as a rest, but similar. Morgan was also right that I couldn't jump into a hundred projects and expect to finish them all. As I spackled some holes in the living room wall I considered why.

Because we only have a finite amount of energy to devote toward thinking, just as we only have a finite amount of energy to devote toward moving our bodies.

"What's with energy being at the bottom of everything?" I asked myself.

The body moves and needs energy.

When our bodies are out of energy, we feel tired.

But the mind...what does it perceive when it's out of energy?

...Tired.

Huh, I thought. *Both use energy, both feel tired. The mind also operates according to physical laws, rather than something metaphysical.*

A couple of days later, as Morgan and I sanded the kitchen cabinet doors, I mused to him,

"The mind and the body are a lot like a computer. Both have a physical part. We have a body and a brain, and a computer has the physical structure we call *hardware*. A computer also has programs that it runs, that are hard to think of as physical...they're electrical...called *software*. The same hardware runs different software programs. The mind is like the software that the body runs. No one would describe a software application as metaphysical, though."

"That's a good analogy." Morgan placed his sanding pad on the floor, then blew sawdust off a cabinet door he'd held in his lap. "Reminds me of this kid Jake I used to live with sophomore year. He was a philosophy major with a computer programing minor. I asked him once why he chose to major and minor in such different fields. He said 'They're not different fields. They're both about performing operations by following logical rules.' I was like, huh, I never thought of that."

"Okay but here is what I don't understand," I said quickly, to see if Morgan could help me find the answer. "The computer is plugged into the wall, and the energy it uses comes from the electricity that comes out of the wall."

"Yup."

"And the mind is electrical, somehow, right? I mean, you can put an EEG on someone and measure their brainwaves."

"Right."

"But we don't plug our bodies into a wall..."

"Ha ha, nope. Hand me that sanding pad? Mine's all gunked-up."

"And we don't eat electricity. Here you go..."

"Right. Thanks."

"So how does our mind somehow *use* electricity? How does it *get* the electricity which it uses to run its programs? It *has* electricity, we just said you can measure brainwaves. Where does it come from?" Morgan rubbed his sanding pad on the next cabinet door—they were lying in a stack in front of the sink—then looked at the sanding pad I'd handed him, which was also full of gunk and old varnish.

"Hmm, I think this calls for a beer in the window...to lubricate our brain cells."

"Sounds lubri-*great* to me."

I sat in the window and looked over Madison Avenue's four lanes. A traffic light hung in front of our window. Morgan carried two beers from the fridge, his body first reflecting green, then yellow, and then red light. I opened the bottles with the end of my lighter.

"Cheers buddy," Morgan said.

His statement made me relax. I realized I'd been scrunching my forehead and shoulder muscles all day. I un-scrunched them and breathed more deeply.

"Cheers Morgan. I'm glad we got this place together. I don't wanna sound…I'm just really glad we live together. I need some human communication."

"Yeah, life is tough buddy. These years are hard. Nobody knows what they're doing. Girls are no help. But we're smart, good-looking guys, we'll figure it out."

"Since you're older than I am, and it's what I want to hear, I'll accept your opinion with no further questions, your honor."

"Ha ha, cheers." We clinked bottles and drank. "There's your answer, by the way."

"The answer to what?" I looked at my beer bottle.

"How the mind works. Think about what you're doing right now."

"If the mind works because I drink, I'll be the smartest man in the universe!"

"Ha — our friends would be Newton, Galileo, Socrates. But no, I mean, ingesting."

"Stop *jesting* and tell me what you mean."

"Ha ha. No, obviously I mean ingesting our food is how we get our energy."

"Yeah but what is food? Chemicals. We eat an apple and break it down into elements, proteins and sugars, which we use to restore our muscles and shit."

"But what are chemicals but little molecules with specific numbers of electrons? We must use our circulatory system to somehow ship those electrons to our brain, where enough of them are stored up to be measured as electricity."

"Ahh, I see what you're saying! We don't *ingest* electricity. We ingest chemicals and *convert* them to electricity, somehow."

"Maybe."

"How?"

"I donno, buddy."

It would be two years before I came to understand the process further, after teaching myself about batteries when researching a design for a fourth raft.

"What do you think about this ceiling," I said to Morgan as we stood in the dining room three evenings later. It was the only room in our new apartment with an aluminum and foam drop ceiling.

"I think it looks pretty gross," Morgan said. "It really detracts from the rest of the apartment, especially now that we've repainted the place and started to work on the floors. Like, who does this?"

Morgan pointed his finger to a ceiling square where, apparently, one of the foam rectangles had been broken and someone had replaced it with an upside-down *Abercrombie and Fitch* poster. It looked like two teen deities peering on our dining room from Heaven.

"I think we should tear it down," I said.

"Ha, well...it does look awful. But...that seems like a pretty large task."

"We'll just pull on the aluminum pieces of shit supports that run cross-wise across the room and hold up the foam," I said. "I was looking at it earlier. It's a pretty cheap construction job. I'm surprised it hasn't fallen down already. Look, I'll show you." I stood on tip-toe and pushed up a ceiling square. I moved the thin aluminum superstructure with my hand.

"It does seem to be just sitting on top of the molding. And it does look bad. I don't want some topless *Abercrombie* guy looking down at me as I eat my cereal in the morning."

"So let's tear it down."

"Hold on a second there, DT. *Downtube DT,* haha. What if the ceiling is all jacked-up, and that's why they have the drop ceiling, to cover up whatever is above it? Then if we tear it down, we could be in a worse situation than we have now."

"Morgan, Morgan, Morgan...sometimes you have to go out on a limb to get the fruit," I said.

"Ha, okay Dallas," he shot me a look that seemed to ask *are you serious?* As an afterthought, or perhaps to stall, he added, "Do you think we ought to ask the landlord first?"

"It's easier to ask for forgiveness than permission. We don't want the ceiling we have now. There's only one way to get another one." I impersonated Ronald Reagan, "Mr. Watson, tear down this ceiling!"

"You know DT, I admire your compulsive enthusiasm. A lot of our friends would look at the ceiling and just say 'I donno what's up there; looks like a lot of work.' And then they'd have an ugly smoke-brown drop ceiling above them whenever they eat. I might do that. But we want the place to look money, you're right. Okay. Maybe my contribution to this little partnership we have as roommates is that I can help you be a little less compulsive, and you can help me be a little more spontaneous. Like, let's think about this for a minute. What if the ceiling *does* look worse above the drop ceiling?"

"Then we'll fix it."

"Okay...is there a way we can peek at the ceiling and see what it looks like before we tear the other one down?"

"We can push up one of the foam tiles and shine a flashlight up."

"Great! Informed decision-making. Let's do that."

So we grabbed a flashlight out of a shoe-box that served as our tool-box. I walked fifteen feet to the opposite corner of the room and pushed up a foam tile.

"Awesome," I said. "The ceiling looks fine above this tile. Looks like a normal plaster ceiling." I grabbed the aluminum overhead. "So, tear it down?"

"One second. I'd just like to look in like, one more place, just to make sure that the ceiling is good not just above where you're standing, but everywhere. A couple of random samples will be more representative than one, which could be a fluke."

"I think your caution is unwarranted, but if it eases your mind, please proceed." I threw Watson the flashlight and he strolled to the corner of the room opposite where I stood. He pushed up a tile exactly opposite the one I'd pushed up, then reconsidered and pushed up a more random square.

"Well...the ceiling looks good above this foam thing, too." He let the square fall back into place and put the flashlight down. "Hard to think of why they went through the work of putting this thing up if the ceiling was fine."

"Who knows why people do things," I said. "But now it's here and preventing us from having a good-looking place."

"It *is* ugly."

"So let's tear it down."

"Okay, let's do it."

"I'll grab the aluminum from this side, you grab it from that side, and we'll yank it together, okay?"

"Okay. Ready?"

"Ready. Pull!"

We pulled the rickety aluminum bars that held the cigarette-colored foam and *Abercrombie* poster ceiling. As the bars bent the foam began falling to the floor. Then there was a rumbling sound like shale sliding down a wooden ramp. Along with the foam there fell wheelbarrows full of white rocks and dust, sending clouds of powder into the room, so that we coughed and choked and had to run out into the hallway to catch our breath on top of the stairs. The dust floated out of the open apartment door. After a few minutes we made our way back inside, waving away the plaster dust as we walked. On the floor of the dining room sat a pile of foam, aluminum and plaster rubble. The ceiling was a pock-marked expanse of chipping plaster, ending three-feet from one wall and giving a glimpse of the attic along one whole side, and in the middle, in a patch shaped like an ameba about three-feet wide by two-feet long, there was a pothole in the ceiling four-inches deep, exposing a diamond-shaped metal mesh that the plaster had originally been affixed to. The only portions of the ceiling which were undamaged were those which had been above the panels where we'd inspected.

"Good thing the landlord gave us free-reign to fix the place up," Watson remarked. "So, uhhh...got any ideas for fixing this?"

"We could put up a drop ceiling."

"Ha ha," Morgan put his arm around me. He was scheduled to move in officially the next day. "I can see that living with you is going to be an adventure, man."

That made me smile, because Morgan wasn't angry. But it also confused me, because I wasn't trying to create an adventure, I just wanted a nicer ceiling. And now we were worse off than we'd been a quarter of an hour before. And the ceiling was much worse than I imagined it could possibly have been. And I didn't have any ideas on how to fix it. But Morgan just laughed, like he had complete confidence in my ability to repair it. So I laughed with him, and smiled, and almost became watery eyed.

"I hope that's not asbestos," Morgan said after we spent a silent minute inspecting the debris. "I don't know what the hell we should do then."

"You just go to work tomorrow, and I'll do *asbestos* I can to get this mess cleaned," I said.

"Ha ha, good one, buddy."

We grabbed two *Honey Browns* from the fridge and poured them into frozen mugs. They were the only dishes in the place. We sat in the window looking over Madison Avenue and the little shops across the street. Straight ahead was the street light and Willet Street, two parallel lines of cars on either side growing closer with distance. To the left were the trees of Washington Park. To the right were a two-story apartment building, then *Little Moon* Tibetan gift shop with a blue awning. Then *El Loco* Mexican Cafe with a white wooden sign with a cactus painted on, then *DiNapoli Optician*. Leaning forward and looking far to the right there was *Lark Tavern* with several people milling about outside. I opened the window to let out the plaster dust. The sounds of cars accelerating over pavement, of trucks air-breaking and bouncing on potholes, became louder. In the distance sirens sounded. I packed a bowl and took a hit. I offered it to Morgan but he said no thanks. I told Morgan about my epiphany of that day: that obligations are like applications on your computer; the more you have open the slower your mind's operating system processes.

"So what windows do you have open that you're going to x out?" Morgan asked. It was becoming Morgan's habit to take my general musings and bring them to the point of some practical application.

"I haven't gotten that far yet."

"You could make a list of all of the *programs* you've got running—all of your *obligations*...It'd be like running 'Task Manager' on your computer." His suggestion animated me.

"That's a great idea! Then I could assign values to each task, based on how much time I spend thinking about it—how often it's in my short-term-memory—which is like how much RAM it takes up in my mind—how slow it's making my mental computer run—that is, how much it's affecting my concentration. Then, when I have a list of tasks, with another column listing the weighted values in terms of concentration-diminishment, I could make another column to see how much physical or mental effort it would take to complete or x *out* each one. Like if 'paying my phone bill' would be quick and is often on my mind, I should do that first. I could make a logarithm designed to show which tasks ought to be performed first, then next, the first ones freeing up mental RAM which could be used to complete increasingly more difficult obligations later, the ultimate goal being to have a mental operating system clear of all minimized windows, AKA a clear conscience."

Again Morgan looked at me as though deciding whether I was serious or fooling around. But when he saw the conviction on my face and how I shook my fists at shoulder height, he deduced that I was sincere.

"You could do all of that," Morgan said. "Or you could just make a list of your bills and homework and people you need to call, and just start doing them." I slackened my posture, which had been very erect.

"Just start doing them. Right. No need for a logarithm." My eyes darted back and forth.

"Too much."

"Got it." Morgan looked at me as I sat thinking, then nodded to himself, then smiled. He made a sweeping gesture around the room.

"For example, you might put on your list, 'Clean up the numerous empty discarded beer bottles which I've strewn across my and Morgan's apartment,' or, 'Pick up the cardboard pizza bases which I've stacked on the radiators over the last two weeks.' You know, little things like that."

"Man, I'm sorry. I totally didn't even realize the place was a mess," I said honestly. Once out of my mouth, those words sounded crazy. I sighed, "I don't want to be weird. I've never had a roommate before. I might need some help...being normal."

"Dude I like that you're weird. That's why I wanted to move in with you. Who else our age plays Benny Goodman records from a phonograph as he paints a wall, musing about the similarities between minds and computers? You know what Jared or Nick says when I play Big Band music? They say 'This sounds like Christmas shit.' Because that's the only time they've ever heard Big Band. So that's 'normal' today. And you know, I've lived with a lot of supposedly normal people and you know what? They're pretty boring. I think as long as you're not going to like, some night just start breaking all the walls with a sledgehammer or something, I think we'll be fine living together. In fact, man, I'm not much for decorating or fixing things up. If you could go ahead and just decorate this place however you want, I'd be happy with that."

"Okay," I said. I realized at that moment that Morgan had a kind of personality that I'd never come across. He really didn't mind if I acted oddly. That was important because people always said I was "unique" and "funny" and "weird" and I never knew what they meant or how not to be those things. The other way of saying it is, I never knew how to be normal. I'd mimic the way people I thought were normal acted, thinking I was doing a good job, only for the others around me suddenly to laugh and joke about how I was acting strangely. So I was comforted by the idea that Morgan thought everybody was odd in their own way and that my version of it was as O.K. as anybody else's. It was a relief. It felt like the apartment was really going to be my place. It felt like the apartment was going to be a place where I *wanted* to go. And indeed it became that. And every night when Morgan came home from work, it was comforting. It was like having a friend.

II. Learning Curves

Morgan handed me a measuring tape as I stood on a ladder. I extended it over a hole in the ceiling. We planned to frame it out and put up sheetrock, which I'd never done before.

"Seven feet, three inches," I said as I climbed down. Morgan held the measuring tape on one end of a 2x4 and I marked the board. I grabbed the circular saw with a wire dangling across the table, which circled on the floor, then hung from an outlet. Morgan grabbed a bottle of beer from the table, which would've been overturned by the cord as I cut.

"Safety first," Morgan said.

"Safety second," I laughed. I cut the board and ascended the ladder. I placed the board over the hole. It was several inches too short.

"How does that expression go?" Morgan chuckled. "Measure once, cut twice?"

I frowned. "We're rushing. My grandmother used to tell me not to rush. That's when you make mistakes."

"Then let's not rush." Morgan handed me the measuring tape again. "I've noticed that there's a learning curve to doing these DIY projects we've been working on over the last month. The first time you do something, you're pretty much inexperienced and figuring it out. The second time, you have a better idea of what the task will take, but you make a couple of mistakes anyway. By the third time you do something, you know what you're doing. I'd say that doing something three times makes you pretty much an expert. At least, you're not a novice anymore. That's how I feel with painting. I never painted a room before and you had to show me the first time. Then the second time I was rushing and you could see places where the old paint came through, because I forgot to finish with horizontal strokes, like you said. Now it's easy to paint a room, and since I know what I'm doing, it doesn't seem like such a chore. In fact, I think I'll paint my bedroom a new color."

"I'm glad I could teach you how to paint," I said. "The hole is seven feet six inches." I got down from the ladder and marked this out on a different 2x4.

"How did you learn how to do all this construction stuff?" Morgan asked. "From your dad?"

"No way," I scoffed. "My father doesn't own tools. It started for me one afternoon in the fall when I used to date Lindsay. She called and asked what I was doing. I said I was about to go out on the tractor to pick up leaves. She said 'You know how to do that?' I was like, 'Of course I know how to pick up leaves with a tractor!' She said, 'You just don't seem like somebody who would know how to do that kind of a thing.' It always bothered me after that that I might seem like someone who doesn't know how to do anything with my hands. We always had to work hard growing up, it just wasn't carpentry or mechanical stuff. It was all just human labor, like clearing brush or stacking wood. Anyway it bothered me, so I got a couple of Do It Yourself books and read them. And then whenever anybody needed help painting or fixing a window, I'd help them out and try and learn like a mini apprentice. And I've often been broke, so it was easy to take a job for somebody doing odd jobs around their house. They don't know any better, that's why they're hiring somebody else to do it. I'd take a job not knowing what the hell I was doing and I just figured I'd 'fake it till I make it.' Then, like you said, you do a thing three or four times, then you do it passably well. You come to understand the order of operations, like, don't paint a wall and then paint the ceiling, because then you might drip down the wall and have to paint it again." I cut the 2x4 and climbed the ladder and somehow the damn board was still too short.

"Or, like learning to measure twice, and cut once," Morgan joked.

"Maybe that's why they say 'The third time's the charm.'" Mike tossed a magnetic dart. He'd come up from his parent's house, and Jared had come down from his midtown apartment, to help Morgan and I finish the last coat of paint in the living room. Morgan bought a pizza and an eighteen pack of *J. W. Dundee's* samplers for our painting party. Jared started to grumble after painting half a wall that it was "mad work and shit," ate a slice of pizza, drank a beer, and then took off. Mike stayed and helped Morgan and I finish. Then Mike and I shot magnetic darts as Morgan stood watching. "It's not a *charm*," Mike continued, aligning his elbow so it pointed at the dartboard. "It's that a person gets the skills on the first two go-arounds and then they know what they're doing by the third time."

"Right," Morgan said. "That's what we concluded." Mike tossed a dart, said "double-five" and lined his arm up again.

"A lot of superstitious bullshit is like that." Mike brought his arm down and looked at Morgan and I. "Like, people say walking under a ladder is bad luck. It's not luck at all. There's shit and paint and tools on top of a ladder and if you walk under it, sometimes it falls on you." Mike lined his arm up and tossed a dart. He said "ten," then crossed out some numbers in a little brown notebook on the table, and wrote new numbers beneath. I picked up the darts and lined up as they continued.

"Yeah, superstitions are pretty irrational," Morgan paraphrased Mike's Anglo-Saxon with Latin-based words. "There're conditions that underlie similar circumstances and produce similar results. Like finding a penny heads-up. Then you notice the first good thing that happens to you and you say, 'It was the penny!' It's just a self-fulfilling prophecy."

"It's something a little kid would do," I added. I threw my darts and scored no points.

"Dallas might want to throw a horse shoe in some holy water, though. I mean, like, if he ever wants to beat me at this game." Mike threw a dart and hit a five, which was the number of points he needed to win. "Victory! Well, what number victory is that? Eighty-seven I believe."

"Yes, it's eighty-seven," I said. Morgan threw up his hands.

"Wait a minute, wait a minute. Now, tell me about this game. Mike has really won eighty-seven games in a row?"

"Not just eighty-seven games in a row. All eighty-seven *series* that we've played since we started playing this game, what, three years ago?"

"Yes," I said. I handed the little brown notebook to Morgan. "If you flip through the pages, you can see the games."

"And you keep playing?" Morgan asked incredulously.

"Of course," I said. "I want to win, and I haven't yet."

"Damn dude. You haven't won one game?"

"We play in series," Mike explained. "Like, best out of three games, or five games or seven. It's not that I'm *way* better than Dallas. He's won some games here and there. Some of the series have been close. It's just that, like, I'm just enough better that over the course of a series I keep beating him. Honestly I don't see how it's fun for him either."

"I didn't say it was fun. I just said I haven't won yet."

"And you never will!" Mike boasted.

"No no, that's where you're wrong. At some point, I don't care if it's sixty years from now, I will win, and then it'll all have been worth it. Let's play another round. How 'bout the best of five?"

"If you want to lose again, sure. But I disagree with what you always say, that sixty years from now if you win one series, then five hundred lost serieses will be like, vindicated. You'll just be a guy who has won one out of five hundred series."

"Explain this game to me," Morgan said. I picked up the darts.

"Okay, you see the dartboard has the numbers one through twenty around the circumference?"

"Yes DT, I know how a dartboard works. Ha ha, come on, man? I mean what are the rules?"

"Right well, okay, so the numbers 5, 10, 15 and 20 are divisible by five. 5 and 20, and 10 and 15 are conveniently located next to one another on the board. Anyway, you start with 45 points, and if you hit one of the numbers divisible by five, you subtract the divisor from your points, and you want to get exactly zero."

"So if you hit a 20, you take 4 points off. What if you hit a triple 20? Then you take 12 points off?"

"Right, because triple 20 is 60 points, divided by 5 is 12."

"And a bull's eye?"

"The big bull's eye is worth 50, the center bull's eye is worth 100, so they're worth 10 and 20 points, respectively. Mike often starts off shooting for the bull's eyes right off the bat. But they're hard to hit and if you miss you get no points for like, hitting an eleven or something. I go for the twenty because a slice of a dartboard is bigger than the bull's eye and if I miss at least I might hit a five and get one point. Slow but steady wins the race."

"Slow but steady loses the race if it's playing against fast and steady," Mike said. He threw a dart and just missed a bull's eye. He threw a second dart and hit dead center. "See, that brings me down to 25 points." He threw his third dart and landed in the double-fifteen. "Six points, so I'm at 19."

"I *do* often get stuck behind Mike after the first throw and then have to play catch-up the whole game. But the triple-20 is as good as you can get outside of a double bull." I threw three darts and achieved eight points. Not a bad turn, but I trailed 37 to 19.

"Now I need 19 points," Mike explained. "You can't go over or you lose any points you got on that turn. So I'm not going to shoot for the center bull this time. Hmm, let's see, I guess I'll go for single-20s. Play it conservative. There's two!" Mike landed a double twenty (eight points), bringing his score to 11. "Now I'll jump down to the fifteens, which are worth three points apiece. Here we go!" Mike threw a dart and struck triple-fifteen, bringing him to two points. Then he effeminately tossed his last dart so that it didn't even strike the board.

"Why'd you do that?" Morgan asked.

"Because he only needs two points to win," I said. "And if he'd thrown his dart and accidently struck anything worth more than 2 points, he'd have lost the 17 points he got, and go back up to 19." I threw my three darts and lowered my score to 21. "I'm catching up on you now."

"But I only need one dart to win," Mike said. "Come on, ten!" He missed. "Alright, ten!" He missed again. Then he shook his limbs like a cat drying itself, walked a pace forward and back, and realigned his arm. "I've shot this dart twice already, right? So according to what we said before, I should now have the experience to hit the ten, ha ha. Third time's the charm!" Mike tossed the dart and won the game.

Morgan shook his head and said he was going into his room to paint. Mike and I decided to smoke a cigar in the window and catch up. We hadn't talked much since August.

"So, if doing things three times makes you a pro, the next time you build a raft, you'll be an expert raft-builder," Mike said. I was surprised he brought up the subject, given his exit on the last raft and his disparaging remarks about the first one in the newspaper. I said nothing. "I'm just joking," he said. "But do you think you'll do another one?" I answered without thinking,

"My urge is to say no. It was a terrible experience that just wasted a lot of time and money. I'm still paying for it three months later." Mike nodded, frowning.

"I guess it was a silly thing we did." I felt I might jump over and strike him.

"It was *not* silly," I said emphatically, "And it was hardly a thing *we* did. It failed because I had nobody to help me. Jared said he'd help, then disappeared. You helped out for like a day. Those other guys were aggravating and controlling."

"Those guys were really mean," Mike asserted. "Like, as soon as I showed up the older guy started attacking me. Everything was 'Appalachian Trail this' and 'Appalachian Trail that.' 'That's not how we do things on the Appalachian Trail!' Honestly man, I don't know where you found those guys but they sucked."

"Okay, thanks for the insight, dude. You know, what else was I supposed to do? I asked Oliver if he wanted to go, he wouldn't take time out of his warehouse job. I asked Brett, he was going on vacation the whole month of August. Jared said no. You had your job at the State. I mean, I had to work with what I had, man. You think I liked spending fucking seven days with those guys who I'd only met once and didn't know? No, of course not. It was supposed to be a trip with you and Jared, my *friends*, not...what it ended up being."

"Anybody want a beer?" Morgan called from the kitchen. His question was obviously timed to interrupt our conversation, which, as Morgan perceived from his room on the other side of the apartment, had grown warm.

"Yes, I'd love a beer," I called back. "Mike'll have one too."

Sometimes it takes but a pause for the heat to dissipate. As Morgan intended, we sat silent as he took his time opening the bottles, and poured them into frozen mugs. Meanwhile, Mike and I considered each other's situation and experience for the first time. Hearing how Mike was hurt by Steve made me feel less abandoned *personally* by his AWOL status on the last trip. And I think he realized, perhaps consciously for the first time, that he'd harmed our friendship by getting off the boat without telling me he was leaving. So that was all in the air as Morgan placed mugs on the coffee table between our chairs and the window, saying,

"You know, the raft…that's one thing I don't really get."

The last thing I wanted was to go into a play-by-play of my motivations and mistakes in front of Morgan, whose respect I appreciated, in front of Mike, who would belittle every point, I imagined.

"There's nothing to *get*," I groaned. "You were there at the first launch. You bought us a round of *Blue Moons* at *Yanni's*. You saw it."

"Yeah I saw it," Morgan chuckled, "but it doesn't mean I got it. Like, was it supposed to be a joke?" The phrase *supposed to be* annoyed me. I pictured a comedian who people expect to be funny, who is not.

"No it wasn't a joke," I said.

"But you were dressed like Indiana Jones."

"Those are my regular clothes," I said.

"Okay DT," Morgan called me out, "some of those things are your regular clothes. Do you wear that *outfit* to the bar, though? Do you wear it to the grocery store?"

"Of course not."

"Okay, so, come on, it was a costume. And the raft itself was pretty ridiculous-looking and unseaworthy, you have to admit. So you're wearing this costume on a raft that's obviously not going to make it to New York City. Okay. So I thought, 'This is a joke.' But then I saw Mike wearing normal clothes, Jared wearing normal clothes, and the newspaper people came and you were very serious, giving inspirational quotes and shit, saying you were definitely going to make it and were determined. So I was like, '*Is* this a joke?' And you and Mike, you guys do these kinds of things, like when you guys ran for Student Government and plastered the school with funny campaign signs and made a website and went way over the top pushing the envelope. Like, that I got. So I thought, 'This is an example of Dallas and Mike's humor, and I don't really get it yet, but a joke is coming somewhere.' I didn't really get why Jared was there—he doesn't do that kind of stuff—but I thought, 'Maybe he's playing the straight man.' So I kept waiting for the punch line, like maybe you guys were going to sink the boat as soon as you pushed off from the dock, and we'd all laugh or something. But then you seemed serious, leaving in the rain...and everybody knew it wasn't going to work but for some reason you guys acted like it was going to, and the story in the *News Herald* and the *Ravena Ledger*. I kept thinking, 'Jeeze, why is Dallas torpedoing his reputation in this town where like, everybody expects him to be Mayor someday?' I talked about it with Andrew Wilsey and Nick and we thought, 'Well, maybe the joke is on all of us. Like, coming down here and standing in the rain, the bullshit Ravena press taking it seriously. Maybe that's the joke, about how nothing ever goes on here and people actually care about three 21-year-olds trying to build a raft. So then it sank and Mike said it was a horrible experience in the newspaper and that he'd never try again, and I thought, 'Well, I still don't get it, but it must've been a joke that fell flat, not a serious thing.' But then Jared tells me Dallas is planning another one and spending every day working on it, and it seems to have cost you your job and really hurt your relationship with Cady, who you say you wanted to keep dating, and now you two who are old friends are getting in arguments over it. So it's not a joke? It was a serious thing? Or what? I don't understand."

"It wasn't a joke," I repeated.

"Did it start as a joke, and then it became serious?"

"No it didn't start as a joke. At least, not for me. It was serious. It was stupid but it was serious. I don't know why I cared so much. It was... It was that...No, how do I explain?" I trailed off.

"It was what it was," Mike interjected, throwing me a life-line. He said that mostly to take Morgan's attention off, because I was flailing. Now Morgan looked at him and Mike struggled to explicate. "You know, sometimes if people are sitting around doing drugs somebody starts to ask 'Why, why, why?' 'Why is it that, I donno, Saturn has rings but Earth doesn't and does that effect the way that life evolved on Earth' and on and on. You know? You can sit around discussing shit like that for hours, why stuff is the way it is. And in the meantime you're not doing anything. So sometimes you have to just say, 'It is what it is,' and move on, or you can drive yourself crazy."

"That's an interesting point of view," Morgan said. "So, what you're saying is there was no plan, no reason, it was just something that you did, and that was that."

"Right," Mike agreed.

"No, that's not really right, either," I said. "We had a plan, we had a goal. We were doing it for a reason or multiple reasons. You thought it'd be fun when we came up with the idea, didn't you, Mike?"

"Well, yeah, when we came up with the idea. And then there was all this work that had to get done that we didn't anticipate."

"Right, so you wanted to have fun, and that was a reason for doing it. And then it wasn't fun, so that was why you didn't want to do it anymore."

"Well, yes, actually. I think that's okay."

"Yes it *is* okay," I said. "I understand it now, like, your motivation. But I had a different motivation. I wanted to get to New York." Ina flash the whole experience seemed explicable by the laws of physics. "Listen, Morgan, I think I just understood what happened in a way that I can explain to you."

"Okay, let's hear it."

"It was a mixture of personalities. It almost couldn't have *not* happened."

"What do you mean," Mike asked.

"I mean Jared and I were on a road trip. I'm on my second date with Cady. We're down there visiting you. So we're all excited, and we're in the woods. We're trying to come up with something casual to talk about, so Jared brings up a movie where they jet ski to the city, and it looks fun. Jared's personality is imaginative and he doesn't like thinking about things deeply, so he just fantasizes about owning a boat out loud, and how he regrets that he can't. Okay. Now me, I'm there with Cady, and I don't want any negativity there, so instead of talking about what we can't do, I say what we *can* do. I just throw out rafting. Now Mike, you're used to going off on projects with me and your habit is to try to reel me back, so you start taking the opposite course, explaining the reasons we couldn't raft. But Cady is there and I'm pumped up trying to impress her, and I want to be in charge and seem like I know what I'm doing in front of her, so every time you list a reason we can't raft, I throw out some reason why, in fact, we can. Now, meanwhile, Jared's personality is that he eggs people on because he enjoys watching other people entertain crowds, especially in clownish ways, so he keeps saying 'I'm in' and upping the ante until you're isolated as the only naysayer. That's not a fun position to be in, so you realize that it's easier just to agree with us that it's possible and sure you'll go along, etc etc. Then we part company. Now, you, specifically, don't work yourself up to doing crazy things unless somebody is there to nudge you often, but I, personally, was hardly in New Paltz over the next 9 months, so I did no nudging, and you pretty much didn't care. Your interest naturally atrophied. But meanwhile I'm living a lot closer to Jared, seeing him more often, and, since his personality is that he likes to egg people on, especially in clownish ways, whenever we'd get together and have a drinking party he'd bring up the subject and then hand me the reigns of the conversation. People would say it's impossible, and my personality is to react in spite with more energy than whoever told me I was wrong, until they admit that I was right. So now, thanks to Jared, I'm doing that a couple times a month, then going home to my parent's basement where I have no other company, to ponder, and it became more and more important to me to do it. But, to go back to you, Mike...in the past whenever I'd done some public extravaganza, it was with *you*. I'm like the idea guy, the big picture guy. I don't know how to fucking, like, cut boards at angles and what knots to use and all that. So I need your help, but you're not around; Jared needs both our help, but I can't seem to do anything unless you're around on these kinds of projects. I'm sitting in the basement just re-affirming things over and over again, so that it seems like we're making progress when we're not, and then pretty soon I've told everybody I know about what we're doing, and calling the papers and the thing has a life of its own, but none of us are actually working on it. Then it's a big failure and you're embarrassed because you didn't really even want to do it in the first place, Jared's not that embarrassed because he writes himself off as a third wheel on a 'Dallas and Mike' project, and now I'm the only one who's told everybody that I'd prove that I could do something, only to not do it. So now out of spite and embarrassment and anger I want to do it even more. And living in the basement with even fewer friends than before, and being even more determined than before, I worked out all the plans in my mind and made the same goddam mistakes I made the first time, failing even more grandly in an attempt to make up for my first failure. So that's what there is to get, Morgan. It was a bad mix of personalities that brought out the bad parts of the other's personalities and led to disaster. And disasters need a human face, and this one got mine. The fucking end."

"Like I said," said Mike, "It was what it was." Morgan looked at us for a moment before he nodded,

"I actually think I understand now. It wasn't a comedy. It was a tragedy."

III. "No More Harry Nielsen!"

That winter of 2006 was the worst period of our lives, for most of my friends. It was like a vapid film previewed to have a great finale. Jess Gadani had moved back home from Ithaca only to realize she was drowning in student debt for a singing degree which would never land her a job. Mike got dumped. He lived at home and commuted to work with his father, leaving at seven a.m. and returning at six p.m. after crunching numbers, the reward for his math degree. Jared had been in love with a blonde girl who started dating someone else. He continued to work at the dead-end insurance job where he'd worked throughout college. Morgan had been dumped; he left the Downtube at eight a.m. and returned every night at five-thirty after filling out spreadsheets in an aseptic office building, making no use of his Political Science degree. We expected the rest of our lives would be a string of meaningless work, in order to receive intrinsically worthless money, to trade for commodities, to give women, to purchase their affection.

I couldn't help but juxtapose the energy and passion of the private times when Cady and I were together, with the loneliness that was like standing in outer space since we'd broken up.

The air grew cold, like a vacuum. The freezing rain clinked the window pane in the library as I tried to study alone at a circular table. At other tables kids conversed openly. No one was studying. Why was I the only one working? Why didn't the librarian tell them to be quiet, so I could focus?

The library is like society, I thought, *it's supposed to be all about learning and becoming a better person, but it's really just a sham filled with shallow people, and those in charge don't care.* People began to look vile. Pimple-faced, scraggly-bearded, sloth-like, with bad posture. Between classes I tried to walk without brushing their bodies.

At twenty-two, if I felt down, there was only one way I knew of to get out. That was through spite. I'd pour myself a beer and address it like an old comrade because that is what society said I should *not* do. At least through spite I could tell myself I was despairing *on purpose.* And then, after hours of vintage, sad music, came the joy of nihilism and the feeling that the whole world was a joke, and only hedonists were in on it, so I might as well be one. Then more drinks and faster-tempo music, and dancing and singing alone and finally, sleep and nightmares, and the sameness of the next day, wondering if I had the will to work my way through the whole process again.

One morning I'd been awake lying in bed devoid of motivation. When I heard Morgan banging around the kitchen getting ready for work, I pulled myself out. He was hung-over and rushing. I grabbed a beer from the refrigerator and sat on the couch, with a coffee table in front of me.

"Your day seems like it's off to a good start," he said.

"Another bullshit day in Shit City," I said.

"Well, I'll be home at five-thirty. Maybe we can tackle painting the bathroom tonight."

"Sure, why not."

"Okay, gotta run. Take it easy buddy."

"Yup." I heard the kitchen door close and Morgan descend the apartment steps. I took a drink from my beer. I stared across the room. I laid on the couch. I sat in the window and saw a cute girl walking her dog. I drank some more beer. "Well, you might as well get the day started," I said. I opened the CD bay on my second-hand computer. I put in a disc I'd labeled "Sad Songs." The opening piano chords to *One for the Road* began tinkling. I finished my beer. "Well, this won't do!" I placed the empty bottle on the coffee table. "If we're going to listen to Sinatra, we better drink some whiskey." So I poured myself some *Seagram's* in a rocks glass and sat on the couch again.

Around 5:30 I heard Morgan climbing the stairs over the blasting music. I heard the door slam overtop of Harry Nielson singing "I can't live...if living is without you!" A dozen or so bottles and cans sat on the coffee table in front of me.

"Dude, what the fuck?" Morgan shouted. He marched over to the computer and practically punched the eject button.

"Hey! I was listening to that." Morgan grabbed the CD and read the title out loud.

"*Sad Songs*? Are you serious?" He snapped the CD in half and threw the pieces on the floor.

"Hey man, that's my Depressed CD!"

"Yeah, no kidding dude! No wonder you're depressed! I come up the stairs and hear Harry Nielson singing 'I can't live' and you're sitting on the couch in the same exact spot you were this morning, with ten beers in front of you?" Morgan paced back and forth, seemingly unable to believe what he'd seen. "*Sad Songs*, dude? Why would you make a CD called *Sad Songs* and listen to it when you're already depressed?"

"Because...because what else are you supposed to listen to when you're depressed. Happy songs?" Morgan slapped his head.

"Yes! Yes! Of course! How do you expect to feel any better if you listen to sad songs when you're already depressed?"

"Well...I don't, I guess."

"Do you like feeling depressed?"

"No of course not."

"Then don't listen to sad songs! Put on something upbeat. *Sublime*, even bullshit Jack Johnson. But not sad songs!"

"Don't listen to sad songs when you're sad," I repeated mechanically. "Huh. You know, I honestly never thought of that?"

Morgan wasn't mad. He paced and said,

"Man, I know how you've been feeling. And I heard that music coming up the stairs. And I thought I was going to come in and find you like, in the bathtub with slit wrists bleeding on the floor or something." I chuckled from the couch,

"Ha! I wouldn't make you clean up that mess, man. If I was going to *off* myself I'd jump in front of a bus or something. That way whoever had to clean up the mess, at least they'd be making union wages." Morgan didn't laugh.

"I'm serious dude. Like, are you okay? I'm worried about you."

That was a nice thing to say. Now I felt like I'd reached a new low, because I'd made Morgan worry. I figured I owed him an explanation.

We sat in the window and I told Morgan about my struggles with Obsessive Compulsive Disorder, which I'd never described to a friend. Rather than a litany of examples, I'll just say that since elementary school I'd experienced a sensation, like my blood was boiling with electricity, if I couldn't align objects the way I thought they should be placed, or clear my throat. The particulars became so prevalent that I nearly dropped out of college by sophomore year, and lost a scholarship. My pediatrician prescribed three different medicines, each with incapacitating side effects. So I decided that since my problem was mental, I'd treat it with will power.

"...Well, so that's what I did. I said, 'This is a matter of perception,' and instead of thinking of myself as 'having a problem' I'd think of myself as just having a different way of thinking than most people had. Most people never learn piano because they don't have the patience to practice a certain progression fifty times a day. Not me! I could practice a hundred and fifty times. It never got boring. Each time I'd play a note, I'd feel that taunting sensation saying 'You won't play that note progression again.' Then I'd play it again, and soon I was learning the blues scale. I took on cleaning jobs, and jobs where my job was to go into the woods and rake and pile things according to size and shape—for Maureen, Jared's boss, the rich eccentric woman. I called it Obsessive Compulsive *Advantage*, because there're some tasks, repetitive ones, and ones that require you to concentrate for a long time, like writing—where it was a real *advantage* to be obsessive. What were the robber barons who made fortunes but obsessive over all the tiny details of their enterprise? What is 'industry' or 'dedication' except the obsessive pursuit of a goal, often in spite of obstacles that would deter most 'normal' people? So that's what it became: spite against normalcy and the behaviors which supposedly lead normal people to be successful; and spite against myself, because I found I was able to taunt myself out of laziness. And then, you know, things really did start improving. I learned about music. I had all this extra time to read because I didn't give a shit about sleeping. I moved out of my grandparent's basement and dated Lisa for two years. So there was no loneliness, then, and no anxiety over missing sleep or failing out of school, and I had all these great friends like Jared who lived a block away, and it was good. Almost no symptoms at all. I didn't even have to drink or smoke after a while. There was just this comfort in the idea that I was equal to the tasks in front of me, equal or even superior to any person my age, because I had this almost super-power to concentrate for long periods and make connections between things that most people never saw. And it was good. Ugh, it was good until like 18 months ago when I had to move back with my parent's because I was broke; when I broke up with Lisa; when I was feeling like I was in a dead-end job and getting sick of college. Everything seemed to be moving backwards. Living in another basement. Then I met Cady, I told myself I only had one semester left, we started working on the raft project, I felt valuable to Cady and like I had an outlet for my creativity with the raft. I was broke and living at home but it was okay because of Cady and the raft, which were the only things I was doing without being forced by some other person. And as long as I could tell myself...as long as I knew that I was in control of things, even in a slow-but-steady way...it was fine. Then the first raft sank and, believe it or not man, it was a big surprise. It was my first, like, experiment of applying my Obsessive Compulsive Advantage against a real-world challenge. And it failed. Then Cady and I started falling apart. Then I thought if I just tried harder, with the raft and with Cady, then it would succeed. Then I had to give up on the second raft. Fail. Then Cady and I broke up. Fail. Extra semester of school, fail; shitty job, fail; car died, fail; parents pissed off 'cause I moved out, fail. Fail fail mother fucking fail! Every day I think about Cady. I think about her and then I note the time and think, 'Damn, another day I didn't get through without thinking about Cady.' And I dream about her. And all the time, man, there's that hopeless feeling like what the fuck are we even trying for, if this is life? And now there's not even a compulsion I can *do* to get a moment's rest from the *obsession*. All I have is the picture of her and the feeling of loss. And the only way to get it out, that I know of, is to drink or surround myself with other people to distract me, because I can't distract myself by concentrating on other things anymore. It's like Cady is a window I can't minimize and its eating up all my RAM and the only thing I can do is try and press Control Alt Delete—I mean drink so that I pass out—so that when the system restarts I can have a little while before her program opens again, like a fucking virus."

"A mental virus."

"Yes."

"Like a computer virus, which is like a physical virus in a body."

"Yeah."

"A mental virus is like a software virus which is like a body virus. Maybe they ought to be treated the same way?"

"And how's that?"

"Well, first of all, you quarantine the problem. Do you have any pictures of Cady, or any of her things lying around?"

"I see what you're getting at. No, I've put them all in a drawer. Although, to be honest, yes, sometimes I open it and look at her picture and other things."

"I think you should either throw that stuff out, or at least bring it to New Baltimore and stash it at your parent's house."

"You know, that's a good idea. I'll do that."

"Okay. Does anything else around here remind you of her? You need to form some new associations."

"Man, everything reminds me of her. Songs I hear. Girls I see that have brown hair who are skinny..."

"Okay well, you can't get rid of everything. And you probably can't erase her memory. But what you can do is make some new memories, with your friends, with new girls you meet, to replace the ones of her." I grew animated because this seemed like a real possibility.

"Yes, I see what you're saying. Like, meet people. Go out to bars. Join some clubs, whatever. I'll probably just go out to bars. But meet people and make new memories, and then soon I'll have all these new memories, to crowd out the ones of her. And if they don't totally disappear, at least they'll have to fight for my attention against other, newer memories!"

"Exactly. So like, how about we go out to bars for a couple of hours a night. Not to get drunk, but just to meet new people and to see where it goes?"

"I like that idea."

"But you've also got to help yourself, man."

"I will. How do you mean, though?"

"I mean you can't indulge yourself. You've got to use some of that spite to your advantage. Don't allow yourself to think about her and if you do, don't dwell on it."

"I think I can manage that. It's a big help being able to talk to you about this stuff, Morgan."

"Of course, buddy. We're friends and this is what friends do. I'm glad to help. Plus I also want to meet new girls. But there is one thing I need to ask...or, no...that I need to demand of you, if I'm going to be your roommate."

"Sure, of course, Morgan. Anything. What is it?"

"No more Harry Nielson!"

IV. It's A Wonderful Lie

When you're lonely you think about how infrequent it is that you meet someone interested in you. Every day that passes reinforces the idea that you'll *never* meet anyone. And then you consider that even if you *do* meet someone, there are numerous contingencies that you have to work through to get to the point that you're spending time with them romantically, and you start to think that it isn't delusional to assume that you will always be lonely, so overwhelming is the process.

Mike started coming up on Tuesday nights. We'd play darts and I'd lose. Then he, Watson and I would walk uptown and go to a bar called *Washington Tavern,* which had a wing special. We drank three beers, ate a dozen wings, and still managed to tip the bartender on $10 apiece. One night I saw a skinny brunette wearing pajama pants and Morgan and Mike convinced me to go over and talk to her. The next week I saw her again, and she gave me her phone number. There followed a few days of potential good-feeling as I tried to schedule a date. Morgan said I could borrow his car to take her out to dinner. But then she stopped returning my texts and I never saw the girl again. I was embarrassed that I'd gotten excited.

One night we went to a bar called *Sadie's.* I'd spent a lot of time there when I was under-age, thinking about when I'd be 21, when I'd come in with some money in my pocket and clean up. I met a girl named Kelly, who was drunk and going from guy to guy. She had red hair and she gave me her number. I thought to myself *remember, Kelly, red hair, Irish name,* so I wouldn't forget her if she called. Then, apparently, I met a girl named Kate, who had blonde hair, and talked to her for hours. But I was so drunk I forgot her. The next day Kate texted me and asked if I wanted to smoke pot at my apartment later. I saw her name on my phone and said "Kate — Irish name, red hair...that's the easy girl from the bar. I'm gonna get laid!" When Kate called I went downstairs to let her in and I had no idea who she was. She came up and we smoked and hung out and talked for four hours. She said I should paint the scene out my window. She said she liked to draw but things like trees were annoying because you have to sketch all the leaves in. Kate was 18 and worked at a hospital, but I'm not sure what she did there. I was so thrown off by the act of playing off that I knew her that I didn't make a move on her. I walked her to her car, and that was that. Kate started calling me when she was done with work, asking if I wanted to hang out at my place. She'd show up with little gifts like macaroni salads, notebooks, and matchbooks with pictures of pinup women, because I had a collection of matchbooks. I'd never met a girl like Kate, who seemed to enjoy just being nice and considerate. It was silly and fun. I put the bar that I'd fixed up, which had been in my parent's basement, in the window overlooking Madison Ave. Kate and I smoked cigarettes looking over the street. When we heard Morgan coming up the stairs we hid behind the bar, because we thought we were going to get in trouble. Morgan laughed and said we were funny, hiding from him like we were kids and he was the dad. It was easy to talk to Kate, and she was pretty. When she asked me a question she looked in my eye with earnest sincerity. But then she said she liked me so much she wanted to introduce me to Jack, who was a guy she was hoping to make her boyfriend. I agreed to the awkward situation, because how could I not? Jack and Kate came over one night and I played the host. They left together and I felt worse than ever.

Then we approached the two worst times of the year if you're lonely: the holidays, and the winter. The holidays are terrible because everything is decorated, so you can't go in public without having your unhappiness thrown like a pie in your face. And the winter in Albany is bitterly cold and drags on endlessly. Thanksgiving wasn't so bad, except for the part where we were supposed to be giving thanks for the great things in life, while all I felt was a vacuum. Then everything was decorated with a holiday cheer that seemed like a mass-produced layer of cover-up.

By the time we went to my sister's house to decorate her tree, the last thing I wanted to do was sit around and talk about the good ole days. I hung a plastic smile from my face as we put the ornaments on the branches, so I wouldn't be the Debbie Downer. When they started playing Christmas movies I couldn't stand it. I blotted tears when Karen cried because Frosty melted in the greenhouse. I fought sobs over the dolly and the jack-in-the-box on the Island of Misfit Toys. I was knotted up and tied up and didn't know which way was up feeling down.

When my sister inserted a cassette of *It's a Wonderful Life* I wanted to run out of her house. It's not a wonderful life, I thought, the movie is a big fucking lie. It's pretty accurate as it follows George Bailey as he's forced to give up his dreams and never go anywhere because of a string of disasters that other people created. But just when George is in the pit of despair, standing on the bridge, the movie loses credibility. In real life there are no guardian angels. Nobody fixes things for you. In real life George Bailey would've either gone to jail because Mr. Potter stole his money, or he'd jump off the bridge and everybody would call him a scumbag because they assumed he stole the money and then abandoned his wife and kids by killing himself. I watched that movie empathizing with each step as George unraveled. How can anybody take it, so many failures and losses in succession? Then the bullshit at the end, where everybody donates to him and the angel comes out of the sky and blah blah blah. It's a bad lesson for kids. The movie should be called *It's A Wonderful Lie*, I spat inside my head. In real life you just fail, and that's that. I got up from the couch and said that I had to call someone and drank a beer outside because I knew I couldn't keep it together through the end of that movie.

At least school is coming to an end, I thought, back in Albany. *At least that will be done, and I'll have a free schedule. I can work and then I can get some money and then things will improve.*

Two weeks before Christmas I interviewed with Kelly Services, a temp agency where Morgan had worked before he got his job at the state. He said that sometimes a temp employee gets hired to a full-time position. I took the bus up to Wolf Road for my interview. I tripped going up the stairs because I'd borrowed Morgan's dress shoes, because I didn't own any, and his were three sizes too big. I either interviewed well, or in those pre-Great-Recession days they needed a lot of temp employees, because they called me back a day later and said I could work for $9 an hour from 8:30 to 5 at a corporation that was a string of letters I'd never heard of. So I said sure, why not.

Then school ended and I skipped the walking ceremony. Then Christmas came and I got some boxes of food from my parents to help subsidize my new city lifestyle. I borrowed my parent's old, leaking gas truck with the crumbling fender and drove it to Albany through sleet and freezing rain, so I'd have something to commute to work in the next day, the 26th, which was my first day of work at my new office temp job career.

In the morning the sky was an invariable expanse of gray cloud. Sprinkles of sleet were still falling from the night before. I pulled off of a gray, five-lane highway onto a gray side road called Metro South Ext. I took the first left and parked in a gray parking lot beside a gray cube building with tinted windows I couldn't see inside of. I tried entering the back door but it was locked. So I walked around the building to the other side. I entered a lobby which was a square room lit by fluorescent lights where there were three identical blue-gray doors. There was a keypad and a buzzer on the wall, so I pressed a button and an electrical voice asked who I was.

"My name is Dallas Trombley. I'm the temp from Kelly Services."

"Just a moment, please." One of the gray doors opened and a woman in her mid-thirties who was neither ugly nor attractive let me in. "Welcome to M.J.O.T.E.," she said. Then she showed me around.

There was a short hallway with bathrooms to the left and a square room with two big copying machines to the right. That was where I was to go if I had a lot of address labels to print, the woman said. Twenty paces farther the room opened into a square lit by fluorescent lights. The carpet was blue, with no pattern. In the middle of the room there was a copier where I would print documents and make copies, the woman said. There was a break-room with a mini-fridge, a microwave, a convection oven and a white table a little ways ahead. It was lit with fluorescent lights. A little farther down the hall was a meeting room where meetings happened. We turned around and walked back into the main square room. Two rows of cubicles divided the room into two equal rectangles. I hoped to have a cubicle on the north-facing wall, where there were windows with natural light coming through permanently-fixed blinds. The woman showed me to a cubicle on the south-facing wall where there were no windows.

"This is where you'll sit," the woman said. There was a black office chair that rolled on top of a square piece of plastic. There was a tan colored phone, a black keyboard and a black computer. To the left of the computer there was a place to stack papers. "I'll get you your sign-on information in a few minutes."

"Okay boss," I said.

"I'm not the boss," the woman said.

"Oh, okay, sorry."

The woman led me over to her desk, where she had a stack of papers.

"The first thing you should do in the morning is come over here and see if I have any of these filings to enter," she said. I brought the papers to my desk and came back. "Okay, great. Now, after you complete the filings, which I'll show you how to do after I get your sign-on information, you want to come over here—" she pointed to a space by a wall where there were several U.S. Mailboxes full of envelopes, "—and see if there are any filings to be sorted. I'll show you how to do that this afternoon."

"Okay," I said.

"In the meantime why don't you sit tight at your desk and I'll get your information."

"Okay, I'll do that."

A few people came over to my cubicle and introduced themselves to me one at a time. They seemed nice enough. They said I wouldn't be working with them, but it was nice to meet me. Then a woman in her fifties with salt and pepper hair came over and introduced herself as the director, but not the big boss. She had a strong handshake. She told me if I needed anything to come to her, and that I didn't need to wear a suit to work every day. She said she hoped I liked it there. The previous girl had liked it, she said. And Fatima was a temp before they hired her full-time. She pointed to Fatima, who had a cubicle that was identical to mine, but ten feet away against the same wall, and Fatima waved. Then I sat down again. The first woman came back and gave me a sheet with numbers and pass codes on it. Then we started up the computer and I signed on correctly and she said I was doing a fantastic job so far. She showed me an icon that opened a program in MS DOS, where I navigated between fields by pressing "tab". Then she pointed to the stack of papers on the desk. There were perhaps fifty sheets in the pile. Each sheet was divided by lines into six fields. Each field represented a "mortgage filing." It was my job to enter the numbers and abbreviations in certain places in each of the fields on each of the sheets into corresponding fields in the computer, by pressing "tab" to navigate each field and F7 when each filing was completed. As I completed each sheet I could put them in a new pile. When I was done with each pile I was to press F12 which would list all of the mortgage filings I'd just entered. I was to compare the list to each of the sheets, making sure I hadn't missed any. Then I was to press F3 to print a report. Then I was to bring the pile of sheets with the report on top to the woman's desk, and she would give me a new pile.

"And that's pretty much it," she said. "Why don't you work on these for a while, and then I'll show you what we do when the mail comes in."

After a couple hours the woman told me to take my half-hour lunch break. I ate a sandwich alone in the break room. Then the woman told me to follow her to see how the mail was done. We went into the meeting room, which had some windows and a long table with sixteen chairs underneath rows of fluorescent lights. On the table there were five plastic U.S. Mail boxes filled with envelopes. The woman removed an envelope from one of the boxes and opened it with a letter opener.

"You can throw the envelopes in the recycling bin," she said. "If it gets too full, just grab somebody else's recycling bin from out in the main office. Anyway, these are mortgage filings. This is what they look like after they come back. These are the hard copies, from the bank. You see this set of numbers and letters stamped in the upper corner?"

"Yup."

"That's the mortgage filing number. Sometimes they're stamped in the bottom corner for some reason. Anyway they're all different, and they need to be sorted by letter and number. You should use the whole table to sort them out. It should take you probably...an hour and a half, two hours to get them sorted. Then pile them up into a stack, and let me know when you're done."

"Okay," I said. She left and I sorted and stacked about two hundred mortgage filings. Then I told the woman I was done.

"Wow, you're doing a great job!" she said. Since I'd finished earlier than expected, I could get to work sooner entering the data from three new piles of sheets she'd produced. When I was done with that it was about four p.m. The woman said I was doing a great job, and since I had an hour left I could help her with the filing. She showed me to a wall of filing cabinets six-feet high by fifteen-feet long. Each drawer had letters and numbers on it. "These correspond to the numbers on the mortgage filings. Each one has to get filed. Now, you've already put them in order, so they should be easy to file."

"Okay," I said.

When I finished the filing it was about quarter to five. I went to the woman's desk. She said there were no more piles of sheets to data-enter, and I'd done a good job, so I could chill out for the last fifteen minutes. I could use the computer's internet if I wanted. So I sat at the desk, but I didn't open the internet browser because I didn't want to get in the habit of keeping it open and checking emails and AIM and such while I was at work. Then at a few minutes past five the older woman with the salt and pepper hair came over and said I was "all set" and that I'd done a good job at M.J.O.T.E. that day. So I turned off the computer and got back in my truck. It was dark by then. I calculated that, including my lunch break, I earned $72 dollars that day, before taxes, for being at the office for 8.5 hours. After taxes it'd be more like $56. At that rate I could pay back Morgan, Mike and Jared the $500 I owed them apiece within a couple of months. That was how I'd be spending five of seven days per week, for the next three months, before I had any spending money.

As I drove home in the beat-up truck I got lost and found myself way on the other side of the city. At exactly six o'clock my cell phone rang. The display showed my parent's telephone number. I answered, it was my mother.

"Hi Dal, are you at your apartment?" she asked.

"I'm on my way there now," I said. "What's up?"

"How was your first day of work?"

"It was alright. The people seem nice enough. There's nothing too demanding about it. A couple of people said there're opportunities for promotion, to a bigger cubicle or something." I pressed the brakes rather quickly and a car sped around me honking as I turned onto a road which was yet another wrong turn.

"That's good. I have some bad news but I didn't want to call you last night, before your first day of work..." Instantly I knew something had happened to one of my grandparents. They were in their mid-nineties. Whenever I got a call from my parents I bit my lip. They were the two nicest people in my life and everybody who ever met them felt the same way. My grandmother never cursed, kept an immaculately clean house until she could no longer get out of a chair without help, and cooked me afternoon meals every school day when I was between the ages of ten and fourteen. My grandfather had no concerns at all except that his wife of 67 years not feel the least discomfort. "Your grandparents were in an accident last night coming home from your cousin's house. They're in the hospital at Albany Med right now. I wanted to tell you in case you wanted to stop by after work. I think you would want to."

"Grandma and grandpa!" I shouted. "Grandma and Grandpa! Why them?! Of all the God damn things that could happen! To the two nicest people! Are they...how injured are they?"

My mother's voice cracked and I heard her sniffle. I think she anticipated a more stoic reaction from me. I very seldom lost my temper in front of my mother.

"Your grandmother isn't doing well. She's in the intensive care unit. She has a couple of broken ribs and a broken wrist, and possibly a punctured lung. She doesn't know where she is."

It was so cruel, the idea of her laying there in pain, maybe at the end of her life, alone. Of all people, she didn't deserve that! I pictured her suffering and writhing and, what with the Alzheimer's that had already affected her, I pictured her waking up in the hospital room and calling for her husband by his name, *Frank! Frank! Help!* and having to be restrained by nurses and doctors because she was hysterical. My grandmother was a second mother to me. As I drove, my chin wrenched back, my hands flew to my face involuntarily, my forehead wrinkled, I bit my fist, all at once, and tears welled in my eyes. I needed to pull over but the street was busy with rush-hour traffic. "What about Grandpa?" I asked when I'd caught my breath, though I dreaded further details.

"He's in another room on the fourth floor. He...he's exhausted and he may have pneumonia," my mother fought to keep her voice from breaking. "His whole face is black and blue from the airbag, Dallas....So is your grandmother's...Dallas...he saved your grandmother's life last night!"

"What do you mean?" My mother's inflection lowered as she exhaled and inhaled rapidly.

"They were coming home from your cousin's after visiting for Christmas. You know, it rained all day, but then after dark it turned to sleet and freezing rain. They were coming back down Bushendorph Road, you know, way out by the golf course, where there's no street lights, and they hit black ice. Your grandfather said they were only going ten, maybe fifteen miles an hour. He said he tried to hit the brakes but he couldn't...he couldn't stop fast enough...Dallas...to hear him tell it. He blames himself for what happened to your grandmother...*hhh..hhh*..."

"So they hit a tree??" I needed to get off the damn street!

"No, well, they slid off the road and went down a big hill—thank God they didn't go off sideways or they'd have rolled over, but they didn't—down a hill and hit a tree at the bottom. The airbag went off, and...and she must've had her hand up because they think that's how she broke her wrist, that her arm came up and hit her in the eye...and that's what broke her ribs...the air-bag...because when you're that old, you know, things get brittle..."

"So what happened? How did they get out? How long were they there? Did anybody see?" I jammed the steering wheel to the right when I saw a one-way street without traffic. It was a cobblestone street that sent my body bumping up and down until I came to a stop, shaking.

"Your grandmother was crying...Dallas...I'm sorry, I'm sad, it's hard to tell the story...and your grandfather's door wouldn't open...God...so he had to climb over your grandmother and get out the passenger side...He...he was afraid to leave her there...he was afraid she'd get cold, but...but he said he was afraid to leave the engine on, in case gas was leaking, he was afraid it'd catch fire...God, Dallas...so he left her there and he got to the bottom of the hill...and you know he has that lame leg, how he did this I don't know, and at 90 years old...he tried to run up the hill, but he kept...he kept falling back down!"

"Stop it! Stop! Okay, I can't hear any more."

"No, no, it's almost over. Sorry. Sorry. Three times he fell down, slipping in the wet grass and the sleet...it was only about 38 last night...and finally he got to the top of the hill on the road, and he knew he had to get help for your grandmother quick, or she'd freeze, and he didn't know if she was bleeding and hated to leave her there, but thank God he did...and he ran a mile through the sleet to the first house he found, and rang the doorbell and knocked on the door and fell down in front of them and begged them to help..." My mother started losing it. "...and...and that's it that's the story they're at Albany Med. Your father is already up there. He's been there all day. I just came home an hour ago. Oh, it's awful. I'm sorry Dallas you've had such a bad few weeks."

"No Mom I'm sorry I love you!" I apologized, feeling suddenly like I'd made her sad by being unhappy at the holidays, and picturing her holidays ruined because of me, and feeling sad, and my father feeling sad, because of me, and my sister feeling sad, because of me, and all of these people now feeling a thousand times more sad because they saw one another sad and in pain, pain and sadness radiating out from everybody else.

"I love you too, Dallas!" My mom said. I was lost on some dark street in a bad truck after a weird day having just heard horrid news and I pictured terrible images and had to get off the phone to collect myself. I told my mother I'd call her as soon as I was home to find out the room numbers at the hospital, which was within walking distance of my apartment.

Then I looked down into my lap, feeling hot water pooled there, and was surprised to see my pants and the back of my hands covered in blood. I brought my fingers to my face and felt it dripping from both of my nostrils. I never had such a nosebleed before or after. Whether it was caused by the cold, dry weather, the bumps over the cobblestone street in a truck with bad shocks, or some psychic reaction to the awful news, I don't know. But I rummaged through the glove compartment and turned a napkin wholly red before I got back on roads I recognized. I parallel parked a block and a half from my apartment, but my nose was bleeding so much I couldn't hold all the blood in cupped hands, and I didn't want to cause a scene walking and bleeding from my face getting blood on the sidewalk. So I called Morgan and asked him to please bring me down a roll of toilet paper and I'd explain when he got there because I couldn't talk. When he came alongside the truck I opened the door and grabbed the toilet paper from his hand and, I imagine, set a new standard for strange behavior in a roommate.

V. Office Work

"One, two, three...heave!"

I felt a juvenile thrill as we threw the Christmas Tree out the second-story window. It was easier than dragging it through the apartment and down the 23 steps, dropping pine needles all over. But we did it, really, to throw out the holiday season.

"Thank God 2006 is over," Mike said. It was the first of January, 2007. He, Jess and I sat in the bow window looking over Madison Avenue. Jess rose periodically to turn over jazz records. She and Mike had started coming up to the Downtube a couple nights a week—sometimes three or four or five times a week—to escape their parent's houses, where they lived in the woods in their high school bedrooms decorated with basketball lamps, collages from grade school, crap they'd thrown up when they were teenagers. "I think, looking back on this decade, people are going to look at it like we look at the 1930s. This ten-year period from 2000 to 2009."

"What's this decade even called?" Jess queried. She stood in a corner reading album covers under a table lamp. "Like, the '80's were the '80s, the '90s were the '90s. I guess the 1910s were the tens, or teens. What were the 1900s?"

"I think they were called *the centos*," Mike said. "Because it was the beginning of the century."

"So should this decade be called *the millennios?*" Jess laughed. "Sounds like a breakfast cereal. 'Come eat your millennios, kids, and get your energy for the next thousand years!'"

"I think they should be called the *ut-ohs*," Mike grumbled.

"I think *the cheery-o's* is better," Jess replied. She liked to take the opposite position of Mike or I in any conversation.

"I agree with Mike," I said.

"Of course you do, Dallas."

"Let's make a list," Mike suggested. "Should we call it the *ut-ohs!* or the *cheery-os*? Hmm. Well, let's see which fits better. Hmm, we have, for instance, 'Ut-oh! Bush was elected!'...'Ut-oh! The polar ice caps are melting away!'...'Ut-oh! We invaded Iraq!'...Jess?"

"Yeah, I got nothing...Jesus...*something* good must've happened...We lost our virginity...hey, that's good! And we graduated from high school and college."

"We have only a few personal things to be happy about, while universally the earth has become more disastrous," I observed.

The next day was the beginning of the new year because the holidays with all the pomp and circumstance signifying nothing were over.

January 2nd, 2007, meant that the last year with all of its setbacks was behind us. It was the day to start focusing. No. It was the day to start *not* thinking. If we could work through January 2nd, then it'd be January 3rd, and then it would be the 4th, and so on. The winter was going to be cold and trying. But we could get through it if we got through one day at a time without extrapolating. If we just got through the winter, then in a couple of months it would start to warm up and we could go outside. That was something to look forward to. We needed something to look forward to.

The second of January, 2007, marked my first full week of work at the corporation with all the letters. It was freezing cold. My truck turned over a lot before it started. I drove Al, my parent's white F150 with the leaking gas tank and the crumpled fender, to Wolf Road. I took a right onto Metro Road Ext. I parked behind the square gray building and walked in through the back door using my new employee PIN. I grabbed a stack of papers from the older woman who was not my boss's desk and brought them back to my cubicle. I resisted the temptation to open Internet Explorer and sign in to Facebook or AIM or check my email. I opened the MS DOS program and started data entering.

By this, the second week, I'd gotten faster at punching the numbers. It was a repetitive series of keystrokes with variations after exactly the same keystrokes for each of the six fields on each of the pieces of paper in each stack. I made a game of learning the strokes and got quicker, so I didn't have to look at the keyboard, but just focus on the numbers I had to enter. I pretended I was practicing a melodic progression on a piano. I hit the keystrokes with a rhythm, each series a little cadence, and ended by striking F7 with force. As long as nothing distracted me, the repetitive motion was fine, even enjoyable. It gave me something to do so I didn't have to think about what I was doing. It was a challenge to see how fast I could work through a pile. I got through the pile without stopping to look around or twiddle my thumbs. The woman who was not my boss was surprised by my alacrity. She gave me another stack and I figured, well, this is one stack, and I'll get through, and then it'll be done, and if I do one stack at a time…that's all I have to do. Same thing with the boxes of envelopes. Open one envelope at a time. Put the letter in its place. I was making order out of chaos. If I thought about it like that, I could get through it. I didn't need the woman to explain how to sort the mail, or file, or data enter, a second time. I didn't mill around making conversations with people. So she said I was a quick learner and a good worker and she was going to tell the woman with the salt and pepper hair who was the boss that I was doing a great job.

I left work and it was dark and cold. It took a long time for the truck to turn over before it started. Then on the way home the lights dimmed and the power steering died. I turned my flashers on and pulled over, but the flashers didn't work. I called Morgan and he brought jumper cables. We got the truck started and drove a quarter-mile and it died again. We were by the University, and by jumping the truck and driving it until it died we got the truck to the parking lot at SUNY over the course of three jumps.

"Of course this had to happen!" I complained when I climbed into Morgan's passenger seat, after leaving the truck at SUNY. "There couldn't be a break from set-backs. Of course not. This way there's a continuum of disasters so that this year is just like the last one."

"Well...it's hard, yeah," Morgan said as chipper as possible. "But it's just a broken truck. It's not the end of the world."

"Just a broken truck that I can't afford to fix, or tow, that I can't keep at SUNY. Just a broken truck that I can't replace. Ugh. Well...so I guess I'll have to take the bus to work and back now. But I don't know how that even works. How do I figure out where to go and which bus to take and when?"

"I bet there's a schedule online or at least a phone number you can call. When we get back I'll help you figure it out. I know how you hate paperwork and stuff like this."

So we drove home and Morgan helped me figure out what bus to take. Then I walked over to the hospital and visited my grandparents who were convalescing. I told my dad that the truck had died. It was the third time in six months that I told him that a vehicle I was using was ruined. First Mindy on my birthday, then when I totaled my grandfather's car in October, and now Al in January. I felt guilty stacking more bad news on my father as he sat next to the hospital bed where his mother had tubes coming out of her nose and a face that was black and blue.

"Well, we'll just have to have it towed," my father said. "I think you should start saving up for a new vehicle." We both knew that was impossible, but I said,

"Yeah," just to avoid having to think about it.

I had to catch the bus at 7:20. It was six blocks from my apartment. I froze in the dead of winter in my hand-me-down blazer with several shirts underneath and a black ski hat.

The bus dropped me down Wolf Road. From there I had a fifteen-minute walk in the tundra to the building I worked in.

"You should buy a peacoat," Fatima, the plump Indian woman who sat in the cubicle nearest to me said. "Men look nice in them. That blazer is old. It looks like it's from the '80s."

"*I'm* from the '80s," I said.

"I can tell." Fatima liked to talk. She told me about her boyfriend and the side business she had, some pyramid scheme she kept trying to get me to enroll in that she had to shut up about whenever another person came toward the place where our cubicles were. Mostly she asked me personal questions and offered unsolicited advice because she'd been a temp, like me.

"So...you don't have a girlfriend?"

"No," I said, typing.

"Why not? You're a young guy. You're not ugly."

"Thank you. Well...having a girlfriend isn't just a choice to make. It involves another person."

"Sure it's a choice. All you've got to do is look and smell good. Like, you should wear cologne. Women love men who smell good. A good cologne is *Calvin Kline*. That's what my boyfriend wears and I love to smell him. If I smell it and he's not there, I think about him and miss him. That's what you want. You want girls to think about you when you're not there and miss you."

"Yeah." I continued typing, but it was hard to keep the keystroke rhythm in my head with Fatima talking.

"And don't bite your fingernails. It looks effeminate. And you should cut your hair. It's too long and short hair is in style now. But the beard is good, although you could trim it a little. A beard ought to be short, really short, like the first setting on the clippers."

"Hey, I appreciate the advice. But I've gotta get this stuff entered and I'm not really good at having a conversation and working at the same time."

"Oh yeah, you're new. So you have to look busy all the time. That's good. I think they like you."

"Thanks."

"They said they liked me too, because I worked hard. It took like six months, and then they offered me my full-time job. So, you know, if you're good and you stick with it, maybe they'll offer you a job this summer."

"Maybe."

"Ugh, this friggin woman at work won't shut up," I told Morgan as we drank beers at *Lark Tavern* that night. We liked *Lark Tavern*, which was across the street, better than *Lionheart*, because there were all kinds of people mixed together at *Lark Tavern*, and the bartenders were all cute girls, while *Lionheart* had mostly jocks and the bartenders were all men. "All she does is tell me about what I'm doing wrong and why I don't have a girlfriend."

"That's really annoying. Is she good-looking at least? Maybe she thinks you're cute."

"No she's ugly and she has a boyfriend. It's like, the last thing I want to think about while I'm at work is how I'm strugglin' with girls. Like, shouldn't she know not to ask about my ex-girlfriend? I hate it. At work, you're trapped. It's got to be clean and clinical and impersonal. I just want to be an extension of the computer when I'm at work. It's bad enough I'm stuck thinking about shitty society and weird shit for forty minutes on the bus each way."

"Yeah and you can't tell her to be quiet because that's rude and then you look like the asshole. I guess some people have so few friends that they latch onto anybody they can corner. Or work is so damn boring that they have to get up and walk around to make the day go faster. That's pretty much how it is at the State."

"I guess it's just a part of getting older and going to work that you have to deal with annoying people to get your pay."

"Pretty much. That's what a job is. It's like, do this annoying shit in a room full of annoying people who are also doing annoying shit. Then you're all co-workers, commiserating because you're getting annoyed together. The trick is to just keep your head down and get through the day so you can go home and do shit you actually want to do, with people you like. Like what we're doing right now. Isn't it nice to have a little spending money so we can come here and have some beers in this cool bar with all these cool people?" I looked around, and Morgan was right, it was a cool place and the company was pleasant. We clinked our glasses.

"I guess I just wish we could do more of this and less of that."

"Well, yeah. That's the goal. We'll find a way. We're a couple of smart guys."

"I hope so, man."

By the beginning of my third week at the corporation I was getting worn from the routine. There were between 227 and 240 steps from my apartment to the bus stop, and between 310 and 326 from where I got off the bus to the office door. I could count these as I walked, or repeat *slow-but-stead-y-wins-the-race* with each step, keeping my chin buried in my popped-up wool blazer collar with my head bent to fight the winter wind. In the office I'd sweat because of the body heat I'd built up marching. It was starting to get hard to stay awake, since I got up so early to catch the bus and stared at the computer screen all day. I'd catch myself nodding off and jerk my head back. I'd go to the men's room and sit in the stall for five minutes of dreaming. Then I'd feel shaky and still exhausted. So I brought in a container of instant coffee and poured piles of it in the bottom of a paper cup with hot water. The bitterness helped keep me awake until the caffeine set in. I'd have four or five of these double or triple cups of coffee and then at night I wanted to run marathons and write Platonic dialogues describing the intricacies of the universe. Then I'd think about the next day and how tired I would be, and I'd want to sleep, so I'd start drinking as soon as I got home in order to relax, and I started to associate drinking with getting rid of the shaky hands the coffee had left me with. But really drinking didn't bring me back to "normal". I'd just start to get drunk while also amped up on caffeine. I refused to go to bed and lay around tossing and turning. So that meant I had to drink more so that I could pass out by midnight or one a.m. so that I could get several hours of sleep and start the process over the next day, dead tired and hungover again. If you've ever gotten caught in that cycle, you know how hard it is to break. Still, I repeated to myself, *one day at a time. Tomorrow is January 9th. Then the next day will be January 10th.* But it was starting to seem less like I was cutting my life into manageable pieces and more like I was listing the days which would repeat, one after another, the same way, *ad nauseam.* I started to get sick from the cold walks and then the hot office and then the hot office and the cold walks without good winter gear—and from the lack of sleep and the up and down cycles and from forgetting to eat dinner because I was drinking.

In the afternoon I spread the mortgage filings out along the sixteen-foot table in the meeting room and started putting them in order. A middle-aged white man entered the room with a sprinkler bucket in his hand. I'd never seen the man around the office before. He seemed surprised to find me there.

"Oh, ah...can I come in here? I'm the plant guy." I looked around the room.

"Yeah, ah, sure. You're not disturbing *me.*"

"Great. I'll just be a couple of minutes." There were a dozen potted plants spaced equidistantly along the perimeter of the room, which I'd never noticed. The guy started going from one to another, sprinkling water into the pots. I opened an envelope as I watched him.

"You, ah...*work* here?" I asked. "I'm Dallas."

"Hi Dallas, I'm Charlie," the man made a gesture and went to the next plant. "No, I don't work here. I bet *you* do."

"Well...yeah...here I am, working."

"Whatcha got there? Looks like a lotta mail." I held up the contents of an envelope.

"Mortgage filings. I gotta put 'em in order." The man nodded and moved to the next plant, so that I had to turn slightly to see him. "So...you don't work here, but you're watering the plants?"

"Yup."

"I confess: I do not understand." The man smiled.

"You're new here, huh?"

"Yeah."

"Whatever company this is, they lease these plants. I guess they figure they gotta put up something for decoration so the people don't go postal. So, yeah, they lease these plants from another company, and it comes with free watering. What company is this?" He seemed to ask this just to keep the conversation going while he watered the rest of the plants.

"Oh, ah, I forget the acronym. I work for *Kelly Services*, I'm just assigned here."

"Ah, a Kelly Girl."

"Well, I'm a Kelly Guy, I guess."

"Ha, you're funny. I'm not an employee either, of my company. I'm an 'independent contractor.' It's pretty much the same thing, except the labor laws only apply to employees. So this way if I work more than 40 hours or whatever, they don't have to pay me any OT, cause I'm self-employed, see?"

"Huh. That's a nice trick."

"Yeah, it's kinda like this corporation that you're working for, but not actually working for, because you actually work for *Kelly Services*. If this company hired you, see, they'd have to pay unemployment insurance and workers' compensation and FICA and social security and all that for you, and do all the HR paperwork and keep files and so on and so forth. Instead, *Kelly* does all that and calls you *their* employee and leases you out, kind of like the plants here, to this place. So this place pays *Kelly Services* something like $15 an hour, which is cheaper than the cost of hiring an employee, and Kelly pays you, I'm guessing, something like ten, right?"

"Nine."

"Sheesh. So, there you go. Kelly specializes in workers, and buys a big group workers' comp policy and all, and so they call that an *economy of scale*, because all Kelly does is do workers, it's their specialty and they know all the loopholes and they get special deals and they do it cheaper than the nameless corporation can hire somebody. So the corporation saves money and Kelly makes a little money on everybody they lease out and you get to say you have a job. What's this outfit do? Mortgages?"

"Yeah...I'm not sure I really understood it actually until you just explained how *Kelly Services* works. The boss guy tried to explain it to me the other day. He said that this company—this one that owns this building that I'm temping at—they only do mortgage filings and nothing else. I guess mortgage filings—to be honest I don't really even know what a mortgage filing *is*—but I guess they're expensive for banks that write mortgages to do. So instead of hiring an employee at the bank to do the mortgage filing work, because there might not be enough to keep an employee occupied, they outsource the mortgage filing stuff to this company, which does it for a lot of the banks. Seems like everything I'm doing has to do with counties in New Jersey for some reason. But yeah, so it's the same thing. The bank saves money because it doesn't have to hire people, and this place charges them a fee per filing that is more than it actually costs, because they've found ways to save money...like, by hiring temp workers. Huh." The guy smirked and moved to the next pot.

"So there you go. I'm a guy who is self-outsourced, working for a company that out-sources office plants, talking to a guy who works for a company that out-sources workers to a company that out-sources mortgage filings." The guy whistled as he moved to the last plant.

"So...that's what you do all day?" I asked sort of enviously. "You go from office to office watering plants?"

"Yup. Set my own schedule, more or less. Spend a good amount of time in my car. Go into the places. Most of the time nobody notices me or asks me what I'm doing. And that's that." The guy had worked himself around the room and was standing in the door with the water sprinkler in his hand about to leave.

"It actually sounds...pretty...*peaceful*," I said.

"Well, it beats sorting the mail." I chuckled, looking at the hundreds of papers I had to arrange on the table.

"It certainly does," I said.

"Well, take it easy." The man hummed as he strolled out the door.

That night my mother called to tell me the truck was dead, but I could borrow an eight-year-old used Dodge Neon which they'd bought to replace the vehicles that had died since August. Then she added that her youngest sister, Michelle, who was thirty-one and used to baby-sit my sister and I, was in the hospital with cirrhosis of the liver and would probably die in the next couple of days. She said she didn't expect me to visit her, and I shouldn't, because I wouldn't recognize her and she wouldn't be lucid enough to recognize me. I responded morbidly that at least she was at Albany Medical Center. That way all three of our family members who were dying or recovering from horrid accidents were in the same place. How nice it was of Life to make things convenient for us in those little ways.

VI. Penumbra

To be without worth—as I perceived myself; with no path—as I projected, was just terrible. Dehumanizing.

** *

It was cold and I was sick, but at least I had the Neon my parents lent me so I didn't have to ride the bus. I sniveled as I sat in my cubicle. My nose was raw from tissues.

As I worked through my first pile of papers I heard the woman with the salt and pepper hair say my name. I looked up as she walked toward my desk. Beside her was a great-looking young woman in a white button-up blouse and tight black slacks. She had brown, shoulder-length hair that curled in around her neck. She was thin, spritely and short.

"Dallas, this is my daughter Katherine," she said. "She worked here over the summer, before college. She did the Jersey mortgage filings like you. Katherine, this is Dallas."

The young woman smiled and extended her hand. I stood and shook it.

"Ah, my old desk," Katherine joked, "I like how you've decorated it, ha ha." The back of her blouse brushed my arm as she leaned in to survey my workspace. "One yellow post-it-note with your sign-on numbers. I like the *feng shui*. Kind of minimalist." As she stood straight I tried to step back to get out of her way, but the wall of the cubicle was behind me. So her head moved past my face and I smelled her hair by accident. I stuttered,

"Well, you know, I just started working here so...I haven't really had time to decorate it..."

"Dallas is very serious about his work," the woman with the salt and pepper hair winked at me. "He's done a great job the last few weeks. If he keeps up the good work I think Bill might ask him to stay on with us." I blushed. I was hot. I wondered if I was sweating. I was suddenly aware of my clothes and felt old and ugly. My hand-me-down blazer and a maroon button-up shirt that was too baggy. It might have looked conservative and professional to the older people in the office, but it was not stylish in the way Katherine was dressed. "When Katherine had your desk you couldn't see the cubicle. She had all her prints and drawings all over the place. It looked like a collage."

"It wasn't that bad," Katherine waved her hand. Someone across the room called out to the woman with the salt and pepper hair, and she excused herself. I couldn't think of anything to say. Finally I asked Katherine why she'd left the company.

"Well, to go to college," she said. "I got into Cornell and I started in September. It's about three hours away so I couldn't keep working here."

"Yeah I know where Cornell is," I said.

"You've been there?"

"No...but my ex, uh, friend, goes to Cortland and it's right around the same place."

"Your ex friend?"

"Well...my ex-girlfriend."

"Oh, gotcha." Katherine asked how I liked working there. I said it was fine, oh, I liked it a lot. She lowered her voice to confide in me, as the only younger person in the office, that she couldn't wait to go back to college the next day, because she missed her college friends and going out on the bar scene. Then the conversation stalled and she said it was nice to meet me and it sounded like her mother liked me. She turned around and walked away as I sat down. Her slacks were tight. They were like the black pants Cady used to wear. Fatima must have noticed me looking too long (or, longingly looking) because she said in a confidential voice from her cubicle,

"Katie is cute, right?"

I pretended to look through the papers on my desk.

"She seems nice," I said, shuffling.

"*Nice*, huh? You don't think she's attractive?" I tapped the pages against the desk.

"Yes, I think she's very attractive," I admitted without looking toward Fatima.

"She's single you know." I straightened the edges of the papers so they made a perfectly square stack, exactly even.

"Well...that's...surprising."

"Isn't it?" Fatima asked with more force, to reel me in.

"Well, yeah." I finally looked over at her. "I'd assume that she has a boyfriend, being really good-looking and personable."

"Nope. We're friends on Facebook. She used to sit right there where you're sitting. So we became friends. She's really nice and, hey...the office manager's daughter." Fatima winked.

"Yeah, well...I'm sure she'll meet a guy in college."

"You'd think so...but you know, girls like Katherine, you think they want a college boy? They want someone mature, to take care of them."

"Yeah."

"You should friend her on Facebook."

"No...that would be creepy. I just met her." I shot Fatima a look and started entering the numbers from the top sheet of the pile into the MS DOS program.

"So what? That's what Facebook is for. To network."

"I-ah...yeah, I don't think it would be appropriate."

"You work in the same place. It's just a social network request, that's all."

"She would think it's weird."

"No she wouldn't. I know her! We're friends on Facebook. Listen, I'm going to send you a friend request right now. Then you can accept me, and she'll see that I'm your mutual friend. There's nothing creepy about it. Here, I'm looking you up on Facebook right now."

"You keep Facebook open all day?"

"Oh, your profile picture is cute! Look at you in a black shirt and tie, cooking something. You look good!"

"Well...thanks...It's an old picture."

"You look hot. Why don't you dress like that all the time?"

"Dress like what?"

"In modern clothes instead of that blazer you always wear. There, friend request sent! Now accept me so I can see your other pictures."

"You know, it's not easy buying new clothes when you don't have any money. I'll accept you tonight. I don't want to start using Facebook at work."

"Oh come on. You can afford a couple of new shirts at *H&M*, and some cologne. Don't be so cheap. Go ahead and accept me now so I can see your profile."

"I'll do it later," I said.

"Just do it now."

"Look, I don't want to open up Pandora's box and start using Facebook at work. Then I'm going to always want to be checking it, looking at...*people's* pictures..." I trailed off. I shook my head and added quickly, "I just have to get this pile of papers entered."

"What, so that you can go get another pile of papers? Come on. Everybody here has their email and AIM and Facebook and Myspace open. What's the big deal?"

"It's not a big deal..." I said weakly.

"Then stop being such a square. This job is boring. You can't just enter numbers all day or you'll go crazy. You need time out to yourself after you get some work done, as a reward for finishing. Everybody does it. It's perfectly normal."

"Fine! I'll sign on now," I said. I clicked the Internet Explorer icon for the first time since I started working at the place. Then I brought up the Facebook page and entered my password. It was the first time I'd logged onto Facebook in three months. I accepted the friend request from Fatima. "There, I accepted you," I said. Then I minimized the window and brought up the MS DOS program again. I forgot where I'd left off data-entering.

"Wow, look at these pictures from a year and a half ago, stud!" I tried to ignore her. I lost my place and had to delete the numbers I'd entered. "You go out at Mad River? I recognize it in some of these pictures. I take back what I said about the beard before. You look better clean-shaven. Or with the five o'clock shadow. Women like men who're a little gruff. You look good in these pictures. You're a sly dog. You're not so straight-edge."

"I never said I was straight-edge."

"Why don't you ever talk about going out? Stephanie and Bill think you don't drink." That made me laugh.

"Look, I've gotta get this stuff typed up," I said.

"Send Katie a Friend Request."

"Later," I said, "After I finish a couple of piles."

"Ugh, fine." Fatima donner her headphones and was quiet finally.

I lost all ambition to data enter.

Her name would *be Katie*, I thought. And she was going back to school, out in the middle of the state, just like Cady was.

There were papers to my left, but my eyes gravitated to the minimized Internet Explorer window. It'd been so long since I used Facebook.

--*Get the data entry done.*

Typing mindless numbers seemed tyrannically mechanical, inhumanely inane.

--*Just look at Facebook really quick, then go back to work.*

--*No, there is no looking at Facebook really quick, don't do it.*

I opened the Internet Explorer window.

I wonder if Cady has a different Facebook picture.

This other girl Katherine couldn't wait to go back to school. *Would it not have been fun to go to college bars with Cady?* Isn't that what Cady wanted to do, and what *I* did for fun? Why did we break up? I couldn't remember.

We broke up because I didn't have any money or a car and it took so long to see her, I reminded myself. *But what if it had been different?* I could borrow my parents' car now. I could drive out to Cortland in three hours, which was nothing compared to the five or more it took to go to Massapequa. And there was no need for public transportation now. And now I had a job...my life was going in the right direction. I'd started to pay back Morgan and Jared and Mike. I had an apartment in Albany. All these things would've made it a lot easier with Cady.

The $60,000 question: *What if I had let the best thing in my life slip away too easily?*

—*What if there is the possibility that Cady is lonely and wishing we hadn't broken up? She* is *stubborn. She wouldn't tell you. But what if she is, and you told her? Wouldn't it solve everything? Wouldn't it make everything easier? Smelling her, touching her. Laughing and singing together? The things she wrote in your notebooks.*

How quickly those thoughts came, the very instant I let myself imagine. Just thinking of how I might make things work was exciting, nostalgic, comforting: identity-buttressing.

It won't be easy. She'll be mad. She'll turn you away at first. But if you show her all that's changed...If you tell her how you've felt without her. If you could have a few hours together...If you could kiss her once…

The ancient philosophers distinguished "man" from "beasts" by calling us "reasonable." But I think it is a mistake to think we use our reason all of the time, or even often. Salesman realized this at the turn of the 20th century:

> Desire means want; and a man *wants* things, *longs* for things with his heart. He realizes a lack, and has a *heart hunger* for something to fill this lack. His mind may oppose his heart, and may hinder his heart from getting what it Desires. His mind has no *feelings*; so it cannot experience hunger...The ache is in his *heart*, the place where he hungered.[12]

I am, frankly, ashamed and embarrassed by the next three months of my life, which issued from one act of unthinking desire, stimulated by a *heart hunger*.

---

[12] Watts, S., *The People's Tycoon (Henry Ford and the American Century)*, Vintage books, 2005, p. 131. The quote is from Norval A. Hawkins in his book *The Selling Process*, describing how humans are motivated by desires regardless of their reason.

I looked at Cady's Facebook page. She'd unfriended me, so all I saw was a picture of a tiger lily as her profile image. So I looked her up on Myspace. There I saw three pictures from *Ski Haus* on New Year's. They were intimate pictures of her and a muscular Asian kid in a red Cortland shirt. She already had a new boyfriend. That desire I'd just re-embraced…it was dashed.

I looked at the pile of papers I was expected to data-enter for 8.5 hours a day for $56 dollars, and thought:

This is your life. It is worthless.

I stood up and said to Fatima,
"If anybody asks, I'm taking my lunch break early." Then I walked out and sat in my car.

Without admitting what I was doing, I pulled into a plaza I'd passed every day for the last three weeks. There was a liquor store. I walked past the liquor store to a shop that sold cigarettes, and bought a pack of *Camels* and a lighter. Then I walked back toward my car. Instead of getting in I turned around and entered the liquor shop. I bought a flask of blackberry brandy, like Kerouac drank in *On The Road*. Back in the car I lit a cigarette. I opened the bottle and drank a mouthful of the burning liquid, loving it for being poison and for burning. I lit another cigarette, and then another one. I was perfectly focused on spiting everything. I fortified myself with another chug and drove back to the office. I told the woman with the salt and pepper hair that I was sick and I couldn't work the rest of the day. It was true. She said she hoped I felt better. I left.

I entered my apartment still with that face like Robert De Niro when he's absorbing someone's insults, before exploding in rage. I threw the three-quarters full bottle of brandy on the table. It rolled and almost fell off, but didn't. I grabbed a bottle of *Seagram's 7* and filled half an Old-Fashioned glass. I held it up and started to say "Hello, old friend," but it seemed too flippant. I wasn't drinking because society said you shouldn't drink when you're unhappy…out of spite, like usual. That sort of thing was a game. It was an act, where I pretended to be an alcoholic because through pretending I convinced myself that I wasn't one. Now I didn't need to pretend. I was drinking because if I didn't drink I didn't know what I'd do, but it would have had permanent repercussions. I went to the record player and dropped the needle on *Getting Sentimental Over You*, but the sad chords were not sad enough. They were too soft and too slow.

"Fuck this shit," I said. I walked to *Lionheart*. It was drizzling. It was 3:30 in the afternoon.

"I'll have a shot of *Seagram's VO*," I told the broad-shouldered bartender. He poured me the shot and said,

"Four bucks." I paid him and drank the shot. Then I saw the scotch bottle on the shelf by the register.

"I'll have a *Dewar's* on the rocks, with one ice cube, no water."

"Startin' off slow today, huh?"

"I'm not gonna bother anybody," I said.

"That's six bucks. You want me to start you a tab?"

"Yes."

At five thirty exactly my mother called. I wanted to ignore it, but I figured someone had died, and I was right. I stepped outside and answered. She asked where I was. I lied and said I was at my apartment. I got sad when she started to cry, telling how her sister Michelle had died. She asked if I would be a pall-bearer. How could I say no after I'd told her all week, "If you need anything give me a call." I listened to her and promised to help, wondering how I was going to help her not to grieve when I was grieving and everything with my dad and his parent's, my grandparents, were already going on, building up on top of each other. There was no sense in trying to think about it because thinking was the problem. So I hung up and felt nice and exquisitely numb.

I first read *Helping* when I was in a creative writing course in 2005. I thought it was alright, but there were other stories I liked better. Now I declared to Morgan in the Downtube,

"*Helping* by Robert Stone is the best short story. He has it exactly right. It's the best description of alcoholism and why and how."

"What makes it so good? It speaks to you because it's about alcoholism?" Morgan sat in the window while I paced around the room.

"No, not that exactly," I said, drinking from a bottle of beer. "It's the imagery. And how you feel you're right there with the guy, and the ending is powerful. It's about a guy named Elliot who has been sober for a while, who works as a social worker. He's a Vietnam vet. Life is the daily grind, you know, but he's getting through barely. And then one day this guy assigned to his counseling sets him off. The guy comes in and he's trying to milk the system by acting like he has post-traumatic stress. He describes his experiences in Vietnam, but Elliot, who was there, knows he's making shit up because the way the guy describes things is all wrong and he's just reciting some shit he saw in a movie or something. So that sets Elliot off, and he gets depressed and feels trapped. Then you wonder where the story is going because there's this whole part where he goes to a library and makes small talk with the librarian and, especially as a creative writing student, you're wondering 'What has this got to do with anything?' But it has everything to do with the story, because Elliot has gone to the library because that's where he used to go before he got drunk, so by going to the library he has put himself on the path of falling off the wagon, and from there he can't escape because he's started the routine. Then the author does *not* describe him drinking. The story just picks up with him arriving home to a dark house with a cassette tape blaring music, and almost in passing, that there's an empty plastic bottle under the driver's seat. So right there you have masterful story-telling because most authors would think that the scene where the guy gets drunk is the most dramatic part and ought to be described. Anyway he goes into the house and then his girlfriend arrives home. She can tell right away that he's drunk and she's pissed off and disappointed. Elliot is simultaneously ashamed and annoyed. Somehow it comes up in the course of a conversation about the girlfriend threatening to leave that some douche bag threatened her that day at her job. She's a teacher or something, and some guy threatened her. So Elliot gets real mad and calls the guy even though the girlfriend says not to. Elliot and the guy get in a fight over the phone and the guy says he is coming over to kick Elliot's ass. That's just what Elliot wants, since he's pissed off. So he goes downstairs and gets his shotgun and loads it up and sits on the couch waiting for the guy to show up. Well, the guy doesn't show up and the girlfriend goes to bed. Now at sunrise the next morning Elliot wakes up still pissed off, maybe even more mad because the guy didn't show up, and he starts thinking about his neighbors who are a bunch of Yuppies who keep skiing on his property even though he marked it No Trespassing. So still itching for a fight he goes outside in the snow into the woods with the gun and decides he's going to hang razor wire where the neighbors cross his property. He chuckles thinking about cutting the neighbors in half. But he doesn't do it and eventually he realizes he's messed everything up. He is standing in the back yard and he looks toward the house and sees his girlfriend watching him from up there in a second story window as he's walking around the yard with a shotgun in his hand and a bathrobe on in the snow. Now he feels pretty stupid and wishes he hadn't gotten drunk and fallen off the wagon the night before. But he also knows that it's hard as hell not to drink and it's going to be hard as hell every day. He needs help. So he stands there and he drops the gun and he looks up at the window toward his girlfriend and he raises his hand to wave to her. He holds his hand up hoping and needing for her to wave back. And that's the most memorable line from the book, because in his head he is asking please, please raise your hand, give me a sign... he needs 'something to build a day on.' That's the key to the whole story: something to build a day on. That's what you need, because when there's nothing to build a day on you have nothing to hold onto and you start to go crazy."

"So, does the girlfriend wave back?"

"The story ends with him holding his hand up, hoping she'll wave back, so he can have something to build a day on, and that's the end. You don't know."

"Wow, so there's no resolution?"

"Right. That's why it's a good story. There can't be a resolution. If there was a resolution it would be fake Hollywood bullshit, like *It's A Wonderful Life*."

"They offered me a full-time job at the faceless corporation," I told Mike a week later in the Downtube window.

"Oh wow, congratulations!"

"I didn't take it."

"Wow, really? Why? What happened?"

"What happened is that I don't want to work in a fucking square gray building for a corporation. And I didn't like the way the guy talked to me."

"Did they say how much they'd pay you or what you'd be doing?"

"The big boss guy came over to my desk. He half-sat on the side of my desk and asked me what my plans were for the summer. I said I wasn't exactly sure, but that I knew I could work installing pool covers with Dan McCrary, and that I had a project I had to finish up and I would need at least two weeks free in order to do it. The guy said he couldn't guarantee two weeks free, or any days off for a while, but they were launching a new division where they'd be outsourcing work for the Department of Motor Vehicles, and they need a director to head up the new unit. He writes a number on a piece of paper and puts it down, saying they'd be prepared to offer me this. I turn it over and it says $34,000. I said thank you and I'm honored, but I need the time off in the summer. He looked at me like I was crazy and said 'Well, okay...If you want to install pool covers...go ahead.'" Mike seemed flabbergasted.

"Wow. I can't believe you turned that down. That's more than I make at the Comptrollers."

"Money isn't everything. I hate my job. I can't imagine being the guy who outsources data entry for the DMV is going to be that much better than the guy who data enters mortgage filings."

"Yeah but, still... I wouldn't have turned that down."

"It doesn't matter how much I bring home in a week if I'm despising every moment that I'm awake," I said.

"You're *that* unhappy?"

"What is there to be happy about?"

"Well, you're young. You're not that unhealthy."

"Wow with all that going for me I'm surprised I'm not jumping for joy every minute."

"Ha. Well, so what's this project that you have this summer that's so important you'd turn down a $34,000 salary?" Mike looked at the grin on my face. "Wait, don't tell me...You can't be serious. Another raft?"

"Shhh, I don't want Morgan to hear just yet. But...yeah. I've got a new plan. You in?"

"I think I need to hear the plan first."

"Okay, but not now. I've got some drawings to show you. This one is bound to succeed, as long as we plan it right and take into account the lessons from the first two boats." Mike looked at me askance.

"You really are a glutton for punishment, aren't you?"

VII. Working Class Animals

Morgan pulled his salt-speckled Subaru to the curb outside the funeral parlor.

"So, how're you doing, man?" Morgan asked after the perfunctory niceties.

"Good. How are you?"

"I'm good. But I mean, how are you doing after the funeral?"

"I'm fine. How was work?"

Morgan turned left onto Main Street in Ravena. We passed a block of boarded businesses, cracked windows, chipping paint.

"Work was fine. What do you want to listen to? I've got Billie Holiday and Miles Davis Quartet CDs."

"Miles Davis. Something upbeat. I'm tired of being dreary."

Morgan pressed a CD into the dash and up-tempo jazz spilled from the speakers. I rested my knees against the glove box and looked out the window.

"You seem like you're in a good mood. I'm kind of surprised. You know...with everything that's happened, I thought you might be pretty depressed."

"Bah, me?" I chuckled. I gazed sternly out the window. Dead branches hung over empty sidewalks. "You know, it's funny. It's like, yeah life is depressing as fuck. Why? Because you expect that good things are going to happen. And they don't. So it's constantly disappointing. You go to a funeral...I've been to a lot of funerals. So you expect it to be sad. But it's more like, comfortable, than most things."

"Huh. And your aunt was only 31 and died of cirrhosis?"

"Yeah."

"Man, that's young. She must have drank *a lot*..."

"She drank a box of wine every day and she popped pills and shit I'm sure."

"Was she depressed?"

"No I think she was pretty happy."

"Sorry that was a dumb question. I've just never heard of someone dying from cirrhosis so young."

"She had a lot of problems. She was never happy. She was really good-looking. She was engaged six times, and six times she broke it off. She was on a T.V. commercial for *FLY 92* one time. When I was a teenager and she was like 26 my friends who saw her at a party or something would be like 'Damn, that's your aunt?' Ha. Well, now she's dead."

"Are you sad?"

"I'm happy for her. Man, if you're really good-looking and everybody likes you and still you're unhappy...that must be miserable. I'm sad when I think about the last day of her life when she realized she was going to die and wished she hadn't killed herself. But that was just the last day, and the rest of the time she wished she could put herself out of her misery. Even Jesus asked God if, you know, maybe he could not get crucified after all, 'yet not as I will, but as you will,' and all that. So we're all *so* happy to be alive that we take that one day of regret that a person feels before they died and we say 'Oh, that was the *real* person coming out! They didn't *really* want to die!' But that's just what people say because really they don't want to admit that the person hated their fucking life for 99 percent of the time, and to force them to keep living is worse than letting them kill themselves. I've never heard this track before. I like this song."

"Well, still...it's sad that she was miserable and died so young when it seems like she had a lot of potential."

"Potential to get older and less good-looking and then run out of potential? That's probably what she thought. Everybody liked her because she was good-looking and fun. Well, that's great when you're young and people want you around to help them have a good time. But then if that's all you have, you must start to feel like nothing when you age."

"I guess that's true. I'm not really sure. I don't know if I really have experience with that kind of stuff with my family. You had an uncle that died from drinking when he was like thirty, too?"

"Uncle Steve. I think he was like 32 maybe. He didn't die from drinking. He was drinking and got in a fight with another guy who was drinking, who ran him over with his truck. It wasn't so much the drinking as the truck in combination with the laws of physics, you know..."

"Well, technically. But it seems like drinking was the common denominator. Not to put you on the spot, but...does that scare you?"

"Drinking?"

"Yeah."

"No I love it."

"Ha, no I mean...these aunts and uncles were only eight or nine years older than you. You do drink...often. I mean, are you afraid that maybe it could happen to you?"

"Cirrhosis?"

"Yeah."

"Man, I hope I die of cirrhosis."

"That's quite a thing to say."

"Well I don't mean it like that, but I feel like that is the least of my worries. Man I'm trying to get through today, tomorrow, the week. I'm hoping to live till 35. If I can do that I'll be successful. Do you mind if I smoke a cigarette?"

"Ha, no, go ahead. You want to drink some whiskey while you're at it? Or maybe shoot some heroine?"

"Chill. I've never done heroine and I never will. Needles make me squeamish. But if you were serious about the whiskey, yeah I'd love some."

"Okay...I don't really know why you're trying to get a rise out of me..."

"Morgan, I'm not. Okay, I'm sorry for being flippant or whatever the word is. The truth is that it just sucks, and it is what it is. There's nothing you can do about it. If you don't die of cirrhosis you die of lung cancer, or you die in a car accident, or you blow your brains out. Or some guy kills you as he's trying to jack your car, whatever. All I'm saying is, yes, I drink and I smoke, and in the long term yes, it's probably going to shorten my lifespan. But if it helps me get through the short term, then drinking and smoking are tools and not vices."

"I'm just afraid that it won't really help in the short term, and then you'll become addicted in the long term."

"I'm afraid that I'm going to hang myself before spring comes. So I'm going to cross each bridge when I come to it."

"Alright, alright...I just want you to be happy. I care about you, man."

"Thank you. That means a lot to me." It was quiet and maybe awkward so I kept talking. "You know what I hate about funerals?"

"What?"

"The whole fucking scene. It's like Christmas."

"Ha, I don't follow you..."

"Like Christmas, man, all bullshit and tradition for no reason. With a Christian bent. And suddenly everybody gets down on their knees and prays, which they never do any other time. And the priest is there, and the person's decaying remains lay there decorated with folded phalanges and a mother fucking set of rosary beads! God. Morgan, you're my good friend, right?"

"Yes, I hope you think of me that way."

"I do. Listen. I want to ask a big favor of you."

"Okay."

"If I die, I want you to promise me that you'll make sure my parents don't denigrate my corpse with religious shit."

"Man, that's a hard request. I mean, don't you think your parents will be upset?"

"Tell them that my carcass is *my* goddam carcass, not a prop in a play to dress up."

"Dude, I'm not going to tell that to your parents if you die."

"I don't want people coming and crying and kissing my carcass. Instead, there should be jokes and shit. People should show up and there should be midgets and clowns and juggling and stuff, something entertaining."

"I think people would prefer to see your body to remember you."

"Hopefully they won't need to see my rotting mother fucking corpse in order to remember me! Jesus Christ, am I that forgettable?"

"Haha, no."

"And my body isn't *me*. It's like the leftover turkey bones and organs after thanksgiving. Who gives a shit?"

"People are attached to the body. It reminds them of the person."

"That's bullshit. Just tell my parents to save the money and throw my body over the hill where we put the leaves every fall."

"Haha, Jesus man."

"Or if they want to have a big ceremony with lots of meaning, they can put my body on a raft, douse it with gasoline, push it off from Coeymans and light it on fire."

"Might be a navigation hazard."

"Oh oh oh! No! I know what I want. These people want to come and see the body so bad? Fine. Print up a program and distribute it before the wake. Then I want my body laid out naked on a steel table under a bare light bulb. In front of the body there should be all kinds of hand tools. Pliers, a Philips-head screw-driver, an awl, a hacksaw. Tell the people that if they want to see the body, fine. But in order to see the body, they have to use one of the hand tools to extract a bone from my dead cadaver!"

"Oh, come on man, Jesus Christ!"

"Wait wait wait...the flier should say in big letters: 'Come Early If You Want The Teeth' ha ha! Because those would be the easiest bones to extract! Ha ha ha. Can you imagine? My little girl cousins trying to pull out like, my femur or something? Aha ha ha!" Morgan couldn't help but laugh at the ridiculous proposal, no matter how hard he tried to be serious. He started laughing and then he had a hard time stopping. "Now I'm serious Morgan, this is the last wish of a dying man, if I die. I'm entrusting you to see this through."

"Ha ha, okay, man. You better leave me some detailed instructions for when I talk to your folks."

"Ha ha, okay. I'll write my last will and testament on a series of cocktail napkins and staple them together for you. I'll keep it in the bathroom under the toilet paper. That way all my most important papers will be together and easy to locate."

Morgan laughed, "I'm really happy to see you laughing again, however morbid and obnoxious the subject matter."

We laughed in the car because we needed to laugh because we were too stressed and serious. Anxiety is like static electricity that accumulates in the air. That's why we describe the mood of a crowd by reference to 'atmosphere'. It's not *like* a physical phenomenon in the air. It *is* a physical phenomenon in the air. Instead of electrical energy, a kind of social energy accrues. And as when electrical energy suddenly channels in the form of lightning, so too does social energy build until we say "You could cut the tension with a knife." ER doctors and nurses laugh as they try to piece together the intestines of a gunshot victim over the course of a six-hour surgery. Desperation is not merely frightening; it is psychically destructive. So we were laughing in the car, to compare small things with great, because it had all gotten so morbid that we needed a release.

When I was an adolescent, I used to read books about alternative medicine, paranormal abilities, UFOs, the Bermuda Triangle, the Philadelphia Experiment, conspiracies and such. One of the books told the story of a man with cancer whose prognosis was six months to live. Refusing to spend his last months in pain and sadness, he quit his job, invited his friends over all the time, bought all of his favorite funny movies, comedian acts, old slap-stick television shows, and spent the day watching such stuff and laughing. Supposedly he went back to the doctor after doing that for a while and all the medical people were astounded because his cancer was gone. Throughout my teens and early twenties, then, I always said that if I ever got cancer, that's what I would do.

"I feel like I have stomach cancer," I said to Mike one day in his new apartment. After living at his parent's house for seven months he decided he'd to move into the second floor of an apartment in the college ghetto of Albany. His roommates were kids two or three year's younger than us, who were moody and into harder drugs. Mike was the older guy who lived in the third room who had a job and saved his money and therefore was the oddball.

"Why do you think you have stomach cancer, Dallas?" Mike asked skeptically. We'd just squeezed furniture into his tiny room, so that there was hardly space to stand. So we went down the apartment's dilapidated back staircase and sat on a piece of plywood that served for a porch in the rear mud yard.

"I didn't say I think I have stomach cancer. I said I feel like I do. Or, like, I feel like I'm on chemo. No, I hate to say that because I've never been on chemo and I have no idea what it's like. But the way I feel every day—nauseous, head-achey, not hungry...I feel like it's hard to breathe and there's a finger pushing on the soft spot at the bottom of my esophagus. I never appreciated how...well, how it must *feel* to be on chemo. Like, weakness; no energy. No wonder people struggle to go through it."

"Yeah it's no joke. Radiation kills rapidly-dividing cells. That's what cancer is. But that's what your hair is too, and your stomach lining. Your stomach has to keep regenerating so it doesn't get burned up by your stomach acid. So then you get radiation and your stomach lining stops replenishing and your stomach acid eats away at it. So you're pretty much fucked because you have to get the radiation to kill the cancer, but now your stomach hurts, and you don't want to eat, so you start to waste away. You know the Hudson Valley has a higher incidence of throat and lung cancer than most of the United States, thanks to the cement plants and shit. That's why ear-nose-and-throat doctors come here. It's a gold mine. Ha, you know, like our high school. Who decides to build a school for kids right in the middle of a cement factory, with the quarry behind the school and the conveyer belt running next to it, and across the road the fucking smoke-stack spewing black shit all day long? The town must've got the land for cheap. On the announcements in the afternoon, remember? '*Blue Circle* will be blasting today,'—ha ha, so that we knew that when the building started shaking it wasn't a bomb or an earth quake. It was just the cement plant. Oh, good!"

"Yeah. I did a video project on *The Jungle* by Upton Sinclair for AP History. I went out on the roof of the school dressed as an immigrant and used the smoke stack and whatever-the-hell-else those metal contraptions are for a backdrop. At least it was interesting to watch the gravel fall off the conveyer belt and make a huge mountain of stones. I always wanted to play King of the Hill on that."

"When I was a kid my sister used to call the smokestack a 'cloud-maker.' She thought that's where clouds came from. 'Nope, it's where soot and carcinogens come from, little girl!' Did you know that *Blue Circle* used to pay *Boxley's Automotive* to give free car washes to people if the wind changed and blew ash over the town? Jesus Christ. My fourth grade teacher said in the seventies they used to come out and have a millimeter of dust on their parent's car that they used to draw with their fingers in. I wonder if in like thirty years they'll be a massive Love Canal style lawsuit against the place. The place should be shut the fuck down. And it's what everybody thinks of when they think of Ravena and Coeymans. It's the place with the smoke stack. There should be a revolution and the people should go to the place with pitch-forks and torches and shit and burn it."

"Well, it's the *people* that want to keep it there. Or, at least, the old-timers who've lived there their whole lives and don't want anything to change from what it was like in 1950...and any, like, report on it being unhealthy is a lie put out there by liberals. Like my dad and his friend Muck. I was complaining to them one day about how when I was a kid and I went with a girl from another school to her prom, the other kids in the limo found out I went to Ravena and were like 'Sweet school with the smoke stack.' Dad and Muck got all defensive like I was an enemy jihadist and went on a tirade about how the cement plant better not close or Ravena will be a ghost town, and how when they were kids they were happy to work in dirty industrial facilities, and that's the problem with the generation today, they don't want to work and they don't care about small towns."

"What'd you say to that?"

"I wanted to say the town already *is* a ghost town, because when you're young and looking to buy a house you don't buy one in the town with the big fucking smoke stack that sprays soot on the town, across from the school where your precious babies are going to go, and that's why the mean age of the town is like 50 years old, and why the fuck would young people want to stick around in a place where the older generation just grumbles and complains about them? Like, it was *your* generation that killed the small town, dude, not mine. I'd love to live in a small town if there was shit to do and young people and a culture that wasn't anti-intellectual and bitter. But yeah, I didn't say any of that, of course, because it was my dad and his friend and I was outnumbered and on their territory. So I said nothing."

"Way to make a stand."

"What would be the point?"

"Yeah, you would've just gotten your dad mad and yourself mad. I guess that's why small towns all across America are dying if not dead already. The politics is all incestuous old families that never want to change. Like Ravena with its Mayor that's been in office for what, like 25 years or something? And keeps getting elected as more people and businesses leave every year. 'Wow, this guy's doing a great job! Let's elect him to another term!' Ha ha, fucking stupid, right? So instead people like you and I move out so we can live in great places like this!"

Mike gestured toward the back yard. It was a field of mud with a few blades of grass here and there. A broken wooden fence separated it from the mud yards of the houses to the right and left and on the next ghetto block. Three black kids who were not yet teenagers moved though the holes in the fences to get from one 'yard' to the next. There was one big oak tree which rose higher than the buildings with its leafless branches juxtaposed against the gray, Sunday-afternoon-in-January sky. We watched a squirrel as he picked up a discarded tennis ball container and held it in his mouth as he climbed the tree. It took him a while to get three stories high. He kept slipping because the tennis ball container was as big as he was. When he got higher than the buildings we said "look at that" because he arrived at a certain limb where there was a bunch of leaves in a pile at the end of a branch. It must have been his nest. We watched, fascinated, wondering if he'd make it, as he started balancing himself on the branch while still holding the tennis ball container in his mouth. It was quite an act. "Oh!" we watched him slip and almost drop the container, but recover, ending up upside-down grasping the branch with his hands and feet. He climbed back upright and crept forward toward his nest. The plastic cylinder would make a great water-proof room for him in his nest, we understood. This whole process took the squirrel about fifteen minutes. Just as he got to the nest he fumbled trying to hold onto the branch while also turning the cylinder around in order to push it into the leaves. He dropped it and it took a couple seconds to fall back down to the mud.

"Ha ha!" Mike laughed loud and mockingly so that his mock reverberated off the dirty vinyl siding of the nearby apartments. The squirrel looked at us and, I swear, he said *screw you guys* with his eyes. He understood exactly that Mike was laughing at his misfortune, and we understood exactly what his posture and squinting eyes said back to us. It was clear communication, so much so that Mike actually straightened up a little and remarked, "Wow, that squirrel is mad at us." The little guy sat there for a moment, defeated. Then he started back down the tree, toward the spot where the tennis ball container had fallen.

"I like squirrels," I said.

"They're funny," Mike said. "But they can also be nuisances."

"I like squirrels and I like crows. Crows are my favorite kind of bird."

"Crows are dirty and they shit all over the place. Plus they're scavengers."

"That's what I like about them. I remember once in high school I was driving to school in a bitter mood. I stopped at the stop sign at the corner of New Baltimore Road and 9W. There were two crows pecking at a dead raccoon that had gotten run over. They were trying to get some meat but a big 18-wheeler was coming. They tried to fly, flapping their wings with intestines in their beaks like spaghetti stringing back down to the carcass. They had to drop the intestines and flew off just in time to avoid getting smashed by the truck. I chuckled and said aloud, 'Ah, the things you have to go through to get a hot meal.' I feel like I understand crows and squirrels. They're like, working-class animals."

"Ha ha, yeah. They're like our grandparents with their lunch pails going off to the railroad or the factory every morning, giving their wife a peck on the beak. 'See ya later, ya young crow. Now, you mind the nest while I'm gone.' Then they take off for the city to earn their living. Except instead of little chunks of metal and strips of paper as pay, they get food and shit to build their nests with."

"And instead of dying of cancer from the factory, they get run over by cars or eaten by cats. Ugh. I wouldn't want to die from a blunt injury or to have my intestines pecked as I'm still in the process of dying. But at least it'd be fast, relatively speaking. When I was a kid I always thought if I got cancer I'd be a survivor, because I'd do a million things like watch funny movies to keep my spirits up, and the positive thinking would be clutch, and I wouldn't allow myself to get down, I'd refuse. But jeeze, I don't know now. I guess I didn't realize just how much the constant headaches and nausea and weakness would wear you down. Like, it's not the baldness that makes people depressed and therefore less likely to get better. I mean it's not just psychological morale decay. It's the constant sickness every day that makes you start to wonder whether you even want to keep living if the rest of your life is going to be like this...like that, I mean... When you're healthy you forget how much it sucks to be sick, and you tell yourself you'll just suffer through it if you get sick and keep working just as hard and being just as happy. Then you get sick and you realize you have this physical body that really can't do whatever you want it to do. Like, it really is limited...it can't just keep working because you want it to. People don't get sick and die because they stopped wanting to live and then just got lazy and thought one day 'I'm going to stop trying.' Sometimes you really want to try but your body just can't. Jeeze, I just got a chill. It's like what they say about young people and how they think they're unstoppable and immortal, and then they get old and they realize they're not. It's kind of true. I think I think about death and dying more than most people. Not in an emo way but like, because I was forced to because of having a big family and having people die and my grandparents living next door and always feeling pressure to be with them because they would be dying soon."

"Grandparents are hard. I guess because they're so nice to you because they don't have to raise you, and you see them when you're young and they're usually the first to go, so as a kid they're the first lesson in like, 'Hey, she was nice, she can't die' unfairness. I think that's what you're saying. I donno if you had a point there."

"I donno if I had a point. I was just describing a feeling, or a new way of thinking or feeling that I just thought of. Is that the same as having a point?"

"Yeah. The point is you had this new thought, that things are unfair. You just didn't make it well because it got scrambled up in other thoughts."

"But that wasn't the point. The other thoughts were the point. I'm not saying things are unfair. They're not unfair. They're incredibly fair. The squirrel drops the tennis ball container; the crow has to let go of the entrails; Muck and Dad have to live in a town that is different than what they pictured it would be; Mom has to bury her sister...But look at that fucking squirrel, man. He's trying again!" The squirrel had retrieved the plastic canister and was once again climbing the tree. This time he held the canister so that the open-end faced his mouth. That way if he made it to the front of his nest he wouldn't have to turn the thing around up in the tree. He'd learned from his mistake and had the foresight to manipulate the canister on the ground, where it was easier. "That squirrel is going to get that canister into his nest, and then he's going to be pretty proud of himself. If he could talk he'd say to the other squirrels, 'Yo, you gotta check out my nest, man, I got this canister in there. The shit is pimp.'"

"Ha ha, squirrels talk like gangstas?"

"Well look where his tree is, man. The ghetto."

"Hey, my apartment's here too!"

"Right, but it's the ghetto. But so what? It's a step up from living at home, right? Or else why would you have moved out?"

"True."

"And you have a job and you only have a six-month lease, and you'll probably get a better place in six months, right?"

"Right."

"Because that's what you have to do. You have to work, and you have to tell yourself that it's going to get better."

"Yeah."

"Just like the squirrel. He's working too, and soon he'll have a better house. But look, man. There is a big difference between my dad and Muck complaining about dying Ravena, and you and the squirrel. Dad and Muck are just complaining, helpless. Nothing is going to change because they live in a place with a whole bunch of people who never try to improve anything. That's their *shtick*. But the squirrel doesn't complain. He acts. And you know who fucking symbolizes that best for me? My grandfather. I mean talk about finding yourself in a situation that almost anybody would consider hopeless. Two ninety-year-olds, one with dementia, crashing down a hill and breaking bones in the woods in the sleet and freezing night. You know? I don't know what *I* would've done. I can't believe he left her there in the car, alone. That must've been the most painful experience of his life. But it was exactly what had to be done. And to get up that hill in the freezing rain and sleet at ninety with a bum ankle? Falling down three times like Jesus Christ? That must've been hard, man. But he did it, because it had to be done. And I'm sure at the top of the hill he was praying to God that he'd see some headlights so he could flag down a passing car, but he didn't. So he ran a mile, at ninety after being in a car accident, wet, after having not ran for what, probably fifteen years? He never had a reason to. And then he did that. I mean I am astonished. I can't believe it. I find it superhuman." I put my hand to my forehead as my eyes darted upward and to the left and right in their sockets. Then they rested and I nodded. "He is my hero. I've never had a hero before. But he is a great man." I paused, then added, "If I could be half the man that he is, I will be successful."

"Maybe you should tell him that," Mike said. And in fact I did, a year later, write him a letter in which I said those things. Grandpa kept that letter and asked my mother to laminate it for him, and told my father that he wanted to hang it on the wall, and that he read it every day. It was a tiny payment from me to him, in exchange for his character, which through emulation would become the most valuable asset I would ever possess.

VIII. Sine Waves

"Life is like a sine wave," I said to Morgan in the window as I paced. I grabbed paper and drew a wave, like a *tilde* or an 's' that fell over. "Life is like a sine wave that goes up and down. Sometimes you're going up—things are improving—sometimes you're going down—things are declining. But the sine wave itself has a trajectory." I lifted a corner of the paper so that the wave angled upward generally. "So like, if you're here, at the bottom of one wave, you've declined compared to where you were a little earlier. But even at the bottom of that particular wave, you're higher than you were at the top of this wave back here. So like, finding yourself in the middle of a setback, your conditions might be, in general, better than they were at best years before. So that's the trick, really. You've got to keep your sine wave generally angled up."

"You know I think you're right," Morgan replied after a silent moment. "Like, I've been thinking about going back to school. I'd like to study psychology. I've got a great subject for a case study living in my apartment. Ha ha, just kidding. But seriously, I don't want to work at bullshit ODSF forever. That's like a sine wave that's not going up. But to get on track to be a psychologist, I'll have to do a lot of stuff that makes my present situation harder. I'll have to take eight undergraduate courses at SUNY in order to pad my resume and take the requirements for applying to grad school. I'll have to study for the GREs, which will be a lot of work and take time. It'll cost a lot of money...probably about three-quarters of what I've saved up working at the State for a year. So that's like being at the bottom of a wave, at least as far as money is concerned, compared to where I am now. But it points the sine wave way up, because now it's headed in the direction of getting paid a hundred dollars an hour for doing something I like. So then, let's say I'm successful and I become a psych. I do well for a couple of years. Then there's a year where I lose some patients or something, and I only make $75,000 instead of one hundred and ten. That's a setback, relatively speaking. But relative to right now, $75,000 is no setback at all. So I definitely see what you're saying. It really depends on what you're comparing it to and how far you want to go back. I mean you can always go back to when you were a year old and compare your life to that, and you're always going to be better off than when you were shitting yourself in a playpen prison."

There was a process, for me, that was almost mechanical. I'd experience an unfortunate setback. I'd list the misfortunes that had already occurred, consider how long anything good takes to blossom, and wonder whether I had enough patience and tolerance. I'd question whether I'd ever experience conditions sufficiently felicitous to justify the work, loneliness, scrimping and planning. Reason based on extrapolation suggested I'd never earn rewards that compensated for my effort.

I felt disqualified for happiness. The things I enjoyed were out of fashion. Perhaps I was over-sensitive in a world of vapid commercialization. It was foolish to think I'd be happy without the space-time-continuum changing.

I'd stop planning, trying to work harder than other people, and go on autopilot. I'd grow spiteful of my own condition, neglect my health, and throw out perversely morbid jokes. That stage would last for perhaps a week, until the lack of self-care, the drinking, the lack of sleep became physically painful, and to rise from bed or go to work or visit my family became torturous. Then I'd shed even the morbid humor. Nothing was funny. Everything was impossible. Life was unsparing. Somehow I'd been born into a world which, merely by coincidence, was particularly set up such that I could never succeed. I didn't feel self-pity, but I wished I could stop feeling and thinking. Then I'd drink just to speed things up, to drown the repeating sounds and images with louder noise and brighter lights.

Then, at the bottom, like "the prodigal son" that my father sometimes called me—he squandered his patrimony and found himself eating from a trough with hogs[13]—there was Guilt.

You are a waste of life.

That was the physical part of me talking. The part that preceded civilization, the reptilian brain.

What is your problem?

It was the part that never articulated under normal circumstances. Un-sparing, critical, focused, yet honest, sympathetic and reasonable. It was the one part without bullshit, where the buck stopped. It was The Body personified.

Your life is so hard that this is how you treat us? This is where we end up, again and again?

There was an opportunity for another part, The Conscious, to speak. But it had nothing to say. It was guilty, red handed. So the primal part went on.

_____

[13] Luke 15:11-32.

Boy, it must have been so hard for you, growing up a white male in the United States of America to a family of average income. What struggles you must have faced, you know, with two parents and enough food and family vacations and a public education. I guess you had it harder than some kid born in Africa or South America or China or Siberia. Your parents must be so proud of you. Good thing they saved up and spent $20,000 on your education, sent you on school trips to Mexico and Florida and Boston, "fronted" you the money for vehicles that you never paid back and ran into the ground. What a great investment they made.

It was calm, quiet, slow, at the bottom. No distractions. Everything shut off. The higher functions had all abdicated. Like being on stage after the setup and rehearsals and preparations, after the other actors had gone home before the big day. And only one light shined down directly. And finally instead of a character — an object of other people's attention — I was the subject, looking out.

The primal part would stop with the sarcasm then. I was shamed into listening, and that was all it wanted. It wasn't sup-posed to have to speak. But since it was speaking, there was no need to be cruel.

Look, I don't ask for much, do I? You are in charge, and that is fine with me. I don't calculate and plan. That's your job. And whatever you calculate and plan, I do. But how about a little help? A bare acknowledgement of my existence? I don't need to be showered with appreciation, but give me a break. You know, maybe a meal every once in a while that has some nutrients in it? Maybe some sleep that isn't poisoned by alcohol? Is that asking too much? I think I do a pretty good job with the minimal resources you provide. I keep working as you run me into the ground. But I have limits. Please, move us to the grocery store. Actuate my arms to put pieces of food into the cart. Go home. Move us around the kitchen. Actuate my arms to prepare the food. When it is prepared, actuate my mandible to masticate, and swallow. I will take care of the rest. It's really not that hard. Then you take over again, and that's fine and great. I never interrupt you. I am trying to have full confidence in your abilities. Eat and drink water and figure out ways to bring us into the company of females. And the vast majority of the time, after you get to those things on the bottom of Maslow's Pyramid of Needs, do whatever you want to divert yourself. Read, have conversations, watch T.V., sit around and don't do anything — I don't care! But come on, I need just a little piece of your attention. We are not living in conditions that require me to be so neglected. Compared to other countries and times we are fabulously well-provisioned. The only problem is your failure to take advantage. Your one real responsibility.

"You know," I said to Mike one night in the beginning of February, "with our technology and everything, we really live better, even us working class people, than kings lived in previous centuries. The variety of foods and drinks we can eat, our medical care, the places we can travel and the sights we can see, our music and theatre entertainments, our access to images and books...it's more than any absolute monarch could enjoy with all his fortune and power a century ago. It's amazing. We really are fortunate."

It was the beginning of the next wave: sweeping optimism after abject despair. Every action triggers an equal and opposite reaction. It started simply enough.

"I think it's time we cleaned up," I announced to Morgan the next night.

"The place *is* getting a little gross. Hmm...I want to get my two hours of GRE practice in. How about we clean for an hour? I'll take the kitchen and you can do the living room. I know how you hate touching the dishwater when there's floating food."

"That sounds great. And we will stop after one hour. No need to kill ourselves. Slow but steady wins the race. We'll do a little cleaning every day, and in a week the place will be clean. Then we can just stay on top of it. 'If you clean a little every day, you'll always have a clean house,' my grandmother used to say."

An object in motion will stay in motion. So, having started to up the sine wave, I moved with momentum. Over a week I saved money, drank less, ate better, exercised, and therefore felt better. I noticed improvements and they were encouraging. They reinforced my recently-remembered-optimism.

But the problem with living in cycles is that the extremes caused the cycles to repeat. Since it took reaching depths of squalor, debt and bad health to trigger virtuous behavior, there were many messes to clean. Before the good behavior paid dividends, late fees had to be paid, cars and apartments cleaned, emails returned, my body repaired. Since there was little real improvement to be expected for quite a while—first I had to do a hundred chores just to get back to being 'even', I thought—I had to really convince myself that it was worth the effort. It had to be a new chapter, a fundamental change. I told myself that "it" would be hard and boring, but I had willpower and industry and spite. Sure, it would take a long time for things to improve, but that was fine. In the long term I would win, whatever life threw at me.

I pictured a struggle: *me* versus *life*. That was helpful to get back to "even"—a clean apartment and enough money to pay my bills. But then that energy and momentum was bubbling and brewing, and there were no messes left to clean.

"Here is my new life plan!" I announced triumphantly to Morgan, who sat in a wheely computer chair in his room, in the middle of his two-hour block of GRE studying on Sundays, Mondays, and Wednesdays. "As you can see I have divided the day into fifteen-minute segments. I will rise at six a.m. every morning and jog. Just the four blocks from here up to South Main and back for the first week, but adding a block each week progressively after. I'll make a good breakfast after my morning shower and shave, to give me the energy I need to work for 8.5 hours. At night I will make a good dinner from 5:30 to 6:30. Then from 6:30 to 9 I'll take a bath and read forty pages. I have a list of books I've been meaning to finish and now I finally will. From 9 to 11 I will write. Then at eleven I will have *Sleepy Time* tea and sleep from midnight to six. By sleeping only six hours a night I will save two hours a day or 14 extra hours a week. Both my physical body and mind will be taken care of, and I should accumulate $75 in savings per month after all bills are paid, including paying back personal loans to you, Mike and Jared. Saturdays and Sundays are the days when I've scheduled particular necessary tasks like laundry, cleaning up around the Downtube, and visiting my parents. With this plan I'll be back on my feet in no time!"

Morgan cautioned that such a plan left no room for relaxation or diversion. But that was irrelevant, because a week or two back into the up-swing, everything was based on the idea that I was *exceptional*.

"I don't need the same amount of sleep as most people do," I said. "Sleep is a waste of time. Pinel in his *Biopsychology* book talks about how sleep gets more efficient when you get less of it. Six hours is more than enough. And it's not like I'm planning to run a marathon every day, that's why the plan starts out with only four blocks. Plus reading is a diversion, and I've scheduled a two-and-a-half hour bath every night. How relaxing is that? 'A change of task is as good as a rest,' right?"

"But there's no flexibility. All your time is planned out."

"That's the point. That's the beauty of the plan! You know, you can sit around wondering what to do, and then you go to the bar, right? I mean, that's what I do. Now there's no wondering what to do. I have a plan! I will follow it military style. That's it. That's all I have to do. All I have to do is pretend I'm George Patton or somebody in boot camp. Then, you know, I get home and I can picture myself like one of the Founding Fathers, burning the midnight oil to pump out an important argument in justification of the new Constitution. Yes, yes yes!" I banged my fist into my palm.

It is only in a vacuum that a moving object will stay in motion indefinitely. In the real world an object in motion will slow *if acted upon by an outside force*. The universe is full of outside forces. By this stage in the sine wave I'd have nothing to suggest that my intricate plans would pay off except for a clean apartment and papers with plans. That was better than what a lot of people my age had, but I was looking for prodigy-level accomplishments, immediate, large rewards to show that the plan was succeeding. After all, the basis for it was my recently-remembered exceptionality! There were no such indicators. So in order not to lose confidence and willpower, which would cause me to deviate from my plans, I sought reinforcement from everyone I knew. Every conversation with Jess, Mike, Morgan, Jared, my parents, or any other acquaintance I ran into, became a verbal dissertation on my plan, the power of optimism and determination. Their confidence in my ability was the added energy I needed to keep going at the same speed. I had to keep going at the same speed, or faster even, because any deceleration signified a change for the worse.

"Fast but steady wins!" I said to Jess. "That story about the rabbit and the tortoise, it is stupid. They shouldn't teach it to children. It makes them lazy."

"Umm, I think you're missing the point of the story. There is no such thing as fast and steady."

"No no, *you* are missing the point of the story. The point of the story is that the rabbit was a fucking moron. Who goes to sleep when they're in a race, just before the finish line? The point of the story is not to be a cocky asshole, and to finish what you start. Then you win!"

"The rabbit had to stop. He was tired from running the race so fast."

"No he didn't! That's not in the story. You're just making that up to support your argument, because you know I'm right and you love to take whatever point of view is the opposite of mine, in order to argue."

"Ha! If I'm always arguing with you, it's because you take obnoxiously wrong-headed positions that don't jive with reality."

"Reality! Ha! From the girl who says there's no such thing as Truth and everything is relative, blah blah blah. According to your point of view, if the rabbit really believes he won the race, then he did!"

"To him he did, if he really believes it. Who's to say otherwise?"

"Come on! That's so stupid. To everyone who is not delusional, he lost. Fast but steady wins, whenever it is pitted against slow but steady."

"Nope."

"Yes!"

"You can't be fast *and* steady."

"Yes you can! Relatively speaking. Look, the whole point of that story is stupid or misconstrued. It's the 'steady' part that's key. If the rabbit had been fast *and steady*, he would've won. So the point of the story is 'be steady.' But there is no reason we ought to therefore put a premium on slowness. The premium is on steadiness."

"The steadiness comes from the slowness."

"Oh my god. You're doing this on purpose. You cannot believe what you're saying!"

"Dallas, Dallas, Dallas. You keep telling yourself that you can run ten miles a day and read a thousand pages a day and sleep for five minutes. You'll see."

"Jess, Jess, Jess. I was just making a simple observation about how stupid that story is. It has nothing to do with me."

But of course it had everything to do with me. I could usually stick to a plan like that for a few days, and in those few days I'd update everyone I'd told about the plan, to prove to them that I was following though. They'd nod and have to concede that I was doing what I said I'd do, and that would keep me going. Then after a few more days I had to talk about other things because people grew bored with my conversation. At that point I lost their reinforcing energy. So, in order not to slow, at this stage I'd announce new, grander plans.

"I am going to do another raft," I told Morgan. "I don't care what it takes or who is going with me. I don't care if I have to do it myself. I'm going to study every inch of the river with *Google Earth*, I'm going to take my time and really design it well, and I will succeed. I don't care if it takes me the whole summer to get there at a mile an hour."

"It's going to be tough to build something like that on your budget, and take a month off of work. Don't you think you should find somebody to help you first, to share the burden?"

"I don't care what it takes. If I have to quit my bullshit job, I'll do it, and I'll get another one when I'm done that is just as mind-numbing."

"Where will you build it? At your parent's house? I mean, you don't live there anymore. Will they mind?"

"If I have to build it in the middle of the woods next to the river bank, then that's what I'll do. That's the thing. Everybody always looks at a project and lists the reasons it can't be done. All it takes is to take the first step and start. Then deal with the problems as they come up, one step at a time."

"Well, good luck. *Carpe diem.*"

Carpe diem. Seize the day. Morgan and I had made that our catch phrase as we worked toward our goals, he slowly but steadily, a little every night; me massively, fast but steady, to make up for lost ground. Everything was possible. I heard about a coin hidden in the woods somewhere in Greene County fourteen years earlier by a historical society, with a cryptic story and a map that had clues describing where it was. No one had found it in all that time, and if found it could be redeemed for $14,000. I was going to find it, I told everyone, so I accumulated maps and Wikipedia articles on cryptology and historical records and dozens of pages of notes where I listed the first letter of the first word of every paragraph, or of every sentence, or ciphers of these letters. I kept all the notes in a three-ring binder. I had dozens of short stories and plays I was going to finally publish. I spread them on the dining room table to be edited and submitted. As soon as I was done getting to New York City on a raft I was going to plan a rafting trip from Albany out the Erie Canal to the Allegheny River to the Ohio River to the Mississippi River to New Orleans. Then I'd write a book about that. In fact what would probably happen was that I'd find the coin and get the $14,000 and quit my job and use some of the money to build the next raft while I edited and submitted my writing, which would then start to be published just about as I got to New York City, so that I'd be a published writer, so that I could write a book about rafting to New York City which would fund my next trip down the Mississippi, and then I'd write a second novel about that and probably be able to retire on the royalties, and that would show Jess that fast and steady wins, and everybody else who said I couldn't do all the things I said I was going to do.

It was ludicrous and at some point the motivation shifted from my friend's encouragement to a desire to spite them. To show them I was really exceptional. I had a picture in my mind of a time when everything would come to fruition at once. Then everything that happened over the last year or two years or whenever I was unhappy would be history, and I'd talk about it the way some old Senator or robber baron talked about the set-backs of their youth, before they worked themselves up by their bootstraps to be masters of their fate. Everybody would be really proud to know me then. Hell, maybe I'd even run for Mayor of Ravena with all the money I made, and fix the place up so my dad could sit on a porch and talk to passersby, like he always wanted. Imagine how happy that would make him. And my mom could retire from the job she disliked. And I could pay to have a live-in nurse take care of my grandparents. God, everybody's lives would be so much easier! All I had to do was just fast-forward a little and then everything would start happening, and it would be great.

That was what the top of the sine wave was like. It was all so simple, it seemed, like clockwork. As soon as one thing started happening, one of the gears would start turning, and that would turn the other gears and it would all play out like a mechanical device. All I needed was to get just one of the gears moving, it didn't matter which. It was so obvious how it would all work that I couldn't understand why Mike or Jess or my parents refused to see it. They must just be cynical, pessimistic people with no imagination or confidence. So I stopped telling them about my plans because it was a waste of time. It was all up to me. No one was going to help. It was all up to me and that was fine, because I had the plan and the will and the energy.

But then, gradually, parts of the plan would fall off. The first thing to go was the clean apartment. It filled with papers and notes and plates and cocktail glasses and cigarette ashes. Morgan said, "Time to clean, *carpe diem!*" and I said "I can't tonight, I've got to focus on finding the coin in the Catskills." So the sink overflowed with dishes, and then the counters, and then there were mice running around leaving droppings on the countertops. But that was alright, I rationalized. Everybody has different working styles. The place was just organized according to how I needed things organized. I'd clean things in a little while, when I was successful and had time.

The next to go was the laundry. The clothes piled up in the closet, and then on the floor of my bedroom, so that the first thing I saw everyday was a mess. Now there was no proof that my plan was working at all. But I wrote this off too. When I was rich I'd buy all new clothes, and I'd have the leisure time to wash and fold them. In the meantime I didn't have the time to take care of such trifling inconveniences. And really, now that I thought about it, it wasn't that important for me to read for two and a half hours a night. Reading was a long process of accumulation that could be delayed. And then in the morning one day I was tired and it was still dark at 6 am, so I hit the snooze button. Running could wait, too. Running was counterproductive, I rationalized, because I needed all my physical energy to go to work and then do more work at home, and also if I didn't run I'd have an extra hour to sleep in the morning, so I could go to bed later, and that meant doing more work at night.

Soon there was no food in the house and I should've gone shopping. But that wasn't necessary either. It took a lot of time to shop and cook, time I didn't have. I'd stored energy in my body over the last few weeks so I could go without good food for a while, just eating bread and frozen pizzas, enough to stop my stomach from growling. People were too concerned with getting enough sleep and eating three square meals with such and such portions from all the food groups every day, like they'd die if they didn't. I knew better.

I felt the nausea and headache growing again. To "unwind" I allowed myself a few beers. And to smoke a few cigarettes. I drank black coffee to stay up and concentrate until it was almost time for bed. Then a few more cocktails to fall asleep. Soon I was sick and tired, saw a mess all over the house, and nothing signified that my plan was working.

"Work hard, play hard!" I said to Morgan. After all my hard work, I needed to blow off steam so that I could focus again. A night at *Lark Tavern* would do the trick. So we went there and made conversation with the cute bartenders and the girls we saw. And that was the point of everything, right? To make it with girls. So why not go to *Lark Tavern* two or three or four or five or six or seven nights a week? That would improve my chances of meeting a girl. And if I had a girl, I rationalized, everything would be tolerable.

The girls were out at happy hour and then again between about ten and two. So the best time to go to the bar was between six p.m. when I got home from work, and two o'clock in the morning. It doesn't take a lot of imagination to see what that kind of lifestyle did to my wallet and sleep schedule and all the plans that required constant work.

Soon nothing was going right and I was wasting time and money and exhausted again. When you're depleted and frustrated, everything becomes annoying. Work was a big pain in the ass and I hated it. Why did I have to go? If I could just spend my time on some productive thing. Or at least make a little more money, or do something interesting. *But all jobs are like, boring and demeaning, so suck it up.*

The questions started popping up. *Is this really working? Will you be able to manage this? Will you ever really be happy and able to relax?* The important thing was to push those questions out of my head so they didn't hijack my mood. It took longer and longer to push them out. More and more noise to drown them. The extra noise made it hard to focus on anything. Now I was barely balancing up there, like a tightrope walker.

I know I'd been at my parent's house for dinner on a Sunday night. I know it was Sunday because I remember wheeling their garbage can to the end of the driveway after dinner in the dark. Walking back I saw the moon through the trees and it seemed so lonely. I realized the place where I'd grown up caused such sadness, and for that reason it was *dangerous* to go there.

I know I was driving back to Albany, and it was before nine o'clock, because Morgan and I had a standing appointment on Sunday nights at nine to sit in the window and listen to Marion MacPartland's *Piano Jazz* on NPR. I was driving up Route 144, where there were no street lights, coming north out of Coeymans, with a view of the Hudson on my right, reflecting the moonlight. Cady texted me. I think we'd sent each other a few texts just to inquire how each other was doing, nothing big. I suggested we catch up on the phone, because I was driving, so that would put a time limit on the call. I wondered if she'd agree, or say no, or just not respond for a half-hour so that I'd be done driving and there'd be no reason to call rather than text. And then instead of texting me back, the phone rang.

That alone shouldn't have done it. It was nice to hear her voice. I'd forgotten how savory-sweet she sounded. It was just casual hey how are you doing, how is class going, how are your folks talk. It couldn't be more than that. Asking about her love life would be a bridge too far. But then she asked if I was seeing anyone, and I said no, and that meant I got to ask her the same question. I remember her tone became cautious and she prefaced whatever she said with "Dal..." to signify that something touchy was coming. Then she fleshed out some of the details. His name was Chris. They'd been dating since early December. That was when she 'knew' that 'we' weren't going to get back together. She was so lonely, Dal. School was hard. She needed somebody. He'd been persistent. They met at *The Red Jug*. He was a sports guy. She pushed him away but he kept coming back, determined. He cleaned her room for her and bought her flowers. He did her math homework for her, and without that, how could she pass her math gen ed. You know how hard a time I have with math, Dal. You remember me flunking that course at Nassau Community College. It wasn't love. He was more into her than she was into him. But it was something.

"Something to build a day on," I said.

"Yeah, that's it. You know. I'm sorry, I shouldn't have told you this. Are you okay?"

I said I was fine and it was nice catching up with her and I was glad that she was happy, sincerely, really, because that was the thing, I said, I didn't want her to be unhappy. That was my biggest fear, I said. She said are you sure you're alright and I said yes, I'm glad we're able to talk again like friends, because that was what I regretted, that our friendship suffered. She said okay, good, that makes me happy, but I really want to know that you're not upset. I said I was fine and it was good talking to you and I was parking in front of the Downtube and had to go. She said Oh! How is your apartment! I wish I could see some pictures. I said oops sorry I really have to go I need both hands to parallel park but thanks for calling and let's talk soon. She said okay are you sure you're alright. I said yes, take it easy. She said Take Care Dal. I hung up.

Then I remember standing in the dining room of the apartment and all the lights were on. Morgan wasn't home. I stood in front of the dining room table with the papers on it.

Then I remember standing in the bathroom and looking in the mirror. I looked old. I remember thinking "How old am I again?" Twenty-two seemed way too young. Thirty-five seemed more realistic.

There was no noise, there was nothing. I just looked out from my eyes like an automaton. I walked out of the bathroom and sat at the table. The only feeling was a heavy sensation in my cheeks, like they were tugged by gravity, so I was conscious of having to keep my chin clenched. To keep my chin clenched required a lot of energy, so I had to breathe deeply and rapidly through my nose. My chin muscles weakened so I had to scrunch my face to keep my mouth closed, and tighten my stomach, and press my fists into my armpits and bend forward a little.

Then I have an image of Morgan's safety razor in front of the toothbrushes on the left side of the sink in the bathroom. It had a blue handle and two blades. Then I have an image of Morgan's safety razor sitting on the dining room table. Then I have an image of just playing around, sort of rubbing it on my left wrist. It was okay to drag it in this direction. It was not okay to drag it in that direction. There was a lot of significance in the difference between those little movements. I tickled the two cords in my wrist with my index finger. Then I closed my eyes and said,

"What the hell are you doing?"

I didn't have an out of body experience in that instant, the way I sometimes do if I completely lose my temper. It was good that

I did not. Instead I started crying, because that is what people do when they have no other way to rid themselves of their frustration, and it is too much to feel. The numbness wore off, and I found myself back in reality. I held the razor with two fingers, like I'd carry a bomb, back to the bathroom. I put it back exactly where I'd found it, so Watson wouldn't know. Then I felt scared, which I seldom do, because it seemed like I couldn't trust myself, and if you cannot trust yourself, what else is there?

I thought a change of scenery was in order, so I crossed the street toward *Lark Tavern*. It was one thing to drink and smoke yourself to death. That was masculine. But slicing your wrist or hanging yourself or eating pills or even blowing your brains out, that's weak shit. Drinking and smoking was like challenging the universe, or spiting it. But what would people say if I had actually used that razor? I couldn't have thoughts like that anymore. Not even fooling around. The repercussions were too serious to play with. Or, like Elliot in the library in *Helping*, it was too dangerous to start upon the opening stages, without admitting I was going there.

"Something has to give," I thought as I started down the sidewalk. The question was what, or how.

IX. Detox Week

"There are nights when I think that Sal Paradise was right:
'Boys and girls in America have such a sad time together.'"
-Hold Steady, *Boys and Girls in America*

On Valentine's Day, Mike, Jess and I met at my apartment to smoke cigarettes and drink black coffee.

Mike arrived around nine. It was snowing for the first time that year, and pretty hard. So it was a novelty. He said *burrr* as he came in and shook the snow off his peacoat. The Downtube was nice and warm because we had free heat. We ditched the black coffee in favor of *Keystones*. Morgan joined us for a brew in the window.

"Here's to Anti-Valentine's Day!" We cheersed our frosted mugs. I said it was appropriate that the day was so cold, and that it would be funny if we saw some lovers slip and fall in the snow.

"That reminds me of a great GRE word I came across the other day: *schadenfreude*," Morgan said. "It means like, taking pleasure in other people's pain. I thought it was a good word because it describes an idea that I understand but never really thought about before. Obviously it's a German word. It's funny how other languages have words for different ideas, and until you learn them you almost don't appreciate the concept."

"I read somewhere that if you don't have a name for something, you almost can't understand it," I added.

"I guess it makes it hard to think about it or conceptualize it," Morgan said. "I think I heard you use the term before, but you called it, like, *schwartzenfroid.* But in the context you were using it, I thought it meant something like, when you go outside and see a bum crying in the rain and you enjoy that."

"I think that's more general *misanthropy*. Like, that's more just hating people and hoping they suffer. I think schadenfreude has more of a...personal...it's more personal," I said.

"Yeah I think it has an element of envy to it. Or revenge, almost. It's not so random," Morgan added.

"Yeah I think it means more like, if my ex-girlfriend fucked some dude and then he got in a car accident or something," I said.

"Well yeah I'd certainly enjoy it if that happened to someone who fucked my ex-girlfriend," Morgan said. Mike, who had not participated up to now, added,

"Me too."

There was silence while we pictured dark thoughts. Then we heard Jess yelling "Dallas!" from down in the street. I threw my house key out the window and she let herself in, saying *burrr* as she entered and stood in the doorway in the kitchen.

"Do you want me to take off my shoes?" Jess called.

"It doesn't matter," I shouted.

"Yeah, the place is pretty messy," Morgan shouted. "Dallas has been in one of his manic spells where everything gets piled up as part of his organizational scheme."

"The Obsessive Compulsive Advantage!" Jess yelled. "Well, what is *order* anyway? I'm taking off my shoes. Boys, boys, it's so good to see you!"

When Morgan finished his beer he left us to go into his room to study for the GREs for two hours. He left his door open, so he could keep half an ear on our conversation. Meanwhile Jess, Mike and I got comfortable. It was nice to watch the snow fall with my friends that night. It was exactly what I needed.

"So, tell me about the new raft," Jess said.

"Ummm," said Mike.

"We haven't decided for sure if we're doing it yet," I explained to Jess. "I learned my lesson last time. I don't want to do it alone. I really want to do it, but I need a dependable *coadjutor*. You hear that Watson?"

"*A colleague or partner on a project*! Nice GRE word!" Watson called from his room.

"Look how intelligent these two are becoming, between bouts of alcoholism," Jess remarked.

"I don't abuse alcohol," I said. "It abuses me."

"Ha ha, okay."

"Anyway, the thing is in the drawing board stages. I don't want to do it unless Mike comes, though."

"Okay, let me see the drawings," Jess said.

"It's in the *pre*-drawing board stage," Mike corrected. "We haven't gotten that far yet."

"Well that's not exactly true," I said coyly. "You see I'm confident that Mike will sign on eventually, so I've come up with some ideas."

"It starts again!" Jess exclaimed.

I rose from the bar and grabbed a hanging file folder from a small cabinet. I had a sketch inside. It was an overhead view of how I pictured the next boat. Picture a square with a triangle adjacent on the right, and two beams running lengthwise, holding another, smaller square to the left.

"What's this?" Mike asked.

"This is the height of practicality. It's simple and straight-forward and foolproof."

"The height of practicality is a fiberglass boat with a gas engine," Mike admonished.

"Not as far as rafts are concerned," I said.

"Okay. But that's because rafts are totally impractical. Hence why nobody uses them. Hence why it's kind of a flawed idea right off the bat. I mean, I'm not saying I won't do it, but let's be realistic about it. Whatever we design should be strong and able to move through the water, and it should keep us dry...Whatever we do it's gonna to be hard. You've failed twice already. It's not gonna be easy. That's why I'm not sure if it's a good idea to try it or not."

"Mike, where is your sense of adventure?" I said.

"I left it in Coeymans the day the first boat took off."

"Oooo, Mike sounds like he'll take some convincing, Dallas," Jess said.

"I'm not here to browbeat anybody," I said. "If Mike's going to join in, it should be of his own accord." Mike nodded to this. "But again, basically it's foolproof. So you see, this is an overhead view. The plan is to get two docks donated to us."

"*Two* docks? Where're you gonna get those?" Mike asked.

"On the last trip when I went to Shady Harbor they said I could take docks and pointed to a pile of 'em. I think they'll give us two more."

"Okay, go on."

"So we take one dock and that's the main structure...the middle square in the picture. We make sure the dock we take floats on foam instead of barrels. They have both kinds. If it floats on foam we know it can't sink, like the barrels. So there is the main problem that we had with the first raft solved, right?"

"Well, yeah, as long as we make sure the foam is attached well and doesn't float off or something. But yeah, okay."

"We take the other dock and we cut one corner off in the shape of a triangle, that we attach at the front of the dock. Now, this second dock is essentially our lumber pile. It also has the cleats and the hardware from the dock, so we know it'll be strong."

"What's *hardware*?" Jess asked. "I thought that was like, tools."

"It's the nuts and bolts and braces and stuff," Mike explained. "The metal stuff that joins pieces together, like screws and nails. Docks have special custom-made brackets at the corners where the wood slides in and the bolts go through, so it's really strong and won't fall apart." He turned toward me. "I like what you're saying because like, with this design, there'd be a big metal bracket corner piece right at the front—because it will be the corner of the second dock. So if we smashed into anything, that metal piece would be there. And there'd be a lot of strong wood that we'd already know is pre-treated and waterproof, since it's a dock. But the thing would be heavy as hell. I mean a dock weighs like, what? A thousand pounds? Where are we going to build it and how are we going to get it to the river? We can't lift two thousand pounds. That's like almost a ton. I'm not sure if you could even put that much weight on a trailer."

"See, Jess? This is why I need Mike's help. A ton is like two thousand pounds? I don't know that stuff. Or, if I had to estimate the weight of a dock...I have no idea. Or how much a trailer can hold. Why couldn't a trailer hold a ton?"

"Well, some trailers could, but I don't know if a regular one could. It depends on how much weight the axels could hold."

"Huh, see? I never thought of that. I always thought an axel was an axel. It's a big piece of metal and the wheels turn on it, so why couldn't it hold indefinite weight? But now I get it. The trailer rests on the axels, so the weight could bend them, because they're made of metal!"

"Yeah exactly. And there are joints and bearings and stuff. All that stuff absorbs the stress of the weight pressing down."

"Okay, so we'd have to find a good trailer, or diminish the weight, or perhaps a dock is not really that heavy. We'll find some way to get it to the river. Anyway we take all the deck boards off of what remains of the second dock, and we build a solid, permanent cabin structure on top of the raft. We cover it in plywood. It has fold-down windows and a door at the front and at the back. You can stand on top of it, so we'll have a ton of deck space, and you can also walk around it because the width of the cabin will be three-feet less wide than the dock, so there will be a foot-and-a-half of walking space around the outside of the cabin. Then we build a quality paddlewheel and put it at the back of the boat, for propulsion."

Mike paused, perusing the picture, then postulated:

"Would it be possible to take the foam out...or maybe stack the foam from the second dock beneath the foam from the first dock...and shape it? What I'm thinking is...could we make the foam into maybe four pontoons that sit deep in the water? Deep enough so that they push up the wood of the dock, so that the wood doesn't touch the water? That way we'd only be pushing four pontoons through the water, instead of trying to plow a dock through the waves."

"If we put our mind to it, I'm sure we could do that."

"And maybe we could cut the foam at the front, into the shape of a triangle, like the bow of a boat, so that it's more hydrodynamic."

"That also sounds like a good idea," I said.

"I'm not sure I follow you on the paddlewheel idea though. Didn't you try that last time, and it didn't work?"

"Well, yes...but that was the first time I tried it. Now I saw what didn't work and you and I I'm sure could design a better one, having learned from the experience."

"It just seems like a lot could go wrong with a paddle-wheel. And then when it does, we'd have this big weight we were dragging along behind us for no reason. And how much power would it really give us? I mean it might be better to just find a couple more people to go with us and give everybody a paddle when we need to steer, and the rest of the time just float."

"Anybody need a beer?" I asked, rising. Mike said yes. From the kitchen I said, "There are a couple of problems with that. The first is 'just finding' some other people to go with us. If we could find a couple of other *dependable* people who bring something to the table, sure, I'm down. But I couldn't find any for the last trip. And then without a means of propulsion...I'm not sure Mother Nature will really let us down the river. You've got the tides, yeah. But then, a raft sticks up a lot further out of the water than it sits in. The wind seems to blow upstream in the summer. When the wind and the tide are going in different directions, the wind wins. I learned that on the last trip. So we need something to push us through the water." I handed Mike a *Keystone*. He snapped it open.

"We could try and sail. How hard would it be to build a mast and a boom and a tarp for a sail? If the boom was mounted at the height of the top of the cabin, you could sail from up there."

"Could you? I don't know what a boom is, or like, anything about sailing. The wind is coming up from the south, so it wouldn't be pushing us in the right direction."

"Right but the wind doesn't *push* when you're sailing. I mean it does if you're going downwind, but that's not even the fastest. It's fastest when the wind is blowing from the side. I don't know the physics, but I've heard it described as like, squeezing a bar of soap between your hands. You're pushing inward, but the soap goes shooting outward. You can go a lot faster than the wind blows. And the *boom* is the pole at the bottom of the sail that's attached perpendicular to the mast, so you can move the sail at different angles to the wind relative to the longitudinal axis of the boat."

"Wow," Jess injected, "perpendicular, longitudinal axis...I feel like I'm back in Mrs. Cushman's math class junior year."

"'The best angle to approach a problem is the *try* angle,'" I quoted from the poster Mrs. Cushman had taped to the cement block walls in the back of her classroom. Mike and Jess rolled their eyes. "If you want to do a sail, man, and you think it would work, I'll help. But I don't know anything at all about sailing, so it would have to be like, your thing."

"Okay. You know another thing that we could do is a rowing station. If we mounted it at the front of the boat one of us could row from there."

"...Well I was thinking we'd have two rowing stations. We could each sit on one side of the front with a paddle."

"Right but *paddling* isn't *rowing*. They're two different things. When you paddle you use...a paddle...like on a canoe...you know, you use the top half of your body to row on one side of a boat with a relatively short paddle. You face forward. When you row you use oars which are attached by oarlocks to the side of the boat, and you row two oars at once, one on either side. You face backwards. And the oars are longer and therefore you get more power." I was starting to understand.

"Ah...it's like, a mechanical advantage thing? Like on a lever?"

"Exactly."

"Okay," Jess said. "So there is enough raft talk for now. You're both doing it."

"Uh, no," Mike said. "We're just talking about what we would do *if* we did do it. There's still a lot that could go wrong that Dallas might not have thought of."

"Right but that's the whole thing," I said. "If you agree to help, then none of those things will go wrong. You'll be right there to see them in the development stages to address them. I'll be there to keep, you know, working away at getting the thing built, and you can provide the expert advice we need." Now Jess pounced on me.

"Oooh, Dallas...doesn't that sound a little *circular*? 'Like in the Bible how it says that God is God and you know 'cause it's in the Bible and God wrote it in the Bible?' Ha ha ha. So Mike is afraid to join in because the raft might not work, so you tell him to join, and then the project will work; so since if he joins in, the project will work, there's no reason he should be afraid to join in? Ha ha."

"*Touchette*," I said. Morgan called from his room,

"You know that means *I've been touched*, literally…it comes from fencing and it's the person acknowledging that his opponent scored a point. It's a gentleman's game."

Mike surprised me by coming to my defense.

"It's not really circular because Dallas is right, what would be different this time is that I'd be able to help design and build it, which I haven't before. So that breaks the circle. Or creates a new circle, or something."

"Yeah Jess, so stop being such a *square*," I said.

"Maybe we should just take a rhom*bus* to New York City," Mike joked.

"Yeah, this whole thing looks like a big pain in you guys' rect-um-angles," Jess laughed.

"I hope we're not walking into a trap…*azoid*," Mike said. We laughed and drank and Jess finished her glass of wine. Rising to get another, she closed the conversation with,

"You guys are ridonkulous." That last word, and how she said it so casually as though it was a real word we didn't know…it was just the kind of thing Jess would say, that nobody else I knew would've said. It was funny and unexpected but also in its own way annoying in its urbanity.

"What the hell is *ridonkulous*," I called after her. Jess did not turn to respond, nor did she speed her pace toward the wine decanter. She just kept walking slowly, with her nose pointed upward and her hands down at her side, fingers erect and curving out from her hips, like a woman from the 1940s.

"You know, it's *ridonkulous*," she said. "It's a word."

"No it's not," I declared. "I've never heard of that word." Jess lifted the decanter.

"Has it occurred to you, Dallas, that there might be words that you haven't heard of before, which exist nonetheless?"

"In fact it has, and this is not one of them."

"Oh, here we go! Dallas hasn't heard of a word, so it doesn't exist."

"That's not what I said." Jess held her wine glass in front of the ceiling light and swirled the red liquid around.

"Until Dallas hears a word, it's not one. Mike, did you know that before July, 1984, there were actually no words?"

"Jess…"

"And then there was this period between July of 1984 and when Dallas started to speak, where the only words were like, *goo goo ga ga, oouchie poo poo wee wee ma ma da da pee pee poo poo*." Mike grinned because I was standing tapping my hand on the side of the bar with my lips pursed.

"Jess. I know that there are words that existed before me, and if I never developed hearing or the ability to speak, there would still be words. Because that's reality, and everything is not relative, despite what you say. Don't project your flawed ideas of truth onto me."

"It's a word," Jess declared, coming back toward Mike and I. "I can't believe you boys haven't heard it before."

"We haven't heard it because it's not a word. It's some slang thing that you and your friends made up at Ithaca."

"Ha! We didn't make it up. It's a real word."

"Well...what does it mean?"

"Oh, I don't know...just how I used it. I'm not the dictionary."

"You know, Socrates would say that if you can't explain something, you don't understand it."

"Socrates *Schmocrates*," Jess said. "What does he know?" That was just like Jess, to sweep away with one grandiose statement two and a half millennia worth of human insight and philosophy. I pointed to the eleven platonic dialogues on the *Greek Philosophy* section of my bookshelf.

"You could, you know, read some of these books here if you wanted to know what Socrates knew."

"Ahhh, of course! That's why Dallas is annoyed! Ridonkulous is a *new* word, and Dallas loves everything that's old. Old equals good for Dallas," she adopted a caveman's voice, "new: bad!"

"Oh, okay, you got it Jess. I'm some arch-fucking-conservative. That's me."

"You dislike it because it's a young person's word and you won't find it in the Oxford English Dictionary at the State University Library. And anything that's not handed down as knowledge from the structures that be...it can't be real for you."

"Are you serious?" I exclaimed. "I'm not like that. I think you ought to be able to just tell me what the word means. Is that too much? Like, how is it different than 'ridiculous'?"

"Is it a really good eye doctor?" Mike suggested. "You know, like a *ridic* oculist?"

I joked, "No, it's an actor with really good timing. Some-one who is *ridic* at being on-que: *ridic-on-que-list*."

Mike went on, "Imagine Morgan studied his piles of GRE words for hours every night for like a year, and memorized them all, and then went to take the GREs and was like, destroying the test—he has a perfect score—until the last question, and it's like 'define Ridonkulous', and he gets it wrong?"

"Oh my God that would *be* ridonkulous," Jess laughed.

"It would be absurd," I said. "So...it means like, 'ridiculous to the point of absurdity'?"

"Right, obviously," Jess said.

"Obviously! Ha," I laughed.

"Yeah," said Mike, "I get it. *Onk* sounds more absurd than *ic*, so if rid*ic*ulous is foolish, rid*onk*ulous is crazy foolish. Makes sense. It's like, I've heard that *duck* is the funniest animal, because of its name."

"No way," I said. "A platypus is the funniest animal. The first part of his name starts with something that sounds like *splat* or like, a beef *patty*, and his name ends with the first part of *pussy*. Plus he has like, all the most ridiculous pieces of other animals all glued together, like God was making a joke. He's got like, two webbed feet but no arms, so he has to waddle. A duck bill..."

"He's got a tail with lines that looks like a *waffle*," Mike said. "Another funny word."

"Yeah and like, a white body with a green head that's balding. Haha, poor guy. Does he also have a unicorn spike?"

"No!"

"Well, he should! That's all that's missing."

"What would a platypus need a unicorn spike for, Dallas?"

"Why, for carrying donuts, of course!" We all laughed picturing this.

Watson emerged from his room and stood behind us. He cleared his throat.

"Boy, what an intelligent conversation you three are having. I excused myself to study, and I didn't realize the education I'd have received if I'd stayed right here."

As we sat up drinking, the snow kept falling in large and frequent clumps. The passing cars no longer left black tracks behind them. The snow accumulated on the sidewalks and in the road as high as the tops of the tires on the trucks and cars and continued to flutter down.

Out of novelty and nostalgia we played the radio, rather than my Window's Media Player. I the dial to "FM/Stereo" on my grandmother's phonograph from the late 1950's, which served as a buffet in my apartment.[14] As it turned to early morning we heard the D.J. announce school closings. These grew lengthier each half-hour, until it seemed that every local school was closed. Then the D.J. announced that some state offices were closing as well. So Mike called a number and found out that the Comptroller's was closed, so he didn't have to work in the morning. We drank a beer to celebrate. With all of those other places closed, I figured, hell, I couldn't be expected to go to work in the morning either. I would have to get up about two hours early just to get there on time, and maybe I wouldn't be able to get there at all. So I declared that I wasn't going to work in the morning either, and we drank another beer, and then several more, until we fell asleep at my place at I forget what time, nice and warm in the apartment with the snow falling silently outside.

The next morning the snow was still coming down hard. It had piled up as high as the mirrors on the parked cars. Nothing had been plowed. So I was safe not going to work.

We felt like we were in *Little House on the Prairie*. I thought about that Whittier poem, *Snow Bound*, where the family gets trapped in their house in a blizzard, and how they passed the time in there. Morgan left for work but Mike and Jess stayed. It was nice and warm and we were together as friends, so we boiled a big pot of water and made hot cocoa. Mike and I dragged the bar to the middle of the room, and then picked up a couch and put it in the window so we could sit and look out. We drank our hot cocoa and watched a brunette march with snow up to her hips to her car with an orange plastic shovel. She held the shovel over her head and took a shovelful off of her roof. Then she looked around, defeated.

I had some *Kahlua* so we spiked our hot chocolates. Then I said I wanted to hear some Hawaiian music to juxtapose our warmth inside with the abominable conditions outside. So I rolled a big cushion-topped chest out of my bedroom hall. It was filled with

---

[14] For almost 15 years I've wanted to resuscitate my grandmother's old phonograph. I've brought it to every apartment I've lived in. My grandmother was going to throw it out after forty years, because it stopped playing records, in 1999. I discovered that although the turntable didn't work, if I rotated it with my finger, an internal apparatus was actuated which dropped a single record from the central pole, then shifted the needle-arm to the circumference of a record, and descended. I needed only to procure a motor that moved at exactly 33 RMPs, and install it. But over the years I've never managed to do so, and it continues to serve as my newer-record-player- and decanter-*holder*.

records that my grandparents had accumulated over the years. We started taking these out one by one and laying them across the floor.

"I love the cover of this one!" Jess said, holding up a record. "*Songs for Grieving Lovers*, ha ha, wow." The cover showed an ashtray with a cigarette burning on a white cloth-covered table, next to a half-full wine glass in the foreground. In the background, out of focus, was 1960s-era furniture and the body of an elegantly dressed woman from the neck down, her hand and arm hanging off a couch, as though she was fainting.

"I love the descriptions on the back of the albums," I said. "It's like...someone took a long time to write these things. Listen to this, from the back of "The Voice" record of Frank Sinatra hits:

'*Next time anyone starts asking questions about what has happened to the snows of yesteryear, the easiest answer will be found in playing this collection of songs. For here they are, just as soft and caressing and artful as they ever were, perhaps, with the passage of time, a little more so. The girls who used to slump into swoons or stiffen with hysteria at the New York Paramount have exchanged their bobby socks for apron strings — ha! — and the Paramount no longer even has regular stage presentations, but Frank Sinatra remains one of the most sensitive singers popular music has ever produced. The program offered here is vintage Sinatra, from the period of his greatest initial fame; here The Voice has its incomparable texture, with that peculiar effect of singing almost into one's ear, and here too is the uncommon communication of ideas that is usually confined to recitalists on the concert stage.*

'It goes on for four more paragraphs! Can you imagine a kid today having the patience to read a description like that? He wouldn't understand half the words!"

"The *NOW 23* doesn't have descriptions, just lots of bright colors and tits," said Mike.

"And the description down here at the bottom: *For the best reproduction of your records, play them on a COLUMBIA phonograph. COLUMBIA, THE GREATEST NAME IN SOUND, is the originator of the modern 'Lp' record and the '360' phonograph. Your dealer can demonstrate a varied line of COLUMBIA phonographs, styled to enhance the decorative scheme of your home. See him today for the pleasure of your life!* Ha! That's funny. Today you just go to *Walmart* and buy a mass-produced-in-Japan CD player to sit atop your mass-produced-in-China IKEA pressed-board bookshelf. Everything is so cheap."

We found three Hawaiian records and played them and started drinking some rum to celebrate our good fortune at not having to go to work that day. I cooked a frozen pizza. We danced around. After the Hawaiian records we started pulling out my grandmother's polka records and playing them, but they weren't as good. Every song sounded the same. As it got to be mid-afternoon Mike said he'd better go home to shovel his car out. I'd lucked out because I'd parked on the "even" side of the street, but he was on the odd side and he'd have to move his car for the snow emergency that would go into effect at 7 that evening. So he took off for an 18-block *Shackeldon* trek uptown, telling Jess and I he'd be back later, and Jess and I continued carousing. It grew dark by 5 pm. Around 6:30 Morgan came home, saying *burrr* and shaking the snow off his peacoat. He said he shouldn't have gone to work. It took him almost three hours to get there and he was one of only two people who went to the office. That made me feel a little better about not going to work that day. Then Morgan made a sarcastic remark about how nicely we'd cleaned the apartment, since the bar was in the middle of the room, the couch was in the window, records cascaded over the floor, and empty beer cans and the cardboard from the frozen pizza were strewn on the radiator. Later that night Mike returned and he, Jess and I drank and played 500 Rummy until midnight. It had stopped snowing by then, and Mike asked if he could sleep on my couch and walk to work from there, because then he'd have a 20- instead of a 45-minute commute walking in the morning.

Waking was hard after drinking the day before, which followed a half-day of drinking. Consciousness felt impossibly heavy. I shuddered when I thought of rising and showering and all the rest...digging out my car...there was no way. So I pushed the curtain aside and looked out the window. It was still a mess out there, although a convoy of snow plows and dump trucks was flashing yellow lights in the dark morning. I told myself that work would understand, and fell back asleep.

I woke up again around nine thirty and rolled around. I got pretty nervous for a second because I realized 'work' would be wondering where I was. I was losing that credibility I'd man-aged to store up over the last two months. I rolled around feeling vaguely anxious, drifting in and out of sleep until eleven.

I stumbled out from behind the louver doors that separated my bedroom/hallway from the rest of the apartment and started to throw soft objects at Jess who laid on the couch. She asked if there was anything to eat. I said there was only oat sodas and cracked open a beer. She said "Umm I'd like something I can chew" and laughed but there was really very little to eat in the apartment. We debated walking to *Dunkin Donuts*, which America runs on, but it seemed like a far walk, since it was across the street one block away.

We hadn't had the *Dunkin* yet, so we didn't have anything to run on to get there, we laughed. So I made us some white rice boiled in beef broth with a tablespoon of butter, which my father used to call "Consumean Rice" and was the only thing he knew how to cook.

Cabin fever was setting in. We took a box of old papers off of a shelf in my closet and I showed Jess some of my old writing back to third grade. We looked at some old pictures from high school. We had a two person dance party to '50s records. Then I had to go dig my car out. I came back and said *burrr* as I walked in, brushing the snow off my threadbare, hand-me-down blazer. I was very proud because a big presumably homeless guy had asked me if I wanted to pay him $10 to help dig my Neon with bald tires out of the snow, and I said no thanks. He stood there watching me, saying "It's going to take you an hour, man! It's only ten bucks!" I said I knew what I was doing, because I'd shoveled my car out more than three times, and I'd have the car out in ten minutes. He laughed and said no way. He'd have dug all around the car to free it up, but I just dug out from in front of the back wheel and two tracks in semicircles in front of the car where the wheels needed to get traction. No sense in shoveling the snow off the top of the car and all that. Then I got my car out in under ten minutes and he couldn't believe it. Jess and I read through some of the plays we'd been in together in high school. Then we went to *Lark Tavern* and had a couple of drinks.

Mike had to walk past us in order to get home on his 45-minute commute, so we texted him and told him he owed it to himself to stop into *Lark Tavern* for a beer at happy hour. We texted Morgan too. We had a good time there and ate meals consisting of substance for the first time in two days. You know, meats and breads and cheeses, all in one bite...crazy. Then since we were buzzed we decided to let the evening wear on back at the Downtube.

"Do you ever think like, maybe we should take some time off from drinking and smoking?" Mike asked, after midnight.

"Oh come on, you're ruining my buzz," I joked.

"No...seriously though. I mean...do you ever think we drink a little too much?"

"Yes," Jess said. "I do. I mean, jeeze, I feel like crap lately. I hate to think about the effect that these binges have on my body."

"Yeah and we do this almost every day. I mean Dallas, when was the last time you went a day without having a drink?"

"Hey why is this about me?" I parried. Neither Mike nor Jess smiled, so I got serious too. "You know honestly...it's probably been about four years."

"Wow, four years without a single break? That's an alcoholic."

"It's not that I'm drunk every day. Actually it's very seldom that I get drunk. I'm not sure it's an *alcoholic* alcoholic. I mean look at the way Jared and those guys drink. They don't drink Sunday through Wednesday, then Thursday, Friday, Saturday they have twenty beers and get blackout drunk. I can't tell you the last time I was blackout drunk. Sometimes I wish I could get blackout drunk and I can't. I get sick to my stomach before that. Maybe because I don't do shots. They make me want to puke. But anyway, yeah...sometimes it gets to be the end of the day and I'll think, Hey! I didn't have a drink today! But then I'll remember I had a beer on my lunch break or a glass of wine while I was reading in the bathtub or something...and it's been like that since my freshman year of college."

"I think sometimes we forget that it's bad for you," Jess said. "Like, it's called in*toxic*ation because it's toxic. In Europe the cigarette packs have pictures of charred lungs on them. Maybe beer cans and liquor bottles should have skulls and crossbones."

"It's also like, a medicine though," I said. "You know, people also die of heart disease and other stress ailments. Alcohol takes the edge off and makes life tolerable sometimes."

"I just want to know that I could go like a week without it," Mike said. "I think I'm going to take like one week off."

"I think that's a good idea," Jess said. "Me too."

"Oh come on. What are we, a bunch of born again Christians or something?" I protested.

"No Dallas," Jess admonished. "Born again Christians are not the only people who forego drinking for a day. You might not care, but some people actually value their bodily health."

"Me? Why, look at me! I'm the *scion* of personal health. A *paragon* of virtue! You hear that Morgan? Oops...I forgot he was sleeping. Maybe we shouldn't be yelling so much."

"I'm just saying like, starting tomorrow I'm going to go a week without drinking or smoking, to prove to myself that I can," Mike said.

"I think that's a great idea, Mike," Jess said. "I'll do it with you." It was awkwardly silent as Mike and Jess looked in my direction.

"Okay, fine! I'll do it with you guys," I said. "It would be nice to know that I can do it too. But a whole fucking week? That's going to be pretty hard."

"Detox Week!" Jess said. "I think it's a great idea. What will we do instead of drinking?"

"Watch T.V.?" Mike offered.

"I, for one, would like a little company if we do this, and I don't watch T.V.," I said. "I think we ought to be able to hang out with one another socially without drinking. We used to do it. We used to stay up at the Hafensteiner's house until 6 in the morning laughing and telling jokes and eating pizza. That's what we should do. Let's do what we used to do like, when we were kids, when we didn't drink. Why can't we do that stuff anymore? Like, I've got all my old *Sega Genesis* video games down in New Baltimore. How long has it been since you've played one of those? That'd be fun. I could bring those up and we could hook them up in the living room and play. I've got *Legos*."

"I've got all my old *Legos* too, in a box. We could set them up someplace and rebuild all the sets. Between the two of our collections we could have a big scene and we could take a picture."

"I like it!" I said.

"I'll get some coloring books," Jess said. "Why not?"

"Yeah, why not? Drawing used to be fun."

"Ha ha, okay," Mike agreed. "So the Downtube is the base of operations for Detox Week then?"

"Perfect. tomorrow we show the world that we can go a week without drinking," I declared.

"Or we fail miserably and have to go to rehab," Mike semi-joked. "But at least we'll know one way or the other."

***

The sun came through the window as I drifted from one nightmare to another, except now my eyes were open. My mouth tasted like garbage; my tongue was a dried-out rag. I reached for the glass on my nightstand. It was empty.

After six months I still dreamt of her. By that point probably because she personified loss to my sub-conscience. My arms embraced an empty pillow.

I rolled off the bed onto a pile of clothes, slid on a pair of pants and a shirt. I kicked open the louver doors to the living room.

"Wake up," I said.

Jess did not wake up.

I went to the bathroom. The cabinet door had fallen off the sink a week ago. It lay on the floor. I knocked over a beer bottle slapping my face with water. The new-fangled light bulb Morgan had installed was too bright. My reflection had dark circles under the eyes and a ten-day beard. I rubbed my hands through my hair and dry follicles fell. I lifted a toothbrush then lost motivation and dropped it on the counter.

"Wake up," I said.

"Ugghhh."

"It's ten thirty. I got fired a couple of hours ago."

"What?" Jess lifted her head.

"I got a sweet voicemail saying I'm fired."

"Hold on." With some effort Jess shifted onto an elbow. "Give me the details."

"Umm well remember how we had that big storm three days ago and I didn't go to work the next day?"

"Yeah—but nobody went to work."

"Right. But most people went yesterday and today."

"Well, did you call them?"

"No. So they left me a voicemail saying, 'Since we haven't heard from you in three days we think it's best to find a replacement.'"

"At least they were nice about it."

"Yeah, fuck 'em."

"Wow. So what are you going to do now?"

"I figure I'll go to New Baltimore and get my *Sega* games and *Legos*, for Detox Week."

"Oh, shit I forgot that starts today. Alright...ugh...do you mind if I lay here for a little while longer?"

"No problem at all."

I took off.

Looking back I feel pretty bad about the way I left those people at that corporation whose acronym I cannot recall. I don't feel bad for the corporation, but for the people who were nice to me and thought they were helping me out by offering me a job. Everybody has a right to decline a promotion at a job they dislike. But the way I left was flaky and unmanly. I should have done that differently. But now it is what it is.

Morgan was amused as Jess, Mike and I moved everything around in prep for Detox Week. I put a folding table in front of the faux fireplace and we spread our *Legos* out there. The sets were mostly in pieces but there were portions of vehicles and buildings. I had town-related sets like a police station and a firehouse. Mike had more pirate-themed sets, a news station with a helicopter and another police station.

"In our *Lego* town every third person is a cop, just like real life," Mike joked.

"The taxes must be through the roof with so many public services and almost no residences," I said.

It was amusing to take out the sets and remember the importance we'd once placed on particular pieces. Like those two-pronged blocks that had a hinge that could fold ninety-degrees or the boat bows or the treasure chest with little plastic gold coins.

"So, you guys are going to quit drinking through *Lego* playing. Interesting. I'm not sure I've heard of this particular dependence-reduction therapy," Morgan joked.

"We're not quitting drinking, just trying to go a week without drinking or smoking," Mike said. "To prove we can do it."

"Well, good luck. I think it's a great idea, if a bit unorthodox in its execution." Morgan excused himself to study for the GREs in his room.

I thought the *Sega* games would've provided hours of entertainment for us. They used to when I was a kid. So we put an old box T.V. that had dials on it instead of buttons on a milk crate in front of a couch. We hooked up all the wires in black spaghetti webs. We sat down to play but the buttons on the controllers stuck and made it annoying. We were kind of jonesing and irritable, so we played a round of Rummy instead and drank orange juice pretending we were drinking Screw Drivers. Then Mike left and Jess drove home because she hadn't drank and hadn't slept in Feura Bush in three nights. I went for a jog, took a shower, then a bath, then read, then laid in bed. So Day One was a success, and I'd proven to myself that I could go a whole day without drinking.

"One day out of 1,277 is a pretty good record," I joked to Morgan the next morning as he made breakfast before work. I'd gotten up early and sat around listlessly waiting for him to wake.

"It's something to build a day on," Morgan said. "And after today your ratio of drinking to non-drinking days over the last four years will be double. Instead of one to 1,277 it'll be one to 638."

"Well, hey, that's quite an accomplishment!" I said in a defeated tone.

"It is, man."

"Ha, okay."

"It *is*."

I thought I was at the bottom of the sine wave and maybe Detox Week was the beginning of the upswing. For all its suffering and nihilism, there was comfort there, at least, in the recognizable surroundings, and the idea that, well, this was my life and it was lonely but I was God's Lonely Man and that was that. It was also disorienting because in such times I usually would've said *well, such is the case, and it is shitty, but it won't bother me, because I will revel in the shittiness.* But with the peer pressure against drinking I couldn't do that. The whole point of Detox Week was to suffer but not to break.

I called my old teacher Adam and he said he needed some spackling and painting done in his apartment. Morgan's father also needed an apartment painted, and the basement and two bathrooms in his house. Maybe they didn't really need those things painted and they were just welfare offerings. But anyway it was work and I needed to pay the bills so I said I'd start the next day. I liked painting because it was just me and I could set the hours and I took pride in knowing the technique and the right order of operations. Plus I was paid in cash at a dollar more per hour than I'd been taxed at the nameless corporation, and I could see the product of my work as soon as I added my labor to a project. So I thought *I can tolerate this.*

That night we completed the structures on the *Lego* sets and started to combine them into a town. It would've been an impressive sight if we'd shown it to an eleven-year-old. We still had a couple of boxes of random blocks that we planned to construct apartments out of, because where else would the workers live? They couldn't sleep at their desks or in their helicopters or police cruisers. After we set up the buildings we started placing the trees and flowers and finally the people.

"And here is the mayor of the town," I announced, placing down a man with red pants and a red torso, with a hard hat on his head and a radio in his hand.

"Nah, nah," said Mike, "this is the leader here." He held up a pirate with a mustache and a hook for a hand.

"*Him?*" I said. "No way. John has always been the mayor of the town." I pointed to the red guy.

"No way, Captain Jack has."

"Man...John has a construction helmet on his head and a radio in his hand. He's been overseeing the reconstruction of the town since the last earthquake that destroyed the place."

"Captain Jack has always been the leader of my *Lego* men," Mike asserted.

"A pirate cannot be a leader. He's inherently anarchistic. I mean, I'm sure John would give him a ship to captain, on the up and up. I mean, feasibly, he could become Secretary of the Navy, with the approval of the Town Council, with good behavior."

"My *Lego* men are used to following Captain Jack's orders. He's led them though a lot of struggles that seemed hopeless. He's a proven leader who's always come through with an unorthodox plan that succeeded. His underdog status and refusal to follow convention are his greatest strengths. I think you should appreciate that. I'm sure he'd give John a job as Second in Command...if the other pirates would go for it."

"If the other pirates would go for it? Ha! They're *crooks*! The cops are on John's side."

"Not *my* cops. John's outnumbered. Maybe we should put the matter to a vote."

"No. John is the leader. A pirate cannot be the mayor."

"He can, and he is."

"No he's not!"

"Boys! Boys! I think you're being silly," Jess picked up one of the few female *Lego* people. "Here, *she* should be mayor."

"No way!" Mike and I shouted simultaneously.

"Why not?" Jess asked.

"Because she's the secretary for the fire company," Mike said.

"Because she doesn't know karate and can't inspire courage," I said.

"You men are hopelessly philistine."

Mike and I were sincerely annoyed. Maybe it was because we'd spent hundreds of hours infusing our *Lego* characters with personalities as children and now it seemed like stabbing them in the back to consider demoting them. More likely, we were on edge because we were trying to quit drinking and everything was annoying. We agreed to disagree but it killed *Legos* as an entertainment. We colored for ten minutes and that was annoying. Then we sat in the window and tapped our fingers looking across the street at *Lark Tavern*. We decided to part company in order to get a good night's sleep. So that was Day Two.

The next night we met up and paced around for about ten minutes. Then Mike said,

"Well, we've proven we can go two days, and that's an accomplishment."

I agreed, so we smoked and drank a six-pack. So Detox Week lasted two and three quarter days.

The next few days consisted of painting for a few hours, and drinking. I need not describe the sensations. I'd been fired, the girl I wanted was dating someone else, I was going nowhere in life, and apparently I couldn't even go a couple of days without boozing and smoking.

March 6th, 2007 was finally the lowest point. Kerouac began his book this way:

> I had just gotten over a serious illness that I won't bother to talk about, except that it had something to do with the miserably weary split-up and my feeling that everything was dead. With the coming of Dean Moriarty began the part of my life you could call my life on the road.

I drove to Adam, my former teacher's, apartment in the grey rain. As I walked up his stairs I felt I had two 25-pound weights on each shoulder. I could hardly make it to the top of the staircase. Inside I said hello to his dogs, Jake and Smokey, and his cat Riley, who were happy to see me. Then I taped the corners of the molding and sat on the floor with the paintbrush. It felt like it felt when I'd started the medicine for OCD my sophomore year of college. I could hardly lift the brush.

"I can't do this," I said. Going to the bar seemed as icky as anything else that day. So I went to the tattoo parlor and asked the man if he could make a tattoo out of the words "Live Free or Die" with old English lettering, and he said yes. He said the ink doesn't disappear because "It gets pushed into the third of fourth layer of skin and the pigment sticks to the cells." Good, I needed a mantra. I scheduled an appointment for the next day. Then I went back to the Downtube and soberly informed Morgan that I was leaving town for a little while, because everything was dead and I just had to get away. I was going to try to hitchhike to New Orleans, where I'd always wanted to go because of its jazz music, history and the Mississippi, which is referenced in all the old Blues songs. Morgan said he understood. So that was that. Jess Gadani said she would sublet my room at the Downtube for a month. I had $600. And so I began what I pictured would be the beginning of my new life on the road.

X. On The Road

I set out the day after Saint Patrick's day. My friend Paul was driving to Delaware to stay with an old flame who'd suggested on AIM that he visit. Paul said he'd drop me off in Philadelphia. I'd visit my friend Tom there, before working my way down to Baltimore to stay with Alan, and then it'd be warm enough to hitch or walk the rest of the way to NOLA.

I'd met Paul at a party at Jared's. He was a nice guy that never said a harsh word against anybody. He was always pleasant and quick to offer help just for the company. Paul picked me up in his hatchback. I threw a mountain-hiking back-pack with hip straps that I'd borrowed from Jess in his SUV. We left at five p.m. from my parent's house, after our annual Saint Patrick 's Day corned beef dinner. As we drove south on the Thruway I looked out the window at the Catskill Mountains.

"The way the trees are sticking up there, like little sticks compared to the big mountains...it reminds me of *cilia*, those little hairs on the outside of micro-organisms, or even the hairs on our bodies. If we were in the second part of *Gulliver's Travels*, where he meets the giants, I bet their arm hairs would look like trees. Anyway I never thought of it before, but I wonder if the Earth itself could qualify as an organism. The crust is like the skin; the magma the circulatory system. You've got air moving around like a respiratory system; lightning fires and makes atmosphere that keeps harmful radiation out and keeps the earth at a stable homeostatic temperature. Maybe all the animals and trees and everything it produces are just a part of the larger organism...the Earth organism...and we're all like cells who don't even realize as we're staying alive that we're also part of a bigger body."

"Huh, I never thought about trees like that, but I see it." Paul worked at a record company and ran several websites. "Have you heard of Gaia Theory? It kind of reminds me of that. The idea that the Earth is an organism itself. I think it's from the name for the earth from Greek mythology. I never understood what role or whatever humans play, though. It seems like we just fuck up the earth and destroy it. Maybe we're the viruses."

"Maybe we're the white blood cells," I said.

"Ha, how's that?"

"Well the earth has all these systems for regulating itself, right? But what's the one thing the earth can't deal with? Shit from outer space like an asteroid smashing into it and setting the whole place on fire and killing everything. Of all the plants and animals the earth has produced, only one of them stands any chance of protecting the earth from that sort of an outside-pathogen, and that's Man. We could shoot rockets out or maybe launch solar sails which could attach to an asteroid. Who knows, in 200 years we could have a ray that disrupts gravitational fields which we could aim just to the left of an approaching asteroid and pull it 'to the left, to the left, everything it owns in a box to the left,' away from Earth."

"Ha ha, we could just *Beyonce* it out of the way," Paul laughed.

"Exactly!"

We crossed the Delaware River into New Jersey well after dark. I thought that was weird because I pictured New Jersey sort of *down and to the right* and Philadelphia *down further but way to the left*. I had a vague idea of the order of the states along the east coast, but no appreciation of the scale of distances between one and another. We stopped off to get gas. Paul laughed at me because I was surprised to see that attendants pumped the petrol for the drivers.

"I feel like I'm in 1950," I said, watching the Hispanic and black attendants put nozzles into tanks in a line in front of us, then walk to the driver's window to get money. It took awhile. The lady in front of us had a minivan and she was talking on her phone as the attendants put the hose in her car and moved to other vehicles. After a minute gas started spewing out of her car...and spewing and spewing...leaking gas everywhere. The attendant came back and looked surprised. He stealthily pulled the hose out, then looked around to see if his coworkers or the woman had noticed. They had not. So he printed a credit card receipt and handed it to the woman. Still on her phone, she signed, handed it back, then crumpled her copy, threw it in the back seat and drove off. I'd like to have seen her face when she checked her credit card statement and had a gas charge for $200. Soon we filled up and got on our way.

There was no such thing as a smart phone in March of 2007. So we had a folding road map. But Paul said we didn't really need it because he'd driven to Philadelphia several times for concerts and knew the way. Then we crossed a bridge and a sign said "Welcome to Delaware," and he said "Fuck, I don't think this is the right way to Philadelphia." It was about ten o'clock at night and we figured the best thing was for me to spend the night at Paul's girl's place, and I'd travel from there to Baltimore somehow, and visit Tom in Philadelphia on my way home. So Paul called his girl. This is what I heard him say into the phone.

"Hi Ashley it's Paul. Yeah, I'm on my way. Should be there in about an hour...we just came over the bridge...Yeah...I was wondering if my buddy Dallas could crash on the couch for a night...I was supposed to drop him off in Philadelphia but we took a wrong turn...well, yeah, on the couch...well...where am *I* going to sleep?...well...I figured I'd be sleeping in *your* room...boyfriend?...what?...well...okay we'll figure it out one of us can sleep on the floor." Paul closed his phone. "What the fuck dude?"

"That sounded like a surprising call."

"I'll say! She has a boyfriend! Who's sleeping there tonight!"

"What?"

"Dude I don't know. What the fuck? Like, she told me to come visit her. I just assumed that that meant come down and hook up. Like, we used to hook up. Why would you not mention you have a boyfriend?"

"Seems like an important detail to leave out."

"Fuck dude. I don't know if I even wanna go anymore."

We parked Paul's SUV outside an apartment complex near Wilmington. As we stepped onto the pavement we heard Ashley shout from her front door.

"Paul! Ya fuck! Your asshole's a stab wound! Ha ha ha!"

"Hi Ashley," Paul laughed. He whispered to me, "Ashley's a little rough. She's in the Air Force." Ashley crossed the lot and put Paul in a choke-hold.

"What's up ya schlemiel? You never drove before? Hi I'm Ashley."

"Hi, Dallas," I said.

Ashley showed us her place. She had white carpets and couches. She said she was sick. We met her boyfriend, a quiet guy who I figured hated us. I put down my bag and we went out to a bar in Wilmington. I was surprised that there was no snow on the ground, because it had snowed almost two feet in New York on Saint Patrick's Day. We played pool and I saw a guy who looked like Matthew McConaughey with a southern accent, and I felt like I was in The South. We played Beer Pong in the bar (with beer in the cups, like you're supposed to play). The Matthew McConaughey character had an unorthodox but effective throw. He would wind up like he was pitching a baseball and roll the ball off his last three fingers, sending it in a straight trajectory before falling precipitously into a cup. It was really something to see. We lost a couple of ten-cup games in a row to that guy, who was the bar champion. After we got drunk we went back to Ashley's because she was feeling sick. She and her boyfriend slept in the bedroom. Paul took the couch and I took the floor, because I'd planned to sleep on floors and brought an inflatable mattress pad. So there I was, living my new life on the road.

The next day we tagged along with Ashley and her girlfriend when they went to the Wilmington Air Force Base to pick up Ashley's paycheck. We couldn't go inside, but as we approached the base down a paved road through unplanted fields, we saw the biggest airplanes I ever saw. Their tails and fuselages rose higher than the base buildings.

"Those are C-5 Galaxies," Ashley explained. "Some of the biggest transport aircraft in the world. They can carry several tanks. Hell, sometimes we transport other airplanes inside them."

"Wow. That's almost...*ridonkulous*," I said.

"Ha! I love that word," Ashley chuckled.

We went to a *TGI Fridays* for lunch and met up with Marcus, a six-and-a-half-foot tall black guy who also worked at the air base. He didn't say much of anything. Then Ashley drove the five of us to an *Abercrombie and Fitch* outlet where they sold clothes at marked-down prices because they had buttons sewn on backwards or something. Since I was on a tight budget I couldn't buy anything. But I found a tennis ball in the parking lot so Paul, Marcus and I went outside to play pitch-and-catch while Ashley and her girlfriend shopped. Then Marcus asked if I smoked cigarettes and I said yes but I didn't have any and he bummed me one and we sat on the curb. I asked how he liked being in the Air Force. He said it was as good as anything else for someone of his background. He was from Texas, he said. He'd enlisted in the Air Force in August of 2001 in order to see the world. Then a month later, 9-11 happened. Then it was constant overtime seven days a week and he'd been stuck in Delaware since, except for a six-month period when he was in Iraq. He said the sand storms were something terrible. They'd spring up suddenly and then you'd have to run for the barracks. After the storm passed, one of his jobs was to bring a step ladder into the engine of the C-5—the engine was so large that this six-and-a-half-foot guy needed a ladder to reach the top of it—and strike it with a sledge hammer to knock the sand out. I said I didn't think I'd like being in the military and constantly getting screamed at. Marcus said it wasn't like that in Iraq, because it's 135 degrees and even military officers know that people will snap in heat like that, so they don't yell at the men. I was surprised to hear that. Now in a couple of months it was going to be time for Marcus to enlist again and he said he probably would, because things were finally starting to slow down and he thought maybe he'd have a better chance of transferring to a different place. So that was Marcus' story. Ashley came out of the store wheezing and coughing and she said she wanted to go home, where her boyfriend was making her chicken soup. So we went back and she went to bed and Paul and I sat in the living room. He offered to drive me to Baltimore, so that I wouldn't have to hitch there, because he said he was tired of being at Ashley's and had another day to kill. So I called Alan and arranged to show up at his studio apartment.

We took off from Delaware, figuring we'd use Paul's map to get us to Baltimore and the directions Alan had given us over the phone to navigate to his building once we were in the city. That was how you got from place to place before you could open your phone and see a blue dot representing your GPS location superimposed over a Google map. We crossed the border into rural Maryland and I saw my first Confederate Flag waving outside a rickety frame house. A while later we passed Charring Cross Road, and Paul mentioned that Maryland was the first really southern state, even though it's north of the Mason-Dixon Line. I'd heard that before—read it somewhere—but I never thought about what it meant until we drove through. Now I understand that it signifies a different culture in rural Maryland than, say, New York or Connecticut. Experience enlightens more than facts in a book.

After making a couple of wrong turns and circling back, we parked on a one-way street in mid-town Baltimore, which I'd never been to before. I grabbed my bag and we walked up two blocks to the bottom of The Standard Oil Building. We entered the lobby and met Alan. Into the elevator we went, up to the fourteenth floor.

Alan's apartment had white carpets, a bed and a desk in one room, a kitchen and island counter in another, a bathroom and a large set of sliding glass doors which opened onto a stone patio overlooking the city. The view was quite impressive.

Alan made *edamame*—which, I learned, are the pea pods you get in Chinese food or eat raw—in a *wok*—which, I learned, is the deep metal pan that Chinese food is cooked in—with rice and beef. Paul knew those words and I learned them for the first time, which is what I was hoping to do. It was a good meal. We ate on the floor because it seemed appropriate. Then it was time for Paul to leave and I thanked him for getting me so much closer to New Orleans, and said I was sorry that the thing with Ashley didn't turn out. He said it was okay, but he wouldn't make that mistake again. So he left and Alan and I sat down to catching up.

I'd known Alan as long as I'd known Mike. I met them the same day, which was the first day of 5th grade, or Middle School, when our two local elementary schools merged. Mike and Alan sat at the end of a brown table with blue circle seats in the lunch room. They had long-haired bowl cuts, which was the style when we were 10. I asked if I could sit across from them and they said sure.

My sister had given me advice when we were very young, from the top bunk one night as I lay in the bottom, about how to be popular. She said the most important thing was to be funny. So that was what I always tried to be. So sitting across from Alan and Mike, in order to break the ice, I said,

"Hey, I made up a new invention. It's called Banana Deodorant. Guaranteed to work all day!" I took a banana from my tray and smeared it on my armpits. Alan and Mike laughed and asked,

"Who is this kid?" So I dabbed it on my neck too, and made farcical gesticulations and facial expressions, incorporating the kind of physical humor I found hilarious in Leslie Neilson and Jim Carey movies. They laughed more. So I squished the banana between my hands and threw the peel on the lunchroom floor and pretended to stroll by not noticing, and slipped on the peel. They erupted in more laughter. So I did that a couple of more times until the lunch aide came over and yelled to stop being an idiot and that was the funniest part of all. Then I made two new friends and we sat next to each other in Social Studies and Science.

Alan and Mike were rich, as far as I was concerned. Their parents' owned more than one car and their houses were twice the size of my parent's. Their parent's had gone to college. The two of them knew a lot more about popular culture than I did, like who the current bands were and how to play soccer and such. I joined the 12-and-under team because I knew Mike and Alan, and then I signed up for modified soccer in 7th grade because I knew them, and that was where I met Jared for the first time. Alan and Mike shared an esoteric humor that was funny for its word play and cultural references. They went to *Woodstock '96* with their parents, at a time when I didn't know what a "hippy" was. My humor was slapstick and vaudevillian.

Playing soccer with those guys was fun but it taught me that I couldn't play the fool and revel in attention without sometimes pissing off the rest of the team. During double-session try-outs in 9th grade we had to run "perimeter runs" around the school campus, then "horse shoe" sprints starting at one goal around the other and back, then "Indian runs" where we all jogged and the guy at the back sprinted to the front, then "hills" where we stood at the bottom of a hill and the coach stood at the top and when he blew a whistle we sprinted, and when he blew again we dropped and did five pushups and then got up and kept running, running always. The goal was to get the weakest players to drop out. One day the coach had the team spread out in a circle to do stretches after perimeter runs. It was the second day of practice, which was always the worst, since we were not yet in shape but we ached from the day before.

"And you, you mother fucker," Alan reminisced, "You fucked it up for everybody!" The coach made us do 75 jumping jacks. We were dead tired when we were done, after having done all the other running. The coach said something like "I hope you're not tired, gentlemen."

"I'd love to do 25 more!" I'd shouted.

"Mr. Trombley would like to do 25 more," the coach said calmly. "So that is what we'll do." The rest of the team groaned and hissed at me. When we got to 100 the coach said, "Mr. Trombley, are you satisfied with 100 jumping jacks, or would you like to do more?" The other players shot me death looks. I was tired as hell, but I couldn't resist. Panting, I responded,

"Boy oh boy coach, this is so much fun. I'd love to do another 50." The rest of the players jeered me.

"Mr. Trombley says you should do another 50, so that is what you will do, gentlemen." So we did another 50 jumping jacks. "Are you satisfied now, Mr. Trombley?"

"Tell you the truth coach, I'd love to do —"

"And that was when I ran over and tackled you," Alan recalled. "And that made me the most popular kid on the team that day. You fucking bastard."

Alan went to college at CASE Western in Ohio and Instant Messaged me about sewing a human ear onto a mouse's back. The first time I visited Mike in New Paltz we IMed Alan and asked him what his favorite song was. Alan typed back some song with fourteen words in its name that we'd never heard of. Mike and I rolled our eyes.

I'd complain about being out of money and Alan would message that I should just demand some from my parents, because it was their responsibility when you're in school. I would roll my eyes because my parent's saved their money in a series of white envelopes

in as little as $5 per week increments for various bills and "funds" —
Alan and I were from different financial worlds, obviously.

We met up during our yearly Symposium but we had less
and less in common as college went on. Now Alan was living in
Baltimore and nobody had been down to visit him, and his girlfriend
had broken up with him, and I didn't know what I was doing, so it
seemed like a nice occasion to get to know each other again. We came
to appreciate how such visits reinforce friendship over time.

We left Alan's place and it was night time. We took a right,
which meant we were headed uptown. Alan asked how long I'd be
in town and I said till whenever, it didn't really make a difference.
He said that was cool and he hoped to be able to show me around. I
said I'd like that. We crossed the street and took another street up a
hill. Alan pointed to a bar and said the place had a bookshelf below a
picture of Vladimir Lenin. Pushing the bookshelf aside exposed a
staircase that brought you to a members-only lounge upstairs. There
was also a coffee house called *Red Emma's* a couple of streets over.
There was a communist theme to the whole Mount Vernon district,
which was where the young people lived, sort of like Lark Street in
Albany, except we had no communist stuff. We got to the top of a hill
and I understood why the district was called Mount Vernon. There
was a public park about the size of a football field beneath a tower
that was twenty stories high with a statue of a man on top.

"That's the original Washington Monument," Alan explained,
built shortly after Washington's death in 1799. "It's got like 229 steps
inside. We should climb it when it's open."

"Cool."

"Then over there is the *Peabody Institute*," Alan pointed to a
classical building with Doric columns a block long. "It's a
conservancy. I've never been inside, but I heard the acoustics are
amazing. A lot of famous musicians attended the conservancy there."
(I had no idea what that meant.) "And over there a block is the main
Baltimore Public Library, but you're approaching the bad part of
town if you go that way, so be careful." I said I wanted to go to the
library tomorrow when Alan went to school at Johns Hopkins, which
was way uptown, and Alan warned me to be careful because in
Baltimore you might find yourself walking on a street that is nice
enough, and then go one block over and get killed because you're in
the wrong place.

We stopped outside of a bar called *The Brewer's Art*. A
staircase ascended to a fancy dining area. We took a descending
staircase that led into a room like a giant wine cellar. The walls and

columns were of exposed brick. Nooks and caverns lined the wall, embracing wood benches and tables. Candlelight augmented the low incandescent bulbs.

The beers listed on the chalkboard were about twice as expensive as in Albany, and came in tulip glasses rather than pints, but they were 10% abv. Alan bought the first round. We cheersed and found a seat at the bar, which is always the best, if you can manage it. The music was mellow and the people seemed nice. Most folks were around thirty. I felt kind of low-class because I only had two outfits with me. I wore an old faded-to-almost-white pair of jeans which hugged my thighs and knees and flared out around my *Samba* sneakers, a white button-up with a subtle pattern, and my canvas adventurer's jacket.

A girl walked in. She had brown hair and brown eyes. She was taller than me and very skinny. She held her hands clasped in front of her as she ordered a beer without greeting anybody. She wore old black pants, work boots and a flannel top. She was rather flat-chested. She had a red ribbon around her neck, like a choker.

"That's my type of girl," I said to Alan.

"She's good-looking, alternative. There's lots of girls like that in Baltimore. You should talk to her."

"I'm no good at that. I have nothing to say. I always play it cool and sit at the bar and then if the girl ends up coming up next to me to order a drink, I'll make a conversation then. Otherwise you look too awkward and they get defensive if you walk over and try and break into their little social circle or whatever."

We had another round, this time on me, and after a while Alan nudged me, because the girl was standing to my right waiting to order another beer. I looked over and smiled. She smiled back. Then spontaneously she said,

"You look like you're traveling."

"Yeah, ha. These are my traveling clothes. I'm only in town for a day or two, so I thought I'd check out this bar. My friend Alan lives here, he showed it to me. How about you? You live in Baltimore?"

"Yeah, for a couple of years now," she sighed. "Where are you traveling to?"

"I'm hitchhiking to New Orleans."

"No kidding? That's great. Everybody thinks it's dangerous now but I've never had a hard time with it."

"You hitchhike?"

"I used to, when I used to live in Texas and Mexico. I'm half-Mexican. My name is Santina, by the way. How about you?"

"Santina, that's a nice name. My name's Dallas."

"Alex?"

"Dallas, like the city in Texas."

"Oh, I like that better. So how long have you been in town? Where did you come from?"

"I came from Albany, New York, which is like three hours north of New York City. I've been here for about six hours. I just got in from Delaware this afternoon."

"I was in New York once, visiting my mother. It was okay. How do you like it?"

"Well, I hardly ever go to the City. It's pretty expensive compared to where I live."

"It is very expensive. I couldn't afford to live there. So, you haven't seen this city yet, huh?"

"No...I'm hoping to sight-see tomorrow when Alan's at work. I guess I'll just sort of walk around and see what I see."

"I'm off tomorrow." Santina's energy was severe but also slightly soft. "My friends and I are having brunch at *Maxie's* at eleven. Why don't you join us, and then in the afternoon we can walk around and I'll show you some things?"

"I mean...that would be great! I'd love to do that."

"Do you know where *Maxie's* is?"

"I can figure it out..."

"Here..." she grabbed my *Moleskinne* notebook from the bar. She wrote "Santina" and her phone number. "Call me tomorrow at eleven and let me know where you are, and I'll give you directions."

"Thank you so much! I can't wait."

"Me either," Santina winked. Then she excused herself and disappeared into the crowd.

"And there you go," Alan said. "You're amazing man. You're in town for six hours and you meet some money girl who gives you her number. I don't get it."

I explained, "It's because I said I'm *leaving*."

XI. Santina

The next morning was sunny and 68 degrees, which felt great, because it was only 36 degrees in Albany. I left the Standard Oil Building and crossed the street. I took a different street up to the park where the Washington Monument was, to see some new stuff. Alan had left me directions, but I didn't use them. I always have a general sense of where x is relative to where I'm standing, once I have set foot in a place. I walked around some side streets admiring the architecture, for it was a beautiful city. The side streets didn't seem as menacing as Alan made them out to be. There were your usual characters sitting on stoops, staring at me for being a single white guy walking through their neighborhood, but nobody said anything to me and I just walked past them. Maybe all the really bad characters were sleeping after having spent the night doing whatever it is that bad characters do.

I found the library and walked through the metal detectors into the main lobby. On the first floor were desks and chairs with homeless people sleeping and computers with adolescents typing or listening to headphones. I thought about how Ben Franklin organized the first public libraries so that people could have access to knowledge in books they couldn't afford. I wondered if, in the future, the function of libraries will be merely to keep the homeless warm and provide internet access to families who can't afford it. I made my way upstairs and found the local history section, which was totally vacant. I leafed through books about Baltimore, mostly just looking at the pictures of the buildings and landmarks and reading the captions beneath. Then I left and laid in the grass in the park in my short sleeves, relishing my good fortune. At eleven I called Santina and she gave me directions to the brunch place.

I can't say I was impressed by the decor at *Maxie's*. It was something Jess Gadani would've liked. A bunch of styles thrown together one on top of another. The floors were black and white checkered. There were chrome railings like a '50s place, but the walls were robin's egg and salmon with orange stripes mismatching. Pictures of Frank Sinatra and Marilyn Monroe fought for space with *Slash* posters. I wandered through, disoriented, until I heard my name called from a table of four. I sat in the empty seat at the head of the table.

Santina sat to my left. Like me she wore the same outfit from the night before, except she donned a black ribbon around her neck now instead of a red one. Proceeding clockwise around the table, next to Santina was an overweight white woman with a sweatshirt and spiky hair. Across from that woman sat a thin, well-dressed white guy in an orange shirt who rested his chin on interlocking fingers and batted his eyes when he introduced himself. Lastly, to my right sat a larger black guy who had a gelled, curly Mohawk and wore a black and white striped tank top with spaghetti straps.

Holy shit, I thought, *Santina is a lesbian.*

We ate brunch as I wondered what I was doing there. The group talked in clichés and inside jokes about people I didn't know and I hoped the whole crew wasn't giving me a tour of Baltimore. Luckily they all had other things to do. So Santina and I left the place alone.

"So...you're a lesbian?" I asked Santina when we were on the street.

"I wouldn't describe myself as a lesbian," she said. "I've dated men and I've dated women. I'm attracted to personalities, not genders."

I can work with that, I thought.

"Are you dating someone now?

Santina smiled. "Do you like to climb buildings?"

"Oh yeah, sure..." I lied.

"Yeah? Okay, let's do that. I love scaling buildings."

"Okay—you're the leader. I'm the follower today."

"Don't say follower. You're not a follower. You're my guest." We went to the Washington Monument, but it was closed so we couldn't climb it. "We can climb my building instead. But first, let's go to the liquor store and get some champagne."

I love Santina, I thought.

We got the champagne and then we walked down an alley that brought us to a courtyard in the back of Santina's apartment building. She told me to wait outside as she opened a door that led to a dirt-floor hallway in a pretty dark and gross-looking place. She came back a few minutes later wearing a backpack.

"We can go most of the way using the porch steps." She started climbing a dilapidated wood fire escape that ascended six stories. I gulped and followed her. She practically ran up the steps. The first couple of floors were okay, but as we came to floors four, five and six, the porch was shaking and rotting. "Watch out for the third step there, it's broken," she called back to me. Then on the sixth story, the last floor, it seemed like there was no place to go. But Santina grabbed a ladder that leaned against a wall. "We can get up on the porch roof through the hole. Just be careful you don't put your weight on the edges. Step like two-feet in and it's fine." I watched Santina and thought *no way*. But she disappeared through the hole and I wanted to keep in her company, so I climbed on the roof too, now seven stories high. "We're almost there now." She walked perfectly erect to the edge of the porch roof. The adjacent building had a foot-wide ledge, at a shallow angle, that Santina stepped onto. She crossed the ledge balance-beam-style, then grabbed an iron ladder that went from the ledge to the roof 20 feet up. The ladder was bolted to the bricks in the side of the building and shook as she ascended. It took all of the courage I could muster to sit on my ass on that ledge and shuffle like a crab across the ledge to the ladder, which I clutched with a death-grip. As Santina climbed I watched her ass in her black pants getting farther away. My palms were so sweaty I thought I'd slip off the rungs, but I climbed after her. I got to the top and slid belly-first onto the roof.

"I'm proud of you," Santina said, standing over top of me looking down as I rolled onto my back. She held out her hand and helped me to my knees. "You don't like heights."

"No, I don't."

"Then why did you say you like climbing buildings?"

"Because I wanted to keep hanging out with you."

Santina seemed touched.

"No, I'm not seeing anybody," she said. She retrieved a camera, a boxy bulky black thing, out of her backpack and loaded film into it. Then she took out a set of black coke-bottle glasses and insisted I put them on. "I love Groucho Marx," she explained. "Everybody I meet, I make them wear these glasses and I take their picture in different places. Someday I'll have a thousand pictures of a hundred people, all having the glasses in common." Santina made me pose with the Baltimore skyline behind me as she snapped thirty shots. I'd love to see some of those pictures, but I never have.

We laid on our stomachs and looked over the roof ledge at the street below.

"I love those things," Santina pointed to a couple of closely-placed black brushes bolted to a stoop down across the street. "They were for brushing off your boots before going into someone's house back when the streets were made of mud and there was no such thing as vacuum cleaners. I love that they're still there. They have no purpose now...not practically, anyway. The past was so much more...earthy and real."

"You took the words out of my mouth," I said.

"And the tops of the windows. You see how the bricks above all the windows are shaped differently? It's to spread the weight of the building out over the windows. Like, a part of an arch. Otherwise the weight would snap the windows...they would sag. The middle piece, the biggest stone, is called the Keystone. Because it's the key to holding the arch together. It spreads out the weight to the sides."

"Poor thing."

We stood and passed the champagne bottle. I felt like I was getting a massage while sitting in a bubble bath eating my favorite meal listening to Tommy Dorsey.

"You see that tall building that looks like a giant chimney?" I said as we looked over the skyline.

"Yeah. I don't know what that is."

"I read about it in the library this morning in the local history section. It's called the *Baltimore Shot Building*, because they made shot there."

"Shot?"

"Like, birdshot or buckshot...bullets. It's fascinating. What they would do was bring molten metal to the top of the tower, which is like 260 feet high. Then they'd drip the molten metal down, and it would fall down all those feet into a pool of water at the bottom. The metal would cool into little spheres—buckshot—by the time it dropped. Funny to think...how else would you make tiny metal spheres back then? Nature and gravity did it for you! It's also known as the *Phoenix Shot Tower*, I guess because of the fire at the bottom."

"I lived in Phoenix for a while. Amazing—I've lived here for years and I never knew what that building was, and now you came here for one day and taught me."

"Well...I didn't know it before today. The library taught me...so...I can't take credit for that."

"You can take credit for going to the library."

"Well...ha...yes."

Santina said she was born in Mexico and only met her dad two or three times. She went to "New York" once and liked it and wished she could go more often. I told her she should visit, and that New York is more than New York City, and that I'd spent very little time in the city myself, which she found unbelievable. Like a lot of people, she didn't realize that most of New York is more like the Midwest than a metropolis. Anyhow her mother had moved back to Mexico and Santina ended up in Baltimore, somehow, never becoming a photographer like she'd wanted.

"What do you mean 'never becoming'?" I said. "You're working on it now. You're an artist, because you produce Art. I write things in a notebook and someday I'll stitch the pieces together into a story, like a quilter makes a quilt. You can do the same with your pictures."

Santina sighed with sad eyes, then forced a smile.

"How old are you, Dallas?"

"Twenty-two," I said, perhaps a tad defensively.

"Twenty-two," she repeated. "How old do you think I am?"

"Twenty-six?" I guessed. Santina paced a half-dozen feet away, then turned back to me.

"I'm thirty-one. Too old for you."

"That's not true."

"It is true. That's nine years. That's almost a decade. A decade is almost half of your life, and not even a third of mine."

"...And six is afraid of seven because seven ate nine. What do numbers mean?"

"They mean a lot. You know what I do for a living? To pay my bills?"

"You haven't told me yet."

"I work at *Starbucks*. As a barista. For a corporation. Making minimum wage."

"Okay. So what?"

"So I'm thirty-one years old, Dallas. I tried the being-an-artist thing. In Mexico...there were no opportunities. So we—my mother and I—came here. Where the streets are paved with gold and all that. But when you reach thirty, you are what you are. You can't make the excuse anymore that you're 'becoming' something. Your life is your life, and you start to realize that what you're doing now *is* what you will be doing the rest of your life."

Santina appeared profoundly dejected. My mood dropped with hers.

"You know, who am I to argue? I mean, I left Albany because basically everything is hopeless. So I'm hitchhiking because there're no options left. It's terribly depressing." Santina paced closer again, and leaned her elbows on the ledge.

"I wish I had some advice for you," she sighed.

"You know what would be better than advice?"

"What?"

"Just...to hold your hand."

Santina looked at me, comfortably sharing melancholy. Then we held hands and looked out over the cityscape.

It was Gin Day, by the Tromblean Calendar. That is, the first day of the year when I don't have anything to do that requires me to be sober, when it is 63 degrees or warmer. (I don't drink gin in the winter. When I was 13 years old the display on my father's Jeep said "63" on a day when I thought it was just warm enough to wear short sleeves. So...you get it.) After I left Santina's, because she had to go to work, I bought a handle of gin from the liquor store, and some sloe gin and lemon juice and made Singapore Slings for Alan and I. Alan had a paper due the next day and apologized for not being able to carouse. I told him it was okay because Santina asked if I wanted to hang out with her and her friends, who were having a little get-together later.

"I'm amazed with you, man."

"Why?"

"Dude, I've lived here for two years. You're here for a day and you're already palling around with a girl and accumulating a group of friends."

"It's because I'm leaving," I repeated.

"What do you mean?"

"I mean I'm a transient."

"Ah...right...and her group is Kerouac style people, who like travelers."

"Yes...but...it's because I am leaving *soon*. There's no risk in talking to me, so the girl's defenses don't have to go up. I'm not going to ask to move in...to try to date. When everybody knows you're here for a moment and leaving in another moment you're...what? Not a *subject*. You're an *object*. Something to talk about, nothing serious. You know...a girl meets a guy at a bar and the guy talks to her...she thinks cautiously, 'How far is this going to go?' 'Will he get clingy soon?' et cetera. So it's nothing special about me that led to me meeting these people. It's just that I'm visibly expendable."

"I donno. It sounds like this girl likes you."

Such words plant seeds that don't help you get back on the road.

Santina had a dozen people at her basement apartment. They got together on whatever night it was each week to watch some *Law and Order* show, which I thought was kind of contradictory to their *shtick*. The place was dirty and smelled of fried onions. There was a cassette player and Santina asked what I wanted to listen to. I said Billie Holiday. She smiled from ear to ear and said she loved Billie Holiday. Everybody was friendly to me — it was the gay brunch crowd plus a few more people. Except one guy kept casting suspicious glances in my direction like I was a home intruder.

We went out to the *Brewer's Art* again and that particular guy took every chance to sit next to Santina. One of the friends was a girl who reminded me of Jess Gadani, with straight black hair and thick glasses who was very friendly. So I talked to her a lot as the guy kept monopolizing Santina and annoyed her. We all moved to another bar and Santina sat in a booth, the guy sat next to her, and I went to the bar. Santina got up and followed me.

"That fellow likes you," I observed to her.

"Brian? Oh, no. We're just friends. He's like a brother. He's just looking out for me."

"To make sure you don't fall into the wrong company."

"He likes you."

"If there was a *Scantron* sheet and he had to fill in a bubble to describe how much he likes me, he would fill in the circle that corresponds to 'little or none.'"

"No...that's just how he is. He's really nice if you get to know him."

"I'm sure."

"Come on, don't be like that."

"Deal."

We all went back to Santina's house to smoke pot and I left as the group started to thin out, in order to avoid any awkwardness. Brian the Chaperone was still there when I left.

I had no agenda. I could stay for a while in Baltimore if I wanted. I wanted to stay in Baltimore for a while. I made a series of perambulatory tours of different parts of the city. The Mount Vernon District was where I'd hung out and met Santina. It was where the young professionals and graduate students seemed to congregate, around the Washington Monument and the Peabody Conservatory. Alan lived in the Standard Oil Building which had been converted to apartments. If you left his building and took a right, you'd go to the Mount Vernon area and way uptown was Johns Hopkins. If you took a left you went toward Fells Point, which was where the clubs and stuff were — not really my scene. But Fells Point was interesting because it was the innermost part of Baltimore Harbor. There were tall ships, and Federal Hill with an artillery piece from the War of 1812. It was here in the harbor that Francis Scott Key wrote *The Star Spangled Banner* as he watched the "bombs bursting in air" aboard a British Frigate negotiating a prisoner exchange. After watching the barrage all night, Key saw the American Flag still there — flying above Fort McHenry in Baltimore Harbor. I liked walking around that area. Then, too, I walked to the residential areas and to the

Ravens and *Orioles* stadiums, and into a museum of history. After four days I felt I'd gotten a good idea of the layout of Baltimore.

Santina showed me some of the more underground places. She drove me around in her red 1960s Volkswagen Beetle. I'd never ridden in one. The engine is in the back; it rattled like riding in a tin can. She took me to a bicycle co-op. She took me to *Red Emma's* for coffee.

"There's a lot of Communist advocates in Baltimore," Santina observed with sympathy. "What do you think of Communism?"

"There's a big question," I observed. "Seems like a lotta bullshit to me." Santina frowned, so I qualified my statement. "It seems like a nice idea, for everybody to be equal and have enough money. But it doesn't really seem to jibe with human nature. Nobody wants to work to fulfill quotas. And then you have to have the Government commanding everybody. No thanks."

"I suppose the American free market society where everybody gets raped like peasants working for corporate Lords and Nobles is better?"

"Marginally."

We took walks in the afternoon and strolled by the bay in the evening, watching the lights of the ships refract in bouncing beams off the black water. I helped Santina as she fixed her bike. Soon five days had passed.

"I suppose I should get hitching again tomorrow," I said to Santina as we drank wine in the afternoon on her roof.

"Yeah...You know, why don't we have a little party tonight? I'll invite all the people you've met and we'll drink. It's Tuesday." She sang, "'*Maybe Tuesday will be my good news day.*'"

"What's that?"

"'*Tuesday will be my good news day.*' It's Billie Holiday. Don't you know it? I always say that on Tuesday morning. It's such a simple, beautiful line. And that's today."

"Huh. Okay, party tonight then. And we'll drink until after midnight. Then it will be Wednesday, my new friends-day."

"Ha...you're cute."

It was festive yet sad at Santina's basement apartment. A score of my new friends were there. The gay white kid and the gay black kid joking. Somebody made a "Good Luck Dallas" sign on pieces of loose leaf paper taped to the wall. I made Sloe Gin Fizzes for everybody. We drank *Franzia* Merlot from a box. We played Beer Pong, having to wipe the dirt and dust off the balls whenever they bounced onto the grimy floor. Brian the Chaperone was gloomy but

Santina ignored him. We went to *Brewer's Art* and had craft beers. Jen with the straight hair and thick glasses hosted an after-party in her nice third-floor apartment with high ceilings decorated with nice paintings she'd made herself. 80's dance music blared. We smoked pot and cigarettes out of open windows. Santina and I danced to Hall and Oates tunes and Michael Jackson. It became the middle of the night and then the middle of the morning. My new friends left, one here, a group there, wishing me well. Brian the Chaperone disappeared. I walked Santina home and she invited me in for a nightcap. It was the first time I'd been alone in her apartment. We'd always spent our time walking around Baltimore, or with other people. She played Billy Holiday, so I could hear the lyric *Maybe Tuesday will be my good news day*. It was from the song *The Man I Love*.

"I feel sad now," I said, as we sat next to one another on Santina's threadbare futon.

"Why do you feel sad? Look at all the friends you've made. And you're going someplace...places."

"And now I have friends that I'm leaving. I didn't expect to meet such nice people."

"You're sensitive, Dallas. It's bad for your health."

"I'm going to miss you."

"You will meet interesting people in New Orleans."

"I'm going to miss seeing you and...our conversations."

"You can write me a letter."

"I'll be coming through Baltimore again on my way back. I'd like to meet up and tell you about my trip."

"I'd like to hear how you made out."

"Maybe you should visit Albany sometime. I could show you around and return the favor."

"Dallas...be real, dear."

"What?"

"Please."

"What?"

"It is what it is, okay?"

"Okay." I didn't understand what she meant. "It's late, and we are drunk," I observed.

"Yeah..."

"I should get going...back to Alan's."

"Probably."

"Okay."

"It's late. If you want, you can stay here. We can share the couch."

We kissed. Santina had soft lips. Her clothes smelled like sautéed onions. We laid down and kissed more, and cuddled. We slept in our clothes. It was warm and innocent.

In the morning Santina didn't stir as I used the bathroom, gathered my things, and left. I walked back to the Standard Oil Building, rolled up my sleeping mattress and clipped it to the bottom of my backpack. I stuffed my clothes inside. I donned my jeans and adventurer's jacket. With all of my things—a change of clothes, some trail mix, my notebook—my backpack weighed about forty pounds. I left Alan's spare key on the counter and strolled to *Starbucks*, to see Santina. When I entered she seemed surprised and unhappy.

"I just wanted to say goodbye again," I said from one side of the barista counter.

"Okay."

"I had fun last night."

"Yeah...well...good luck."

"Thanks. I'll see you when I'm on my way back, in a couple of weeks, okay?"

"Yeah..." She wouldn't look me in the eye. "I'm pretty busy the next couple of weeks...I'm going to be out of town...so..."

"Oh. Okay. Is anything wrong?"

"I've just got some things I have to do and you know..."

"Okay. Well...I'll try and find you and hopefully we can get together for a drink or something?" Santina paused, then said mechanically,

"It was nice meeting you."

"Okay...It was nice meeting you, too," I said honestly. Then Santina said she had to get back to work. I stood outside on the street wondering what was the matter. I said aloud, "Well...I guess this is how you know it's time to hit the road."

It was ten thirty in the morning. I walked through Mount Vernon, past the Standard Oil Building, downhill to Fell's Point. I took a right at the Museum. A mile farther I walked past the *Orioles* and *Ravens* stadiums. I walked past a bus station, under a bridge by a railroad yard. The buildings became smaller, residential, made of brick. Young black men sat on stoops. I walked over a bridge over a bay and arrived in Anne-Arundel County. I saw Baltimore behind me. Up a hill on a highway I walked and stuck out my thumb. No one stopped. It became mid-day. The highway had three lanes and the right-hand lane was for exits, so anybody close enough for me to thumb down was getting off the road. To pass the time I sang songs.

I picked up my bag, went lookin' for a place to hide…

There was an expanse of highway with no buildings, just trees and fields on either side. They grew into a small town. Still no one stopped. I must've looked as out of place in that town as anyone dressed like me would've looked walking down Main Street in Ravena. A pickup truck with three Hispanic men in the front seat, with a pile of junk appliances in the bed, drove by and laughed at me. I got hungry and my legs got tired. I came to a cemetery and jumped a guardrail to get inside. There was a tree on a little hill next to some graves. I sat in the shade and ate some trail mix. It was two o'clock in the afternoon. I napped for a half-hour. Then I went to the road and walked some more. My stomach grumbled. I found myself in a little town with a diner. I decided, what the hell, I'd eat a good meal and find out where the nearest bus station was. It'd be better than walking until night-fall and having to sleep under a bridge or something. So I asked the waitress at the diner, an old woman with white hair, where the nearest bus station was. She said she didn't know, but she asked the cook, who was her husband, to come out. He told me the nearest bus station was…in Baltimore.

"But that's about eleven miles away, son."

So, feeling confused about Santina and defeated in my hitching scheme, I left the diner and started walking back where I'd come from. I got back to Baltimore at seven o'clock at night, having walked 22 miles with a forty-pound backpack, accomplishing nothing. I called Alan and asked if I could spend the night at his place again, and he said sure, but he wasn't going to be home until 9, and I'd left his spare key in his apartment. I was famished, so I stopped into the first restaurant I came across.

I went into a restaurant in Baltimore wearing my backpack and ripped jeans and adventurer's jacket, sweaty and probably smelly from walking all day. A black maître d' stood on the other side of a host desk, wearing a tie and vest. I asked if there was any room and he motioned to follow him. He led me across the restaurant, where every table was full of young black couples in ties and dresses, sipping Martinis. The only open spot was a stool at the end of the bar, where I pushed my yellow backpack under the foot rest. Here I was the dirtiest, low class person in a restaurant of cosmopolitan folks of another race. I'd thought casually about what that must feel like; now I had my *aha!* moment. I ate my soup quietly and left.

XII. Evolution

We sat on the floor in Alan's apartment that night.

"So what's your plan now?" he asked.

"I don't really have one," I said. "I've only got about $200 left. I could never afford a bus or plane ticket to New Orleans, but now I really can't. And I don't think I can hitchhike. Nobody stops to pick you up."

"Yeah, it's not like the old days. People are very suspicious now of strangers, and you look pretty strange."

I was running out of options and grasping at straws.

"I know what I'll do!" I declared. "I'll get a bike, and I'll ride a bike to New Orleans."

"Dude, you can't ride a bike to New Orleans from Baltimore."

"Why not?"

"Because it's two thousand miles. You'd have to train, exercise, get in shape."

"Ha! What better way to *get* in shape!" Alan exploded in laughter.

"Haha! Okay man. That's like saying 'Hey, I'm overweight and obese. I'll just climb Mount Everest real fast to get back in shape!'"

"Sigh...you're right. Fuck. That won't work either."

"Don't you have a credit card or something you could buy a ticket with?"

"Negative."

"I don't know then. You can stay here as long as you like."

"Thanks. I can't stay here though. I've begun to wear out my welcome with Santina I think."

"I thought she liked you?"

"I thought so too, until this morning. Inexplicably she's cold now."

"Huh. That's broads for ya."

"Yeah. A good reason to keep on going."

I decided I needed to get farther south and judge things from there. The next morning I walked to the bus station with my bag. For sixty bucks I could get to Virginia Beach. I'd be almost out of money, but it would be warmer there and I figured I could sleep under the boardwalk and figure something out. So I bought a ticket and boarded the bus.

Sitting next to me for the six-hour trip was a kid with crooked teeth named Skip. It was an appropriate name, because he'd left town after his girlfriend had a baby, to move to Colorado and work at his friend's pizza place. But after a year, guilt had set in, and he was moving back.

"Gotta make some duckets for my bucket, ya know?" I'd never heard that expression before. Anyway the kid chatted my ear off and gave me his number, saying we ought to meet up when we were both in Virginia Beach.

Crossing the *Chesapeake Bay Bridge* was a discomforting experience. We sped along at 55 miles per hour a hundred feet over the water. The bridge is so long that you can't see land when you're in the middle of it. I was afraid a breeze would topple us over, or we'd hit a curb, ricochet through the guardrail and fall to the water.

The bus pulled into the station in the early evening and I was surprised to learn that the it was a couple of miles outside of town. So I picked up my bag and walked along the highway toward the seaside.

By the time I got to the boardwalk it was twilight. My plan of sleeping on the beach was foiled by a cold front that had moved in. I thought it was going to be seventy degrees, and instead it was fifty-three and getting colder. So I needed to get a hotel or motel room, but I had less than a hundred dollars left. I needed to keep some cash to buy a ticket back to Baltimore if something went wrong. Kerouac knew where to find Skid Row places to sleep, but I didn't.

I walked along the boardwalk past the hotels where the signs read $75 a night—too much. At the very end of the strip was a hotel undergoing repairs. It had a sign that said "low rates," so I went in to talk to the clerk, a guy in his early thirties. He glanced at my outfit and bag and scrunched his eyebrows.

"Hey, man," I said. "I need a room pretty bad and I'm at the end of the line. Do you have anything really cheap?" The guy shot me a look and hit a few keys on a computer.

"Single or double bed?"

"Whatever is cheapest, man. I'll take anything."

"We've got rooms for $49 a night I could offer you."

"Man, help me out. I'm broke. I can afford like, $20 a night. I'll be real quiet. You can give me like, the room where you'd put the janitor's brother if he comes to visit." The guy chuckled, considered, nodded.

"Okay look, I'm going to give you this key for room 401. You're not here. It won't be cleaned. If someone else comes and they need the room, I gotta kick you out, alright?"

"That's fine. I really appreciate it, man."

"Yeah...I know how it is. I been there. I work nights. Don't talk to the day staff, don't make a scene."

"I promise."

"Okay." The clerk called a Mexican custodian who showed me to the room. It had a bed and a T.V. and a dead cockroach near the bathtub.

As I unpacked I turned the T.V. on. A newswoman was reporting that Merriam-Webster had added three new words to the dictionary. Number three was "ridonkulous." I laughed aloud.

Mike called me as I finished unpacking.

"How's your trip going? Where are you?"

"I'm in Virginia Beach at a cockroach hotel," I said. "New Orleans is looking pretty unlikely."

"Yeah, but it always was, right?"

"Yeah, I guess."

"I can't believe you're that far, actually."

"Really?"

"Yeah. You know, I'm actually pretty jealous of you. You just took off and you're having an adventure. I'm at work in my cubicle all day. I kind of wish I could've gone too."

Mike was not liberal with compliments, and things had been a little strained since the last raft debacle. I assumed that he and everybody else thought I was a nutcase. To hear him say he would've liked to join me — well, you need that kind of reinforcement every now and then. And, too, he reminded me that the adventure was the the goal or the objective, rather than a specific place, like New Orleans, which I'd picked rather arbitrarily. The point was that I was doing something. It didn't matter what it was. It took courage, one had to admit, to up and leave with no plan and few resources. That single statement from Mike made me remember that it's acceptable, even respectable, to *fail*. What is unacceptable is not to *try*.

I had a miniscule amount of dried pot in a plastic bag, and some rolling papers. I rolled a pretty terrible joint and made my way to the boardwalk. I walked to the boardwalk's southern terminus, then down wooden steps to the beach. It was an hour after dark. There was a jungle gym where two eleven- or twelve-year-old black boys were climbing and singing,

Goin' down, down baby
Your street in a Range Rover
Street sweeper baby cocked
Ready to let it go

I chuckled as I walked past them. They probably thought I, an older white dude, had never heard that song...which was played at every high school dance I went to.

It must have been low tide because the water was quite a ways out. It was night, and the wind was blowing. There were no stars. I ambled far, just in from where the waves lapped, and sat in the sand. I gazed at the rolling waves beneath the rolling clouds over the very place where life first emerged from the sea. The air was cold and salty and fresh. The sound of a thousand undulations melded to a rhythmic roar. In that space were the primordial elements, the earth, the water, the air. With my lighter I created fire. I had to cup my hands to light the joint, and even when I did, it was hard to smoke because I'd done a poor job of rolling it. I threw it away after two semi-hits.

I sat, and all of civilization faded behind me, out of sight. I was alone, in the dark, where the elements mixed, in the birthplace of life. There, in that place, a continuum formed between thought and matter, light and shadow, all of history through now to the future.

In that gradient, that borderland, after all of the death and failure and hope and chaos of the last year, there was climactic calm—piercing perspective tipped with diamond-sharp epiphany.

Look at yourself, I thought, *honestly...and that is how others see you.*

What is potential, but that which might come to exist? You have it, but it cannot be sensed. Others must deduce it from signs that you give them.

You crave companionship, romance, the Good Life. You wish others to have confidence in your plans.

It is not reasonable for you to expect others to respect your potential, which cannot be seen, when all of the outward signs you present suggest failure.

You control how you present yourself, and therefore you control how others see you.

You have no money. You are unshaven. You have a messy apartment. You wear old clothes that are out of style. You cannot expect intelligent, successful people to see these traits and conclude that they are temporary conditions rather than character flaws.

It is not the case that society is shallow and uncaring and selfish. That is an excuse. Society is made of people, and groups coalesce with others who are similar.

If you dress and act like a vagabond, your company will be vagabonds like Santina, confused, wallowing in their own unhappiness. The paradigm of such groups is cynicism, misanthropy, despair. Happiness is not to be found there, only the kind of camaraderie that comes from mutual misery.

Dress better, act respectably, keep your affairs in order, and you will be surrounded by others who are on the cusp of prosperity. Therein lies the key to happiness: the intelligent control of the signifiers you use to describe yourself.

Human happiness depends on the respect of other people – this is true, no matter what philosophers say.

Respect from others depends on how you present yourself. Therefore to present oneself well is not shallow, but rational.

That which is rational is Good. That which is Good is Virtuous. As Socrates said, the Good and the Virtuous and the Happy are all the same thing.

In other words, don't be a drunk, disheveled buffoon. Be a sober, well-dressed sophisticate.

It's so simple that you must laugh at yourself for having to go through all of this to understand it. But that is the difference between knowledge and wisdom. Wisdom comes from bad experiences. And good experiences come from wisdom. How beautiful and poetic and simple, and how tragic that some people never realize This.

I felt a warm liquid in the chambers of my chest that radiated out to my toes and fingertips. I had been erratic and confused for so long that I forgot what it felt like to be confident. The experiences on that beach on the dark night in April of 2007 changed my life forever. The good and the bad, death, failing, succeeding, everything became light and airy suddenly.

So I was on a beach out of money... ha ha ha!

So I wasn't going to make it to New Orleans, and I'd have to go back and explain to my friends...no. There would be no explaining. They wouldn't *care* if I made it to New Orleans... ha ha ha!

I would have to get a job...well, yeah, of course... ha ha ha!

And this is where I am right now, and this is my life. All things considered...this is pretty fun! Ha ha ha!

I smiled and waved goodbye to the sea, and said Thank You. I pressed the butt of the joint into the sand. Hands in my pockets, I turned and strolled back toward the lights of the boardwalk, sort of humming, thinking about how pretty the skyline was.

As I got back to the boardwalk I passed the jungle gym where the kids were still climbing. One of them hailed me.

"Hey white guy! Got any weed?" they laughed.

"Sorry guys," I said.

"Aw, come on! We know you was smokin'!"

"Yeah, but I smoked it all."

"Aww, shit! Well, at least you tellin' the truth 'steada playin like you wasn't."

"Yeah, true. Well, take it easy."

"Yeah, take it easy white guy." I took a couple of paces forward and then I turned around, unable to resist,

"Hey, by the way guys—If you need me, 'You can find me in Saint Louis rolling on dubs, smoking them dubs in clubs and blowing up like cocoa puff.'"

"Ohhhhhh shit!" the kids laughed so hard they fell off the jungle gym and rolled around in the sand. Imagine a white guy like me knowing a Nelly lyric. Ha ha ha!

In the roach hotel room I was eager to get back to Albany to start putting the pieces of my life back together. But if there was one thing I'd learned in my conversations with, and through observing, Morgan over the last six months, it was not to go from zero to sixty, burning the wick on both ends and running out of fuel too quickly. No, there would be no grand announcements about how I'd just discovered the key to human happiness, no time-sensitive objectives wherein I would, through superhuman application, accumulate x amount of money, quit drinking and smoking all at once, undergo a complicated exercise regimen, save every nickel and dime, and so on. Rather, calm confidence was the key—confidence in the benefits that would accrue slowly over time as a result of doing the right thing, meeting my obligations. It was not half as important to make great leaps forward every day as it was simply not to move backward and then have to make up lost ground. Most importantly, there would be no proclamations creating self-imposed obligations. The thing was merely to clean up, to get to neutral. Words mean nothing but they have the potential to embarrass you. Better to have modesty, balance, and let others deduce what they will from the good fortune you create for yourself.

I stuck around an extra day in Virginia Beach and spent the whole duration watching movies I'd never seen. What a waste of time! But I was on vacation, after all, wasn't I? There was a conclusion: it is not wasting time to waste time every now and then, if it helps you regenerate so that you have energy and concentration when you want to use it.

Then I went back to Baltimore. I met Santina at *Starbucks* and she was cold and distant. I went to *Brewers' Art* and ran into Jen with the strait hair and glasses. She explained the situation. After I'd spent the night at Santina's, Brian the Chaperone had slipped a note under her door the next morning, saying how I was someone she ought not trust and how he had deep feelings for her. So that explained that. The next day Santina and I went for a walk to the harbor and I told her it was pusillanimous of Mike to sabotage an innocent fling, sliding a note under a door like a 7th grader. She said she was confused and I said I understood, but the whole thing left a bad taste in my mouth and I realized I ought to stay away from women who are in love with their own existential crises, because they suck the energy out of you.

I put my ATM card in a machine and it let me take out $200, even though I had no money in the bank. So I put my ATM card in again and took out another $200. Ordinarily that would have caused me a lot of anxiety, but it didn't. I got an Amtrak train to Philadelphia and spent a couple nights with Tom, as I was supposed to have done at the beginning of my trip. That was a real nice visit because we hadn't really been that close before, but there is a bond created when you go to another city and stay as someone's guest. The Greeks realized that, which is why they treated hospitality as a religious duty. While I was there I met a girl who gave me a tour of Phili while Tom was at work. We smoked a bowl and she showed me South Street with its buildings covered in colored glass. Then I took an Amtrak to Brooklyn and spent a couple days with Kate, the nice girl I'd met months before in Albany. Again, that could've been awkward, since she lived with Jack, her new boyfriend, and I am male. But I was feeling so happy-go-lucky that there was no awkwardness at all. We all went out drinking together and had a nice time. While we were waiting for a train I glanced at a subway map, and that was the first time I realized that Manhattan was an island. It sounds pretty dumb, but as I told Santina, "upstate" New York is practically another country from New York City, and although I'd taken busses there when I dated Cady, I never studied the geography.

"But you were going to take a raft to Manhattan...and you didn't know it was an island?" Kate wondered.

"You learn something every day, ha ha ha!"

I took a bus back up to Albany, but there was a week of April left and Jess Gadani had paid to sublet my apartment for the month. So my parents brought me to their house and I spent a week in New Baltimore under the radar, visiting my family and reading a lot for the first time since I'd graduated.

That was the end of my hitchhiking trip, during which I'd done no hitchhiking, and I felt thoroughly rejuvenated. More than that, it was the end of my blue period. I wouldn't go so far as to say it was the end of my youth. But it was the end of that part of my life I would call "The Lyrical." Henceforward The Practical would take precedence.

The first thing I did when I arrived at the Downtube on the morning of May 1st, 2007 was plant a 50-gallon trash can in the middle of the living room and declare,

"It's time to clean up!"

Morgan's door was closed but I heard stirring. I surveyed the room. *Sega* cords were braided in tangled piles atop mangled *Lego* models across the room. Juvenile objects for wasting time, they were. They were machines with which I'd spent hours, days, as an adolescent, palms sweating surviving final levels with few extra lives. Into the trash can. Beer cans, empty liquor bottles—the place had obviously not been cleaned since I'd left—into the garbage. Morgan's door opened.

"Heyyyy welcome home!"

"Greetings, good sir!" I shook Morgan's hand.

"You seem in good spirits."

"I am in excellent spirits. I feel I have acquired a new paradigm for making my life prosperous, according to my definition of that."

"Wow, that must've been quite a trip you made! You're cleaning the place up this early in the morning?"

"It is 10:15. I don't think that's very early. If you were to go to work, you would have gotten up three hours ago. That is approximately when I got up in New Baltimore, and I am coming to the job of repairing my life. I ought to approach that as seriously as I approach an occupation, ought I not?"

"Ha, wow, I agree. Big questions for the morning. 'Some of us drank last night,'" Morgan quoted a familiar Jaredism.

"That's okay. This is mostly my mess anyway. Feel free to go back to sleep for a while."

"No no, I want to take advantage of DT's enthusiasm for cleaning while I can. Plus it'll be a good way to start off your return, and you'll associate the place with relaxing instead of clutter and shit."

Morgan went into his room to change. There were many dirty plates, beer cans, solo cups and silverware cast around the rooms, so I brought these to the kitchen counter, until the counter could no longer hold any more, so I began rinsing out cans and bottles if they were returnable or chucking them if they were not. Jess moaned behind the louver doors that led to my room.

I divided the *Legos* into two boxes, one of Mike's and one of mine, and stacked them by the door. Morgan emerged and said,

"I'll take care of the dishes because I know how much you hate to touch the water with the floating food in it."

"Thank you very much, you are right, it disgusts me."

I stacked Jess's belongings in a pile in the kitchen. Soon the two couches and the backs of the dining room table were cleared of clothing. The louver doors opened and Jess shuffled out, rubbing her eyes.

"You're ambitious today."

"Is that a bad thing? Morgan...is ambition a bad thing?"

"—Oh here we go—"

"No I don't think it is," Morgan shouted from the kitchen. "After all what is ambition but the pursuit of what motivates you? As long as your ambition isn't like, to kill hundreds of thousands of people, I think it's a good thing."

"Yeah but what about those people who *do* have that ambition?" Jess groaned, "That's why we ought to get rid of *all* ambition *everywhere*, so that nobody wants to do anything, ha ha ha."

"I leave for one month and you all become Communists?"

After four hours the place was as clean as one would expect two mid-twenty-year-olds' apartment to be. I wasn't yet satisfied, but we'd gotten our space back to par, so although we might not gleam with pride, we wouldn't be ashamed to have company. I'd removed most of the clutter by filing papers into boxes and throwing out with merciless anti-nostalgia the toys we'd accumulated over Detox Week. The result was four contractor trash bags full of crap stacked awaiting garbage night. Morgan ran the dishwasher continuously which resupplied our cocktail and wine glasses, which I dried and placed in several display cases, after dusting them for the first time in months. Morgan filled several black bags with beer and soda cans. As I continued cleaning, he brought them to "Ghetto Chopper" as we called the *Price Chopper* around the corner. Using the money from the cans he bought a 12-pack of *JW Dundee's* beer bottles and a frozen pizza. Morgan, Jess and I sat in the window for lunch, surveying our progress.

"The place hasn't looked this good in months," Morgan commented contentedly.

"It is amazing to me that we let it get as bad as it was, when spending a morning cleaning together would've taken care of the problem," I replied.

Jess had taken a while to get moving and at first I felt bad stacking her stuff by the door. The implication was Time To Go. I think she hoped to stick around a little longer before understanding that I was instituting a return to normalcy.

"I think you have fleas, or something, in your bed," she said.

"Have you seen fleas, or your skin just itches when you sleep there?" I asked.

"My skin itches and I have little bumps."

"Ah, yes. Sorry about that. That's not fleas. The pillow with the checkered pillowcase is about fifty years old and the material is disintegrating. It gets in the bed sheets and gives you a rash. I thought it was fleas, too, until I figured out what it was."

"Umm, I wish you would've told me that before I used that pillow for a month."

"I assumed you would bring your own pillow."

"Why would you even keep a pillow like that? That made you itch? How long has it been like that?"

"For several months," I said.

A "ha!" escaped Morgan's throat as he brought his hand to his forehead, not, as Jess or I would have done, in order to illustrate that he was confounded, but because he was truly so confounded that he did it involuntarily. He said,

"You're saying that for three or four months you slept in an itchy bed when you could've just thrown out a pillow and solved the problem? That's amazing. I don't understand how someone could, like, suffer something continuously when you could've solved the problem in two seconds."

"Yeah?" I was surprised my Morgan's myopathy. "I'm not saying it wasn't lazy, but you ought to understand it, at least. In a way it's a trait that our whole generation, and our parent's generation, suffers from. At any given time, it's easier to 'suffer' some small annoyance than to fix the problem, even if the problem is simply fixed. At any given time, it's easier to scratch and say 'I'll get a new pillow this week,' than to clean all of my sheets, vacuum the mattress, drive to bullshit *Walmart*, buy a pillow, and drive back. Having rationalized that the problem will be dealt with later, we forget about it. Buying the pillow and all that isn't hard *per se*, but the *process* is more annoying *at any given point* than scratching and rationalizing."

"I'm not sure you can really generalize that to the whole...generation. I think most people would've just got a new pillow," Morgan said.

"Yeah? How about that cabinet door in the bathroom? The one that falls off the wall every other day, and has fallen off the wall every other day for seven months, exposing the gross inside of the cabinet beneath the bathroom sink. How many times have you walked into the bathroom, saw the damn thing on the floor, and picked it up and balanced it just right on the hinge so that it stays there for a little while, before falling off again?"

"Ha, geeze, you're right. I must've done that fifty times since we've move in."

"Fifty times it has annoyed you. Fifty times you've taken 30 or 45 seconds to balance the thing. How many times have girls come over and used the bathroom and thought 'Gee I thought this was a nice place until I saw the cabinet door falling off,'? Add my fifty times fixing it and getting annoyed by it and now you've got a cumulative total of a man-hour of temporarily fixing that door and a hundred instances of annoyance, at least. Meanwhile there's a drill on the back porch. We could use a bit to drill through the cabinet door. We replace the drill bit with a screwdriver bit. We take a screw from the back porch, and then we screw the door into the cabinet. It would never fall off again. It would take, what, a minute and a half to really fix it, and yet we never have, because at any given point it's been easier to put it in place without a screw, knowing it'll fall off again. At my parent's house they have a closet door with a little knob that fell off when I was a kid. The knob has been sitting on the bathroom counter for twelve or fifteen years now. It only needs a longer screw. There is something in this, I declare. All of these little annoyances repeat, sometimes daily, like debits periodically charged against our time, concentration and energy. Added together and multiplied over time they have a tangible effect on our standard of living."

"Well, you're right. It does seem kind of stupid that we keep being annoyed by certain things when we could fix them easily. I think it's that we're always busy so we just don't make the time to fix things. We say to ourselves that we're going to fix x, y, and z later, but then we never schedule a time to do the things."

"I was just thinking of the repeating scene in *It's A Wonderful Life* when George Bailey walks up the stairs and the railing knob comes off in his hand and the second time they show it happening he looks like he wants to slam the knob. Anyway, the lesson is this: remember that accomplishing numerous small, easy tasks can produce as much good, in terms of saving you time and from annoyance, as a large task that takes the same amount of time to accomplish. If a person was to have, say, four hours free on a

Saturday, it might be a better idea to fix the closet knob, the cabinet door, the broken drawer, get a new pillow, and so forth, than to spend the time doing one big thing like painting a porch. Especially when one considers that such annoyances will repeat and accrue over years and even decades. A couple of hours of menial work can save dozens of man hours of time spent temporarily dealing with menial annoyances. It's not the key to human happiness, but it's a good habit: fix things as they come up."

"*Good habit*," Jess laughed. "I mean I agree with you, but the term 'good habit' is funny. It reminds me of my grandparents telling us to say please and thank you and walk with your hands behind your back. I always thought of 'good habits' as like, an adult, controlling...almost religious idea, and I thought it was bullshit."

"I mean evolutionarily there must be some benefit to having good habits," Morgan postulated. "I mean, yeah, they're wrapped up in religious shit today in this country but a good habit is *good* because it's *healthy* for the organism. It's a good habit for a squirrel to bury nuts all over the place in the fall, so that he has shit to eat in the winter. It was a good habit for, I donno, Native Americans to spend a few hours every day making arrow heads, because they needed them to hunt."

"It's another example of a word or an idea that has been hijacked to mean something more than it originally meant. Jess—and I know what you mean, Jess—feels like there is a *moral* component to a good habit, and since she rejects the idea of moral *authority*, she thinks good habits must be meaningless or hollow. But it's not *morality* that makes a habit *good*, it is: *the tendency of the habit to promote health and happiness.* Cigarettes are bad habits because they tend to destroy health and therefore happiness. The other word for a bad habit is a *vice*. The opposite of a vice is 'virtue.' So everybody thinks that *virtue* is some religious thing, like going to Church on Sunday, when virtue need not have any connection to religion at all, and if it does, it's coincidental. That which is virtuous *is simply good for you*, in terms of making you healthier and happier. So like, temperance and moderation; not biting your finger nails; spending your money wisely; these things are all virtuous, not because the Bible says they are, but because they help you. Never taking the Lord's name in vain—whatever that means—isn't really virtuous or un-virtuous at all, because it has no impact on your happiness or health. Religion says it's responsible for *the idea* of morality and virtue; we come to associate morality and virtue with religion; then when we start to despise the excesses of organized religion—when we start to disregard it as outdated and irrelevant—we think the same about *morality* and *virtue*. If you think that because you don't subscribe to a religious sect that therefore you can't know what's good for you...well, you're going to be a pretty unhealthy and unhappy person. But if you take virtue as the opposite of vice: *something good you do constantly*, then as Ben Franklin said, 'Long habits of virtue have a sensible effect upon the countenance.'"

"Makes sense," Morgan acceded. "If you sleep on dirty pillow cases, never wash your face, smoke cigarettes and eat greasy food, you'll have pimples. If you do the opposite you'll have clear skin."

"Which reminds me, Jess, I'd like to go shopping with you for face washes," I said.

"Wow, really? Ho, ho ho. I distinctly remember suggesting that you buy a good face wash and you said something like, hmm, what was it? 'I'm not going to use a face wash like an effeminate pee pee boy?'"

"I don't think I used those words exactly..."

"Ha ha, Dallas Dallas, it's good to see you're learning that there's nothing wrong with taking care of how you look. It's worth the extra money."

"I admit that you were right to give me that advice, and I should have followed it."

Jess clutched her chest with clasped hands and affected a painful expression, as though undergoing cardiac arrest.

"Dallas! I was *right*? Jess Gadani was *right* and Dallas was *wrong*? What happened to you on this trip?"

"Many people lead bad lives that would gladly lead good ones but do not know how to make the change," Franklin said in the 18th century. It is true today. So much of human *un*happiness stems from bad habits that people cling to as part of their psychological constitution. There is nothing immoral or bad about recognizing what society values and adjusting your habits to concord when harmless. It's practical; it's virtuous, which means it's good. Over the lifespans of two individuals, one with good habits and one with poor, it makes a big difference—years of extra time, thousands or tens of thousands or hundreds of thousands of extra dollars. The great tragedy is that some people never develop good habits—they never *mature*. Instead, they spend a lifetime lamenting their condition, blaming a fate which they create.

Now that my apartment was clean and organized I had a base of operations. A living space is an extension of one's mind and body.

The next task was to acquire money. My new job would have to be intellectually stimulating or I wouldn't be happy. Since I had connections at my former high school I applied to be a substitute teacher and tutor. I submitted the paperwork to the Board of Education and provided my fingerprints. As I awaited approval I went to Adam's house and then to Morgan's father's house and finished the painting I'd left half-done a month before. At least I partially made up for my previous flakiness. I began to exercise and to read.

Morgan lent me *The Way You Wear Your Hat*, a series of anecdotes about the style of Frank Sinatra. I made it a rule never to leave the house unkempt, even if I was tired, because even at the grocery store or for a walk I'd run into people, and I felt healthier and more productive if I looked my best. Dressing with taste shows respect to the rest of society, who has to look at you. Sinatra was known as a big drinker, yet he never allowed himself to appear intoxicated. He was always seen with a cocktail in his hand, but never an empty glass. The book said he'd often merely hold the cocktail, like an accessory to his outfit, and put it down when it was half empty, then order another. In that manner he *seemed* always to be drinking, yet always exuded self-control, which is another way of saying he was "cool." Morgan and I adopted this habit and although I continued to spend a lot of time in bars, seldom did I reach the point of even a buzz. I was amazed at how different the other males became as the evening wore on, and vowed not to drink to intoxication, to avoid looking foolish.

It was absolutely necessary to have such poise when I began substitute teaching. Since I was only five years older than the students at the time, the way I held myself and the language I used were my only means to establish authority over a group of 25 or 30 teenagers looking to produce chaos in order to gain attention.

"Hey teacher, do you smoke pot?" was a standard question from the back of the room as I took attendance, followed by giggles and laughter. Without poise and self-confidence, how do you deal with such a question? To yell "That is not a question a student asks of an adult!" would merely make them laugh. I knew from slipping on banana peels in 5th grade that an explosive response from an exasperated adult was the funniest possible outcome. To lie and say "No, of course not," would be to descend to the defensive, and to say "Yes, fairly frequently" would be inappropriate. "While I am honored that you want to emulate me, which is why, I presume, you're asking about my personal habits, the question goes beyond the scope of today's lesson, which is the Russian Revolution, a fascinating topic," became my standard response.

While substitute teaching was interesting it barely paid subsistence wages on a per diem basis. Tutoring, on the other hand, was more profitable, if also more challenging. As a kind of independent contractor, I could choose to accept pupils, or not. As the only young, male tutor available to the district, I was often asked to tutor students, in their homes, who were mentally or physically ill, long-term behavior problems, or awaiting court appearances while forbidden to attend school by injunction. I took every assignment offered and was soon very busy between subbing and tutoring. Over the course of a month I was able to pay back much of what remained of my loans from Mike, Morgan and Jared. And so after being back in Albany for 30 days I was feeling and looking better, paying off my debts, meeting women, and living in one of the nicest apartments among my group of friends. That was the reward for thinking and acting practically. Cumulatively I felt very content, and looking back on the winter and the way I'd felt before, I thought, "Never Again."

II. The Manhattan Project

Life was going about as well as I could hope. I was genuinely happy and satisfied with the way my job and friends and avocations were progressing, almost for the first time. My new perspective affected how I perceived the world; this affected how the world perceived me; a salutary feedback loop developed. And yet there was this one open, unfinished goal from my *past life*, if you will. That was rafting down the Hudson.

Mike and I had talked about it hypothetically during the winter, but we made no plans. We merely noted that this or that improvement would overcome particular problems we'd encountered on the first two attempts. So the idea was out there, but we were taking no steps to make it happen.

The extra time it would take to build a raft alone, compared to with one or two other people, made partners a necessity. Although I earnestly desired to try again, I didn't talk about it much, because without friends it would be foolish to try a third time.

One day Jess and I took a stroll down Lark Street. It was a pleasant May morning as we admired the architecture and the verdure of the blooming foliage. Albany is pretty in the spring. Trees broke up the cityscape as tulips sprouted from sidewalk planters. At the corner of Lark and Central Avenue, the latter of which marks the path of the first railroad built in New York State (from Albany to Schenectady), was the main branch of the Albany Public Library. We decided to tour the place. As luck would have it, we came on a day when the library was giving out free books acquired from an estate sale. On top of the first pile I perused three books: *Shoreline and Sextant: Practical Coastline Navigation*, by Mike P. Budlong; *Seamanship*, a book detailing the trade of a deckhand, by Peter Kemp; and another book also entitled *Seamanship*, which was an anatomy of boat types, navigation rules, knots, nautical terms, marine practices and laws.

"This is a *sign*," Jess said.

I pointed to a placard that read *Exit*.

"*That* is a sign, Jess. *These* are books."

"Oh come on. Of all the places that we could have ended up, on all days, you of all people ended up here finding those of all books. Fate is telling you to read them and finish sailing to New York City."

"Your *Fate* sure has a complicated way of actuating people to do its bidding."

"The Lord works in mysterious ways," Jess laughed. I flipped through the pages of the books.

"These are absolutely fascinating, invaluable. I can't believe I can get these for free," I admitted. "Look, an illustrated appendix on kinds and uses of various knots! Ha! There are different uses for different kinds of knots. Amazing. Who knew? Look at this book—how to lay an anchor and back up an anchor...*How to Pick Up a Mooring in Slack Water; Against the Tide; With the Tide; At Right Angles to the Tide...Weather Patterns and Prediction...Construction; Ropes and Rope Work; Sailing Regulations and Etiquette*! What a wealth of knowledge. Amazing. I wouldn't understand what any of this stuff refers to if I hadn't had our first two rafting experiences. I would have no context; it would be like reading about how to fly a spacecraft. But I understand what these situations mean now. Boy I would love to read these books and have all of this information in my head. You know, it would be knowledge that would legitimate me being called the *Captain*."

"You see? I'm telling you, there is a method to the madness of things. Maybe not God, but something has a plan, and part of it is for you to raft the Hudson!" I closed the hard-cover book and looked at Jess, trying to gauge how facetious she was.

"Jess, I would love to believe that."

"Then go ahead and believe it."

"Yeah...but I can't believe that. Just because I want to."

"Bah, what difference does it make?"

"It makes all the difference."

"Why." I paced away and came back.

"You're preying on me. I'm ripe for suggestion because of this odd coincidence, and I really want to do this trip again. But the idea that there is this thing called Fate and there is a grand plan and somehow me building a boat out of docks and sailing to New York City is a part of that plan...it is ridiculous."

"No it isn't."

"It's *ridonkulous*! How self-centered of a thought. Could it be more self-centered? That all of the universe has a plan for *me*?"

"It has a plan for everybody, not just you."

"Oh, pah, this is an old conversation. I hate this conversation. Part of Fate's plan is for babies to die of malnutrition in Chad? For a boy to have his feet amputated because he's from the wrong village in Congo?"

"Maybe, I don't know."

"How do you manage to push my buttons so easily? I'm aggravated at you."

"You make it easy, Dal."

Jess took a collection of Hawthorne's short stories and a copy of *The Book of Laughter and Forgetting*, by Milan Kundera, one of my least favorite authors, and we were happy with our harvest.

I cleaned the bathtub, scrubbed it to the point of scratching the enamel. I lowered myself into the hot water. On a little shelf to the right of the porcelain I laid out a copy of *Seamanship*, a pen, a highlighter, a glass of water, a cup of tea, and a bowl of mixed nuts. I realized I hadn't read an entire book in almost six months, since I finished my undergrad. More than anything else that illustrated to me how dysfunctional I'd been. Long baths were the most luxurious pampering I indulged in. I trickled hot water to keep the bath from cooling. By the time I was finished I'd relaxed my muscles, cleared my sinuses, and read two chapters about seamanship.

I started spending three or four hours a day reading. If I didn't get called to substitute teach, I likely took a bath and read for three hours from 6 a.m. to nine, ate breakfast, read on the couch, ate lunch, took another three-hour bath in the afternoon, and read more at night. In the previous twenty-two years I'd only once read more than a hundred pages in a day. Now a hundred pages became a rather moderate objective, not at all uncommon.

I finished reading *Shoreline and Sextant* and the smaller of the two *Seamanship* books, not really remembering or understanding everything, but trying just to expose myself to the material and bookmark those sections which I wanted to return to. The larger of the Seamanship books was a tome, six or seven hundred pages, hard cover, with small print. That was going to be work to get through, but it was so fascinating I could hardly put it down, and I started to carry it with me everywhere, reading a paragraph or two whenever I had downtime. I imagined that someday I'd pilot a boat down the Mississippi, and then it would be necessary to know all of the rules and etiquette of navigating inland waterways.

Then I went to the bookstore and bought *The Hudson* by Morgan Lewis and read about the geological and cultural history of the river valley, gaining an expansive new appreciation of its importance to American History. While not as wide or as long as some of the other rivers in North America, the Hudson was a main access point for colonization; the scene of important strategic developments during the Revolution; the inspiration for the Hudson River School of Art, the new Republic's first homespun aesthetic movement; the scene of the short stories of some of America's first writers; the river where Fulton tested the first steamboat; the trade artery which, after the construction of the Erie Canal, made the Midwest a breadbasket and New York City a thriving metropolis; the place where the first legal wrangling over pollution took place, and where the "environmentalism" movement burgeoned. Practically across the river from my childhood home, in Kinderhook, was the hometown of an American President, Martin Van Buren. I started to shed the image I'd held since childhood, of the river as a rural muddy stream where now and then a barge would pass. The river became a personality, a character, a scene where history unfolded, existing long before any of my friends, which would continue long after we all expire. And what characters lived along its shores! Boy, did I want to get out on the river again and see the places I read about. Boy did I want to get out there and try and put some of my new knowledge into effect. But, I had to keep reminding myself, I needed help, and it had to be voluntary help. I couldn't push anybody or I'd find myself right back where I was the year before, responsible for everything, doing all of the work. That would be foolishly impractical.

These things that I was doing *instead* of building a raft were increasing my chances of finding help to achieve that goal. There is an object-lesson in this which warrants consideration.

Whatever you want to call it, Group Psychology or Interpersonal Politics, there is a sociological component to every interaction between multiple individuals. It is a component of raft-plan-making, job acquisition, family dinners, dating. We enjoy participating with others toward an end. In many ways, it is what gives meaning to our lives. But we seldom think about the factors that affect in what and with whom we participate.

The previous summer, when I tried to execute the second raft trip, I begged and pleaded for help from anyone with arms and legs. On the one hand I built the thing in order to have a vehicle *if* I managed to convince someone to join me. On the other hand I made extravagant projections on the likelihood of success while scrambling like a chicken with its head cut off. The discrepancy between words and actions was destructive to *trust*. Instead of convincing people, as I was trying to do, that it would be *in their interest* to join me because of the fun and experience, the whole thing seemed like a mess that would cause stress.

Appearing to need other people's help, asking everybody and anybody, was bad policy, plain and simple. It was similar to a single person who goes around constantly saying how lonely they are, imploring others to set them up on dates, remarking how just meeting someone would change their whole life and they would do anything to meet and be with anybody. It is unmanly and unattractive.

Desperation dissuades, because it suggests a poor *partner*. After all, anyone who is desperate for company to pursue a goal must have already been rejected by numerous other people, or they wouldn't be desperate. When one solicits the help of one person, then the next, then the next, the person who is asked for help *later* feels entirely un-special. It's like being invited to a wedding by a person who has already asked, and been turned down by, four other people. You might like the person and want to go to the wedding, but it feels demeaning to be anybody's fifth choice. When a person pushes and provides justifications and explanations and seems obsequious, anyone they approach tends to think "This person is too much. I don't care how nice they are, I don't want any part of this noise. I've got my own problems to deal with." Practically speaking, over-eagerness is a turn-off in any context. No matter how much one yearns for something, one ought never to *seem* too eager for another's attention. The point can hardly be over-emphasized.

I hardly brought up the raft trips throughout May. I didn't realize it (because honestly, I avoided talking about it due to embarrassment), but this caused people to wonder if and what I was planning. Instead of appearing stressed-out and crazy, broke, drunk, and anxiety-ridden, I seemed kempt and confident. People are magnetically repelled from over-eager personalities, but gravitate toward those who *seem*, at least, to have their affairs in order. So instead of talking about the raft with everyone I met, I seldom discussed it, and others began to bring it up.

"So...how's your next raft plan coming?" Paul, my friend who drove me to Delaware, asked.

"Honestly, it's something that's on my mind; I'd like to try it again. But I'm not going to do it until the conditions are right." There was something in an answer like that that made people assert,

"You know, I think the next time you do it, you'll make it."

Over the course of the month, conversations on that topic changed 180 degrees from a year earlier. Whereas before people would bait and taunt me about how such a trip "could not be done," and that I was foolish for trying, now other people tried to convince *me* that it was possible, and that I *ought* to try again.

I would like to claim credit for developing some sociological strategy for getting others to support me, like Reverse Psychology or something, but I really only stumbled into it as I tried to focus on other things, and understand what happened in retrospect. The important thing is not to be omniscient, but to use your powers of introspection to abstract lessons from your experiences and apply them in the future.

As it happened, Jared mentioned in an off-hand manner one night that he would "be down" for another trip, but one that didn't require "mad work." I told him I appreciated that, and that if I tried again I would want to go with four people. Knowing that he wanted no part of building the boat, I said that nonetheless I'd be happy to have his help for the trip itself, since I pictured a raft where four people would paddle to provide the movement casually. But, I emphasized, it was all speculative, and we might as well not assume that anything was happening unless I found two others to participate.

TJ was an old friend of mine, a serious young man whose school papers I helped edit, who disliked attention, who worked industriously and had no discernible vices. A good-looking kid, who grew up with a single mom who verged on crazy, he had little patience for tom-foolery and was actuated above all by a desire to obtain a good job with good income in order to be financially stable. He was athletic and liked the outdoors.

"If you ever wanted to canoe to Manhattan, I'd be down to go with you," he said one day.

I told him that the next "raft" I pictured would be much like a canoe trip. The boat would sit on two rows of foam pontoons which would cut through the water like canoes, and we would paddle, as on a canoe.

"I would love to see the whole river," TJ said. "But I don't want to be in any headlines or dress up like characters and stuff."

"I'm not interested in dressing up or being a joke," I said. "There's a new seriousness to my life that I want to continue. But I would like to close the chapter on this raft thing. I wouldn't go unless we built a boat that we tested ahead of time, to know it will not sink; unless we had two other people to go with us to help; and unless we brought an electric trolling motor and some batteries in case we need propulsion."

"I thought you couldn't have a motor?"

"I can't use fossil fuels. That was the original goal and that's still a parameter. But a battery is electrical energy. Could be charged, say, by someone's solar panels before we go. So it wouldn't use fossil fuels, but it would be there as a safety device." Without pushing, I showed TJ some of the highlighted sections in the books I'd read on marine navigation, and the notes I'd taken. I told him that what was fascinating was the science behind it all. There is, for example, a formula that you can apply to determine how much "scope" — length of rope — to let out when anchoring, based on the depth of the water. Based on the composition of the river bottom (e.g. mud or rock) there are different types of anchors to use. "It is the shape of the anchor — rather than its weight — in addition to the scope, which provides the holding-power. Therefore, the choice of anchor and the length of line can be determined by a formula. Knowing the formula for that, or any other application, is what constitutes good seamanship." TJ was intrigued by the science, and thought a river trip, under safe conditions, could be fun. He also wanted to learn more about building things. So he said he would help me build another boat, if I got all of the materials together myself, and would join me on the trip, if I found two others to go and kept his name out of the newspaper. So now there were two friends willing to help me, to different extents, if I designed the boat and got the materials myself, and found another person.

Of course only one person would suffice for the job, and that was Mike. No one else had the mental independence and understood the idea completely. One night he came over to the Downtube and I said in a speculative way,

"You know, if I ever did a raft trip again, I've come to realize the importance of doing it with the help of other people. Different people bring different things to the table. I'd really prefer, if it ever was to happen again, to be more of a coach or a facilitator, than a Captain."

"Yeah. You're very good at like, convincing people to give us docks, coming up with a general design, doing the manual labor and stuff. Also providing the place where it'd be built, because I assume it'd be built at your parent's house."

"Naturally."

"But I think you need a little help like, translating your design into something practical that can actually be built. I feel like that's the part that I'm better at."

"I feel the same way. And anything that had to do with sailing, or cutting angles...it was your idea to make foam pontoons for the sake of hydrodynamic-ness. The trip would need innovations like that."

"And you really think The Boat House would let you have two more docks, to build the design you were talking about in February, with the cabin and stuff?"

"Yes, I'm certain."

"And your parents would really let you build *another* boat in their yard?"

"I could convince them."

"Huh. But you'd have to find a couple of other people to help row, right? Because you said you wouldn't go unless you had four people."

"Well, it's funny you mention that, because just this week Jared and TJ both brought it up, and said they would go with me if I tried again, and help row."

"Really? Wow. TJ? He'd be good at rowing."

"Yeah. He said he wants to learn more about building stuff and he'd lend a hand building it, too."

"Wow, no kidding. It would be nice to have someone else's help during the building stages."

"Yeah."

"Huh. And you have a trailer to get the thing to the water?"

"Yes. I'd want to have it built a couple of weeks before we launched. That way it could be tested out." Mike's eyes moved around and he nodded as he considered. Then, to my surprise, he suddenly smiled and said,

"You know? I'm down to try this again. I think this plan would work. Yeah. I have a week vacation I could take this summer. I think TJ would be a big help and Jared would be fun to go with. What the hell, let's try it again."

"Yeah? I mean, I'm serious. If I try this again, that's it. It would take work to build it and try it out ahead of time. We'd have to work on designing it and building it together."

"I'm serious too. I mean, I get out of work at five, I have weekends free. I'm sure between me, you and TJ we could build the thing in a couple of weeks. Yes. I'm actually really excited. I'd like to try this again."

With that we both grinned and shook hands emphatically. Mike was the keystone, as far as I was concerned, the last and most necessary piece. He would be a significant asset. Now we had a real chance of success, and I would finally be able to check 'rafting to Manhattan' off of my list of things to do. It was a red-letter day. Immediately we sat down to sketch the design.

Getting the materials to my house was not very difficult. As with the previous summer, Charlie, the proprietor of Shady Harbor, let me take two old docks from the stack in the woods. This time I selected two docks with foam floatation instead of barrels. There would be no chance of sinking. As a sign of good faith I asked Jared and TJ to help me get the two docks to my parent's house. The first weekend in May I managed to get most of the materials we needed in one place.

The next problem was orchestrating everybody's schedules. I made the mistake of asking what weeks worked for Jared, TJ, and Mike. Each had different times that would work or not work, and for a week the project floated in a sea of relativity as we discussed dates, which affected the construction schedule and delayed Mike and Jared putting in time-off requests. Ultimately as the facilitator I chose Thursday, June 28th as the launch date. The hard target became a tangible thing around which everyone's plans coalesced. If you're planning with other people you have to choose a date to prompt them to start planning, otherwise nothing gets done.

The plan called for an updated version of a paddlewheel. I thought it would give us a chance to use some of our leg muscles for propulsion, to give our shoulders and arms a rest. But as time passed and we took no action to build the wheel we realized we had neither the tools nor the understanding to construct it correctly. Instead we decided to rely on paddling and sailing.

One of the docks served as our scrap lumber pile. The deck boards were nailed, rather than screwed, to the joists of the dock. We removed these deck boards using a crowbar, and now we had thirty pieces of 2x6 planks 12-feet long. That was plenty of feet to build the frame of the cabin. Next, Oliver Cross came down with his chop saw, which I found to be an amazing labor-saving machine for cutting angles in lumber. With a chop saw you simply set the angle on the tool's built-in protractor and it cuts a machine angle without having to draw a line.

Mike suggested that the cabin would be sturdier if he cut 20-degree angles into the bottoms of the joists, so that a front view of the cabin would look more like a trapezoid than a box. I didn't really understand what he meant, even as he cut the tips of all of the boards at angles. The next day, TJ and I went down to work on the boat, and decided to assemble the frame of the cabin from the boards Mike had cut. Not understanding what Mike was planning, we were annoyed that the boards didn't sit perpendicular to the deck. So we cut all the boards again at 90-degree angles, and assembled the cabin so that, from a front view, it looked like a box instead of a trapezoid. When Mike came down after work and saw what we had done, he smacked his head.

"I spent two hours cutting all those boards so that the sides of the cabin would angle down to the deck. Then you guys cut all the boards so that they would stand straight up. You just spent two hours undoing what I did for two hours!"

Well, so I was no carpenter. We agreed that henceforth we ought to understand exactly how every part of the boat was going to be built before any of us started working.

Since we figured we might need to make repairs to the boat along the way after we set sail, we built a square, floating "trunk" at the back of the dock. It hung off the stern as a 4x6 foot rectangle, with foam underneath for floatation. We bought hinges and made a plywood cover for the trunk, so that we had a big toolbox to keep things in, floating behind us. Next we nailed plywood to the outside of the cabin frame, and made doors at the front and back out of plywood. Now we had a shelter to protect us from rain and horseflies. The cabin was strong but heavy. We enjoyed climbing on top of it and picturing ourselves jumping off the top into the water once we got under way.

One of my tutoring students was a fifteen-year-old kid who was forbidden by court order to attend school, because of an ongoing criminal case in which he was the defendant. His father was non-existent and I could tell he had few male role models. During our first couple of sessions, which occurred four times a week for two hours, he tried to distract me so he wouldn't have to work.

"Me and my friend went rafting this weekend," he said one Monday.

"Yeah?"

"Yeah, in the Hannacroix. We took a refrigerator box and floated on a piece of foam we found in the back yard. It was fun! But we only went a little ways and it broke apart."

"That happens sometimes," I said. It pleased me that he spent his weekend doing something like that, obviously having gotten the idea from me, instead of getting into trouble. Since he was supposed to be learning trigonometry, I took a risk and asked his mother if she felt comfortable allowing him to come to my parent's house as Mike and I constructed the triangular bow of the boat. She was very happy to drop him off that Saturday.

"So, here is the problem," I told him after showing him the dock with the cabin on top of it. "Right now, the front of the boat is square. Now, over here we have the frame from another dock. Where two sides of the frame come together, they make a corner, obviously. They create a Right Angle. How many degrees are in a right angle?"

"Ninety," the pupil smiled.

"Right. Okay, now what we want to do is keep that right angle as the tip or bow of the boat, and cut both boards that shoot out from that angle at exactly the correct length so that we can put it at the front of the dock, with the front of the dock forming the base of the triangle."

"Yeah I get it. You want to cut the boards, like, rotate it, and attach it to the front so the front of the boat is a triangle."

"Right. So how do we figure out how long to cut the boards that will be the sides of the triangular bow?"

"Uhh, trial and error?"

"That won't work, because if we cut the sides of the triangle too short, well, we can't lengthen them."

"Alright, I give up."

"No giving up! Let's think about it, eh? Now, what information do we know?"

"We know that the tip of the triangle is going to be ninety degrees."

"Yes. And the base of the triangle is going to be how long?"

"Uh...however long the width of the dock that you're attaching it to is."

"Twelve feet."

"Okay...so the base of the triangle is twelve feet, and the apex of the triangle is ninety degrees. I donno what else."

"How about the sides? We don't know how long they need to be. But what do we know? What ratio will one side be, to the other?"

"Ratio...hmm...well, the sides'll be the same length, right?"

"Right. So we'll have a right triangle with two equal sides."

"Isosceles."

"How do you know?"

"Because it's got two equal sides."

"But doesn't isosceles refer to two equal *angles*?"

"Yeah but if you have two equal sides, the angles across from them will be equal."

"So what are the angles of our triangle?"

"Uh, one is ninety, and the other two are equal, so 180 minus ninety is ninety, so whatever times two equals ninety, that's the degrees of the base angles."

"Okay, and what is ninety divided by two?"

"Oh, duh, 45."

"So the triangle we want to construct for our bow will have a 90-degree apex, and two 45-degree angles at the base, and the base will be 12 feet."

"Okay but I guess this is what I don't get. You know the angles; how do you figure out the fucking lengths?"

"Chill with the F-bomb. You figure out the length of the sides because they have a relationship with the angles across from them, like you already said. So we have a right triangle because it has a 90-degree angle. So across from the 90-degree angle is our base, which we said is twelve feet. So we know that one side squared, plus the other side squared, is going to equal 12-feet squared, which is 144."

"Okay so a squared plus b squared equals 144. Now what?"

"Well so a and b — the sides of our bow — are equal, we already know. So it's like saying 'What number squared, plus the same number squared, equals 144?'"

"What number is it?"

"We gotta work backwards. First we take 144 and divide it by two. Then we can take the square root of that number."

"Okay so 144 divided by two is 72 feet. So the square root of that is…?"

"Now we need the calculator." The kid took out his scientific calculator, which was lent to him by the school district. He punched in the calculation. "Okay it says 8.4852 blah blah. So what does that mean?"

"You tell me."

"Well, it means that our sides are going to be 8.4852 blah blah feet, right?"

"Yup. Since we're not making molding or something let's just say 8.5 feet, because it's pretty close. Remember we have to convert that *decimal* to *feet and inches*, so we're not talking 8 feet 5 inches, but eight-and-a-half feet, which is 8 feet 6 inches."

"Holy shit, I actually get this. So we'll have a triangle with a 12-foot base and two sides that are 8.5 feet. Man, you're a good teacher. Every kid should have to build rafts to learn trigonometry."

"Yeah," said Mike, who'd been listening to and watching us figure it out. "Except you didn't use trigonometry at all. That was all Pythagorean Theorem stuff."

"Shit Dallas he called you out! I guess Mike would be the principal, if you're the teacher."

"The lesson here is that there's more than one way to skin a cat," I said. But of course the real lesson was for the kid to learn that math has a practical application, and there are better ways to spend your time than doing things that get you arrested. As Mike set about cutting the bow 8.5 feet from either side of one corner of the spare dock, the pupil and I worked our way through the problem again, this time using *sine, cosine* and *tangent*. The kid was helpful lending an extra hand as we screwed the bow to the front of the dock and completed the outline of our boat. Three years later I ran into him randomly, and he re-introduced himself. He said,

"Doing that raft building shit at your house was fun."

I was pretty proud of that.

(Building the third raft. I'm on the left working on the bow. Mike sits on the driveway cutting and duct-taping the tarp sail. Note that the triangular bow and rear floating 'trunk' have not yet been attached. May, 2007)

Some of my friends started stopping down to see the boat as it was under construction, to help with the building or just to satisfy their curiosity. My friend Harry drove down on his motorcycle and helped us cut and attach the foam pontoons to the bottom with straps of fire hose, and to cut the ends of the foam pontoons into triangular bows so they would slice through the water.

"But Dallas, my question is: how the hell are you going to get this thing to the river? It must weigh 2,000 pounds."

"To be honest, Harry, I don't know yet." We leaned against the craft drinking cans of *Coors Light* after an hour's work. "I figured one way or another, the first step was to get the thing built, and I didn't want to delay building it because I didn't have a way to move it. But now it's almost built and we're supposed to sail in two weeks and I don't know how the hell we're going to get it onto a trailer." Harry smiled.

"I thought you'd say that. I have an idea. Seth my roommate works for *Nolan Propane*. They have a truck that has a crane. I bet in exchange for a 30-rack he would 'borrow' the crane, and use it to lift the boat onto the trailer for you."

So that became the plan. Such is the value of knowing a lot of people, who all know other people, each who have different resources at their disposal.

My friend Bri came home for a visit from NYU and stopped over. She took pictures of us as I painted the boat and Mike constructed a sail from a blue tarp and duct tape. She tagged me in a picture on Facebook, and then I got a message from Sean, my friend who lived in Boston, who was tech savvy. Sean suggested I send him some pictures and text, and he'd create a webpage for the project. That would lend extra credibility when I sent a press release to newspapers, he said. It was a good suggestion. Meanwhile Morgan's sister Julie offered to be the press liaison and wrote and sent the press releases.

The project was starting to become a real *thing* that people were following. Folks commented that this time they thought we'd succeed. After getting such positive feedback, Mike and I figured we might as well push the envelope. In Albany in the summer on Thursdays the city sponsored free concerts called "Alive at Five" at a riverfront park. Thousands attended. And we lived in Albany now. We decided to launch from our new home town. By leaving from Alive at Five we'd attract more attention and our friends wouldn't have to drive 15 miles south to see us off. But that created a new problem. We'd be putting the raft in the water in Coeymans, where we'd test it for a week before the launch. But how would we get the boat up to Albany, 15 miles north of Coeymans, for the launch itself?

"My dad has a boat. He thinks your rafting adventures are fun. I bet he'd tow you to Albany the day before your launch," Jess Gadani informed Mike and I one night at the Downtube. So that took care of that logistical quandary. "What is the name of the raft, anyway? I'm sick of calling it *The Raft*. It needs a name. And please tell me it won't be *The Crab Legs 3.0*."

"Definitely not," Mike declared.

"How about *The Third Time's The Charm*?" I suggested.

"Eh, that's weak and hokey," Mike said.

"Well, what would you call it?"

"How about *The Best Angle To Approach A Problem Is The Try-Angle*," Mike joked.

"You need a name, not a sentence," Jess said.

"You could call it *Carpe Diem*," Morgan shouted from his room, where he was reviewing GRE words. I liked that suggestion but Mike did not.

"Well, it's a raft project," Mike said, "and we're trying to go to Manhattan. We could call it *The Manhattan Project*."

So that became its name, and the website became TheManhattanRaftProject.com.

One or two nights per week I spent a few hours at Mike's new apartment on Eagle Street across from the Governor's Mansion. We'd come to realize the importance of making drawings and deciding on designs prior to driving to New Baltimore. Otherwise we'd waste half or three-quarters of our time near the boat merely deciding how to interact with it. I carried a clipboard and graph paper to figure out the measurements for, say, the rowing station we planned to build, or the height of the mast. Then when we got to New Baltimore we merely had to reference the plan and start measuring, cutting and screwing. There was still plenty of unforeseen work—we had by no means become skilled engineers or boat builders—but our written and oft-reworked designs on paper helped us establish an order of operations and to complete the work on schedule.

One night Morgan called me while I was in Mike's basement apartment.

"I think you should come back to the Downtube. There's somebody here who wants to meet you." Morgan had started seeing Alison, the daughter of a family friend he'd known since childhood, after meeting her again at a wedding a couple of weeks before. "Alison's here with her sister, Nicole, and they want to hear about your boat. I figure I wouldn't be able to do it justice, and you should come regale them with stories of your adventures yourself." Morgan whispered, "I think it's in your interest to come up. You'll think Nicole's cute."

"I will be there post haste," I said.

Walking up the hill past the Empire State Plaza, into Center Square where Madison Ave is skirted by three-story brick apartments, I thought, *Girl wants to hear about my raft failures? Must be hurt-looking.* I opened the kitchen door and entered the apartment to clapping and laughter. I wore an old pair of jeans, a blue striped button up, and a leather fedora. I looked the part of an adventurer at least.

"Grab a beer, DT!" Morgan called from the window, between Alison and Nicole. "Grab four!"

I introduced myself in the process of distributing *J. W. Dundee's* bottles. Nicole was blonde, about five-foot-two, maybe a hundred pounds, a little shy, yet when she talked she spoke assertively.

"Do you always wear a fedora?" she asked.

"More or less, yes. I have a couple of different kinds. I wouldn't wear this one with a suit jacket, since it's leather. But I wouldn't wear one of my other ones when I'm on an adventure, because it would just get dirty."

"Huh. That makes sense."

We all sat in the window talking about life and work and rafts, and then we played rummy. Nicole and I chatted and I found her very pleasant and pretty. Moderate might be a good word to describe her personality, which was refreshing. Because most of the other females I found attractive were either alpha-female boozers, like Cady had been, or boring squares who cast condescending glances on anyone enjoying themselves. It was impossible to avoid the double-date atmosphere, so I talked a lot about anything besides love and relationships to keep it from getting awkward. I must've done an alright job because the next day Morgan said,

"Alison said Nicole said she liked talking to you, because you actually talk about *real stuff*. Ha! I was wondering how jumping right into the raft stuff would go over as soon as you meet a cute girl, whether they'd yawn and get glassy-eyed. But I guess at least with Nicole it worked!"

III. "This This This This…Monstrosity!"

We finished the raft, more or less, a week before our launch. We'd created a boat that sat on four foam pontoons that was 20-feet long and 12-feet wide, with a trunk compartment. On top, the cabin was 6-feet wide, 8-feet long and 5-feet high, with plywood sheets attached to hinges that folded to protect us from the elements or provide a screened-in room. It was plenty strong to walk on top. Attached to the middle of the cabin and extending from the frame of the boat 16-feet high we'd constructed a mast from interlocking wood beams, with a crow's nest another 4-feet above the cabin. From the top of the mast hung the tarp sail, with a "boom" extending 12-feet from the mast aback toward the stern, which we'd made from an old wooden railing I found in my parent's basement. On a Saturday morning Mike, Jared, Jess Gadani, Harry and his roommate Seth assembled at my parent's house, Seth having driven down in a diesel truck with a crane.

"This is really getting to be quite the project," my dad commented. Several of the neighbors moseyed over to catch a glimpse of our goings on.

Seth extended stabilizers from the crane to the ground. I attached the trailer to Al, my parent's crumbling white F150 — recently repaired with a new alternator — and backed the trailer in front of the The Manhattan Project.

"Okay here is problem number one," Mike noted. "The trailer is 10-feet long and 6-feet wide. The raft is 20-feet long and 12-feet wide. There's going to be a lot of overhang."

"We'll have to attach it really well to the trailer. You know, with a lot of ropes."

"DT I'm more worried about this trailer," said Seth, a tall, good-humored kid I knew from high school. "You said you had a trailer…I thought you had a *trailer*. That trailer there is for like, moving your lawn tractor from place to place. You sure it's strong enough to transport that ship of yours?"

"There's only one way to find out, sir. It's time to give it the old college try." We ran ropes around the underside of the bow of the boat, and Seth used to crane to lift the bow six feet in the air. I backed the trailer up until it struck the underside of the boat about eight feet back from the bow. Then we untied the ropes and ran them underneath the stern of the boat and ran them back up to the crane pulley. Now when Seth lifted, the front of the boat rested on the trailer and the back was suspended by the crane. Next Seth lifted the back of the boat higher, pushing the whole thing forward onto the top of the trailer. When we'd pushed it as far forward as it would go it still hung 9-feet off the trailer, precipitously threatening falling. So before we untied it from the crane we secured it to the trailer with a bunch of "bowline" knots—the most useful of all knots, according to *Seamanship*. Still we held our breath as Seth let the crane ropes slack because we were worried that the boat would simply crush the trailer or break it off the ball-hitch. But everything held together, if unsteadily and awkwardly. The wheels of the trailer were crushed almost into ovals instead of circles. But nothing snapped or cracked or broke so we considered ourselves successful. I pulled the truck ever so slowly forward and the trailer with the oversized boat inched forward behind me.

Then a new problem. As we inched out of the driveway onto the dirt road on which my parent's house was located, Jared yelled "Stop!" Hanging wires swagged across the road from one telephone pole to another, and the mast of the boat—almost twenty feet high now that it sat on top of the trailer—was just a little too tall to pass beneath them. Mike and I got out from the front seat of the truck to assess the problem as my friends and neighbors coalesced.

"Well, I guess we didn't think about how tall the mast would be *after we put it on the trailer*," Mike noted.

"Fuck, dude. We're like six inches too big," Jared complained.

"I bet you never thought you'd hear yourself say that," Jess commented.

The whole scene felt ad hoc, which I found exciting. There were murmurs in the crowd about whether 'That was it'—meaning no shipping the boat to the river, or about how 'He simply needs to remove the mast,' which would've been no easy task.

"Okay, here is what we'll do." I handed Jared a discarded plank from our lumber pile. "I'm going to inch the boat forward ever so slowly, and as I do, you stand on top of the cabin of the boat and push up the wires with this board. After we inch underneath, let the wires down behind the mast." There was general murmuring among the onlookers.

"Dude am I gonna get like, electrocuted and killed?"

"I doubt it."

"Okay then."

So that's what we did. Jared stood on top of the cabin, which was on top of the deck made of docks, which was on top of the trailer, lifting wires as I drove at a snail's pace. It worked. The wires had enough slack that Jared could lift them over and let them down behind the mast.

At the end of the dirt road where my parents lived we formed a convoy. My friend Carly drove her car ahead and Jess followed up the rear with hazard lights blinking. We pulled onto the paved New Baltimore Road as Jared lifted another set of wires. We repeated the process a mile farther down when once again wires transected the road. Extremely slowly we made our way down a moderately steep hill to Route 144, keeping my foot on the break and wondering if the old truck had enough breaks to hold us.

Route 144, or River Road, is one of the main drags to Albany and we started to accumulate a trail of cars behind us. I felt I couldn't drive faster than a mile an hour, because every bump was amplified through the lever-like situation of the boat balanced on fulcrum-wheels, hanging off the back so far. If we went too fast might shake the raft off the trailer. My palms sweat as I imagined a hundred cars honking because the road was completely blocked by an overturned, 2,000-pound boat, and it was all my fault. So we pulled over to let a dozen cars pass, then pulled out again going a mile an hour.

"Thank God we only have to go two miles," Mike said from the passenger seat. "Two hours to go from New Baltimore to Coeymans. I think we might set a longest-ever record. Horses go faster than this."

"Paraplegics with flat tires on their wheelchairs go faster than this," I grumbled.

Then a new problem. Halfway to Coeymans, Route 144 crested the top a hill. The telephone poles were set back, down the hill a bit, and the wires swept lower than elsewhere. I crept up so that the truck passed under the wires and the mast was just about to touch, but then I saw Jared in the rearview mirror gesticulating for me to stop. Mike and I got out of the truck.

"They're too low," Jared shouted from atop the cabin. "I can't push them over."

Adding to the problem, a skinny gray-haired man now emerged from a nearby house and stomped up to us, screeching.

"No! No! No!" he screamed with each slamming footfall. "Stop! Stop it right now! I don't know what this is, but stop! No. This is illegal, absolutely! Who's in charge here?"

"I am, sir," I intentionally avoided glancing at Mike or Jared in case they made a face and the man noticed.

"What the *hell* are you doing? What is this? You can't *do* this! You're out here, disrupting traffic, probably ruining the road, making a disturbance, touching wires that are attached to all these houses! I'm calling the police."

"Sir, there's no reason to call the police," I tried to reason. The man refused to look at me, but paced back and forth toward the truck/trailer/boat and back to his yard. He had bedroom slippers on his feet. I wondered if he was very liberal and thought we were rednecks, or very conservative and thought we were liberals. Either way it was obvious that he didn't like us. "We'll have this problem solved in just a moment."

"No! No! No! I've watched you pushing up those wires. I wondered what you were going to do when you got to these lower ones. No, not the ones on *my* house, so help me God." The man continued his tirade and I figured the best thing was to absorb his wrath and reason when he was done. "This is just plain irresponsible. This, you, you you you, you can't have this, this, this, this *monstrosity* on the road!"

"Sir, please, I understand that now." I lied, "This is a college project. We've built this boat to go from Coeymans to Manhattan without using any fossil fuels. Obviously we need to cut the mast in order to lower the height of the boat so that we can safely pass underneath."

"Obviously! You never should have been allowed on the road in the first place. This, this, this...this is just *poor planning!*" He emphasized the last two words as severe criticism. I affected profound disappointment.

"You are absolutely right," I kicked the gravel on the ground. "We didn't think about the wires. I guess we were so focused on how to overcome the challenges we would face in the water that we forgot to consider the challenges we might face getting the boat there. Now I've learned my lesson. Maybe we should have driven along the route ahead of time and made observations on any obstructions we might encounter. I really failed at that point."

"Well, I would say so. You should've thought of that."

"I'm sure it'll be reflected in my grade. But now the immediate problem is right here. I can't go backwards, sir. Not backwards with a trailer going up a hill and around a curve. And I can't make a three-point turn. The road is too skinny. The only choice is to go forward, and to do that, we've simply got to cut the mast. Not a couple of inches, but cut about three-feet off the thing so this doesn't happen again. But there's no need to call the police, who'll take a half-hour to get here and just tell us to cut the mast anyway, and maybe give us a ticket and ruin the whole project, and then we'll have to call the newspapers and say it's all cancelled. Just give us fifteen minutes and we'll have this thing out of here and you'll never see us again. Okay?"

"If you damage my house or these wires, so help me—"

"Ten minutes. No damage. You'll never see me again."

"Ten minutes then I'm calling the State Troopers, you hear me?"

"Loud and clear, sir. I apologize for the inconvenience."

Jared, Mike, Carly and Jess stood listening anxiously as the man and I ended our exchange. For his part, the man stood pacing and watching us, emphatically glancing at his watch. This was my first experience as the party responsible for dealing with some significant crisis with a stranger. Aware of our ten-minute timeframe I looked at the whole situation and began directing the others immediately.

"Carly, Jess, will you guys stand in front of your cars and direct traffic? Jess, could you stand at the top of the hill within sight of Carly, at the bottom, and wave cars on from either direction, so that we don't keep people stuck here?" I retrieved a hand-saw from the "toolbox" attached to the back of the boat. "Mike, will you cut three-feet off the mast? We can reattach the severed piece at the river using other boards to brace it."

"Yes," Mike said, looking nervously towards the guy.

"Ableman, go around and check the ropes between the trailer and the boat, okay?" Jared shot me a quizzical look. I rolled my eyes and pursed my lips as if to say *Dude, I don't know...we're trying to look busy and professional in front of the guy in the bed slippers.*

"Okay Captain, I'll get right on that," Jared said, and went around the outside of the boat, looking at things.

The truth was that if we hadn't had to interact with that guy we'd have fixed the situation and been on our way already. It only took Mike a couple of minutes to cut the top off the mast, even with my grandfather's rusted, 50-year-old hand saw, and then we had no problem driving underneath. Just to be sure, though, Jared stood on the roof of the cabin with his stick. The guy disappeared back into his house so we were quick to depart in case he'd called the police. We high-tailed it, driving at 150% of our previous speed, or, approximately 1.5 miles per hour, to Coeymans Landing. On the way, Mike said, to my satisfaction,

"You handled that situation well, Captain. I wanted to deck that guy."

As we drove up to the boat launch a small crowd assembled on the dock and river bank, as on the previous two occasions, to see what we were doing. The crowd assumed that we'd struggle to back the awkwardly-shaped load onto the ramp. But this was my third time executing that maneuver, so it was no problem backing straight onto the launch. The problem was that someone had taken a boat out of the river a few minutes before, so the ramp was wet. When I rolled the rear wheels of my parents' crumpling F150 onto the launch, we lost traction. Mike and I felt the truck slide downhill even as I pushed the brake pedal to the floor, and for a few seconds I thought my parent's truck was going to slide into the river. However, fortunately the boat hung nine-feet off the rear of the trailer, so the stern splashed into the water and became buoyant, and we skidded to a stop within inches of submerging the exhaust pipe. My friends and the strangers on the shore laughed and clapped at disaster averted.

This time it was a simple affair to untie the boat from the trailer. The *Seamanship* bible I'd been carrying taught that a knot is more than a tangle of ropes. While a knot will never untie itself, it should be capable of being untied with one hand by anyone who knows what kind of knot it is. This time I untied the raft quickly and preserved all of our *line* ("Rope...Is Called Line" was the title to the chapter) intact. Within fifteen minutes *The Manhattan Project* floated in the Hudson. We secured it to the end of the dock and looked on in satisfaction. It was definitely sturdy and, with all the foam underneath, almost impossible to sink.

We planned to set out from Albany in front of thousands of people, as announced on our website, ten days later. In the meantime, there was still finishing work to complete. Mike and I judged it better to put the boat in the water, loaded with tools, than to get her completed at my parent's house but then worry about getting it in the river just before the launch. We loaded a circular saw, a power drill, and a 100-foot extension cord into the cabin, so that we could, over the next week, tie up at the marina and run the lead cord to an outlet on shore. In addition to the power tools we loaded screws, nails, a toolbox with a hammer and screw driver, extra pieces of wood, a sixty-pound electric battery and a trolling motor. On top of the cabin sat the severed mast, the sail and boom. We loaded several buckets of paint which I planned to use before launching. So the cabin was cluttered about to capacity.

And now the next problem.

"What are you going to do with it for the next week?" someone in the crowd asked.

"The police'll do something to it, tow it or something, if you leave it here," Jess noted.

"No, I can't leave it tied up here in Coeymans for a week. I don't want people to mess with it or whatever. We're going to anchor it in the river and use the canoe to get out to it and back."

"You can't anchor it in the middle of the river," an old man interjected. "You'll disrupt traffic. It'll be a navigation hazard."

"Right," I rejoined, "but outside the channel I can. Outside the channel the water isn't consistently 35-feet deep. That's why people can have docks and tie up their own boats next to their property, close to shore. So I'll anchor close to shore, out of the way of traffic, where there are no houses or anything on the riverbank."

"What if your anchor lets loose?" Jess asked. We strolled to the end of the dock and stepped aboard the boat. It supported six or seven of us without sinking more than an inch deeper into the water. I opened the plywood doors to the cabin and emerged with an anchor on a six-foot chain.

"I bought this at the marina. Last time we used, what, a brick, Mike?"

"A cement block."

"Yeah, and we'd throw it into the water and just drag it. But then I read about anchors. This is called a *Danforth* anchor. You see, it's got these two big metal teeth like canines? Depending on what way you're drifting when you drop the anchor, you let it loose, and the chain drops this vertical bar to the ground. You use a Danforth anchor in water with a mud bottom, like the Hudson. As you drag the anchor with the teeth pointing down, it digs into the mud, and that, rather than the weight *per se*, is what secures you to the river bottom."

"In theory," Mike said.

"In theory and in practice. You see boats anchored all the time. This is how they do it."

"But this will be the first time *you* have ever done it. I think it might be a good idea also for us to run a rope from the boat to the shore, in case something goes wrong with the anchor."

"A rope is called *a line* in nautical terminology."

"Alright, you should run *a line* to the shore, for when something goes wrong with the anchor." This seemed prudent and I agreed. "I also think we should have some kind of lock mechanism or something. It's going to be just floating out there for anybody to come up to. We have a lot of tools and motors and shit. We should be able to lock them in." This point struck me as emblematic of two ways of thinking, one practical and helpful, the other impossible and therefore futile to worry about.

"I would like to have locks on this boat," I pointed out. "But Mike, I don't think I have to remind you that the cabin has two doors each at the front and the back, made out of plywood. And the cabin has two shutters that stay up or fold down based on little latches.

We're already at the river, and we have to do something with the boat. How can we possibly create locks, to secure our stuff?"

"I don't know. I guess we can't."

"Maybe we should've thought about it before, but we didn't, and now it's too late. So it doesn't do us any good to worry about that. What we *can* do is try and find a place to anchor this boat that's out of sight and hard to get to, and then hopefully no one will fuck with it."

It was an hour before twilight now. I parked the truck and trailer out of the way as Mike attached the trolling motor to the front—er, *bow*—of the boat. The motor had a red and a black wire with o-shaped metal eyelets on the ends. Mike set a car battery next to the motor, which had bolts protruding from the positive and negative terminals. He put the red eyelet around the bolt to the positive terminal, and the black to the negative. When he turned the handle on the trolling motor, it buzzed and jerked forward, pulling the boat. This seemed like some magical occurrence to me—that power and propulsion could be generated from this little box called a battery, enough to move a 2,000-pound contraption that I had constructed.

"We forgot champagne!" Mike noted. "Isn't it bad luck to sail a boat without dedicating it?" But Jess smiled perversely,

"Don't worry boys, I thought you might forget about that. Here, I brought you this!" Jess unzipped her backpack and held out a bottle of *Colt 45*. "If you had two zig zags, baby that's all you'd need!" she quoted the *Afroman* song.

We decided to test out the boat and find a place to anchor it before we dedicated it. So Jared and I joined Mike onboard, and we thanked Carly and Jess, who stood on the dock, for their help. We detached our line and drifted a couple inches away. Then Mike turned on the motor and we moved north at a mile or two an hour.

"You're the pilot," I said, a tad pedantically, to Mike. "He's the person who actually directs the boat in rivers and ports. That book, *Shoreline and Sextant*, talks about how it's actually more dangerous to sail a boat within sight of land, because of reefs and outcroppings and all the other kinds of underwater obstructions, not to mention more boats moving in close proximity, than it is in the ocean."

"Makes sense," Mike said, bent over near the bow. He was getting a feel for how the motor worked. We wanted to go north to get above the little string of buildings that constituted Coeymans in order to find an uninhabited shore. The first obstacle was a marina which lay directly in our path. A ramp extended from the shore, to our left (or port side) in front of us. It connected to two rows of docks to our right (or starboard) where three or four dozen boats of various sizes were tied up. So Mike turned the handle of the motor toward the port shore, which turned the propeller so that it pushed water toward the port shore, and our boat turned to starboard. (We moved to starboard because the motor was mounted at the front of the boat; if it'd been mounted at the back, our bow would've moved toward port.) When we faced the middle of the river Mike straightened the motor and we gurgled away from the shore. When we'd travelled farther toward the center of the river than the docked yachts, Mike turned us north, and we began to pass by the yachts twenty feet or so away. Mike experimented. "You can adjust the height of the propeller," he said. "Do you know: is there an optimal height?"

"I don't know," I said.

"Well, if I put the head of the motor just below the water, it makes all of these bubbles and noise. I feel like that can't be the right setting or whatever. It seems like if I lower the motor about a foot below the top of the water, it runs more smoothly. But I don't know how shallow the water is. I'd hate to hit a rock or something and break the propeller. Then we'd be screwed."

"These boats are tied up to the docks here, right? So there must be a channel...like a mini-channel off of the main river channel, that gives access for these boats to the marina. That makes sense right? I mean, they can't be worried about hitting rocks with *their* propellers."

"Right. Okay so we know that we're not going to hit a rock while we're close to these other boats. I'll keep the motor extended." These might seem like trivial realizations, but the *feel* of it was invigorating. We were learning; we were using that which was in each of our minds discretely and putting that information together into a practical plan of action. From atop one of the yachts, we passed a man and a woman, reclining with drinks, who waved to us and smiled. Us three waved back with the enthusiasm of children. Mike noted that we seemed to be moving at around three miles an hour, "a lot faster than I thought a little electric motor would move. How long does the motor last?"

"About three hours, according to Dick Brooks," my fourth grade teacher and polymath who lived in New Baltimore, who had lent me the motor and battery. "He said something about how electric motors work differently than gas ones. Like, they're stronger at pushing heavy loads really slowly, but they can't push anything fast. Something about *torque*...I didn't really understand it. But he said a trolling motor can push even like a barge really slowly."

Slowly but steadily we passed the line of yachts at Coeymans Marina. A quarter-mile farther north, on the Coeymans Creek, seven boats were tied at a dock near a clearing where a green and yellow triangular flag reading "RC" flitted above a pavilion. It was the Ravena-Coeymans Yacht Club where Rutherford Clines, Oliver and I had gotten the leaky barrels for the first raft. Two middle-aged men in tight tee shirts and black hair stood on the dock, unsmiling. Twice I'd been to that place and both times it struck me as decidedly unfriendly.

The sky was starting to turn that pink and cyan color it becomes just before dusk, and the tree line on the shore to port was shadowy brown. About a half-mile above the yacht club, on the western shore, there was a clearing. The beach was covered in bricks and brick pieces, smoothed by the glancing action of waves over a hundred years. In 2007 this area was abandoned. As far as we could see along the shore, up to the next bend in the river, were barren hills and a couple of condemned warehouses. I knew from passages from *Coeymans and the Past* that the area had once been the *Powell and Minnock* brick plant. There'd been many brick-making factories along the river, which mined the clay from the river banks, combined the silt with straw, poured the mixture into molds, and fired the molds to make masonry. Along with farming, ice harvesting, and railroad work, brick-making provided seasonal employment for local men prior to 1900. Now, like a lot of the town, the place sat there uninhabited. A line of circular wooden pilings extended in an arc into the water, perhaps the remains of an old wharf or pier, forming a kind of rampart that protected a circle of water. The pilings were placed approximately eight-feet apart, but one of the pilings was missing, so that there was a sixteen-foot gap in the rampart.

"Can you pilot the boat between those?" I pointed to Mike.

"I think so."

Mike aligned us with the hole in the pilings and we motored close. Meanwhile Jared and I grabbed two paddles. Just as we were about to pass between the pilings Mike pulled the motor out of the water, so that it wouldn't strike anything, because we'd passed into the shallows. We glided through the hole in the piling-rampart and now *The Manhattan Project* was protected in a shallow puddle surrounded by wood posts.

"No one else will be able to get a boat in here. Not a good motorboat, anyway," Mike noted. And we were satisfied that we were far enough from population to be safe. We ran a line to a tree on the shore, and I dropped our anchor for good measure, although it'd be pretty useless in such shallow water.

"And what about this?" Jared held up the *Colt 45* bottle.

"Time to dedicate the boat!" I said.

"And yet, it'd be a pity not to drink it first," Mike said.

"True," Jared agreed. So we drank three quarters of the forty, poured a libation to Neptune, and Jared did the honors of smashing the bottle. In order to avoid the problem of the first trip, where my mother tried to break the bottle against wet wood, and it didn't smash—an unlucky sign—Jared hit the bottle against the iron "bullnose" bracket at the front of the boat—and sent broken glass all over the deck. Then, feeling we'd done all we could really do, we loaded two paddles, the trolling motor and the battery into the canoe, got in and canoed the mile back to Coeymans Landing.

That night I laid in bed in Albany thinking of the boat unattended in Coeymans. With all that the boat signified for me, I felt a lump in my throat wondering whether it would be seen, washed away, towed by police, or vandalized. I hadn't considered how anxious I'd feel leaving the boat alone like that. I knew I had a sleepless week of worry ahead.

IV. "Liability"

"*Liability* is a word I never thought much about," I told Nicole at brunch the next morning. She was in Albany for a summer job interview. (She attended college three hours away and would return in the fall.) We had eggs and coffee in my apartment. "I wonder if I've ever used the word. I mean, like Morgan says when he's studying for the GREs, a lot of words, before you really learn them, you understand them kind of...like, you have a vague idea of what they mean, you understand a sentence they're in, you know they're associated with other words, like in this case, *insurance*. But that's a shallow kind of understanding...just barely passing for understanding. When you really think about a word because you read its full definition or because it becomes important to you for some reason, then you come to understand it as an idea and all that it entails."

"Liability," Nicole repeated. "So, I would say liability means what you're responsible for. Like, if you get in a car accident and it's your fault, you're liable."

"Right. I wonder if it's connected to the word *libel*. If someone says, wrongly, that you're responsible for something, because you did something that you didn't do, that's *libel*. You can sue them for *libel*. Or *slander*. I know there's a difference but I don't know what it is."

"Well, so now you're liable for this boat, and it has you thinking about what it means. Did you think that liability was something you'd learn from your boat adventures?"

"No."

"I think I like that about what you're doing. At first when Morgan said you were building a boat to go to Manhattan, I thought it was funny and it was cool that you were doing something instead of just drinking and watching T.V. like everybody else. I guess I thought it was pretty straightforward and easy. But listening to you talk about all the things you have to do and manage and all...I think the interesting part is the things that you've learned." I blushed and thanked the young woman across the table from me.

"The thing is that this is a *thing*," I said. "Like, a physical thing, the boat is, and it *is* a liability. I mean, you and I, everybody knows what it means *to be* liable, as a verb. Like, for our actions, and stuff. So I always thought of liability as a function of my...person. I was liable for what I did. But now there is this other thing which is not my person...it's the boat...and *it* is a liability."

"Because you have to care about it and worry about it."

"Yes. Why?" I asked sincerely, and the answer came as I thought aloud. "Why? Because *my actions* created *the thing*. It's mine now. It's like, now it has value, because I created it with my labor, and now I have to care about it. I didn't expect to have to devote a portion of my concentration to worrying about *it*."

"It didn't bother you on other boats?" Nicole folded her hands on the dining room table.

"On other boats I was there the whole time. If we got into a bad situation, I could row to shore or something, or talk to people who came up to us if we were about to get into trouble—like if we needed a tow or something. The problem with this is that I'm not there, and there are all kinds of things I can imagine happening to it. I almost wish we hadn't put it in the water a week ahead of time, so I wouldn't have to worry."

"Well, you needed to test it, and you waited too long other times to put it in, right?"

"Yeah. So I guess I had no choice." Nicole sighed,

"Still, I wouldn't want to have to worry about that. I could never do something like what you're doing. I worry enough about other things already. I couldn't take the suspense."

"Well, if it was important to you, then you'd do it."

"It would have to be really important to me for me to do something where I had to worry all the time about something important to me getting wrecked. I'm not sure anything could be that important to me, except maybe my family. I mean, I'm always anxious, I hate it. I feel like all I want is to not feel anxiety. So anything that created anxiety would automatically not be worth it. I think that's something I like about you, Dallas. You're not afraid of spending all of this time and something going wrong."

"There's no sense in being afraid. Or, there's no sense of *not* doing something because you're afraid of being afraid. I don't know, I hate the feeling too. But I guess the feeling of *wanting to succeed* is stronger than the feeling of anxiousness. Besides, I keep reassuring myself that nothing is going to happen anyway. We put the boat in a safe place."

"But people are mean," Nicole said emphatically. "That's what I would worry about."

"I'm not so worried about people, like, strangers, as I am of the police. They're the ones who'll go out of their way to stop you from doing something. People are generally nice."

"I wish I was an idealist like you. I don't trust strangers. I feel like 90 percent of people will fuck up your stuff just to make you have a bad day. That's just like, *society*."

"Well, I refuse to believe that about human nature."

"But believing something doesn't make it true."

That night after work Mike and I drove to New Baltimore so we could check on the boat and start the finishing work. We put the canoe in the water in Coeymans and paddled past the marina and the yacht club. But when we got to the spot where we'd left the boat, we found that rather than bobbing in the water, it sat fifteen feet ashore, marooned atop the brick-strewn bank, completely grounded. Mike was exasperated. He threw up his hands before our canoe touched the masonry beach.

"There goes our whole trip!"

"Well, let's not throw in the towel yet," I used the paddle to stand up straight, then walked up the canoe to the beach.

"Dude, the boat is a dozen feet from the water. We had to use a crane to move it in your back yard. There's no way to get a crane back here. We can't lift it. Ten guys can't lift it. The trip is over."

"Look, it's low tide. Obviously the boat drifted up there at high tide. All we have to do is wait until high tide comes again, and then we ought to be able to get it floated again."

"And if that doesn't work?" I hated such questions.

"If that doesn't work then we'll have to try something else. But it will work." I jumped aboard and rummaged through the cabin, to retrieve a copy of *Boating on the Hudson Magazine*. On the deck I flipped to the section with the tide charts. "Okay, tomorrow morning, high tide is at 11 am. I'll canoe up here and see if I can get the thing unstuck. I'll call you either way in the afternoon, okay?"

"You're going to canoe here yourself?"

"Yeah. I've got to learn how to do it sometime. I'll bring the trolling motor and use that instead of paddling if I can't manage to go in a straight line."

"Okay, yeah, sorry," Mike said. Worrying weighed on him too. "That would be great."

The next morning I backed the truck down the boat launch and pulled the canoe from the bed into the water. I sat in the back and paddled away from the dock. It felt very awkward. I didn't know, as Mike would later teach me, that when paddling a canoe alone one should sit in the middle. My weight at the back made the front of the canoe rise out of the water. Nor had I perfected the "J-stroke," by which one paddles with the face of the paddle flat for three-quarters of the the stroke, and then rotates the paddle to push the water away from the canoe. The combination of the two parts of the stroke cancel sideways motion to the bow and propel the canoe in a straight line. Instead I paddled on the right side, then ended up facing left, then paddled on the left side and ended up facing right, and traveled in a serpentine fashion generally north but covered three times the distance. It took me nearly an hour to canoe the mile to the site of *The Manhattan Project*. Though the tide was rising, she still sat severely stuck.

My brother-in-law had given me a water-proof watch after hearing about my overboard debacle on the previous raft. I saw that I had about an hour before high-tide. I recalled from my *Seamanship* book that "slack-water" — the period when the tide neither rises nor falls — begins about a half-hour before a tide is reached. So the water would continue to rise for another half-hour or a little more.

The boat was transfixed atop a row of bricks that formed a kind of ledge below her amidships line, with the bow suspended and pointed toward the shore and the stern descending downhill, a few inches into the water. Obviously when the water rose it would provide some buoyancy at the back, but it was unlikely to float the front half of the boat. If I were to tie a line to the back of the boat, I could try to drag her off the ledge using the canoe, but it seemed unlikely that I could paddle and drag a 2,000-pound chunk of wood even a couple of inches. Instead I calculated that my best chance was to apply force to the bow, using the brick ledge as a fulcrum, and try to spin the boat and slide it downhill. First I secured a line from the cleat at the front of the boat — the bullnose — to the anchor. I put the anchor in the canoe, paddled to deeper water, and dropped it. That would at least prevent the boat from floating farther ashore once the back became buoyant. With the water still rising I climbed ashore and tried to lift the bow by bracing my legs and pushing upward with my chest and arms. It wouldn't budge. The tide had risen such that the back quarter of the boat was now in the water. I tried standing in the water and heaving the back upward, but this was impossible. Next I climbed onto the boat and went into the cabin. I stacked all of the tools, extra wood, anything not nailed down, toward the stern, on the water-side of the brick ledge. This made the bow of the boat rise a couple of inches higher, yet still I couldn't lift it.

I leaned against the bow to catch my breath as a speedboat sped by on that hot June morning. A moment later its wake reached the shore, and sent the buoyant stern bouncing a few centimeters. I realized what must have occurred the evening before: *The Manhattan Project* floated up the shore at high tide, and the wakes of passing boats lifted it even farther, onto rocks, where it was stuck when the waves receded. Presently, motoring north past Coeymans in the channel, I saw a tugboat pushing a hundred-foot barge, and had an idea. I recalled Archimedes' adage about mechanical advantage: "Give me a lever long enough, and a place to stand, and I will move the earth." I ran to the top of the cabin where the boom pole was laying—the section of railing I'd taken from my parent's basement—and threw it to the brick shore. I grabbed the severed section of mast which Mike had sawn when the guy in the slippers yelled at us, and threw that to the shore. Then I set the severed mast, which was about eight inches squared, on its side, just in front of the bow of the boat. I stuck the boom railing under the bow and used the mast as a fulcrum. As the barge passed and sent foot-high waves onto the shore I jumped onto the boom railing and hung there. The bow rotated an inch, then another, and slid off the brick pile. Mostly buoyant, it was relatively easy to use the lever to get the boat off of the little rocks it caught on after that, and she was buoyant again.

"I love it when a plan comes together!" I punched my right fist into my left palm. To avoid the same predicament the next day, I used the trolling motor to move the boat south, about halfway between the abandoned brick plant and the Ravena-Coeymans Yacht Club. Ten feet from shore a crumbling cement dike, designed to prevent erosion, extended for a quarter mile along the river bank, which would keep the boat from grounding again. I used the canoe to drop an anchor in the river, and tied the boat to a tree with a lot of slack on the river side of the dike. The two slackened lines would allow the boat to rise and fall with the tide, and the base of the boat was sturdy enough not to be damaged by washing against the stone dike. Since the boat was in sight of the Yacht Club, would-be vandals would be deterred. As I canoed back to Coeymans Marina I was happy to have found a better spot to work on the boat, and we'd only lost two days of finishing-up time. We still had five days before we had to tow her to Albany.

That night I met Mike at his apartment. He was surprised that I'd been able to get the boat floating, and was visibly encouraged. He paced and nodded to himself, then declared,

"Yes. You know, I'm sorry for being defeatist yesterday. I should've had more faith. I just—I saw the boat up there and I didn't see how we could possibly get it off. I won't do that again. You're right...I mean, we're smart people. Leverage, tides—these things have been around forever. We can use them. From now on I'm going to look at how we can get over any problem instead of just getting down and thinking it's over." I quoted that formative film from our childhood, *Back to the Future*,

"You can do anything if you put your mind to it, Marty."

"Ha, yeah." Mike grew serious as he drew papers out of our raft folder. "Okay, so we still have five days to work on this before Jim Gadani tows you to Albany. That's good, but not great. We still have a ton of work to do."

"Agreed."

"Tomorrow I think we need to go down and work on it. Let's say the goal tomorrow is to get the top of the mast re-attached. And also to run the rigging from the top of the mast to the sail, and get all that working. We really ought to test out the sail soon. And we should stop by the marina and get some legit oar locks so that we can row. We're going to need electric hook-up so we can screw those in. Jeeze, and we really, really, need to get Jared and TJ down there in the next couple of days so we can all practice rowing and paddling together, so we can get an idea of just how fast we can move the thing."

"And then, when all that's done, we still need to take the power tools and stuff off the boat and load our supplies."

So we met up in Coeymans after Mike got out of work the next day, and canoed up to the boat site. But now a new problem. As we approached the boat, we saw that its starboard side was suspended a foot out of the water; a large, broken tree branch lay atop the cabin; and there was a note tacked to the front door. I jumped aboard and read the note.

"It's from the police," I called to Mike. "It says *There have been complaints that this vessel poses a navigation hazard. The owner must remove it within 48 hours or it will be impounded.* There is a sergeant's name and a telephone number."

Mike tied the canoe alongside and boarded. While we were happy that the police hadn't towed the boat, they'd nonetheless damaged it. I'd left enough slack on my anchor line and the line I tied around a tree so that the boat could rise and fall with the tide. But apparently the police had tied two more ropes, without any slack, from the starboard cleats to two overhanging trees during high tide. When the tide receded, the weight of the boat hung by those cleats, lines and trees. The weight had snapped one large branch, which now sat on the roof of the cabin, where the force of the fall had crushed the plywood in two places. The cabin wouldn't be water-proof now. The other rope didn't break, but it suspended the starboard bow in the air as the rest of the boat angled into the water at 30-degrees. The "trunk" that we'd attached to the stern had snapped off as it dangled unsupported, and it was nowhere to be seen. In this trunk was our extension cord and several power tools.

"So what do we do now?" Mike asked. "Call the police and ask them not to tow us?"

"Hold on." I removed my knife from the lanyard on my belt and cut the remaining rope so we splashed into the water. "Someone obviously complained about our boat being here. It might be an eyesore, but it's not a navigation hazard." I pointed toward the Coeymans Yacht Club where several people were looking up at us with arms akimbo. "Somebody over there doesn't like us and complained to the cops," I concluded. Mike agreed.

"And if it's us versus the Yacht Club, the cops aren't going to let us keep the boat here."

"So we've got to move it."

"And where do you suggest, Captain?"

"I think our only choice is the bay at the mouth of the Hannacroix Creek, just south of the Coeymans Filtration Plant."

This was a mile and a half downstream, right on the border of Coeymans and New Baltimore. So we set up the trolling motor and started south. As we passed the Yacht Club the three men stared, unwaving. It seemed that they hoped we wouldn't move the boat so they'd see it towed. We motored by the boats of Coeymans Marina, passed the boat launch where we'd put our vessel in the water. We rounded the little peninsula that had taken 45 minutes to pass on the *Crab Legs 1.0*, and motored past a little island where there's a beach on the north side and a water treatment plant on the south. Just past this island is a bay formed where the Hannacroix Creek divides Albany and Greene Counties and empties into the Hudson. The first time Mike took me canoeing, a year before, we paddled into this bay and discovered that it is extremely shallow and lined with sandbars. At the entrance to the bay one long sandbar has accumulated where the silt carried by the creek meets the river current. One can only get a motorboat over that sandbar during high tide. So this would protect us from police boats. We motored into the bay until we grounded on a shallow mud shoal. By this point it was getting dark. We'd lost some of the tools we needed to fix the mast, and we still had to canoe back to Coeymans. So we left *The Manhattan Project* in the bay, and I told Mike that TJ and I would return the next day, with new tools, to make repairs.

It was a Monday, the last week the of school year, and I had three students to administer finals and Regents exams to. I scheduled these in the morning and late afternoon as best I could, leaving a few hours in the middle of the day to check on the boat.

As we canoed from Coeymans to the bay, TJ and I discussed how we'd have to move the boat again to fix it. We needed electrical power to operate the circular saw and a drill to finish the rowing stations and reattach the mast. When we got to the mouth of the creek we found the boat sitting peacefully. After inspecting her and tying the canoe to her side cleats, we pushed her off a sandbar and started motoring south. There was a municipal park in New Baltimore a mile downstream where we could plug in the extension cord.

TJ was obviously disturbed as we got underway.

"Man, this is as fast as you go?" It took fifteen minutes to motor out of the bay.

"Believe it or not, this is a pretty good clip compared to our other trips. Still...we don't seem to be moving as fast as the first day we put the boat in the water. I wonder how many hours, in total, I've used the battery. It might be starting to die."

As we motored from the bay into the river we were hit by the wind that stopped me the year before, which blows up from the ocean all summer. Our rate decreased noticeably, so we decided to paddle along with the motor. After being on the water for an hour or so, TJ wiped his forehead and asked,

"How many miles do you think we've gone?"

"It's two miles from New Baltimore to Coeymans. We were halfway between, and we haven't gotten to New Baltimore yet. So, less than a mile."

"Oh my God," TJ exclaimed. "I didn't realize it was *this* slow. Man...why don't we just take canoes to New York?"

"Because the point of this trip is to go on a raft," I reminded him. Looking at the water I saw we were barely outrunning a twig of driftwood.

"Yeah but it'd be so much easier!"

"That's beside the point," I rejoined.

"Yeah but I mean, dude...you really want to do this, like this? What's the big deal about using a raft?"

"The big deal is that that's the project, man. Look, you've been out here what, one hour? Do you know how many hours Mike and I have invested in this? We can't just, *pow*, like that, get rid of this thing and go in a canoe. The whole point is to go *in this*."

"Okay, okay...I'm just saying..."

I'd never been on a boat powered by a trolling motor that was running out of batteries, but it was pretty easy to conclude that that was what was happening. As we came around a bend we saw the docks to Shady Harbor. Beyond *The Boat House* was a small bay, and on the other side of that, on a small peninsula, was the park we were aiming for. However the wind hit us just as we motored past the docks of Shady Harbor, which extended a third of the way into the river, and we began to be pushed upstream and away from shore.

Not wanting to appear unequal to the situation, I suggested quickly that we aim for the end of one of the docks, where there were three open berths between two yachts, so we could show the proprietor, Charlie, what we'd done with his donation. Really I felt I needed a minute to figure out what to do if we couldn't motor south any farther. We successfully landed and tied up. We walked ashore, unsure of ourselves, and I asked around for Charlie, hoping he might offer to let us dock at Shady Harbor for a couple of days. But he wasn't present and the employees doing dock-work didn't appear overly charitable. We got back aboard and motored into the bay to the south successfully. Although the peninsula on the other side of the bay sheltered us from the wind slightly, our motor was almost completely drained and worthless. So we motored as close to the rocky shore as possible on the southern side of the marina, and dropped the Danforth anchor. Once we turned the motor off we slid backward in the breeze. I let out 30 feet of line, since the formula requires six feet of line per foot of water depth, and I judged that we were in five feet of water. The anchor held and I secured it to the bullnose cleat at the bow. The boat was now anchored in the open in the middle of the bay. Along the shore were three-story colonial houses with river frontage, so someone might complain of the eyesore, but there was little we could do. The situation was a set-back, certainly, because we still hadn't made repairs or practiced using the boat. Nonetheless with no other option we canoed back to Coeymans with an apparently-dead battery, making plans to charge it so that we could propel the boat the remaining quarter-mile to Cornell Park *the next day* — for I had two tutoring appointments and would be unable to return that Monday afternoon.

I picked up Nicole after dark.

"Would you mind if we stopped by the river on the way to Oliver's house? I really want to check on the boat. It's only about ten minutes out of the way."

"Sure. I'd like to see it."

"Yeah?"

"Of course. You've been talking about it. I'd like to see what it looks like in real life."

"Okay, cool." We drove south out of Albany on Route 144. "I'm starting to get nervous about this whole thing," I confided. "Don't tell Mike."

"I'm nervous for you," Nicole said. "It's a thing that would make anybody nervous. Why can't Mike know that you're nervous?"

"Because... that's not part of the plan."

In New Baltimore Route 144 passes close to the river, a hundred feet in the air, overtop of the cliffs that supposedly look like those in old Baltimore. I tried to look out of the driver's window to spot the boat through the passing trees, but it was too dark and the cove was too far away.

We parked at Cornell Park and walked through some weeds and trees, through someone's manicured back yard, complete with a gazebo, to the end of the peninsula that formed the southern section of the bay. By the light of a nearly full moon we saw the raft bobbing in the bay where I'd left her earlier that day.

"There she is," I exhaled.

"She looks so small out there. Smaller than the pictures on the website."

"It's an optical thing. Really she's rather big. Maybe too big. I'm so relieved to see that she's still there. I do not like having a liability, I've decided."

"Yeah, but it's something that you have to have, if you want to do anything." My shoulders and neck muscles were tensed up, I noticed all of a sudden. I tried to unloosen them by breathing deeply. Then I rubbed my hand through my hair, and thought about how I'd rather be simply enjoying myself with Nicole that evening instead of babysitting a boat.

"I just can't wait for it to be done," I sighed.

"Like when you're going on a vacation and the day before seems really long?" Nicole offered. I smiled.

"In a way. But on a vacation you're...well, you're on a vacation. I can't wait for this trip to start so that at least I can be done worrying about starting the trip. But the trip itself will be no vacation, it'll just be more work for ten days straight." We were looking over a river on a clear June evening, and it should have been romantic. Instead we stood close, but not touching, talking about rafts, and then trailing off.

"I think what you're doing is really cool," Nicole said.

"Yeah?" I wasn't surprised, but wanted to hear her say it again. "I think it's really cool that you think that this is cool." Sinatra would've grabbed Nicole's shoulders, said a line that would fit in an old movie, and kissed her passionately. Instead I merely stated, "I feel really lucky to have met you. I can't believe you find this stuff interesting."

"Why? It *is* interesting," she insisted. "Anybody would find it interesting."

"Yes but you are an attractive, nice, intelligent *girl*."

"I'm not used to hearing that from handsome, adventurous, intelligent men," Nicole said. "But what difference does that make to your raft anyway?"

"It makes all the difference," I said, stealing a glance before we both looked back over the black water. "The difference is that it's worth something."

"If a *pretty girl* likes what you're doing," she turned as though to lecture me, "it makes it worth something?"

"If a pretty, nice, intelligent girl does, yes." I spoke sincerely as far as my desires were concerned, and looked her in the eye.

"Well, I'm not any of those things..."

"I think you are, and you make me feel like I'm *not* a loser for doing the things I want to do." Nicole stepped forward and hugged me. I asked if it would ruin the moment if I kissed her under the full moon, by the river, in the summer of our youth.

"No..." she paused, then added, "I mean no it wouldn't ruin it, not no you shouldn't do it, I mean." So we kissed. She smiled and said, "Sorry that was awkward, what I said a moment ago...but the way you framed the question was awkward, so it made it awkward to ans—" and we kissed again. Then it wasn't awkward to kiss after that, if either of us felt like it.

We stopped by my folk's house in New Baltimore so I could get a bathing suit, and I introduced Nicole to my Dad and Mom. They were watching television, because it was a week night. Then we went to Oliver's parent's house, where he was having a nighttime pool-happy-rafting-party for Mike and I. Symbolically, in retrospect, Jared and TJ were unable to attend, but Mike and Oliver and Jess Gadani came, so it was like a mix of a rafting send-off and a symposium. We drank wine and laughed swimming in the moonlight, as jazz played from the pool-house speakers. As I drove Nicole back to Albany the stars disappeared behind a blanket of cloud. As I lay in bed, sheets of rain smacked my window, punctuated by claps of thunder and lightning that illuminated my room. I pictured the boat bucking in the wind seventeen miles south, in New Baltimore, and didn't sleep.

It was imperative that Mike and I work on the boat the next day, Tuesday, because our launch was two days away and I was supposed to get towed by Jess' father in 36 hours.

I tutored a pupil in the morning and got to New Baltimore in the early afternoon. As I drove south on Route 144 I looked out the driver's window down toward the bay. It was easy to make out the boats in the daylight, but my boat was not there.

I sped to Cornell Park and ran through the foliage, through the manicured yard, and stood atop the rocks that formed the peninsula at the southern end of the bay. I looked down and to the left. There was *The Manhattan Project*, grounded again atop a pile of rocks, completely out of the water. A hundred yards up the shore the rocks of the peninsula crumbled into a cobblestone beach. Two teenage girls sat on a checkered blanket, in wet suits, next to jet skis. A yellow Labrador retriever wagged its tail and ran toward me.

I climbed down the rocks to where the boat was grounded, climbing on the deck to survey the damage. The dog jumped aboard, too, and licked my hand. The girls started walking over.

"This is your raft, right?" the taller of the two girls shouted. She had blonde hair, the younger had red.

"Yes," I said, standing on the deck. I jumped down when they were within conversation distance. "She seems to be marooned."

"Appears that way," the shorter, red-haired, girl observed.

"This is your house?" I asked, pointing toward the three-story colonial on shore.

"No, that's Roger Cook's house. You don't know him? You're Dallas Trombley, right?"

"Yes," I smiled, surprised. "Ah...how did you know that?"

"Who else has a raft in New Baltimore? I'm Veronica and this is my sister Bernadette. You probably don't remember us but we know you from the summer camp you used to be a counselor at, and through the [New Baltimore] Conservancy. We live up the hill but Roger lets us use his beach. He's real nice. We've seen you working on your raft over the last week up in Coeymans and around here. The storm brought it here last night and beached it."

"Huh. Wow. Foley, I remember your last name. How are you doing?" We shook hands. "Man, can you apologize to the guy who owns this beach for me? I bet he's annoyed to see my junk here. I'm going to try to get it out of here as soon as possible."

"Roger doesn't mind. He said you should've asked him to keep it here to begin with, if you didn't have a place to store it. He's real nice."

"Wow. Really? I can't place his name..."

"He's in the Conservancy too. He remembers you from when you got a scholarship. Everybody read about your other boats in the *News Herald* last year." I looked out at the bay and pointed toward Shady Harbor where there were dozens of high-end yachts docked.

"Oh my God...can you imagine if the storm had been blowing the other way...and blew my boat into all of those rich people's yachts up there? The amount of trouble I'd be in right now? How much money I'd be liable for?"

"That's what Roger said," Bernadette, the younger sister, observed.

"So what's your plan now?" Veronica asked.

"Hmm, that's a good question." The three of us climbed aboard the boat. I showed them the cabin full of tools and paint cans and books and hardware. When we walked from the bow to the stern the boat did not shift on the rocks. It was obviously stuck. "I think the only choice is to wait until high tide and try and float it off the rocks," I said. "Do you think Mr. Cook would mind if I waited until high tide and got it off immediately after? I think high tide is around 9 o'clock tonight."

"Nine forty-five," Veronica corrected. "We figured that'd be your plan, so we figured out the tide. Do you have someone to help you?"

"My friend Mike," I said.

"The Admiral," Bernadette observed.

"We followed your stories in the *News Herald*," Veronica reminded me. I smiled,

"Yes, Mike. He's the Navigator on this trip. We figured we didn't need any admirals anymore, but we could use a navigator to figure out where we're going."

"Like, not into a pile of rocks," Bernadette joked.

"Yes...like not into a pile of rocks," I agreed.

Mike came down after work and we went to the peninsula to assess the situation. The dog was still sniffing around, and he lifted our spirits as he tagged along with us, walking over rocks and jumping onto the marooned boat's deck. We kept throwing sticks and he kept bringing them back.

"We could use a raft dog," Mike said. "Let's bring him with us."

"Ha, unfortunately I think he belongs to a couple of really nice girls who are wise for their years, who would miss him."

"That's too bad," Mike said, bending. "Isn't it *Rafty*? Rafty the Raft dog. Aww, you're a cute dog aren't you?"

Since we had to kill time we drove up to *Yanni's* and had a beer at the bar. It had been a rough week and we were happy that this would be the last night leaving the boat unattended. I told Mike that the *Times Union*, the largest Capital Region newspaper, had called me that afternoon to schedule an interview.

"Wow, the *Times Union*? That's huge. I guess Sean McGrath's website and Julie Watson's press release paid off! What's the TU's circulation? It's got to be over a hundred thousand readers between Albany and all the surrounding towns."

"It's really something now," I grinned.

With the big Albany newspaper coming to do a story, and the smaller Ravena papers, and the website and Facebook announcing our launch, there was no way we could avoid setting out from Albany at Alive at Five, two days later, whether we were ready to go or not. On previous trips I'd risked my reputation in front of *my friends* — but now thousands of people were going to read about the adventure. If I failed to show up with the boat the failure would be a thousand times worse.

It was the darkest part of dusk when we parked in Cornell Park and made our way to the peninsula. The water had risen so that half the boat was floating while the other half was still transfixed on the shore boulders. In the full-moonlight we pushed and lifted until we freed the boat. Then we used the motor to move around the tip of the peninsula to Cornell Park, where we tied it to shore with three mooring lines and dropped an anchor out in the water. It would take a tsunami to move the boat now. Then we sat on top of the cabin, drank a beer, and, like the water, reflected.

"Here we are again," Mike said. "If you asked me if I would be on another raft this time last year I'd have shouted 'No!' I guess a lot can change in a year."

"This time last year we were both dating college girlfriends, living with our parents, and working in dead-end jobs."

"Now we represent the epitome of success!" Mike joked. "But seriously, you're right. How much better is having an apartment than living at home? And I have a salary and a retirement plan...it's a big improvement. And with girls, it's just a time thing. It's easy to get annoyed or whatever when you're single, but if you have a job and an apartment and you go out and meet people, sooner or later you meet somebody. And the girlfriend thing is really the only thing, at least in my life, that's not an improvement over last year. So, hey, cheers...at least it's not 2006 anymore!"

We cheersed and felt pretty good. We decided the best plan was for me to do whatever repair work I could on the boat during the day tomorrow, after tutoring and between newspaper interviews, then I'd get the tow from Jim Gadani around four p.m. with help from TJ, and then at night Mike, Jared and TJ would load their supplies aboard in Albany. I'd sleep on the boat tomorrow evening so that nothing could happen the night before our launch in Albany.

We jumped to shore and walked to the car. I realized I'd dropped my wallet while we moved the boat. We spent half an hour searching the bank with a flashlight, but I never found it.

V. Storm

It was humid and hazy that Thursday morning. I skipped breakfast. Grumbles gnawed as I drove into the Hamlet of New Baltimore and turned down a winding road past the old Methodist church. After descending an acute angle past the old fire house, I arrived at Cornell Park, where I had a view of the riverbank across the tiny park with a gazebo and one street light.

There she was! Beyond the boulders of Cornell Park, six feet down, but with her mast rising high above the shore, Mike's American flag furling vigorously in the wind gusting toward Albany. Yet after I parked, as I walked closer to the rocks that formed the riverbank, a sense of vulnerability struck. Both of the boat's mooring lines were severed and she only sat stationary in the water because it was low tide and she'd beached upon some shallowly-submerged boulders.

An old man with a fishing pole, who I'd seen there the day before, stood at the north end of the peninsula. He neither smiled at me nor in any way acknowledged the obviously homemade boat in distress in our mutual vicinity. He just looked annoyed.

I thought to myself, giving strangers the benefit of the doubt: the mooring lines I'd used were not made of steel, they were normal climbing ropes, and a clothesline. They were under two-thousand pounds of stress holding the raft to rocks that were not smooth. The lines could've snapped, and I supposed I was lucky that they hadn't snapped over the previous week, when I ran a line to shore in other places. Still, I was troubled by the fact that the lines had "snapped" in the middle of the line, rather than around the points of contact with the bounders to which I'd tied them, where abrasion would've occurred. Also they were severed clean, as though they'd been cut with a blade.

Alas, what was I to do? I had to administer a final exam in a half-hour. I retied the mooring lines, figuring any vandalism must've occurred the previous night, and knowing I still had a couple of hours of low tide to administer the test and return while the boat was beached. With the knots retied, I sped to my session. It was out in Feura Bush, nine miles outside of Albany. Then I drove eight or nine miles back to New Baltimore, by 11:30 a.m. I was scheduled to meet Jess Gadani's father in Coeymans at 4:00 p.m. for the tow.

As I drove back from administering the exam I considered my limited finances. Tutoring checks took three weeks to arrive, I'd spent most of my excess cash on last-minute materials for the raft, on gas, and on bills generally. So now I had no money for contingencies. I couldn't use an ATM because I'd lost my wallet with my ATM card in the river the night before. I knew I could manage for a week with little or no money, eating things like cans of tuna fish and drinking water from marina spigots, but the crew might mutiny under those conditions.

Back at the river I received a call from an unknown number. It was the *Times Union* reporter, Brian Nearing. A friendly man with brown hair and a beard, he explained upon arriving that he'd been assigned the story because he ran the environmental-themed "Green Blog" under the newspaper's aegis. Yet what really attracted him to the story, he said, was the lyricism of the adventure.

"I like that you keep trying," Mr. Nearing said as the photographer, Mike Farrell, arrived in a different car and assembled his equipment. "This isn't really so much an environmental story as it is a story of a guy who won't let failure stop him." His perception was invigorating. I gave the reporter a tour of the boat, which he found fascinating. The old fisherman stood on the shore casting glances. When Mr. Nearing tried to get a comment out of him, he wouldn't speak. Meanwhile the photographer, a stylish, middle-aged man who sported a goatee and a fedora of his own, set up an umbrella-looking apparatus with a remote flashing mechanism and told me to stand on shore. He snapped dozens of pictures as Mr. Nearing continued asking about our previous trips, how long we expected our current endeavor to extend, what provisions we would use, and whether we thought we'd succeed. When he was finished he asked me to call him an hour before we left Alive at Five the next day, so he could do a story on our departure. Then he shook my hand and wished me luck. As he was leaving, the reporter from the Ravena *News Herald*, Tom Tucker, arrived, and we repeated the interview *sans* high tech photo equipment. Then he left and it was just me and the fisherman alone again.

I drove to my parent's house a mile up the hill to meet TJ at noon. TJ's role was Quartermaster, or, the crewmember responsible for provisions and cargo. Time passed quickly as we organized our supplies for transport from my parent's house to the river. We made sure to pack all the supplies from the Quartermaster's List which we'd compiled over the previous week. Into the back of my parent's truck, we loaded our charged battery, my clothes, hand tools, and other odds and ends. Just then I remembered I'd promised to run several errands for my parents before getting towed to Albany, including picking up some cash and an old car battery from their mechanic's garage in Ravena. (They'd sold their Jeep.)

As we loaded the supplies I noted the time: 2:00 pm. We had two hours to unload everything onto the boat, before we were scheduled to rendezvous with Jim Gadani up at Coeymans Marina. That would be enough time. But I was nervous after the morning's mooring-line incident, now that the boat had been unattended for two hours. So, half loaded, we drove to the river just a few minutes away to check on the boat.

"Where's the raft?" was the exclamation that had become a refrain over the last week. We should've seen her wooden mast with flying colors as soon as we pulled into the gravel lot at Cornell Park. But there was no boat.

Imagine you're hiking through mountains, moderately tired, yet sure of your step, when suddenly the ground crumbles and you fall into a cavern where you're completely blind to your surroundings—yet you know you're in trouble. I was momentarily stunned with that awful dropping feeling that accompanies surprising news. The possibilities came to mind:

-The raft has been towed by police and I don't have any money to get it back for tomorrow's launch, which will now be delayed;
-The raft has been stolen and my trip is over;
-The raft's lines have been cut and it has floated into the middle of the river where it will be smashed by another boat and I am now liable for damages or injury to other's property and persons;
-The raft's lines have been cut and the two-thousand-pound raft has floated into the nearby marina where it is now smashing against yachts worth hundreds of thousands of dollars for which I am now liable.

I am proud of my parasympathetic nervous system. When other people tend to become hysterical, I feel rather calm. TJ had the opposite reaction. His presence, rather than the raft's absence, worried me most. After an instant I collected myself and figured we'd locate the boat momentarily, but I thought the scare might make TJ drop out of the project altogether.

We ran to the mooring rocks. Our ropes were tied around the rocks with neat knots. A limp line continued toward the river, severed clean at the same distance on both lines. So that was that: someone had cut our lines and pushed the boat adrift.

Then the big scare. We ran to the northern side of the peninsula (the flood tide was ascending and a south wind was blowing so I knew the boat would've drifted north) and saw our boat in the waters of the shallow bay, floating directly toward the docks of Shady Harbor, with its boats worth hundreds of thousands or millions of dollars. With the wind whisking north and the flood tide pushing, our wood and metal vessel would soon smash against the expensive fiberglass of aristocrat's yachts. Even the tiniest scratch on those million-dollar boats would bring rich-men's wrath upon me— and there was the potential for my raft to puncture and even sink one, and then I'd be in really deep trouble. I judged it would take the wind and tide a half an hour to push the boat north into Shady Harbor.

"Alright this is what we're going to do," I said quickly. "We're going to run to my house, get the canoe, bring it here. You're going to canoe to the boat and stop it from drifting. I'm—"

"How am I going to do that?" TJ exclaimed.

"Any way you can. Meanwhile I'm going to speed up to Ravena to get the other battery from my parent's garage, then speed to Coeymans to meet Gadani at the docks. If I can't get Gadani down here in time to cut off the boat from hitting the docks, you've got to stop it, and vice versa. Any way we can." We started running back to the truck. "There's no way we can get the supplies from my house on the boat now. I'll load the supplies onto Gadani's boat and transfer them to the raft when he tows us." We slammed the truck doors as I started the engine and hit the gas. Stones flew behind us.

"What if I can't get the raft to stop, what am I going to do then? You should come with me."

"Listen," I sped onto the main road. A car horn told us we'd cut someone off as we accelerated up the hill. "You *have* to stop it from drifting."

"How?"

"Find a way! Use the anchors. Throw the anchors down to slow it, then tie all the ropes end to end and canoe to the shore and tie it to a tree. It's imperative that you stop it from drifting. I'll come back after I get the battery and see how you're doing before I go to Coeymans to meet Gadani."

"Oh man this is bad," TJ kept repeating. "This is bad."

At my house we threw the canoe in the back of the truck. I sped TJ down to the river and we got the canoe in the water. I gave him a walkie-talkie so we could stay in contact. We had no cell service by the river in New Baltimore.

"Good luck," I yelled as I sped off.

Now it was three o'clock. The timeline was constricting. I set a speed record driving to my parent's garage, where I was given an envelope with three hundred dollars, which I stuck in my back pocket, and grabbed the car battery. I sped back to my parent's house and threw a bunch of my personal supplies and clothes, and the rest of the raft's supplies, in the back of the truck. As I had my hand on the door handle, I noticed the weather. It was hazy, still and hot. All day the wind had blown north at a fifteen mile an hour clip. But now not a single leaf flitted and the cicadas had stopped screeching. It was dead silent and dead calm and humid. But there was no time for noting the intricacies of the atmosphere. I rushed back to the water. I tried repeatedly to reach TJ on the walkie-talkie but there was no response. I skidded to a stop at Cornell park and ran across the peninsula with a pair of binoculars. There I saw the raft floating closer to the yachts. TJ was in the canoe with a line stretched behind him, one end tied to the boat, canoeing toward the shore. I hoped he had things under control and sped to Coeymans to meet Jess and her father.

As I hit the brakes and jumped out of the truck in Coeymans I remembered that it was Jess's birthday. Her friend from Ithaca, Liz, was in town, and her father had left work early to meet us for the tow. Thus it was an inconvenience for most of the Gadani family to tow us to Albany that day.

I regretted skipping breakfast and lunch. I sweat in layers, dirty, salty and hot. I wore a thin plaid shirt but still I was soaking. The humidity was a smothering weight, inhibiting movement and rendering it hard to breath. A light breeze, only a couple of miles an hour, had resumed blowing north, but it was too weak to cool us.

I felt bad because it was Jess's birthday and I showed up like a madman. Right away I started running equipment down the docks to their boat, almost without saying hello: heavy marine batteries, oars and life-jackets, a duffle bag full of necessary supplies (the "Raft's Bag" as we called it, with lantern fuel, lighters, a first-aid kit and hand tools). Liz and Jess helped as I tried to convey to them the need for urgency, while seeming grateful for their service and not being too pushy.

"Here's Mr. Dallas now!" Mr. Gadani bellowed from the boat's drivers' seat. He'd clothed his ursine body in a gray tank-top and measuring-tape-patterned suspenders over a Santa Clause paunch. He bellowed his words from under a big brown mustache, good-willed. Like everybody, he was sweating profusely, and nervous.

"I'm sorry I've got so much stuff to load on here," I said. "We were planning on loading it in New Baltimore but somebody cut our lines."

The vandalism didn't seem to register with Mr. Gadani.

"Oh no problem Dallas," he said. "Load her up here. Jesus you've got a lotta shit." Indeed, I did. When we'd conveyed everything from the back of my truck into his boat it sat inches lower in the water. I tapped my feet and fingertips on the side of the boat because I still hadn't heard from TJ. I pictured him sitting on a dock at the Boat House next to all those expensive yachts while the raft smashed around, shaking his head and repeating "This is bad."

We had to stop to fill Mr. Gadani's gas tank. It was a small fishing and pleasure boat, about twenty-feet long. Filling the tank took forever as I bit my nails down to their nubbins. I got a *Snickers* bar from the marina gas station.

"'Not going anywhere for a while?'" I repeated the phrase from the *Snickers* commercial as I unwrapped the candy. I considered saving half of it for later in case something went awry with our towing plan. But then I thought, *I'll be in Albany in a few hours*. I joked to the candy bar, "Maybe *I'm* not going anywhere, but you are!" as I demolished the thing in less than one minute.

"Oh, honey, you look exhausted," Jess said when we got underway.

Of course when you're on a boat moving through the waves you're going to feel wind in your face. But looking at the clouds and trees on the sides of the river, everyone observed that the wind was gathering force. No longer was it blowing leisurely at a few miles an hour upstream. Now it blew a steady belt of waves against the boat, pitching us up and down over each crest, and there were stronger gusts which came from the east and west, and even from the north, that made it hard to determine the wind direction. It was as though all the atmosphere in New York was converging on the Hudson River at Coeymans. The wind whipped up the water and slapped it into waves with little white peaks.

Mr. Gadani looked worrisome.

"Now Dallas," he said. "They're saying all over the radio that we're supposed to get a big storm this afternoon in from Syracuse…"

"Let's hope they're wrong." That didn't quell his fears.

"Well yeah we'll hope they're wrong. But I mean let's just think…you know, in case we can't get all the way to Albany tonight…do you have a backup plan to get it up there tomorrow?"

"No. This is it."

Gadani looked at the sky, the trees rustling, the choppy waves. He looked very nervous indeed.

We sped past the inlet where we'd "hidden" the boat for a few days the week before, at the mouth of the Hannacroix Creek. We would be at TJ's position in another couple of minutes.

Attention is a finite resource and I couldn't worry about hypothetical disasters like storms when there were practical disasters to avert *at that very moment.* I knew we'd find a way to deal with bad weather if it came and that was that. The thing at present, in an order-of-operations sense, was to get the boat towed. To Jess and Mr. Gadani the weather seemed the most pressing issue—but at that exact moment, as we were about to rendezvous with the raft, we had to consider the angle to approach the raft in the hard wind; whether our towing lines were secured to the transom of Gadani's boat; and which knot to use to tow. The weather would have to wait; there were too many other things to worry about first.

We got to The Boathouse. A long dock at the restaurant jutted a third of the way into the river. The yachts moored along the dock obstructed our view of the downstream shore, so we had to speed past the restaurant to see whether *The Manhattan Project* was banging against the boats on the south side.

Finally—and I say finally because I hadn't taken a full breath in the last two and a half hours—the raft came into sight. It was anchored just where TJ had found it, floating up and down in the choppy waters about seventy-five yards from the restaurant docks. I let out a sigh. I tried to reach TJ on the walkie-talkie but there was no answer. When we got closer I saw him sitting in a camping chair with his shirt off, sunbathing. He had a pair of sunglasses on and *I-pod* phones in his ears. I jumped up and made ready the lines.

We had to come alongside the anchored raft and tie up to it with the heavy wind pushing Gadani's boat, without slamming and damaging its fiberglass hull in the choppy waters. And it was really whipping us by that point. People from the restaurant and shore watched us approach wondering what we were doing piloting a good boat up to what looked like a floating tool shed in deteriorating weather. We came along too far away on our first approach and had to circle back. All the while an ominous cloud of gray and brown crept behind us, slinking in the northern sky, shadowing the trees and waters upriver in dust and dusk.

We got alongside on our second approach and tied to the raft. I jumped from the Gadani's boat to the raft to tie the cleats like a good First Mate. I almost lost my hat in the process. We began transferring the supplies to the raft bucket-brigade style. It was hard getting the two batteries onboard. Each weighed about fifty pounds and the girls couldn't pass them. TJ and I had to reach out over the bow of the Gadani's boat and hope that when Jim handed us a battery it wouldn't topple us head-over-heels unbalanced. It occurred to me that a couple of handles mounted to the side of the cabin would've been a nice addition to the raft.

The wind was causing considerable consternation now; Mr. Gadani developed a tick as it began to whistle. We were rushing and that degraded everything. TJ and I threw the supplies haplessly inside the cabin. TJ was tired and nervous now. He explained an errand that meant he couldn't accompany me on the tow. So I tried to organize the supplies as the Gadanis conveyed TJ to the dock at the Boat House, which was walking distance from my parent's house and his car. By the time Jim, Jess and Liz motored back to the raft, I had the tow lines set, so I brought up the anchors and jumped back to Jim's boat, where Jess and Liz steadied me because it was hard to jump around in the up and down water.

Jim left the helm and helped me tie the tow lines to the stern cleats of his boat. We held the raft by the tow-ropes and tried to keep it from floating away, which took a lot of strength and made it hard to tie off at the same time with a free hand.

"What kind of knot should I use?" I shouted, although Jim was right beside me bent over the stern.

"I don't know knots!" he said. That surprised me.

Without thinking I grabbed the tow line from our boat and the lead line from Jim and tied a bowline in one. Gadani promptly wrapped this around his boat's stern cleat. He did this deftly. I grabbed the towline from the raft, tied a reef knot at one end, added a slip-knot and tied this to the rope Gadani had secured to the stern cleat. In under half a minute we had, using knowledge we thought insufficient for our purpose, worked together to secure a spliced towline from stern cleat to bow cleat: not an uncomplicated maneuver. After a few adjustments Gadani increased the throttle on his boat and the raft made white lines in the bubbly water as we began motoring north on our trip toward Albany. We slowly accelerated, the surf spraying our faces, carried in a mist above the increasingly choppy waves, like steam. The wind whistled above the drone of the motor in low gear.

"Anybody want a soda or a beer?" Jim offered.

"I'd love one," I said.

Jim reached into a cooler and gave me a cold bottle of *Bud Light*. I set a *Guinness World Record* swallowing it. I think I absorbed half the liquid through the dried kiln that was my tongue and throat. We were all breathing hard—you could see everyone's shoulders rise and fall as we slumped into our chairs to recoup after the exertion of the previous minutes. For a moment a tired, pensive quiet floated awkwardly in the humid afternoon atmosphere. I looked at my watch. It was five o'clock. We were scheduled to depart from Albany in twenty-five hours.

Jim sat at the wheel. He twisted to look at the towlines.

"This is a lot bigger than I pictured, I gotta tell ya..." He was nervous about the weight of *The Manhattan Project* pulling on the stern cleat of his boat. "Check that stern cleat Jessica babe," he kept saying. "Jessie babe, check that stern cleat will ya? Jesus I was picturing something smaller." He tried to be positive but his face betrayed his consternation. "I'd love to stay out here all afternoon and drink beers—hell that sounds like my kinda day! But it looks like it's getting pretty bad up there." Jim pointed to the sky upriver. A grey-brown cloud layer was creeping south—as though the clouds had swept up dirt and were carrying it toward us. I was silent. "If it wasn't so choppy and we had the tide this might be easier." We were getting bounced and pushed now both by going over waves (which are caused by wind) and the wind itself, which began blowing in circles. The gusts were erratic, the result of two pressure fronts converging and fighting for supremacy a mile above us. "We're the only schmucks on the whole fucking river right now," Jim noted. I looked up and down the river and there wasn't another boat in sight. "Now, in case we can't get all the way to Albany tonight, do you have another place you can tie up for the night?" I did not. But I conceded that, if extreme circumstances made it impossible to go to Albany, I could tie up at Henry Hudson Park, which was about halfway there. I didn't want to think about that idea. I knew the chances of getting the raft to Albany within twenty-four hours would decrease one-thousand-fold if Jim couldn't or wouldn't tow me that night. "Henry Hudson sounds like a good goal for today," Jim concluded.

Our sluggish speed was infuriating. The raft was built to float, not move through the water, and we had to tow her so slowly that our speed didn't register on Jim's speedometer. The trees on shore slothed south like snails on Sunday strolls. We trolled toward the storm gathering directly in our path.

To make matters worse it was impossible to tow the raft straight. It yawed about fifteen degrees to starboard and threw off Jim's steering, because the starboard towline was shorter than the port towline. Rather than pulling the bow of the raft out of the water, as a bullnose towline would've done, the two side cleats tended to jam the bow into the water and increase the drag. I suggested we switch the lines to a bullnose tie—Jim didn't want to stop. Jess and Liz looked from Jim to myself without knowing what to say.

After towing for an hour we'd only moved two miles upstream, just past the abandoned brick plant north of Coeymans. At that pace we'd arrive in Albany at four o'clock in the morning the following day. Jim had become a kind of Simon of Cyrene.

Now lightning began flashing between clouds in the sky ahead. A moment later thunder rumbled past our position. We saw the storm descending — a shadow and a haze like a sandstorm creeping south toward our sorry spot, throwing the river and trees below it into premature dusk. We were in the middle of an uninhabited portion of the river, with nothing but a dense tree line on either side of us, except a barely visible railroad bridge upstream, juxtaposed against a leaden blanket of cloud. The wind blew so hard we had to shout to hear. I reached up and grabbed my hat as a sudden gust blew it, and several other light objects, upwards and backwards.

"We're not going to make it to Henry Hudson!" Gadani called back to me.

Now we were really in a bad spot. Returning to Coeymans would take too long. We were going to be caught in the storm in the middle of the river — there was nowhere we could go on either shore to wait it out. Gadani thought there was a marina on the other side of a peninsula a hundred yards upstream where I could wait it out while he sought shelter with the girls. The raft and I would have to be detached from Jim's boat.

When we rounded the peninsula there was only a cove with a sandy beach and a huge uprooted tree.

"Fuck!" Jim shouted. I could barely hear him because of the wind. He cut the motor so that we drifted while deciding what to do. We couldn't stay in the river.

A weird silence fell everywhere. As though orchestrated, the wind quieted with the motor. Leaves and branches that had been waving like windsocks suddenly limped. We looked around feeling eerily alone. Viewed from the sky we were a tiny shiny speck adrift in suddenly calm waters, surrounded by eclipse-like darkness.

Tick…tick, tick, like rice falling on a linoleum floor, we heard the sound of raindrops tap the boat, a metronome musical score. A rotund wave moved us up and down, silently, serenely, as it rolled past. We looked at one another, hearing only *tick, tick.*

Then a tearing peel of thunder ripped across the sky and made us jump and put our hands instinctively over our ears and eyes. A great streak of white-hot lightening spewed from a cloud at exactly the same time, and chaos erupted. Rain the size of marbles pelted the boat, sounding like metal nuts shaking in a coffee can. The wind bashed us from different directions, at the same time pushing us backward and broad-siding us so that the whole boat moved up out of the water. We were unable to stand without holding onto something. A wind burst hit the boat so hard we turned forty-degrees to starboard and the Plexiglas windshield, which had been open on a hinge, slammed closed, almost smashing Liz who was standing next to it. The sound of the percussion made us jump. Then another crack of ear-splitting thunder and our boat up and down and tossed around. The most terrifying aspect: circular vortexes of wind suddenly appeared and whipped the surface of the water into miniature whirlpools. The wind and tiny sand particles danced spiraling back and forth like tiny tornados twisting and courting one another.

Jim wasn't going to wait for those tornados to become full-sized. He jammed the motor into high gear.

We were jerked almost off our feet as the towline, which had slacked when we sat motionless a moment before, became once again taut. We had nowhere to go, we were just moving to seem to be getting out of there, wherever there was.

The Manhattan Project and I had become a liability.

Jim revved his engine. Our faster tow speed and the awkward way we'd tied the raft sent the bow of *The Manhattan Project* diving under water. I looked back and saw waves crashing over her bow, into the cabin and all over the equipment inside. The starboard hinge on the aft cabin doors had been broken when the police tied the boat to a tree the week before, so there was a real threat that the water might inundate our supplies and carry them right out the back door into the river.

Jim got the boat moving even faster. He was really gunning it now. The bow of the raft dragged so low that the triangular front section was completely submerged beneath the boiling brown water. I envisioned the whole ship sinking in the middle of the river and the thought of the immense futility of the vessel — if it were to sink now — made me feel sick and faint. I noted, too, that Mike's canoe was missing. As I squinted I saw that it was being dragged beneath the raft completely underwater. I thought *we cannot lose the canoe without jeopardizing the entire mission*. It was essential for taxiing, docking, re-supplying and exploring. The thought of the canoe's lines breaking because of the drag, or its hull being punctured by the raft's weight, made me shout in objection to our quickened pace.

But no one heard my exclamation because a huge discharge of lightning obliterated the space between two clouds above us and sent a sound so deafening down that everyone shouted and felt the percussion against their shirts, skin and eardrums.

"Bring me in to the shore!" I shouted again.

"What?" Jess yelled.

"I'll tie off to the shore! You guys need to get back to Coeymans fast!" I had to yell because the wind was whistling and the sound of the rain, semi-frozen, drowned out everything.

"Okay!" Jim shouted from the front.

"Just get me in as close as you can!" I shouted. My goal was to transfer to the raft, create a length of rope as long as I could by tying smaller lengths together, and swim to the shore to secure it to something solid there. But the wind was blowing in such crazy directions (even up and down) that I needed to be well into the cove before untying from Jim's boat, or the wind would blow the raft up or downstream, with me getting dragged along. I figured I had about a thirty percent chance of tying together enough rope to achieve my objective, but if we got far into the cove there was a chance that the raft would crash into the banks of the cove's surrounding peninsulas and hold me in one spot in case I couldn't swim to shore. That was my contingency against the raft being set adrift in the river. It wasn't the best plan, but I made it in a split second and there were really no other options to save Jim's boat. The inundated canoe meant I had to swim or stay with the raft and the equipment no matter what happened.

"I can't get any closer," Gadani shouted when we were about seventy-five feet from the shore. "I'm about to bottom out!"

"Okay!" I shouted back. "Turn off the engine so I can get some slack on the rope!"

Jim killed the engine. The wind raged, blowing us toward the shore and the shallow water. Every moment Jim's boat was blown closer to beaching or grounding out. From the force of the tow the knots around the cleat had gotten so tight and wet that they wouldn't budge. In a moment of exasperation, I grabbed my knife from its belt sheath and severed the line, holding the length attached to the raft.

Suddenly a wave pushed the bow of Jim's boat up in the air, then we fell down again, and the raft's towline, now severed, slipped out of my hand. Without thinking I jumped and grabbed for it and caught it by the last knuckles of my fingers, but I was so outstretched over the water that my feet slid and Liz shouted "Dallas!" and grabbed me by the legs to keep me from being pulled overboard.

All this happened so quickly that until Liz's exclamation the Gadanis were anxiously watching the approaching shoreline as the wind pushed us closer to the bank. Just as Liz grabbed my legs and kept me on the boat Jim throttled up the motor. I was just able to bend my knees and get my feet angled on the stern of the boat in such a position that I could pull the raft toward us with all my might when suddenly Jim's boat lurched forward under power. I found myself, still clutching the raft's towline, flung into the air. I just had time to close my eyes and tense up when I felt the warm water hit my face and the sounds of the storm and shouts soften beneath a swish of water rushing into my ears. Still holding the line, I kicked to stay afloat but found that I could stand in the belly-deep water.

Back on the boat the girls were shouting and pointing. When they saw my head pop out of the water they looked frightened. I stood up to show them it was shallow.

"Get the fuck out of here!" I shouted to Jim.

Mr. Gadani did not waste time following that good advice. He made a perfunctory "Are you sure?" gesture as he opened up the throttle and high-tailed it out of the cove.

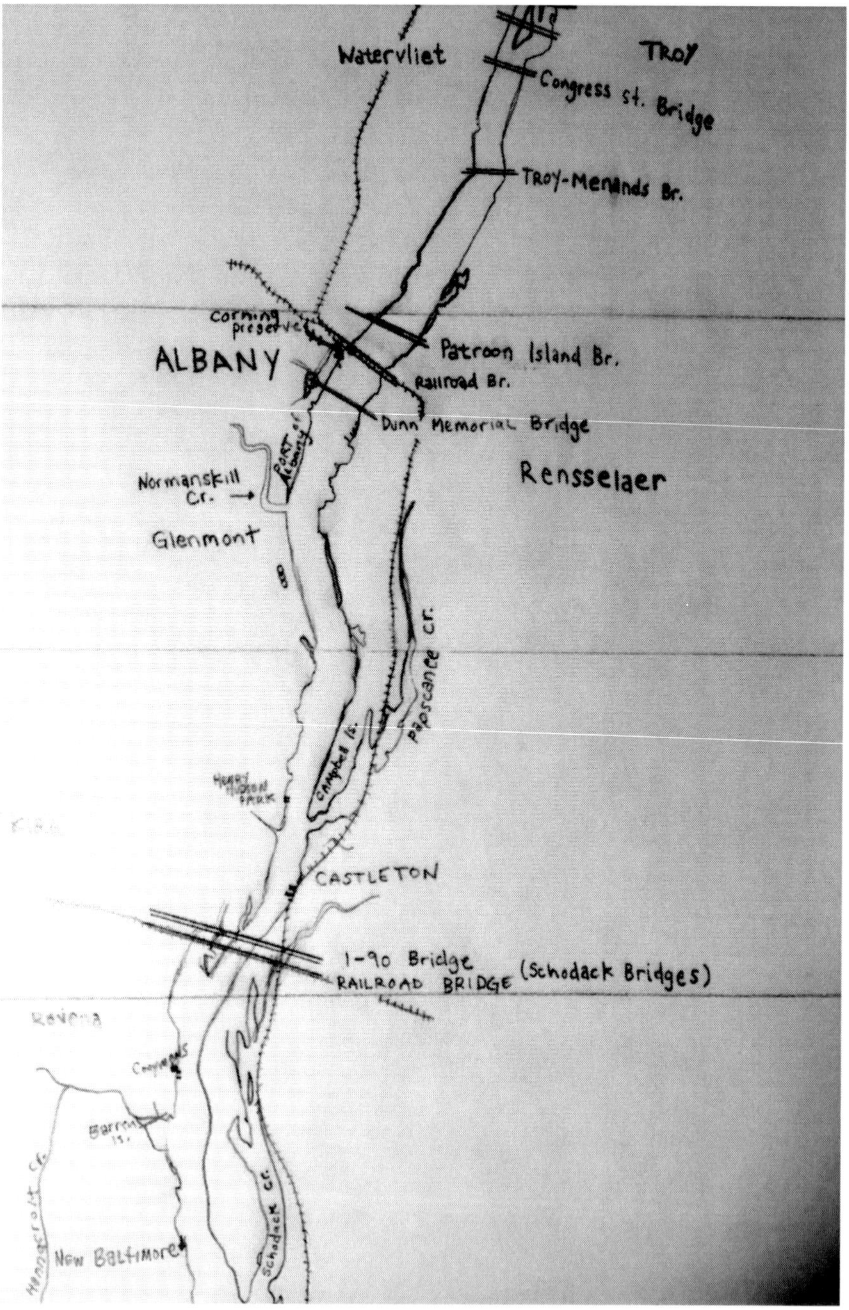
Watervliet
TROY
Congress st. Bridge
Troy-Menands Br.
Corning preserve
ALBANY
Patroon Island Br.
Railroad Br.
Dunn Memorial Bridge
Normanskill Cr.
Rensselaer
Glenmont
Papscanee Cr.
Campbell Is.
CASTLETON
I-90 Bridge
RAILROAD BRIDGE
(Schodack Bridges)
Schodack Cr.
New Baltimore

VI. Captain's AWOL

After the Gadanis' boat sped away I stood in the muddy water up to my stomach with a feeling like I was watching everything happen from ten feet above. But there I was with my feet in the muck and the rain falling hard and cold (much colder than the water, which was warm) and the storm like something tropical blasting the side of my face and pushing the raft toward the shore and downstream.

I had to act quickly. I grabbed three lengths of hundred-foot rope that were sitting on the bow and tied them together. I waded to the shore where an uprooted elm lay with its roots reaching like fingers into the water. As I waded and tied, the wind whisked the boat downstream. I hoped my ropes would hold so I didn't end up helplessly adrift. I tied triple knots with redundant ropes to the tree and the raft in different places. Then I ran knee-deep through the water and climbed aboard into the cabin to wait out the storm.

It was totally dark and I was soaked to the skin trying not to shiver. My eyes adjusted as the rain beat the plywood. The equipment had been thrown into in piles from the surf and our rapid loading. As a result, there was no room to sit. The roof was dripping. I stood half-bent. I took a deep breath and looked around. I tried to consider my options.

"First thing's first. You're not going to die. Okay, so things aren't that bad. You're probably not in any danger of getting badly injured. Okay. Well, then, first thing's first—get out of your wet clothes and get warm." I remembered that advice from watching *Survivor Man*.

By a fortuitous accident Jess had grabbed a plastic bag from my truck with some of my dirty clothes in it, and stowed it on the raft. So by luck I had a relatively dry tee shirt and a pair of exercise pants that buttoned up along the legs. I think they're called "breakaway" pants. I found some twine that had rolled out of a duffle bag and made a clothesline to hang my wet clothes. As I stripped off my pants and jacket it hit me that my cell phone, walkie-talkies, and watch had all been submerged when I was pulled off Gadani's boat. I hoped the phone might dry, so I took it apart and put it in the medicine cabinet I'd brought to act as a dry box—a necessity according to *Seamanship*. I also found three soaking wet one-hundred dollar bills in an envelope in my pocket—the payment for the Jeep from my parents' garage. I opened the bills and laid them in the dry box across two pens so that as they dried they wouldn't stick to the shelf. That money was another stroke of good fortune—I only had one other dollar in my pocket and I had a feeling I might need more, especially since I'd lost my wallet the night before. I hung my clothes to dry and found an overturned camping chair. I cleared a space and sat naked to dry myself. Then I tried to think logically.

In the chair, every couple of seconds, drops of cold water fell on my head or the back of my neck and dripped down my spine. I could hardly see because the storm-clouds had turned the late afternoon into night and all the shutters and doors were closed to keep out the rain. I groped around to find a flashlight—I could recognize bags by their texture—but most of their contents had been scattered by the rough ride. I couldn't find the flashlight. I got cold-naked-mad and started shouting and kicking blindly. I found my adventurer's jacket with a box of matches in the pocket. They were matches Kate had given me, with a French maid on the cover of the box. I'd carried them across Delaware, Maryland, Virginia, Phili, New York and Albany, but now the old reliables were soaked and wouldn't ignite. I opened the front starboard cabin door to let a little light into the cabin, but with the light came a wall of rain, so I jumped around naked getting hit with spray trying to find that wretched flashlight. I found a long-stemmed barbeque lighter and slammed the door closed so it was dark again. But to my frustration the barbeque lighter wouldn't light, so I stood there in the dark with my fists clenched shaking my head for a minute, until I remembered the Bic lighter in the dry box. I found that and got a flame going, then I looked around and found the "raft bag" with its plastic bottles of lamp oil. I found two rickety dollar-store lanterns and filled their reservoirs with fuel, only to have the lighter run out of fluid as I held it in the air to light the first one. I shook it and tried to light it again but it wouldn't ignite. After rolling the flint knob and hurting my finger it lit for a second and I got the lamp ignited. I turned the flame on the lantern all the way up. It illuminated the cabin and felt warm, at least. I could see then that the ceiling was leaking in a straight line where two pieces of plywood joined, so I placed my chair along the wall and sat naked drying in the light now, without being dripped on, and tried to think again.

I sat for several minutes, exhausted, looking around at the inside of the cabin the way a person might read a page of text while thinking of things that happened throughout the day—I moved my eyes over everything but didn't comprehend what I saw. After my skin had mostly dried I donned the dry snap-on pants and tee-shirt, then sat down again, warmer with only my feet still wet. I listened to the rain pounding the sides and top of the cabin, but I no longer felt the up-and-down motion of waves. The raft had evidently beached.

"Well," I said as I sat there biding my time, "no matter what happens I'll benefit from getting this cabin organized, and the sooner the better. *Carpe Diem.*" I rose and put the miscellany back in bags and cleared a space on the floor so I could walk bow to aft. Then I sat down again.

"Well okay, what can I do now to help my situation?" I asked aloud. There is always something you can do during the instant we call the *present* to help your future an instant from now. For the next half-hour I re-organized the cabin. I put the hand tools in one box. I tied the loose lengths of rope in coils and hung them from the ceiling beams, by lamplight. I put fragile equipment like the extra lantern in the holds we'd designed beneath the cabin floor. I chris-crossed the six-foot paddles to contain the life jackets between the wall joists. The batteries and motor I lined at the base of the walls with the toolboxes in neat rows. After thirty minutes the cabin was organized so I could lie down if I wanted and I knew where everything was so I'd be prepared for contingencies. The activity gave me a feeling of agency. I checked to see if my phone or watch were working—they were not. Then I sat down with *Seamanship* to see if I could get any ideas.

The lamplight flickered shadows across the plywood walls and bare stud supports. The light on the wood made the tiny room feel like a miner's cave or a tall ship marooned away from port. But soon, visible where the boards came together, I noticed rays of sunlight. I put down my *Seamanship* book and opened the front starboard door. Into the cabin flowed a wall of evening light. Outside, the storm had been carried off by the wind or expended itself, as a flame in a bottle, before evaporating. The sky was a pale blue expanse. Birds tweeted behind the bush beyond the beach. A breeze, nearly imperceptible, stroked my face and carried the aromas of flourishing foliage and muddy musk. It was like waking to see the primordial earth take shape.

I jumped from the bow of *The Manhattan Project* onto shiny, firm dirt that continued fifteen feet to the water.

Across the river, perhaps two miles downstream on the opposite shore, barely visible, was the terminus of the conveyer belt of the factory that blasted stone across my high school campus. The sheet metal structure was the only suggestion that humans ever inhabited that portion of the Hudson River where the boat and I now stood. The rest of the shoreline within eyesight was a jungle. I was in a cove with two peninsula points jutting into the river a hundred feet to the south and four hundred feet to the north. I'd purchased a fold-out, water-proof map, which was in the cabin. I could determine my location once I'd viewed the topography better. Far upstream, when I squinted, I barely descried a faint line that represented some kind of bridge.

I walked around the ship's perimeter to assess the damage. To my surprise and satisfaction there appeared to be none at all. The raft had been pushed under the waves and had her foam dragged and beaten—she'd beached and smashed against rocks over the last few days—and here she sat a specimen of endurance. I felt a lot of pride looking at what Mike and I had built, with help from friends here and there. But then I saw our Achilles' heel and my stomach sank again: the canoe was filled with water.

The canoe had been tied taut to the starboard side of the raft so it would mimic the movement of *The Manhattan Project*'s hull as she was towed. But when Gadani had sped up and forced the bow of the raft underwater the canoe had been inundated and, the more it filled, the lower sank. As Gadani moved faster the canoe had been forced beneath *The Manhattan Project*, and my fear was that the one-ton vessel would come to rest atop the aluminum canoe and crush it. Luckily, the canoe had come to rest aside the raft, though filled with water. I bent and grabbed the sides of the canoe in order to turn the water out. I grunted as I tried to lift one side. I was unable even to ripple the water inside.

"Okay," I said aloud. "One-two-three, mind over matter. Ready Trombley? One! Two! Three! Grrrahhh!" The bastard canoe sat there and wouldn't budge a half-millimeter. It was like an extension of some granite formation underground.

"Fucking canoe!" I shouted and kicked the side of the thing. I jammed my right big toe, because I had no shoes on, because my sneakers were soaked. I hopped on my left foot in the brown muck and stepped on a sharp stick. When that happened I very nearly lost my temper. My hand flew into the air above my head in the shape of a fist in order to pummel the stick, which was the size of a twig, into the earth. But just then I caught myself and, smiling, I bent down and plucked the twig from the mud with two dainty fingers, like lifting a fragile teacup. With perverse pleasure tingling in every extremity, I delicately placed the injurious object on the deck of the raft, which was waist-high when beached. Then I climbed into the cabin and slowly and thoughtfully removed a hammer from its spot in the tool box. With perfect posture and poise I marched back to where I'd stood a moment before. Then, first raising the hammer above my head with two hands, I smashed that twig into pulverized pulpy sawdust with a dozen violent poundings. After, breathing heavy, I placed the hammer back where I'd found it. I returned, said to the canoe, "Okay canoe, let us fix you," and cracked my knuckles.

I knew what I had to do, which was get the water out of the canoe. I tried bailing it with cupped hands but that would take forever. I tried digging a ditch next to the canoe to tip it into, but that was equally unsuccessful because the ground was packed hard. My attempt to locate a piece of hose-like material on the raft or on shore in order to fashion a siphon was also futile. Finally I rolled up my pant legs and sat on the side of the canoe, bailing, saying in unison with each dripping handful, "I'm going to fix you, canoe," in a kind of song.

I'd searched for something to use as a container in order to bail the water more efficiently but found nothing. Then I remembered the plastic solo-cups we'd brought for navigation lights. (Their green and red translucent color atop flashlights mounted on the side of the cabin worked well as port-and-starboard night running lights.) So I began bailing the canoe with those. I got a good rhythm going, straddling the canoe, reaching into the canoe water with a solo cup in each hand and then throwing the water out either side. I started singing, "Row, row, row your boat, gently down the stream; merrily, merrily, merrily, merrily, life is but a dream," to the rhythm of my bailing. I laughed at the absurdity of the situation.

As early-evening faded to dusk I was still marooned on the muddy beach in the middle of nowhere with no means of communication and only a vague idea of my location, with an inundated but improving canoe and no food or water.

The canoe was still half-full of water and immovable. As I was bailing, I remembered that I was supposed to meet Nicole that evening in Albany aboard the boat. I'd looked forward to spending the evening listening to music on the water, drinking wine under a starry sky. I was supposed to call Nicole at six o'clock. The thought that I should've been hanging out with a young woman, and the angle at which the sun had descended (signaling the rapid approach of evening) pressed my spirits into my ribcage. My arms ached from repetitive bailing. I looked toward the tree line and noted that the *melancholy hour* had arrived, when the sky is still bright but everything on earth is cast in shadow. Quite tired, I got out of the canoe barefooted and walked along the beach at sunset.

The tide slowly began its rise as I strolled toward the southern peninsula to scout. My muddy feet left footprints in the sand. I thought about my grandmother's music-box that told the story of a man who, at death, saw his life pass before his eyes as a set of footprints on a beach. There was a second set of prints that represented God walking with the man. "God," the man said, "why is it that during the hardest parts of my life there is only one set of prints? Why did you abandon me in my darkest hours?" and God replied (as a little magnetic seagull glided around the text and mechanical wind-up music chimed) "My son, I did not abandon you. Those were the times when I carried you." I thought about that music box because of its association with footprints on a beach, not because anything about the story could help me.

I grew morose. *You find inspirational lies like those strewn around people's houses to comfort them*, I thought. I thought about Adam, my former teacher who I painted for, whose dog had recently died. On his refrigerator he hung a piece of paper with a picture of a lab frolicking through a forest, with a short story that read roughly as follows:

> When our pets die they walk through a path in the forest until they come to a bright rainbow, the Doggie Rainbow. When they pass underneath the Doggie Rainbow they find themselves in a great field full of other dogs, and flowers. And they all frolic together and play and are never hungry or sad or in pain for ever more.

Both of those stories are total bullshit, I observed angrily. *The fact that they're comforting doesn't justify belief in such nonsense… hanging on one's wall and refrigerator as if such things were True.* I paced a few more steps, shaking my head. *In fact, it's almost harmful to individuals and to humankind. Faith in what we wish was true, rather than what is, is at best un-pragmatic and often detrimental.* I looked back at the raft and my trail of muddy footprints and knew I was being carried by no deity. In all probability, I was going to be rescued that night by no human either. And I was starting to get hungry and extremely thirsty (I couldn't drink Hudson water because it'd been poisoned by a century of industrial pollution). So with redoubled resolve I straightened my posture and walked with purpose toward that southern peninsula to scout, knowing that whatever was to happen would be the product of my own effort, endurance, and sense of determination.

The human body is a complicated machine with many interconnected parts, and is therefore susceptible to a range of injuries. I'd always pictured *injury* as damage to a gross muscle group or an entire appendage. But as I walked toward that southern peninsula I was stopped by a strain to a very small portion of my musculature.

To get to the lookout point, I had to walk barefooted across an expanse of moss-covered stones cobbled smooth by waves. The now-returning tide had covered the stones with an inch or so of water. To walk on these slippery spheres required bending my toes and gripping them like a monkey might clutch a softball with his foot. After a few steps a Charlie-horse shot up the bottom of my right arch. It grew so intense that with every step my foot felt stabbing pain. I shouted aloud. I stood on my left foot in the ankle-deep water and massaged my arch. It felt as though two of my toes had burst from their sockets. If I lifted the foot the pain disappeared, but as soon as I tried to place my step it shot up with incapacitating severity. I was the length of a tractor-trailer from the point I wished to scout but I couldn't move. Some little belt in my foot, some ligament a podiatrist might study on a flash-card and forget again, had stopped me in my tracks.

The failed scouting expedition cost me about half an hour. When I got back to the raft it was almost completely dark. The water had risen so it just lapped the bottom of the foam pontoons. Since the water was rising, I was missing my opportunity to travel upstream on the tide, because I was beached. My chances of getting to Albany, where newspapers, family and friends were scheduled to see the crew and I the next day, were slipping with every second. I stood looking out at the river, growing cognizant of crickets chirping. It seemed that I was going nowhere that evening — and that meant postponing the trip indefinitely if I couldn't get a tow the next day, because I would lose the crew. With my hands at my sides I stood there, a solitary man juxtaposed against a black foliage background. A moonbeam flashed over the trees on the southern peninsula. I turned and watched the moon rise over the horizon, slowly, orange, alone.

On the beach I nodded to myself. It was dark and there was only time for necessary tasks. I found the "navigation lights" in the cabin, where the lamp was still burning. I attached these to their port and starboard designations. I carried the heavy battery and trolling motor out of the cabin and put them on the stern section, which was still only roped to the back, having broken off when the police tied our boat to a tree earlier in the week. I wasted time trying to nail it more strongly to the back of the raft but I couldn't lift the section and nail it at the same time, so I reinforced it with more ropes. I spent another fifteen minutes bailing the canoe and I was able to tip it over easily because it had extra buoyancy sitting in a couple of inches of water. When I finally tilted the canoe and the water flowed out I literally jumped for joy and exclaimed "Yes! Take that!" to the canoe and circumstances in general.

Now the primary preparations were set for the decision I'd made basking in the moonbeams. When the tide was high enough, I was going to try to get the raft un-beached. If I could do that, I was going to travel as far north as the wind, the tide, and my batteries would take me. Then the next day I'd be closer to Albany, and more likely to attract a good Samaritan or convince a friend or acquaintance to tow me, if I could get to a phone.

I'd become exceedingly thirsty. It was hard to believe that that same day I'd woken up in Albany and administered a final exam to a student ten miles away. All I'd eaten was a *Snickers* bar; I'd only drank two cups of iced coffee and a beer.

I had about another half-hour before the raft would be buoyant enough to push it off the mud. So I got into the canoe. I paddled it north, to scout what was immediately beyond the peninsula that formed the northern boundary of my cove. As I paddled from the raft I fixated on finding a water spigot or a fresh-water tributary to drink from. If worse came to worse I could drink the Hudson water and suffer the diuretic and bacterial effects later. But if I drank the water and had to relieve myself of liquefied excrement every ten minutes the trip would be ruined. Yet the dehydration dried my patience and monopolized my attention.

I was a terrible canoer, having canoed alone only once three days before. With every stroke the bow shot to one side. I couldn't move in a straight line. My arm was tired and achy. As I zig-zagged I felt my blood reach a rolling boil, so I stopped to rest. But the river current turned my canoe broadside so it faced the channel, and then I had to realign myself before I could paddle north again. To keep making progress I used a method I'd taught myself during soccer tryouts: make it to a landmark a couple dozen yards away, then trick myself into thinking, "Oh, I was looking at the wrong landmark. My goal is really _____ a hundred feet farther," and repeat that until I made it to my ultimate destination without resting. But as I paddled on and on, passing vertical beam after vertical beam of a wooden dike that ran northward parallel to the shore, as far as I could see, all I could think of was finding water.

"Just make it to the end of this dike and there might be something there," I said to myself. My lips were a layer of dried broken skin, as in wintertime; my tongue and throat were liked the baked rocks at the brick plant downstream. "Fuck the end of this dike!" I shouted. "I'm thirsty. There's nothing up there. The raft might be floating by now, turn around!" So I did.

When I got myself turned around the raft was a tiny flickering light far away, like a star that fell into the tree line. Now I was even more annoyed because I realized I had to paddle against the tide on the way back to the raft. Everything was a variation of black, the deepest and darkest of all the water, which seemed like a river of oil in the moonlight. It was sheer strength of will that kept me from reaching over the side and drinking handfuls of the black liquid.

I thought about the people on the B-52 bomber *Lady Be Good* who over-flew their landing strip in Morocco in World War II and crash-landed in the African desert. When they found one of the bodies decades later there was a journal in the skeleton's pocket. The men had survived the crash and walked for days before succumbing to the heat and the lack of water. But as the days passed, the entries in the journal became indecipherable. Was it because of weakness? No. As the body loses water one of the first things to desiccate are the mucus membranes, like the eyes. As the men of the *Lady Be Good* grew more and more dehydrated, they lost the ability to tear and wash sand out of their eyes. After a few days in the desert their eyelids became sandpaper, and the reflex of blinking—well, every time they did it, they grated their retinas until they blinded themselves. The last entries were so sloppy because the man writing them couldn't see what he was writing. I reflected on that and paddled on, employing two tricks. The first was to get myself closer to the shore where the current is sometimes less than or even opposite to the tide, and the second was to sing as I paddled in order to maintain a rhythm. I sang *That's Amoré, Moon Over Parma, There's a Moon Out Tonight,* and *Dancing in the Moonlight,* in celebration of my celestial companion so prominently shining just above the blackened trees. I was on the second verse of *Blue Moon* ("What is a blue moon?" I was thinking), when I got close enough to the raft to jump out. I had a great idea just then as I saw the blue tarp-sail hanging on the cabin's roof. I climbed up quick as a monkey. Like Indiana Jones finding some Aztec treasure, I grabbed the torch lamp and held it close to the top of the cabin, bending my head to examine.

What I saw there made me grin from ear to ear. A puddle of rain water collected in the folds of the tarp! I dove into it with pursed lips and sucked it dry. I could feel it absorbed by my tongue, then the back of my throat, and hit my belly and make gurgling noises. I got half a cup of water and was satiated, more or less. My mind knew I'd get more water soon. The half cup quieted my body for a while at least and made the pangs bearable.

I lashed the canoe to *The Manhattan Project*, untied the lines that moored her to the roots of the fallen elm, transferred as much weight to the port side of the raft as possible (for that was the side in deeper water), and waited for nature to do the rest.

I'd flat-out rejected the idea of piloting the raft solo the week before, when I needed to move it per police request. I'd waited for Mike to get out of work. It was hard to steer, even with two people. Without a completed rudder, the only way to direct the raft was to paddle on one side or the other in order to increase that side's velocity and slowly turn it in the opposite direction. Forward progress required at least two people paddling in unison. However, now I had the trolling motor to move me forward, so as long as that continued to work I'd only have to steer the thing. If I ended up in the middle of the river and the motor died I'd surely go wherever the tide took me — which was likely to be downstream if the tide changed before I could get the raft to shore — or possibly into another boat, which would be even worse. If I couldn't steer the boat and a barge came along a collision was possible. There was also the possibility of police interception, because my "navigation lights" were below the required candle-power, I had no reliable steering and the police were known to stop people for less than piloting a 2,000-pound raft alone at night. Also, I had no idea how long my batteries would last, how much of the flood tide was left, or if the motor would even push me out of the cove where I was beached, since it seemed to be flowing with an opposite, downstream current.

Fifteen minutes passed. I rolled my snap-up pants above my calves, jumped in the water up to my knees, and pushed. After a series of rocking movements and pushing at the bow rather than amidships, I succeeded in floating all but the stern of the raft, which still rested upon the muddy bottom. The bow bobbed, facing the channel and upstream. I thought, "Is this really what you want to do?" and then I pushed her out and jumped aboard.

Silently, the momentum of my thrust pushed *The Manhattan Project* into deepening waters, leaving a v-trail of illuminated ripples dancing outward behind. I flicked a switch on the trolling motor and lowered the four-inch propeller into the water. It made a dull hum that was just audible as it moved the boat slowly from the shore toward the channel.

What a serene, peaceful scene! It must've been around ten or eleven p.m. Not a single cloud, nor any city lights obstructed my view of a full moon and full complement of stars twinkling dazzling above me like spilled diamonds on black silk. The oil water, motionless, reflected the great white sphere of the spring tide moon, biggest it would be for thirty days. The pitch tree line, enveloping the river on either side all up and down—I could only perceive by an absence of stars where the forest began. Forward and behind, red and green channel markers undulated on and off, reflected in the black water and elongated by perspective into rippling trails of color. Out past the peninsula in the open water a summer breeze scented with shades of blooming and musky river water nudged me northward. There were no crickets. No sounds of waves. Only the gentle hum of the motor and the free American outdoors pushing me and lifting me. I wished I could bottle that evening air, the liberating scent that only summer and youth with its potential can carry, for spritzing in wintertime. But fresh country air would spoil in a bottle. And it is experience, rather than aroma, that liberates.

A mile or so upstream an illuminated line was a bridge. When I'd gotten myself almost into the channel I ran to the bow and paddled on the port side to straighten out. A few too many strokes—I stopped paddling when I faced straight upriver but momentum carried the bow to starboard. I jumped and paddled on that side to straighten out. I faced north again only to overshoot to port this time and jumped up and paddled on the port side. This happened a couple times until I began to cease paddling before my correction had completed. The bow of the ship had a natural tendency to wander to starboard, so after a few trials I sat on the starboard side and paddled about six times a minute to compensate. By that method I achieved a fairly strait trajectory, and was even able to lean my back against a lifejacket and the cabin to relax a little, because all of my muscles were achy. I looked toward the tree line and saw the vertical posts of the wooden dike moving back, and tentatively assured myself that I was making good progress.

After a while I got brave and left my post to see if I could get more comfortable. I retrieved a wind-up radio from the cabin and tuned in to a local rock station. It would've been a gorgeous night to have rendezvoused with Nicole on the boat, but as it turned out I was enjoying my solitude even more than her company. Periodically I had to run to the bow and paddle to straighten out. Every time I stepped into the stern section where the motor was clamped, my feet got wet because my weight pushed the unattached stern section under water (good thing I was using marine batteries). I could never achieve a really straight trajectory but had to realign the trolling motor every couple of minutes as the boat veered in lazy wide zigzags. Once I even got the thing turned completely ass-backwards and cursed before pointing north again. But pleasant work it was, silently overtaking the objects ashore. As I passed the first green blinking buoy I smiled, and every one after was a marker of progress. I passed a marina lit up to the east. I aimed between two supports of the railroad bridge and was satisfied when I passed beneath the bridge just where I'd aimed.

Passing beneath the bridge was really something. The breeze picked up as the gigantic stone pillars grew with uniform speed. Beneath the bridge, yellow light shined on its concrete pillars, scary because of their size. And just as I was underneath the bridge a freight train crashed across the top and rattled everything.

Later I passed a sleepy town of four or five brick buildings and two streetlights. At a bend in the river I crossed the channel to take the shortest route. I overtook an anchored tugboat with its white anchor light glowing atop its mast. And then I nearly shouted as I suddenly saw the mast of an anchored sailboat silhouetted against the shore, sitting directly in my path only fifty yards away! I threw the motor full to port and got the boat facing perpendicular to the river, facing the channel, then pushed the motor forward only to pass the sailboat so close I could've touched it. I cussed the sailboat as it faded into the distance and out of sight, like everything else I was slowly overtaking.

I was on the water for a long time, probably about four and a half hours. I kept hoping the D.J. on the wind-up radio would tell me the time but he never did. I had to wind it up every ten or fifteen minutes and after a while I just sailed on listening to the breeze and every now and then a train passing on the tracks beyond the tree line. Most of what I passed that night was unpopulated foliage. Not a single watercraft went by. I could have been the only person in the world.

Eventually my eyes grew puffy and heavy; yawns followed in quick succession. My progress slowing, I figured I'd better find a place to tie up for the night. As luck would have it a park appeared around the next bend, to the north of which was a boat launch and dock. I aimed in its general direction.

I could "steer" only in the grossest sense of the word. My inability to maneuver was exacerbated by the shifting tide and the slow death of my battery. Trolling motors are supposed to be used for short spurts to steer light watercraft. I'd used it continuously for hours. I had no way of really getting close to the dock except by getting off the raft and using the canoe. I found this loathsome, but I made this my plan: I'd tie together as many lengths of rope as possible, tie one end of this new super-rope to the bullnose cleat at the bow of *The Manhattan Project*, put the coil of rope into the canoe, and paddle to the dock, letting out line as I went. Then I'd tie up to a cleat on the dock and pull *The Manhattan Project* in. I pointed the raft toward the western shore and left the trolling motor on while I got into the canoe so that the raft would propel itself toward the shoreline as I paddled. I did this to compensate for any tendency of the current to pull the raft, and by extension, the canoe and I, back toward the middle of the river.

I tied a lot of rope together and put it in a coil with one end attached to the raft. When the raft was about fifty yards from the dock (well within reach of the ropes I'd tied), I got into the canoe with my paddle. The rope was in front of me in the middle of the canoe, so I could let it out over my shoulder.

It was a good plan, anyway.

As soon as I pushed off from *The Manhattan Project* the whole coil of rope flew over my shoulder, instead of a little at a time, and splash-landed in the water behind me.

"Fuck!" I shouted. I paddled in reverse to grab the line from the water. In doing so I got the canoe facing every which-way except toward the shore. Tired, thirsty and hungry, terrible at canoeing, I felt in the joints of my fingers frustration mounting. I plucked the soaking rope and threw it in my lap all knotted now although it was perfectly coiled only a moment before. Meanwhile the raft with the trolling motor moved without a pilot toward a thicket of trees and weeds just north of the dock and boat launch. After a few minutes of agitating, deep scoops into the water with the paddle, I finally got the canoe facing shore again. But with every paddle the nose of the canoe went left, then right, then left—any direction but a straight line toward the dock. Still the raft crept quietly toward the trees upriver. Every few feet, kinked, knotted sections of rope came out of my lap; I couldn't manage to let out a straight line. It was as aggravating as trying to comb through a crying kid's knotted hair, forcing the brush through to rip the knots apart as the kid screeches.

"Son of a bitch!" I shouted at the rope. Each time the line came out in twisted knot sections my rope got a couple of feet shorter. Meanwhile the raft, behind me, was twenty-five feet from shore, then twenty. A knot came up from my lap that forced me to grab the line to keep the whole coil from going overboard. The canoe jerked to a halt. I struggled to untie a little wet section and get the canoe facing the shore all over again through the left, then right, then left routine. All the time I noticed I'd been grinding my incisors harder and harder; tensing my shoulder muscles like I was going to fight someone. What should've taken ten minutes was, after fifteen, still not completed.

Finally, I was the length of a school bus from the dock and literally "at the end of my rope." I was so frustrated to be so close to the dock only to run out of line thirty feet away that I started yelling all kinds of obscenities at the canoe, the rope, the raft, fate. "You fucking God-damned son of a bitch canoe! God fucking damn it! Jesus fucking Christ all God damn mighty you son of a fucking bitch!!" I mean I really, really lost it. At the end of a cascade of complexly constructed cusses I found myself screaming in an hysterical voice. My eyes tunnel-vision-focused on one particular cleat on the dock—as I looked at it, it seemed to grow in size juxtaposed against a red, fiery background. Involuntarily I lowered my voice to a guttural growl, clenched my fists with my eyes popping. I put the rope between my teeth and paddled with all the strength I could muster, only to be jerked back, then jerked back a second time, then when I tried to paddle hard again, jerked back a third time. I was ten feet away when I got so aggravated and violently angry that I grabbed the rope with my left hand and jumped out of the canoe. Under the water it was warm and weirdly quiet like swimming in a glass of chocolate milk. I had almost no strength. My sneakers, shirt, and cotton pants dragged me down. I kicked and grunted and pulled until I got above the water. Then I saw the dock and I pulled and grunted more, doing the crawl until I just reached the cleat. I stretched my right arm way out, with the tips of my fingers reached the dock, and with the last of what little energy I had I pulled my water-logged body, shaking leaf, up onto the dock with the rope between my teeth. My breakaway pants were so heavy that the snaps unbuttoned as I pulled myself up—they fell down around my ankles. I had no underwear on because I'd hung them out to dry in the cabin after the last time I went overboard. On my knees, I wrapped the rope around the dock cleat a couple of times, and then I fell backwards naked from the stomach down lying on my back on the public dock in the middle of the night. I closed my eyes.

Then I remembered the canoe and sat up. It was floating upstream thirty yards away. For a second I sat, completely limp, soaking, with my mouth open. I thought about letting it float away. But then, with every appendage like granite, I threw my sneakers and pants on the dock and jumped without any muscle tone into the water. I swam as hard as I could toward the canoe. Halfway there— so tired and a bad swimmer—I thought I couldn't make it and closed my eyes. But I kept kicking and putting one exhausted arm over the other without the energy even to form a conscious thought, and mechanically somehow I reached the canoe. There I was able to hold myself above the water by folding my hands around the bow, and after a few minutes I kicked backwards and got back to the dock where I tied the canoe up to the same cleat I'd tied the raft up to. Meanwhile the raft had crashed into some trees fifty yards upstream. Still naked except for a red tee shirt, I lifted my bare, white, ass cheeks onto the dock and once more collapsed backwards. If a cop had driven by at that moment I'd have had quite an explanation to make. For a good ten minutes I lay there on my back looking at the stars fully exposed in the park's streetlights, thinking absolutely nothing, just breathing.

When I'd regained some strength I sat and pulled on the rope to draw the raft to the dock. The rope became taut, but the raft did not come closer. It was tangled in the trees upstream.

"Just let it stay there," I said to myself. But I knew that was laziness, not reason, talking. The oil lamps were still burning on the raft and could start a fire if the concussions from colliding with the shore had knocked them over. The trolling motor was still on and would deplete the valuable battery if l left it on all night. The tide might go out and beach the raft if I didn't move it, and then I'd be trapped the next day. Besides, where was I going to sleep, if not in the cabin? A couple more hopeful tugs did nothing. So with an exhausted sigh I got into the canoe without any pants and used the line between the dock and the boat to pull me to the raft so I didn't have to paddle. I extricated *The Manhattan Project* from the trees and pulled myself, with the raft beneath me, back to the dock. I blew out the lanterns and tied off.

The entire docking process took forty-five minutes and left me angry, soaking, and tired. When I'd tied everything up I put on the pants that I'd hung to dry in the cabin that afternoon. The dampness made me shiver as I pulled them on. I made my way up the dock to the shore with my canteen to scout. On the shore facing a parking lot was a sign that read *Henry Hudson Park Boat Launch*. I laughed out loud thinking of Jim Gadani's statement earlier that afternoon, "I think *Henry Hudson* is a good goal for us today."

I spied a water spigot and held my mouth upside down under its rusty nozzle. Then I filled my canteen. There was a blue plastic port-a-potty but, having eaten nothing all day, I only peed a little. I found a pavilion and looked around for an electrical socket so I could recharge my boat batteries, because I'd stowed a charger onboard for just this sort of opportunity, but there was none. There was a paved road that continued out into the shadows of the early morning, surrounded by the bended bodies of two rows of majestic trees, but I'd seen enough for one day. I made my way back to the raft, spread a camping mattress inside the cabin, and laid down.

The cabin was not nearly as screened-in as I'd hoped. All night I was tortured by incessant buzzing in my ears and bites from mosquitoes that forced me to curl in a fetal position so I could wrap the sleeping bag around my body for protection. That didn't do much, except make me hot and damp. I still felt creepy-crawlies all over me, whether they were in my mind or real. Between the damp clothes, the humidity in the sleeping bag, the bugs, and the fear that I'd be woken up by a patrol cop at any minute, I slept for a total of eighty-seven seconds all evening.

VII. The Old Man and the Sea

I couldn't delay in the morning. Only certain action would get me to Albany's Corning Preserve in time to rendezvous with the crew and begin our expedition at five o'clock.

I figured my best chance of getting to Albany was to call a friend for a tow. But I had no idea what time it was and my cell phone was *kaput*. Luckily I happened to have two quarters and my notebook had Jess' cell and Mike's work numbers written in it. I made a cursory check of the raft's mooring lines and then walked up the dock.

In front of the dock was a parking lot and a paved road. I looked up and down this road and saw buildings off in one direction. As I walked toward them I saw the effects of the storm from the previous afternoon. There were wood chips and pieces of broken bark and mulch scattered all over the place, and dismembered branches and limbs. Two of the massive trees had trunk sections ripped off where the branches forked out. They looked like casualties of a titanic battle, with the green, living flesh oozing where they'd been torn by the wind. The grass by the road was wet with rain or dew. A breeze rustled green leaves in a constant thrush. Gray skies pressed above the canopy.

I came to an abandoned house and a small concrete municipal building with restrooms, which were locked. I walked twice around its perimeter: once to see if there was a telephone anywhere, and a second time to make sure I hadn't overlooked a phone the first time. There seemed to be nothing else down the road, so I turned around and started back toward the raft.

On the way back I saw an old woman power-walking in my direction with headphones in her ears. She crossed to the opposite side of the road. I tried to ask her the time but she power-walked past me as though I was invisible.

When I got back to the raft there was a thirty-something man with a young son sitting on a dock adjacent to the dock I'd tied my raft to. They were fishing. Excitedly, I walked down to them. They turned when they heard the hollow concussions of my footsteps on the metal planks. The kid smiled when he saw the outfit I was wearing—I probably looked like some cartoon adventurer in my white linen jacket and brown pants—but the father did not smile.

"Excuse me, sir, but do you have the time?" I asked.

"It's seven thirty," he said flatly.

"Do you happen to know how far it is to the Corning Preserve from here, by river?"

"Nope sorry," he said, staring at the river.

"Man…" I said. "I'm really kind of in a desperate situation. Do you happen to have a cell phone I could borrow to make a call? I'll only be one—"

"—No."

The guy at the dock annoyed me. I thought mean things about him as I walked barefoot back to my boat. My stomach gurgled.

The sky was gray, the water the color of bark. The evening before, as I was traveling north on the river, the wind blew at my back. It continued to puff and would help me get north if I set out immediately.

The ship was not ship shape. The authors of *Seamanship*, *Modern Seamanship*, and *On Deck* would've gasped at the sight of my vessel. Cardinal Rule Number One in all the safety and etiquette chapters warned of the dangers of leaving line strewn about, and here was mine tangled and trailing overboard.

"Keep the deck clear of debris," they said. I had a cement block and two anchors, a hammer, a wind up radio, a plank with nails sticking out of it, a life jacket and a camping chair lying on my deck. The plywood door hung open on a broken hinge with my wet clothes strung over. I hoped they'd dry overnight. They were still cold and damp.

I yawned, scratched my stomach and looked over the choppy waves. My pants were missing a button so I'd tied twine through the belt loops to keep them up. I saw no reason to don my wet socks or shoes. I wore my adventurer's jacket and hat and knife. I'd accumulated a two-day beard and a day's worth of sweat and dirt. My eyes were puffy.

I knew I was at Henry Hudson Park but I couldn't find my exact location on the map. I guessed I was about eight miles from Albany. I thought about walking up the road at the park or trying to flag down a passing car, but it seemed like I was pretty far from any main street, and even if I could find a phone I wasn't sure anyone would help me get a tow to Albany. Eight miles was just about the maximum travel range for one tide, and the wind was blowing upriver. I figured the battery was almost dead, but maybe there was enough juice left to steer. I knew the tide wouldn't change in my favor for an hour or so, but I remembered the effect the wind had had on my second expedition, and figured the wind and my motor could push me upstream against the current until the flood tide began. Any progress I made in the morning would increase my chances of getting help in the afternoon. And there was still one ebb tide left where I'd have to anchor, and one final flood tide between now and Alive at Five that night. So I made ready my ship.

The first thing was to get out into the middle of the river where the wind would be strongest. I could use the trolling motor for that. Then I could open the sail and test it out.

I untied *The Manhattan Project* from the dock cleats, and stepped onto broken back section. My feet got wet as it sank a couple of inches under the cool water. I turned the motor on, grabbed a paddle, and jogged to the front to steer. In a moment I was making very slow headway toward the river channel.

In fact, it was excruciatingly slow. I seemed to move only a few feet per minute, and I'd attached the battery that I thought had the greater charge of the two onboard. It took a five minutes to get fifty feet from the dock, while the man and his kid intentionally looked away as though disgusted at my existence.

Then I wanted to curse or bite the raft, because when I looked at the dock, I saw I was actually floating very slowly downstream, in the direction of the father's and son's fishing lines. The last thing I wanted was to lose ground, and to have that guy give me a dirty look and grumble because he had to reel in his lines as I took fifteen minutes to drift past him. I paddled hard on the starboard side so I faced diagonally toward the opposite shore and upstream. Then I waited a minute to see what effect that had on my position relative to the shore, which proved to be none. I put myself at a sharper angle so that I faced almost directly upstream, just so that I didn't get pushed downstream by the tide. That barely had an effect either, and for the next few minutes I sat so that the cabin was between the man's gaze and I, and anxiously marked any movement I made toward the channel or upstream, which was hardly noticeable.

I made it almost to the center of the river, but no farther upstream. When I looked to the shore I saw a cop car driving past. It slowed and pulled into the marina. I was far enough from the shore to be out of casual conversation's range. Nonetheless I decided I had to get moving.

Knowing I was being watched, I climbed to the top of the cabin and untied the rope coiled around the boom. Then I climbed the mast (it was pitching back and forth in the wind) and strung the tarp/sail-line through a loop at the top. I climbed down and heaved. The blue triangle with the white money sign (a decorative touch Mike had added) rose fifteen-feet into the sky. I tied it off to the mast and jumped behind the cabin to direct the boom.

On the shore the cop had gotten out of his car and a utility truck was there too, with a guy in a hardhat standing next to him. In the parking lot their postures suggested they'd both been driving by and stopped along the road to see and discuss a spectacle. I shivered; the wind was blowing hard out in the channel. Downstream, I saw a rescue squad practicing maneuvers with an orange inflatable raft with an outboard motor and wetsuits. On the other shore was nothing but a jungle of foliage.

When I tried to catch some wind with the sail I looked like an idiot. The problem with sailing without a rudder is that as you pitch the sail to one side or another to catch the wind you swing the whole stern of the boat around. You need the rudder to keep your vessel pointed straight, otherwise all you do is spin. The sail got me turned around so that I faced directly toward the opposite shore, and after facing that way I couldn't get the sail at an angle to catch wind again, and I began drifting downstream because the current was still heading out. I swung the boom all the way around so that its port side was windward, but all that did was get my bow pointing back toward the shore I'd just come from, and I didn't even want to look there to see what the cop and the utility man and the son and father were doing. I pictured them pointing and laughing, or calling reinforcements to haul me to a salvage yard. I tried using the trolling motor as a rudder by turning it perpendicular to the sail, and tying the sail off so that it kept the wind. But somehow that got me facing downstream. So with fists clenched I directed the motor completely perpendicular the raft to start to me back upstream, jumped up on the cabin, untied the mast line and let the boom crash to the deck so there was no more sail, then jumped back off the cabin, splashed my feet and straightened out the motor in time for the momentum to carry my bow upstream. Now at least I faced the right direction.

I started second-guessing myself. Maybe I'd read the tide schedule wrong, and I was in the middle of an ebb tide after all? Why else would I be staying smack still in the middle of the water with a fifteen mile-per-hour breeze and the trolling motor pushing me upstream? I couldn't even move to the west or east, let alone to the north. I seemed tied to the bottom of the river.

And there I sat for half an hour, going nowhere but draining the valuable battery.

A second police car pulled up along the road and an officer in a uniform got out. I could see the two policemen and the utility man standing with their hands on their hips looking out.

I began to get nervous after being in the middle of the river for forty minutes. Since I couldn't make any headway, I pointed my bow back toward Henry Hudson Park. I went nowhere. In the process I slipped downstream a little, losing ground and time, so I pointed north again. I was right in the middle of the channel and nervous that if a barge approached I wouldn't be able to get out of its way. The cops on shore took off, but I wasn't too relieved because by that point I thought I might have to flag someone down just to help get me to shore. Downstream the EMS team ran their maneuvers; I debated trying to get their attention. The tables had turned from the night before. Without another person on board I was really struggling. I kept hoping the EMS crew would take a ride by me out of curiosity and then I could confess to be in trouble. After being on the water for an hour, even the EMS team packed in their bags. With my binoculars I watched them load their raft onto a trailer and drive off. Now I was the only human in the middle of the river.

I had to get off the water and figure out a new plan. It would be vastly more beneficial to return to the western shore and Henry Hudson Park, where presumably there was a road which I could take to a town. But I was about a third of the way closer to the eastern shore with its jungle thicket. The exhausted battery necessitated I make for the closer, uninhabited shore.

I switched to the almost-dead battery from the night before, because the battery I'd used all morning got me nowhere. It made a bit of difference. Very slowly I crept toward the jungle shore, standing at the bow with a paddle. After twenty minutes I heard scraping as the foam met some old, wooden poles which were part of a dike just below the water. I switched off the motor and jumped onto the wooden poles, climbed up some rocks between the dike and the shore and tied off the raft, at bow and stern on the starboard side, to the crook of a fallen tree that stuck out over the river.

I surveyed the situation. Standing on slippery stones, I looked past my bobbing, bruised boat across the choppy water at the park, on the other side of the river now. The tide was still ebbing. I could tell because the boat pulled downstream on its mooring lines. I guessed I had an hour before the tide changed.

Behind me were a few feet of mossy rocks, splashed by breaking waves, and then a thicket of brush that was almost impermeable. I could see I wasn't going to bushwhack a trail. My boat wouldn't convey me anytime soon. If I was going anywhere, I'd have to hoof it along the shoreline.

Back aboard the boat I gathered some trekking supplies. I always carried a knife on a lanyard affixed to my belt. I grabbed my little black notebook filled with running ink numbers, and put my sneakers on. I only had a dollar, but I put one of the hundred dollar bills from my parent's car sale in my pocket. I attached my empty canteen and my machete sheath too, and with my jacket, my damp clothes and my adventurer's hat, I set off to the south toward a little town I'd seen in that direction the night before. My goal was to find a phone, food and water.

It was slow going along the shore. At first it was slippery rock terrain, but then it became a mud beach and my feet sank five inches. With every step my quads ached as I *schluck*ed my sneakers from the sand with a sucking sound.

I remember my trek as a no-dialogue movie with scenes spliced together. First I picture a scene filmed from fifty yards away, a panorama of the shoreline with its bright green vines and its cool, moist rocks and I, a tiny figure at the bottom of the screen, marching across the beach like an ant. Then the next scene is spliced in, filmed looking down from my point of view to my mud-soaked sneakers, my feet landing tired and flatfooted on one rock, then another, the only sounds the clapping my soles against the stones and the *caw-caws* of a few independent birds out for a morning flutter. Then a scene filmed from the brush, with vines in the foreground framing a view of the choppy river reflecting the morning sun breaking behind the clouds as I walk across the screen silhouetted in black against the yellow water. Then spliced in the shot from far away again, with me as an ant, jumping over a log by some cattails.

After a while I came to the mouth of a wide stream. It looked maybe five-feet deep near its delta. It was about sixty-feet across, with a mud bottom. I couldn't go around it and I didn't want to go up to my chest in water. The remnants of a very old dike spanned the delta, connecting the point where I stood to the opposite shore. But the wood was so rotten from soaking for decades that it looked like it had the consistency of peat moss, and if I fell off the side — it was essentially a slick decaying balance beam — I'd land in the deepest part of the water and be soaked and maybe over my head, and have to swim to the shore with my shoes and pants and jacket and hat on. Still, I'd waste a long time trying to find a way around the stream, so I went for it. I climbed on top of the dike. The beam stood about four feet above the water supported every three feet or so by posts like cut-off telephone poles. I crawled on all fours. At one point in the center of the dike I had to lie on my stomach and shimmy forward while hugging the beam, because in the center the support posts were missing and the beam was like a grease pole with nothing to put my hands or feet on. A ways farther the beam itself was broken, and I had to stand up and step from post to post. It was like jumping from banana peel to banana peel. I could still see Henry Hudson Park on the other side of the river, and make out some cars in the parking lot over there. I wondered if anyone was watching me climb on my hands and knees like a nervous chimp across a dirty stream on a rotten dike. When I got to the other shore I jumped down and looked back across the stream, satisfied. I was no worse for the wear save some dark brown mud spots on my pants and a wide muddy streak down the center of my jacket, and some peat-moss-like residue on my hands and under my fingernails, which I washed off in the stream water. I couldn't see the raft anymore because I'd made progress walking along the shore, but I figured it was still bobbing back there.

Another fifteen minutes or so through the mud and rocks and weeds and I came to the bottom of a fill. It was a mound of gravel a few feet inland, a big hill of the stuff. I climbed up the fill and reached a kind of plateau. Through a thicket of weeds I saw beer cans and a *Frisbee* and garbage, so I figured I was getting close to society. I found a little path that some kids or homeless person had made, which took me up a hill past some telephone poles that had fallen sideways, pulling their power lines dangerously downhill. I climbed a slope of fine gravel and fell backwards because it was too loose and steep. Then I took out my machete and stabbed it into the gravel halfway up and used it to ascend, in the process getting my sneakers full of tiny stones. I could see through the brush some railroad tracks a dozen yards ahead, and a chain-link fence. So I left my machete in the gravel and weeds and made for the tracks. Sure enough, when I got to the tracks I found there was a road on the other side of the fence.

The fence made me pause. I didn't know how to tell if it was electrified. So I stood there, looking, wondering if I could touch it. I spit on the fence and nothing happened. I grabbed a stick out of the brush and threw it at the fence. I guess I figured if it was electrified the fence would go crazy and start sparking and I'd see electricity fry the stick and burn it or something. But it just hit the fence with a *chink* and fell to the ground.

Hmm, I thought.

I didn't know what that meant. I was afraid if I touched the fence I'd get shocked and get paralyzed touching it and continue to get shocked until I died. I always thought that was the problem with electrocution, that you'd grab some power lines or something and you wouldn't be able to let go as you were getting electrified because the electricity immobilized you. So I thought up this brilliant plan. I'd swing my arm really fast and just barely graze the fence with the tip of my finger, so that if I got shocked, the momentum of my arm would ensure I didn't continue to touch the fence even if I got paralyzed. I brought my hand way back like I was going to throw a softball from the outfield to home plate and then I whisked my hand past the fence and brushed it — and absolutely nothing happened.

Hmm, I thought.

I didn't really know what that meant either. Finally I said to myself, "Well, no guts, no glory," and I grabbed the fence with both hands with my jaw clenched and my face turned away toward the ground — and absolutely nothing happened. I stuck my foot in a diamond-shaped hole and got a leg over the top. It was shaky at the top and I added a new hole to my pants and a new gash on the inside of my left thigh that wouldn't heal for a couple of days. When I jumped down I was on the side of a rural, paved road with no lines and no shoulder.

Now that I didn't have to worry about climbing over obstacles the only thing on my mind was how tired and hungry and thirsty I was. It had been a day and a half since I'd eaten. I started walking along the road, and walking. I didn't care about the pebbles in my shoes. I drew willpower from recalling having walked twenty-four miles that spring in Baltimore. I was only a little less exhausted by the end of that trek. The trick was to just put one foot in front of the other and march with a rhythm, one-two, one-two. Keep your head up and think about making it over the next hill, then around the next bend, then to the end of the next fence. Small goals strung together and realized equal substantial accomplishments. I walked with that bile in my stomach, churning and making gurgling noises. A couple of times vehicles passed and I stuck out my thumb but nobody stopped. Once a rusty red pickup with three hick teenagers in the front seat sped down the road and blew their horn laughing.

Eventually as I got to the top of a hill, I saw I was entering a town. I felt like a desert nomad stumbling upon an oasis. A block away, a *Stewart's* gas station! I jogged to it, or rather shuffled my feet along. I swung open the door with a tired but triumphant posture.

A bell announced my entrance. Three scruffy old men sat at a table in the corner drinking coffee. They saw me and grimaced. It was in a real working class town, apparently. It felt like one of those *Pace Thick and Chunky Salsa* commercials where all the rednecks respond at once, "New Yawk City?!"

Right away I got a bottle of water and drank half of it in a single swig. I made myself two juicy hot dogs from the rotisserie with cheese and onions and mustard and sauerkraut and chili on both of them, and I grabbed a *Strawberry Charleston Chew* and a bag of

Munchos and cradled everything up to the counter. The woman at the register was middle-aged with smoker's white-brown hair, chewing gum. I laid out a damp $100 bill, which she looked at, then at me, then back at the bill. She held it to the light and flipped it around like it was the strangest thing she'd ever seen, and gave me my ninety dollars and change.

"I got washed overboard and my boat is beached a ways upriver from here," I said. She stood chewing gum like a cow mouthing cud.

"Uh-huh?"

"I had to walk along the shore and then climb a fence just to get here," I said.

"To *Stewarts*?"

"Well, to this town. What town is this anyway? I haven't eaten since two nights ago!" I bit off a quarter of a chili-cheese dog and chewed it at the counter.

"Schodak."

"Schodak!" I said. "Like as in Schodak Landing?"

"Guess so."

"Well, is there a marina around here?"

"I donno."

"You don't know if there's a marina in this town?"

"My brother Joe has a boat," she said. "He'd know. But he's in Castleton this morning."

"Well, thanks anyway," I said. I drained the rest of the water out of the plastic bottle. "God, this is good."

"I like *Poland Spring*."

"Yeah. Well, thanks."

I sat at a table and let my stomach settle. Jim Gadani had told me Schodak Landing was just north of Coeymans. So either I'd traveled all night and not gotten anywhere, or he didn't know where Schodak Landing was. Or things seem closer when you're in a speedboat versus a raft. Either way I figured I was close to a lot of boaters and I could call my friends for a tow with the pay phone. I hadn't talked to anyone in eighteen hours.

I put two coins in the pay phone. I found Mike's smeared work number on one of the pages of my notebook. It was a good thing I'd written down all of my important numbers when my last cell phone fell in the river. I dialed and heard Mike answer on the other end of the line at the Comptroller's Office,

"Good morning, *Withdrawals*."

"Ahoy!" I shouted.

"Jesus Christ, you're alive," he said in almost a whisper. I marked a real sense of concern in his voice.

"Yeah I'm alive," I said. "I've had a hell of a night. I haven't eaten since two nights ago; I went all night without water, got washed overboard."

"Where are you? Everybody went looking for you last night!"

"They did? I'm across the river from Henry Hudson Park. I think I'm in Schodak."

"Henry Hudson Park? How'd you get there? Jesus. Jess and TJ went across the river looking for you but they couldn't find you anywhere. People were scared. Why didn't you call anyone?"

"What was I supposed to call with, a phone I made out of rocks and sticks and shit?"

"Ever heard of a cell phone?"

"It got ruined when I got pulled overboard off Jess's Dad's boat. My walkie-talkies, my cell phone, my 'waterproof' watch, everything. They all got wet and ruined. I didn't even know what time it was all night, or if people were coming to look for me or what."

"Well how'd you get to Henry Hudson Park? We weren't looking anywhere near there. I thought about driving down there to see what I could see but I figured you couldn't be that far north. How did you get there?"

"Well, I sat there after the storm passed—"

"—Please deposit fifty cents," the phone said.

"—Shit. Hold on I need to get fifty cents from the counter, just a—"

"—Please deposit fifty cents,"

"I'm going to! Jesus Christ, gimme a chance," I said.

"—Please deposit fifty cents. Goodbye!" There was a click and the phone disconnected.

"Fuck!" I shouted, "fucking phone!" The old men in the corner sneered at me. I went to the counter. "Can you give me like, two dollar's worth of quarters please?" She did, and I dialed Mike again.

"Good morning, *Withdrawals*—"

"I've got 'em."

"What happened?"

"The phone ran out of money and hung up on me."

"No, what happened last night?"

"Oh. Well, I didn't know who was coming or if anybody was coming. So I just assumed I either had to sit there and wait for someone to find me, or try and sail as far north as I could when the flood tide was coming up."

"Wow so you sailed it yourself?"

"Yeah, and it was nice. Really beautiful and peaceful at night. But no water or food or anything, and today I had to trek forty-five minutes through the woods to find a phone. I called as fast as I could. There's literally nothing along the sides of the river, it's like a forest for miles."

"Shit. Well, I'm glad you're alright. Well..." I read Mike's mind.

"I need to get a tow from Jess or Oliver," I said. Mike was tentative.

"It didn't sound like Jess's dad was really looking forward to giving it a second go."

"Well we gotta find something. Maybe Oliver can help."

"I don't know."

"Could you call Jess and see if her Dad would give us a tow?"

"I don't know man. I've been getting calls all day at work from people asking about you: Jess, Oliver, TJ, your parents, it doesn't look real good..."

"Shit. Will you call my parents and let them know I'm alright?"

"Yeah, but still, I don't think you're going to get a tow."

"Well then what am I supposed to do?"

"I think you might have to think about what you'll do if you can't make it up to *Alive at Five.*"

"Out of the question. There are reporters there. Everyone is going to be up there. All our friends who we told we'd be there. We said we were going to be there, that's that."

"Well, good luck. Hey did you see the *Times Union* today?"

"No, why?"

"There's a big picture of you on the front page of the Capital Region section. It's a funny picture. You look weird."

"Well that's pretty cool."

" — Please deposit fifty cents," the phone said.

"Fuck me. Can you call Jess and ask if her dad will give us a tow?"

"Well, I mean, it's pretty much a *No.*"

" — Please deposit fifty cents."

"God damn it, alright. I'll call her. Call my parents will you? Please?"

"Sure, when will I hear back from you?"

"This afternoon!"

"Okay because —"

"—Please deposit fifty cents. Goodbye!" The phone disconnected.

"Fucking phone!" I shouted.

Sometimes I feel like I'm playing with one of those plastic, spherical children's toys that have shapes cut out of them, the ones where little kids have to find the right corresponding square or trapezoid or circle piece to fit through each hole. Except that I feel like the shapes I'm trying to fit don't match the cutouts — like my pieces came from a different toy manufacturer and aren't meant to be used with the sphere somebody gave me. And then I think I know something about my own character, because if I were a kid and that happened to me, I'd probably get mad and smash the shapes through the holes they were never designed to fit. Or maybe I'd shave them down to the right size. But one way or another, the shapes would be inside the sphere at the end of the day — even if I had to cut the thing in half and tape it back together — and then I would be satisfied.

That was how I felt with the raft. It wouldn't be easy, it would be an inconvenience to others, it might even be illegal, but somehow I was going to get the thing to Albany that day. I just had to, and that was that. Even if I had to smash some pieces or tape the river back together.

I grabbed a newspaper from the counter and took a look at the Capital Region section. Sure enough, there was my mug strewn across the page, and a picture of me standing in a Napoleonic stance with one leg up on a rock and the raft in the background, flag flying in the wind. I got another bottle of water and said goodbye to the woman behind the counter — she didn't seem too impressed when I showed her my picture in the paper. I opened the door and the bell chimed as I stepped into eleven-in-the-morning-on-the-sidewalk, with birds cawing and a truck motoring by. I took a breath and smelled the damp earth, the fresh worms, the evaporating rain. It was time to force things.

When I left *Stewarts* I had a feeling like Michael J Fox in the first *Back to the Future* when he wanders into the town square hearing *Mr. Sandman* playing from the speakers in the movie theatre. He reaches into a trash can and removes a newspaper — it reads *1955*. Suddenly the director layers in eerie, warping sounds as the happy do-whop of the Andrew's Sisters fades and the sounds of chaos — cars moving, the steps of passersby, kids jumping on moon-shoes — takes over. As the camera pans out to show the whole town square we get the feeling that Michael J. Fox is a disoriented speck in some bizarre microcosm of a former day.

That was the feeling I had while walking down the street in Schodak. It really is a shame what has become of these once quaint towns that dotted the banks of the Hudson. I walked the crumbling sidewalk, past brick buildings with white and red paint flecking; past a flea market with a chandelier in the window that read "For Sale" — was it the chandelier, or the building? — past two younger, scummy-looking girls with baby carriages; past an open doorway where I was startled by a woman screaming — *screaming!* — for her daughter across the street to "Get here now! Now! What the fuck you doin' cross dat street? Get in here now I ain't fuckin' jokin'!"

A few minutes later I came alongside a chain-link fence and a gravel parking lot. Past the lot by the river were docks. I moseyed inside.

Some marina. Only one boat was tied up. There was a wooden shack that looked like it might be an office, so I figured I'd try my luck there. Just as I pushed open the storm door a skinny old man appeared in the doorway carrying a length of rubber hose in his arms.

"Hi," I said urgently.

"Can I help you," he said as he brushed past me, trailing the hose.

"Yes. Could you tell me — is this the marina at Schodak Landing?" As I said this, one end of the hose fell from the man's arms and started dragging on the ground, so I picked up that end. Then the man dropped the hose by a spigot near the gravel parking lot as I held the end in my hand. He turned.

"What're you doin' with the hose?"

"Nothing," I said as I let it fall. "I really need to have someone tow my boat from here to Corning Preserve in Albany. Can you suggest any way you think I could make that happen?" The man stared at me while scratching his hair.

"Well, we don't have a salvage service here. You'd have to call...closest one's Coeymans I imagine."

"Well...I wasn't really looking for a salvage service..." We stood there for a minute looking at each other. "...Do you know anyone that would tow me with their boat? I have some money I could throw somebody a few bucks." The man rubbed the back of his neck.

"Nobody's here yet. You could wait around a couple of hours and people might show up."

"I don't have a couple of hours," I said. He frowned.

"Well, as I said, best bet's Coeymans. You can use the phone inside if you want."

I left the old man and went inside the office, which looked like a tiny Knights of Columbus hall with water damage to the wood paneling, and used the phone after looking up the marina number in a phonebook. The Coeymans salvage man was "not in" and the woman who answered the phone didn't know if Albany was in range, when the salvage man could possibly tow me, or how much it would cost.

"Thanks for all your help," I hung up.

As I let the storm door swing shut I heard the old man hail me from down by the docks. The gurgle of a motor rumbled up. At the riverbank I saw the man helping tie up a red speed boat. Inside the boat stood a black haired, middle-aged man with one foot on the gunwales.

"This is the guy, Joe," the old man said.

"What is it you're tryin' to do?" the man asked.

"I really need someone to tow me from just upstream to Corning Preserve in Albany."

"You the one with that pink, wooden thing looks like a floating shed tied to the dike up the other side of the crick?"

"It's beige," I smiled.

"Ha! Yeah, saw that this morning. What are you tryin' to do?"

"It's a long story," I said. "I'm trying to go to Manhattan."

"Ha! Manhattan! Good luck! You know Albany's the wrong direction, right?"

"Yes I'm aware of that."

"Well, I wish I could help but I'm going the opposite way. But I'll let my friends know if they happen to be going that way by river this morning."

"Thanks," I said.

"I will too," said the old man.

"Thanks," I repeated.

So that inland expedition was a failure.

Back down the crumbling streets of Schodak through Marty McFly Square. Back into *Stewarts*, the old men were still there. I called Mike again and told him I had no tow, no help — that I'd make contact with him if I was able, but he, TJ and Jared ought to proceed according to plan, bringing their bags and supplies to Alive at Five, and I would do everything in my power to get the raft to the concert on time.

"I mean, look—maybe we ought to just cancel tonight," Mike said. "I mean at some point we just have to admit it's not going to happen."

"I'll be there," I replied.

"...Well, okay. Good luck!"

"I don't believe in that luck bullshit."

Back down the no-line county road, back over the not-electric fence, across the railroad tracks, down the gravel hill. I found my machete sticking out of the ground. Then, like a storyboard in reverse, I've got the snapshots of my trek back along the shoreline: my feet schlucking through the sucking mud; balancing on the wooden dike crossing the muddy stream; back across the slippery, moss-covered rocks—all done this time with a *Stewarts* bag tied to my belt with a couple of bottles of water and some *Nutragrain* bars for sustenance. After about forty-five minutes I got back to the mooring point and threw my new provisions and gear aboard.

It was around half-past noon. *The Manhattan Project* bobbed in brown water as I stood next to her on a rotting dike pole. Nothing all morning had gotten me closer to my goal, though I'd been trying. The batteries were almost dead. At least there was a northerly breeze and the tide was beginning to flood. I reached into the water and untied the boat from the log I'd affixed it to earlier, which had become submerged in the rising tide. Then I pushed off, jumped aboard, switched on the motor, and ran to the front starboard side to steer. It was getting to be familiar now.

Using that battery was like asking a 90-year-old woman to put a towline around her waist and swim me to Albany. But in a few minutes I'd directed my boat into the channel and pointed upstream, and the breeze and tide combined to help me make steady, albeit slow, northerly progress again.

The afternoon had become quite pleasant. There wasn't a cloud in the sky, yet the breeze cooled things off in fluttering fashion. I kept checking over my shoulder to make sure there were no barges coming up behind me since I was pretty much at the mercy of the wind and tide for direction.

At one point a thirty-something kayaker paddled to my port side and kept pace with me easily.

"Howdy!" he shouted.

"Afternoon," I replied.

"So, this is the *Manhattan* boat."

"Yes!" I said. "*The Manhattan Project*—"

"Haha, that's right."

"—How'd you know?" I was impressed with the kayaker's pace given the leisurely way he paddled.

"I read about it in the newspaper this morning. Where's your crew? Can you control that thing with one person? It's bigger than it looks in the *Times Union*."

"I'm meeting them up in Albany. I was supposed to get towed up there last night but that storm came and it got so bad the guy towing me had to drop me off on the side of the river and head back."

"You're trying to leave from *Alive at Five* aren't you?"

"Yeah."

"You think you'll make it up there in time?"

"I don't know. I'm going to try like hell."

"I've got a kind of speedometer on here and we're not even registering—and it's five or six miles upstream."

"Yeah," I said.

"And it's almost two thirty now."

"What can I say, man? I'm gonna try and get up there and every inch closer I get, that's an inch closer to being there. Maybe you could grab a rope and paddle ahead of me and together we'll get there in no time."

"I'm actually headed downstream I just saw you gliding by and thought I'd say hi since I saw you in the paper."

"Thank you." The guy dug his port paddle in the water and broke off toward the opposite river bank.

"Good luck pal!" he said. "I didn't mean to like, ruin your dreams or anything I just don't think you'll make it up there."

"It's alright," I said. Then I shouted, "Hey man, you don't know when the tide is changing, do you?" He shouted back from twenty feet,

"Not sure—but you're in luck since you're going to New York. Wind's forecasted to blow south starting sometime this afternoon." Then he paddled away and I felt nervous.

That nervousness grew to desperation over the next hour. First I noticed it got harder to steer with the trolling motor. I'd been staying close to shore for safety's sake, but a half-mile ahead and sticking out a tractor-trailer's length from shore I saw a "No Wake" buoy with a sailboat anchored twenty feet away from it. I tried to aim my boat toward the channel to go around the buoy and sailboat but the current kept pushing me onto a collision course. I tried to point myself directly toward the channel to avoid a collision, but the motor had no effect and I skirted a crash by so small a margin that I actually passed through the twenty-foot space between the sailboat and the buoy, and then I had to use a paddle to push my boat off of an embankment of rocks just north. A quarter mile farther north I'd just begun passing the remains of a concrete dike when I was hit head-on by a burst of wind which stopped all progress completely. I began floating back south. I lost ground so quickly that I had to do something.

"Son of a bitch!" I yelled. I got the boat pointed toward the dike to starboard, which was just fifteen feet away, but by now the battery was dead and I moved no closer to shore. I picked up speed blowing backwards. I looked back at where I'd just come from (and now, floating backwards, where I was going). The broken concrete dike extended along the shore into the river only twenty-five feet back. Then it crumbled and disappeared beneath the water while the shore receded into a cove by the anchored sailboat and "No Wake" buoy. The dike was a strip of hope, a concrete causeway, extending into the river. I had to get to that dike to starboard and tie up the boat before the wind pushed me back beyond it, or I'd be far from shore with no way to steer.

I grabbed a paddle, ran to the bow and furiously began digging at the water to slow her slide toward the dike's terminus. No noticeable effect. I floated toward the end of the broken concrete dike twenty feet back, and closing. I jumped to the port side of the boat and paddled there to get my bow pointed toward the dike, and then jumped to the front again to paddle and try and pull the boat within reaching distance. The wind gusted and blew me sideways. I ran to port and paddled. Only ten feet of dike remained. I stroked until I smashed the front of the boat against the concrete dike with seven feet left. But that sent the boat bouncing back into the river and I had to paddle to get her back again with five feet of dike left. When I got the bow close enough I grabbed a rope and jumped onto the dike but in the rush I hadn't put on my wet sneakers and I cut the soles of my bare feet landing on the cracked concrete. There was no time for epithets because the boat was still floating backward and I needed a place to tie her off before the end of the dike four feet away. But there was nothing to tie to. You can't tie off to a slab of concrete. I wrapped the rope around my hands and held the boat in place. The wind blew the raft just past the end of the dike, dangling. I braced my legs and pulled the boat toward me a couple of feet with my arms, holding it like a heavy kite. I tried to brace myself but I stumbled and cut my feet as the raft in the wind dragged *me* along the dike instead of vice-versa. I tried to lean backwards and bend my knees to get some leverage but every step felt like fifteen arrowheads jabbing the flesh of my feet. It got to be too hard to bear and I sat on my ass and braced my feet against one of the severed telephone-pole-looking logs that'd been pounded into the river at intervals along the dike, which now sat rotting just below the waves. The water felt good on my soles, and in a moment I was able to brace myself in that position and hold the boat from pulling downstream any farther.

I was seething. I saw the boat through a telescopic lens surrounded in a circle of boiling blood red. I breathed through my nostrils, and ground my teeth. Hungry, thirsty, tired, the sweat drops dripped down and stung my eyes. My hands hurt from nail wounds, my legs hurt from fence wounds, my feet from concrete wounds, and I had mosquito bites all over. I looked behind me and saw that the dike ran along the shore as far as I could see upstream.

"Alright you fucking cuntbag cocksucking piece of shit asshole," I growled, rising to one knee. "Come on you fucker, you think you got me? Huh? You fucker? You think this is it?" I jumped up, faced upstream and clutched the towline in my hands, letting it extend over my shoulder back to the boat. I took a step forward and jerked the boat with me. "Come on!" I shouted. I took another step, and *The Manhattan Project* inched northward again. I was going to drag that boat to Albany. "Come on!" I shouted, and took a step forward, only to be pulled backward because the boat had gotten caught on top one of those protruding wood pillars I'd braced myself against a moment before. "God damn it!" I walked back to the boat and got on my ass on the dike in order to kick the boat off the pillar that impaled her. Then I got up and grabbed the tow line again and took two more lurching steps forward like a mule on the Erie Canal. Then I took a third step and lurched back because the boat had gotten impaled on the next underwater pillar. With teeth set and seeing red I marched back to the boat, got on my ass again and kicked at the boat to get her off the pole. This time she wouldn't move. I pulled at the rope from different angles but still she wouldn't come unstuck. So I jumped back aboard and stood on the port side to see if shifting my weight would get her off her starboard obstruction. It did not. I tried jumping. That didn't work either. Almost pleading I jumped ten or fifteen times, and that did nothing, so I sat Indian style and all the red I saw changed to indigo and cyan and I confess I had to wipe my eyes out of insurmountable frustration.

"If I just had one other fucking person!" I yelled to the boat, out to the river. "If I only had one other person," I repeated to myself. I sat there alone.

I thought there must be something I could do with the time I had left. I donned my soaked sneakers and climbed back onto the dike. I walked north on the dike to a point where the shore was close enough to jump to. I worked my way through a thicket of tangled vines and discovered some dirt-bike trails. I followed one of the trails for a few minutes. It meandered and seemed to lead nowhere, at least not to anyplace to get to Albany within the hour. So I went back to the boat.

I didn't want to beg for help. I hated that idea. Yet I could see no way out of the situation. The *Seamanship* book described the protocol for signaling distress. I mounted the American Flag upside down, and took off my red shirt and tied it to a canoe paddle. I stood on top of the cabin and waved this at a pleasure boat that passed going north, starting as a speck beneath the line that was the bridge I'd passed under the night before. The boat didn't stop. There was a lengthy period before another boat passed. This time I grabbed the flashlight and, in addition to waving my red shirt, I flashed three short, three long, three short flashes: SOS. That boat didn't stop or slow, either. Looking at the river in both directions, then, I saw no more boats.

By my estimate it was five o'clock. Mike, TJ, Jared, Morgan, Nicole, Jess, various other friends, Brian Nearing from the *Times Union*, everybody must've been gathering at Alive at Five. All the work I'd done building the boat, all the effort I'd put in pushing north that day and the day before, and all it did was get me stuck wherever I was. Not only was I in the process of letting everyone down and looking like an idiot again, but how was I supposed to get out of wherever I was? It was overwhelming to think about. I laid on top of the cabin on my back and gazed up at the sadly pleasant blue sky.

Then I heard a motor.

"Hey...there...are you in trouble?" I heard an old man's voice.

I sat up and looked down at the water. A grey-haired man in an aluminum fishing boat had pulled alongside.

"Yes!" I shouted, jumping down to the deck. I winced because I'd forgotten about the cuts on my feet.

"Say, yeah, I thought so. I saw you tie up here a couple of hours ago and figured there was a problem when you didn't go anyplace. You got a motor on this, Captain?"

Captain! Like, the driver of a real boat! Ha!

"I had an electric motor but both the batteries are shot and I got caught in the wind."

"Well, you can't stay here. There ain't nothing 'round here for miles. This is a big island, or used to be, it's a peninsula now I guess, but nobody comes or goes. Where're you trying to get?" Now I was happy that I'd bought a copy of the *Times Union* that morning. I grabbed it from the deck and held it up. There was the close-up picture of me standing on the boat, and a caption that read "Raft Crew To Voyage Downriver."

"Sir," I spoke quickly, pleadingly, "You see, I must get to Albany by five o'clock. I'm meeting my crew there, everybody. See? It's in the newspaper. I was supposed to get there yesterday but the storm...I was being towed and the storm came..."

"...That was a bad storm."

"—Yes! And it messed everything up and my phone, my wallet, everything was destroyed. So all these people are waiting for me in Albany and I can't get there. Sir. Wait a minute..." I took one of the hundred dollar bills from my pocket. "Sir, I will give you $100 to tow me from here to Albany, please!"

"Well, now, I'm supposed to meet my daughter...Heck, you're in a tough spot. I couldn't take any money."

"I've tried to flag down other people, no one will stop. I insist on paying you."

"Well, Albany's five or six miles from here. That's a big boat. I'm not sure this boat could pull it."

"It could. It definitely could."

"Well..." The man looked at his watch, at the boat. "Okay. Let's get going right now. Just up to Albany, you say?"

"Riverfront Park, the Corning Preserve."

"You'll have to show me where to stop."

"Deal!"

I jumped for joy in front of the old man. Quickly I threw anything that might blow away into the cabin. Then I threw the man a line and tied it off to my bullnose. The man throttled up his motor. *The Manhattan Project* made a scraping noise as she was pulled off the wood pillar she'd been impaled on.

"Go ahead!" I shouted when the man looked back. He opened the throttle and pulled the boat off.

What a feeling! In less than a minute we were out in the channel. I sat on the triangular bow and let the mist from the bubbling water spray my face. Everything held together fine. When the man looked back periodically to check on me I waved enthusiastically and showed him a thumbs-up—and he smiled, because I was smiling so much. I watched the dike on the eastern shore pass by, then disintegrate into natural shore. A few houses dotted the sides of the river. Then a couple of minutes later we passed the Normanskill Creek which marks the southern boundary of the City of Albany. I jumped and clapped. I saw emerging on the western bank the piles of compacted cars, the moored hulls, the cranes and salt piles of the Port of Albany. Then to starboard a moment later, the Albany Yacht Club. As we kept motoring north I saw the top of the Corning Tower, the tops of the shorter Agency Buildings, the Alfred E. Smith Building, and then the New York State Capitol. The man looked back for me to indicate where to stop.

"Just a little farther sir, thank you so much!"

Past the *USS Slater*, the *Dutch Apple Cruise Lines*. We passed under the *Dunn Memorial Bridge* and the anticipation was unbearable. Then we rounded a slight bend in the river and the concert park came into sight, with a crowd of thousands along the shore, behind railings that stood atop boulders that rose out of the river thirty feet high.

"Is this the place?"

"Yes! Anyplace here would be great!" The man pulled me up among dozens of pleasure boats which were anchored to hear the concert. On shore I saw people press against the railings to examine the strange wooden raft that had just been towed by an old man in a fishing boat, and me with my fedora and adventurer's jacket standing on the bow. I dropped my anchor and the man untied the tow line. "Thank you so much sir! Please, let me give you some cash! You've just saved my day. More than you can imagine."

"No no. Thank you anyway. I've got to see my daughter now. Good luck." The man motored off without further comment.

VIII. Outside Forces

I let out extra scope because the tide pushed me downstream and it appeared the anchor wasn't holding. Imagine floating downriver in front of everyone as soon as I arrived. I tossed rope in the canoe and started paddling toward shore in order to tie a redundant line. I got jerked around because of the knots in the rope, as I had the night before. I'd paddled two thirds of the way to the riverbank when a police boat motored up to *The Manhattan Project* with blinking blue lights.

"What are you doing there?" an officer with short black hair shouted through cupped hands.

"The boat's being pulled downstream even though I dropped an anchor," I shouted back from the canoe. "I'm bringing this line ashore to tie it off."

"Why don't you come back out here so we can have a conversation about the vessel. I'd like to make sure it's safe and legal."

Oh Jesus Christ, I thought. I shouted, "Do you mind if I tie this off first? I don't want it to drift downstream."

"Come over here now it looks like your anchor's holding," the cop shouted. So I paddled back and boarded my raft for our "conversation" with a hundred people looking down from behind the railings on the concert shore.

"Do you have a registration for this vessel?" The cop asked after we'd both boarded my boat.

"No sir I built it myself. I'm intending to use the tides to propel me."

"Is that a trolling motor at the back of the boat?"

"Yes sir."

"What's your name?"

"Dallas Trombley."

"Where do you live Dallas?"

"New Baltimore."

"Dallas do you know that it's a violation of the New York State Navigation Law to pilot a vessel on the navigable waters of the state if it's mechanically propelled without a valid and current registration from the Department of Motor Vehicles?"

"I thought that was only for gas and diesel powered engines, not a trolling motor. This motor moves me less than two miles an hour."

"Sir is that a knife hanging on your lanyard?" The cop pointed to my belt.

"Yes sir."

"Sir do you mind if I hold onto that while we talk?" I handed him the knife. "Do you have any other weapons aboard your boat sir?"

"I have a machete," I said.

"Please give it to me." So I handed him the machete which happened to by lying on the deck just behind me, and he said, "Any other weapons aboard, sir?"

"Well it depends what you mean by weapons," I said honestly. "I mean I have a hatchet for cutting wood, a handsaw for cutting boards, a utility knife for cutting rope."

"And what did you need a machete for?"

"Honestly, for the theatre of it, mostly."

The cop gave a look up and down the boat, up and down me. Then he retrieved a clipboard and started reading from it.

"Do you have a lifejacket sir?"

"Yes," I said.

"Do you have a Type-IV throwable life preserver?"

"Ah—no. I don't think so. I have a piece of foam that I could conceivably toss to someone if that counts."

"That does not count. The life preserver must be circular or seat-cushion shaped and Coast Guard approved. Each vessel greater than sixteen feet in length requires one in addition to the PFCs required for each passenger on board. Do you have a fog horn?"

"Yes sir," I showed him.

"Do you have a visual distress device?"

"Yes actually. In fact I just used it. It's a red shirt tied around a canoe paddle."

"Do you have three nighttime flares?"

"No."

"Do you have a green light marking your starboard side and a red light marking your port side if you're planning to travel at night?"

"Well, what I've done is to tie two flashlights to each side, and by putting on top of them a red translucent Solo Cup on one side and a green one on the other, I can mark the port and starboard. I have the white one atop the cabin and at the back as well."

"Are these visible in a 112.5-degree arc at a distance of one mile?"

"You got me there."

"Do you have a fire extinguisher?"

"That I do."

"Can I have your license?"

"Actually I lost my wallet a few days ago getting this thing in the water. I can give you my address though." I told him my address.

"Sit tight," said the cop. While he boarded his vessel I walked around cleaning the front of my boat as the crowd looked on, many rolling their eyes and laughing. The cop flipped through a bunch of pages on his clipboard and wrote things. Then he said "Well, here's a ticket for the trolling motor. You need to have it registered if it's on your vessel even if it's in a cabin and not being used. So get that off your raft or get it registered. In the meantime you need nighttime flares and a throwable life preserver or every cop in every county is going to give you a ticket on your way down. But I'll let you go on those. Don't try piloting this thing at night, it's too dangerous. Have a good trip." He handed me my knife, machete and the ticket, which I put inside the cabin in the 'dry box' medicine cabinet. Then I canoed to shore.

For all of the previous two day's challenges, it was a hell of an entrance as I climbed the boulders on the bank of the Hudson and leapt over the iron railing into a circle of friends. Mike was there, and Morgan and Jess and TJ and Jared of course, but also many acquaintances I hadn't seen for years, who'd read about the launch in the *Times Union* or on the website my friend had made, or who were at the concert anyway and recognized me and wanted to know what was going on. In any case I was greeted with congratulations, remarks about The Man giving me a hard time, and, from my closest friends, with relief.

"I can't believe you made it," Mike said. He shook my hand enthusiastically, smiling ironically, then became serious, then shook his head. "If you asked me what the chances were that you'd make it up here by *Alive at Five*, I would've given you about a 2% chance. I can't believe this. Who was the guy in the fishing boat who towed you?"

I explained the events of the previous thirty hours, and Adam, my former teacher whose apartment I painted, handed me a plastic cup full of beer.

"Here, I think you could use this."

"I sure could!" Man did that beer taste good after such hunger and thirst. Others handed me tickets for beer and a hamburger. Then a young brunette woman pushed her way through the crowd.

"Are you the one with the boat? I'm Megan Lynne with FOX 23 News. Do you mind if we get a couple shots of you and the boat?"

"Sure!" I said. I hadn't considered the possibility of getting on television. Mike was facing away from the woman and grimaced before saying lowly,

"Dude, Fox News? Fuck them." I think he pictured a Bill O'Riley style interview. Anyway he and TJ who hated headlines backed away and I talked to Megan Lynne for a few minutes. Although I missed the broadcast, it was on the 6 and 11 o'clock news, people told me later.

We drank a few rounds as I basked in the attention. But when I saw Nicole I excused myself. We stood at the railing looking down at the river.

"When I'm done with this, I want to go out to dinner with you," I said. "To a fancy place where we get dressed up, and it's romantic."

"I'd like that a lot," Nicole blushed.

Then, since the boat was being held from drifting downstream only by the anchor, I announced that we had to launch, because the tide was going out. There were calls for a speech. I merely explained that it was difficult to get the boat up to Albany and it would be more difficult to get it to Manhattan, but with friends on board it would be fun, rather than desperate. Jess snapped a picture with her Polaroid camera, which she carried as an intentional anachronism.

With TJ murmuring, *I can't believe we're doing this. Shouldn't we wait a day?* With Mike gleefully assisting, and Jared just going with the flow, we jumped the fence, and Mike took turns taxiing each of us out to the boat.

We left Alive at Five to cheers, and "the psychedelic sounds of Jefferson Starship," as the *Times Union* quoted my website, playing at the concert. What a euphoric feeling, having the attention of hundreds of people directed at you, wishing you well. To give the crowd a little show I climbed the raft's mast and from atop the crow's nest drew out my machete and pointed it toward the sky, as TJ and Jared paddled near the front of the boat. That made the crowd clap and laugh. Then Mike climbed the mast and unfurled our big blue sail, with the white "$" made of duct tape. Mike enjoyed the spectacle. Then my crew of three and I sat each at a corner and paddled. It took nearly half an hour to float beneath the *Dunn Memorial Bridge* .3 miles downstream. A number of curious onlookers continued to watch us by strolling along a sidewalk that led south from the concert. As concert goers began to depart, they headed down this sidewalk toward their cars and easily overtook us by walking. It was a source of humor to several buzzed men who yelled from the shore about how many years it would take to reach Manhattan at our speed. From the bridge it took another hour to paddle .56 miles to a little cove on the west bank, with a dock comprised of floating plastic cases tied to shore. By then it was dark, the tide was slacking, and we needed to collect ourselves now that we'd gotten out of sight of the crowd.

It was an odd little park, where we found ourselves after dark. It was a patch of green in a part of the city full of industry, pavement, and concrete bridges spaghettiing over one another. A

Mexican man was walking up the dock with a fishing pole as we paddled into the little cove. We tied up to the end of the rectangular plastic dock, and stepped off to stretch.

We all felt different things. TJ was nervous.

"Dude, I think we should just take canoes," he repeated. I was dismissive after all I'd overcome the previous day.

"I'm not even going to address that suggestion, as we stand here with the boat we built for the purpose of going to New York this week."

Mike was helpful, very positive, as if my unexpected arrival at *Alive at Five* proved that anything was possible and we couldn't fail.

"Yeah, we have this boat, man, this *is* the project. I still can't believe you made it up here. I didn't think I was going to be on this boat tonight. Man!" Mike looked around and chuckled. It was the first time it hadn't rained while launching, and we were surrounded by crowds wishing us well, instead of cracking jokes. "This is a real, like, *thing* now! Launching from Alive at Five was a great idea. How many people do you think saw us? A thousand? And Fox News and the *Times Union*? I gotta hand it to ya, Captain. Like, I guess I never thought anyone would care about this, and it'd just be a joke...but it's become something where everybody wants us to make it." I smiled and thanked him.

"But I wouldn't say 'everybody.' In New Baltimore the mooring lines were cut twice; the police have given us a hard time two times now, and apparently we can't use the motor. The Coeymans Yacht Club was unfriendly; the guy who called it 'a monstrosity' with his power lines was not very helpful." But then I weighed the balance. "On the other hand when the boat washed up on that rich guy's personal beach in New Baltimore he was nice to me; those high school girls even looked after it for a day for me; the *Times Union* reporter and photographer were really friendly, and all the people seemed to like it at the concert."

"Until they made fun of us when they saw how slow we were going," TJ added.

" — So on balance, I guess most people support the project."

"I just think it would be way *easier* to take canoes," TJ repeated. I didn't feel I needed to list the reasons why that was impossible, but I did.

"And what are we to do with this boat, which is in the ghetto of the Port of Albany, if we take canoes?"

"Well...I'm not sure. We'd have to take it out."

"Where're we going to do that? And we have one canoe, but four people, do you have another canoe?"

"No."

"And," Mike added, "what about all those people who we just told that we were taking this boat to New York City? The newspapers are going to wanna do a follow-up story."

"Yeah, but I said at the beginning I don't care about newspapers, I don't want to be in them or anything." TJ glanced at Mike and I, who were frowning, and Jared who was wandering around looking at parts of the boat. Finally, TJ shrugged. "Okay, I don't want to be a downer here, alright. But I think we need to be smart. I'm the so-called Quartermaster, right? So I think we'd better get organized tonight and figure out what supplies we need and all. I'm not doing this trip like you guys did the first one, going hungry and eating like, nuts and shit. We need water, food. None of us have supplies on board right now."

"Now you're talking TJ! See? We're making a plan, and then we'll take steps to follow that plan, and then we'll be on our way to succeeding."

"Yeah," TJ said. "And we need to stay clean. The Hudson is disgusting. I think we should bring a bunch of bars of soap and wash ourselves off every time we pass a stream." Mike looked at me and tilted his head to the side. I winked at Mike and said to TJ,

"Sure, good idea."

Several problems had to be addressed immediately.

First was *provisions*. There was no food on the boat, and we were hungry. We knew there was a truck stop within walking distance of the park, and decided we'd trek there after we figured out our plan for the night. The next day we'd somehow have to shop for enough food for four people for ten days, and load those supplies onto the raft.

Then there was the problem of *propulsion*. We had to spend the night in the park because the tide was going the wrong way. The cop warned that I'd get ticketed for having the trolling motor on board, even while not in use. Yet I was not about to discard that important tool. So we decided we'd hide it in the cabin. (That an electric motor that moved us at a mile an hour had to be hidden like contraband struck us as ridiculous.) Yet the batteries were dead. I'd brought a battery charger and a 100-foot extension cord. We searched the park for outlets but there were none. We decided we we'd carry a battery and charger to the truck stop after we were done making our plan, and beg the clerk to let us charge a battery overnight.

Thirdly was a *personnel* dilemma. Mike had been able to take the entire *next* week off of work. It was a Thursday night, however, and he had to work the next day, Friday. He'd joined us for the launch ceremony, but he had to work 8:30-5 tomorrow. Once TJ and Jared realized this, they both decided that they needed to have the next day off too. That would give them the ability to pack and shop (I wished they'd done that already). But that would leave me alone with the boat yet again. Compounding that problem, when we'd made our original raft-schedule prediction, we judged that given three tides, four paddlers, and two fully-charged batteries, we'd have travelled from Albany to Coeymans, about 15 miles south, between Thursday and Friday evenings. So we'd invited our families, their friends (rural people who didn't go to city concerts), and some of our closest friends, to meet us at *Yanni's* the next evening, where we could talk more intimately and everyone could have a chance to see the boat up close. Twenty-five or thirty people were planning to come the next night. So I had to get the boat to Coeymans, and I needed, at an absolute minimum, one other person to help me. Mike was necessarily out, and TJ, I felt, could use a night to sleep and rest. I asked Jared if he'd help me get the boat to Coeymans during the next day, and he agreed.

There was the further problem of lacking numerous 'safety' items that the policeman had queried me about, but I figured it'd be easier to ask forgiveness than permission if we got pulled over again. And last there was my personal exhaustion over the last few days. I'd maintained myself by setting "reach *Alive at Five*" as a goal. Now that was over and I had circles under my eyes and I was filthy and hungry. I was about to eat at the truck stop, then sleep, and so I repeated "I will work harder" in my head, in imitation of Boxer, the work-horse from *Animal Farm*.

"So, this is the plan. Let's grab a battery and charger and go to the truck stop. TJ, you can go home tonight and get some sleep, and tomorrow shop for supplies. We'll split the money with you, and you can meet us in Coeymans at *Yanni's* and we'll load everything up tomorrow night. Mike, you'll go to work, get your stuff, and meet us at *Yanni's* at nine. Jared, you're with me. We'll get the battery from the truck stop in the morning, and set out when the tide changes at 6:45, and we'll paddle and motor, when we can, down to Coeymans. If we wear out the battery tomorrow, we can always charge both batteries at Coeymans. Then we'll have a good meal at *Yanni's* tomorrow night, the whole boat will be organized and loaded, everybody will be onboard for the duration, and we'll set sail when the tide changes at 10:30 at night." This seemed like a reasonable plan, and all agreed. I was satisfied that I was learning to form a logical plan quickly, and that other people had begun to acknowledge it and assist. So we grabbed the heavy battery, taking turns lugging it, and walked through the sketchy, dark, broken streetlight streets until we came to a parking lot with the truck stop lit up. We asked the middle-aged fat guy behind the counter if we could plug in our charger. He agreed without saying much. Then we got luke-warm aluminum foil-wrapped cheeseburgers and left.

Outside the truck stop, sitting at a picnic table in the dark, there were two white, skinny, hippy-looking kids, about twenty years old. One of them hailed us.

"Hey, guys! We're trying to hitch-hike to Boston. Any chance you guys are going that way and want to give us a ride? We don't have any cash to offer you, but we could smoke you up once or twice." I walked to their picnic table.

"Hey dudes, sorry, we don't have a car. Actually, we built a raft and that's how we got here...or, down by the river."

"Wow you built a raft? That's awesome. We built a raft too! On the Mississippi though, not this river. This is the Hudson, right?"

"Yeah. You built a raft too? No shit." I looked at Mike. "What are the chances?" I looked back toward the kids. "What was it like? Where you coming from? I mean, what are you guys doing?"

"Coming from Portland, in Washington, the state. We hitch-hiked across the northwest. We got to Cairo, Illinois and we figured what the hell, why not go down to New Orleans? Or whatever, let's just see where we go, because we don't really have any place to go, we're just traveling along seeing things."

"Wow and you got all the way to New Orleans?" Mike asked.

"Ha, naw, not even close."

"What happened?"

"Our raft fell apart. We built it from like, these barrels that we found along the shore, and we put pallets on top and tied them on."

"Yeah! That's how we built our first one."

"Your *first* one?"

"This is the third one we've built. Anyway, what happened?"

"Wow. Ha, well, so we just got on and started floating. It was pretty hard to steer. We had some pieces of wood we could push off things with and paddle a little. Anyway the ropes came untied about ten miles away and the barrels floated off, and we had to swim to shore. I lost a damn cell phone that way, and haven't been able to replace it yet."

"Ha, me too! Damn man, everything you're saying is like, something that's happened to me."

"It's a raft brotherhood," the kid said. "Man, we'd love to see the one you built."

"Yeah?"

"Yeah, we're not doing anything else. It'd be cool to check it out and swap stories."

So we left, six of us now, and started walking through the dark back to the ghetto cove. I was pretty amused by these two kids who reminded me not of myself, but of the kind of person I wanted to be a couple of years before, traveling around, meeting people, hitch-hiking.

"Hitch-hiking is a drag," I said. I told them about my experience in Baltimore, not catching a single ride.

"You gotta avoid the big highways, man," the taller of the two kids pointed out. "Like, on the highway everybody is going 70 miles per hour, and there's three lanes. Nobody wants to stop. Now, you can camp out on the on-ramp to the highway and then if you can find somebody you prolly got a ride for a long way, because people go long distances, that's why you take a highway. But the cops'll kick you off if they see you camped out on the ramp. We did a lot better sticking to county roads that go between small towns and cities. We had an alright time getting rides from Portland to Illinois, even Ohio. But it's been tough since then, in New York. We've been asking truckers for rides all night here in this city."

When we got to the cove the kids threw up their hands and said that our boat was "way better" than the thing they'd made, and we were "real serious" and "like, fucking, professionals." I showed them the little conveniences like the cabin with hinged shutters protecting screened windows, how we'd fashioned the foam into pontoons and attached it with fire hose, cut a triangular bow, and fashioned a sail. They were impressed. TJ left as the rest of us smoked on the dock and talked about our adventures on a clear June night, bobbing up and down. Then we all went to sleep, Mike, Jared and I on the raft and the two kids on the dock, all of us feeling a little more secure in our numbers, given where we were forced by circumstances to sleep.

When I think about the two days before and after the launch of *The Manhattan Project*, I see a microcosm of Life in One's Early Twenties. Expecting fun, the reality was a lot of work and repeatedly-delayed gratification. It was a sine-wave couple of days, with the troughs and peaks exaggerated. For thirty hours before *Alive at Five* I'd faced some of the toughest physical challenges of my life, alone, and it seemed almost delusional to think I might get to

Albany. Then, arriving there against the odds, supported by friends and strangers, the peak was higher than normal, like a K-complex in an EEG readout. I'd seldom felt so successful, a result of the organic outpouring of goodwill from so many people. The closest I'd ever come, perhaps, was the applause after a drama club production, or getting elected Student Council President. But those were adolescent achievements—basically I'd done well at playing a role in a program run by teachers in comparison to fellow students. As soon as I graduated there were other Student Council Presidents and other male drama club leads. *The Manhattan Project* was *my* creation.

Important older people, like news reporters, were interested. "If Huck Finn had encountered obstacles like those Dallas Trombley has, there might not have been any adventures on the Mississippi," Brian Nearing began his *Times Union* article. A year before, the rural Ravena *News Herald* had penned a piece with a humorous, almost sardonic tone—which we deserved—before concluding, "It's great to be young." This time beneath a close-up of my face looking rather haggard, the urban *Times Union* explained, "Failure forged Trombley's resolve. Since hatching the idea as a lark with friends almost two years ago, harsh experience has transformed him into someone who can read a tide chart, navigate a river channel and tie a variety of nautical knots." That was *adult* stuff, and the reference to harsh experience was written before any of the problems I'd had getting to Albany. Coming as it did amid a progression of set-backs, that article and the happy launch made me feel like I was right, after all, in sticking to this goal of mine. So the night of the launch was a high point. And like a lot of successes in your early twenties, it was ecstatic and short-lived. The sine wave crested, and now it was time for everything to start falling apart again.

The next morning Jared and I woke at six. Mike had left to walk twenty blocks to his apartment before work, and the hitch-hiking kids had left during the night. We walked to the truck stop and saw that our charger was unplugged. The same guy was working who'd been there the night before, and he said he'd just unplugged it. Yet when we attached the terminals of the charger to the battery and glanced at the analog readout, the needle on the "charge" display barely bounced above "0". It takes about eight hours to charge a depleted marine battery, so we guessed that the guy had unplugged it early in the night. We hoped there was *some* charge in the battery in case we needed propulsion.

As I looked at *The Manhattan Project* moored in the river with the rising sun gleaming behind her, I felt a connection to the craft, like she was a living entity. We'd spent so much time together the previous days. It was uniquely mine, different from any other boat ever made in color, construction, and intended use. I'd sweated and even bled upon her. I'd learned to steer her by sitting on the starboard side and paddling six times a minute to correct for her tendency to pull to that side. I'd jerry-rigged a system for keeping the aft cabin door closed after the hinge had broken. In particular ways only *I* understood how to work the thing. Even Mike who'd helped build her had almost no experience sailing her. And she'd been abused and bruised. The paint was chipping, the ceiling of the roof had cracked — little injuries to both the boat and my body had accrued almost continuously since we put her in the water. I could cite the place and manner in which every part had broken. It was an intimate connection such as I'd never had with an inanimate object, not even my old car Mindy, because I hadn't built Mindy, or understood how and why everything was put together the way it was. *The Manhattan Project* was the product of my labor and imagination, and my protection. I laid my hand on the outside of the cabin and patted her.

It was windy when we set off. The wind blew from the east, as it almost never does, and inhibited our progress greatly as we headed south. We made two miles, arriving just north of *Scarano Boat Builders* at the southern tip of the Port of Albany by 8 a.m. But the batteries were dead and without our motor — and minus two crew members — we were unable to steer in the wind. Twice we hit the piers lining the western bank in the Port and got turned around in circles floating uncontrolled. It was obvious that we needed the help of the others or the motor to steer.

Just south of the Port is the Normanskill Creek, which marks the boundary between Albany and the town of Bethlehem. Since the tide was nearly over and we'd only made two out of the fifteen miles to Coeymans, we concluded that we wouldn't reach Coeymans by that evening, so we had to change our plan. We needed food, and we needed to charge the batteries. Yet I was afraid to leave the boat someplace where a person might find it and do something to it. So the plan became this: we used the little bit of juice that was left in the battery to propel ourselves up the mouth of the creek. When we got to a little bend we motored to shore and tied the boat beneath the bough of a big overhanging tree. The tree branch and the bend in the creek prevented the boat from being seen from the river, and the shores on either side of the creek were nothing but a thicket of prickers and vines. I felt it was a good place to hide the boat until we returned with supplies.

Jared and I each toted a fifty-pound battery in one arm, and I carried the charger, too. Everything else we had to leave on the boat, because we ran out of hands and didn't know how far through the woods we had to trek before we reached Route 144.

"Man, mad work," Jared grumbled as we trudged uphill with weights in our hands getting lacerated by thorns. "There is no way we can carry these fucking batteries all the way to your apartment, dude. Maybe we can call Mike and ask him to pick us up. It's only like eight o'clock." This was a good idea, and Jared had a working cell phone. So we called Mike and asked him to meet us at a bridge where 144 passed over the Normanskill Creek. Mike agreed as long as he could pick us up quickly so he could get to work on time. After we hung up with Mike we reached a little hill where there was a narrow path that made it easier to walk. We followed this through a quarter-mile of woods until it opened perpendicular to railroad tracks. We crossed these and then a gravel lot and we were on 144. Mike picked us up in his second-hand melon green Geo.

"Dude, fuck that walk," Jared said as we loaded the batteries and then ourselves into Mike's car.

"Dude, you're telling me," I said. "I'm starving and exhausted."

"So what's the new plan?" Mike asked.

"Well it's going to take eight hours to charge these batteries. So that's going to take until five o'clock. I'm tired as fuck and I need need need to take a nap. So I was thinking I'd charge up one of these batteries and sleep, and then when you get out of work we can all go shopping for the supplies that we need, in your car. Now, you're out of work at five thirty. We're supposed to meet everybody in Coeymans at seven thirty. Okay, so we drive down to Coeymans, at that point we plug in the other battery and start charging that up. We meet everybody at *Yanni's* so that we're not no-shows, and explain our setback. Anyway, we have a good time, eat well, and get a good night's sleep at my parent's house, because we need it. Then in the morning we'll take all of our supplies and batteries and drive back up here, and we'll load them on the boat and get going, Saturday morning, one day behind, but fully stocked."

Mike agreed because there seemed to be no other plan. But changing plans so frequently did not cultivate confidence. Now Jared reminded us that he'd have to skip *Yanni's* and all day Saturday, because he had a party for his grandmother in Long Island.

"That's why I didn't want to go this weekend. I told you that when you were planning the trip. The plan was that I'd call you on Sunday and meet you wherever you are for the rest of the trip." He was right, but I'd forgotten. So there was one quarter of the crew gone. Decay was setting in. I felt like I was herding cats just trying to get the others to show up two and three days after we were supposed to all embark together. But there was so much to think about that it threatened to overwhelm, and I was so tired and hungry, that any plan which offered the prospect of relief from constant concentration, however momentary, seemed best. So Mike dropped me off at my apartment and went to work, and I plugged in the charger, attached it to one of the batteries, and fell asleep on my couch, which felt like some kind of royal luxury, until early afternoon.

I forced myself to get off the couch at two p.m. although I wanted to keep sleeping. I checked my email and found that the *Metroland*, "Albany's alternative news weekly," as its masthead proclaimed, wanted to interview me. Chet Hardin, a reporter, had read the press release Julie had sent and emailed me three days before, asking to meet up at *Alive at Five*, and gave me his number. I hadn't had internet access in the last three days and I couldn't call Mr. Hardin because my phone had been drowned. But the *Metroland* office was only two blocks from my apartment. So I walked over in order to meet the reporter so he didn't think I blew him off. I was conducted to a small room with a table. Mr. Hardin, a young white male with black hair and a beard, came in. He seemed surprised by my disheveled state: I'd been wearing the same 'adventurer's outfit' for three days, my eyes were swelled and dark, and I'd lost several pounds through not eating while doing lots of laborious stuff in the hot weather. At first, Mr. Hardin seemed not to know where to start. Perhaps inconvenienced by my unexpected arrival, he didn't smile as he asked questions about the first two boats, and how we constructed the third. But as I started to describe the cutting of the mooring lines, the storm while being towed, dragging the boat along the dike, and so on, he stopped asking questions and scribbled notes on a pad of paper. It took forty minutes to explain the last few days. When I was done describing the challenges of the previous week, the location of the raft at present, and the most recent tentative plan, the reporter leaned back in his chair, looked to the side, then at me, and pointed his palms upward, asking in a cut-the-bullshit tone,
"So...okay. Do you really think this is going to work this time, or what?"
"It *has* to work this time."
The reporter tapped his chin.

"And what is your contingency if you find yourself, say, six days from now, halfway between here and Manhattan, and your crew abandons you, and you can't steer the boat yourself, yet you have this 2,000-pound liability that you can't get out of the water, either?"

"I have no contingency," I admitted. Mr. Hardin accidentally rolled his eyes, then caught himself. "Look," I explained, "there are all kinds of what-ifs in life. I can't predict the future. What's the sense of listing all the things that are beyond my power to control, that could go wrong, like the crew abandoning me? Constant second-guessing isn't helpful. The only choice is to keep telling yourself that you have the power to do this...you are equal to the task. It seems to me that a lot of projects fail not because some insurmountable obstacle stopped progress, but because the person came across an obstacle and called it insurmountable and gave up. If I threw in the towel whenever someone pointed out that I *might* not be able to overcome this or that challenge in the future, the thing would still be in my back yard. Can I say something off the record?"

"Go ahead," Mr. Hardin set down his pen.

"I am terrified at the prospect that I might not make it to New York on this boat. The idea is so awful that I can't stand to think about it, like not being able to stand picturing a loved one who died alone during that last moment when they knew they were dying alone. So I must succeed. There's something that's been set in motion here and I can adjust the trajectory with a lot of work, but I can't stop it from happening. I can't, say, delay going, because Mike can only go this week because of work, and I need Mike, and where would I put the boat? I can't leave it anyplace people might find it, because people seem to like harming it. But that's not the ultimate, what? kernel of truth at the heart of the matter. The thing is I can't *not* do this...it's become such a thing associated with me, almost an *existential* liability...it's a fucking albatross is what it is, hanging around my neck, and the only way to get it off is by passing under the George Washington Bridge."

Mr. Hardin considered this and smiled for the first time since I'd met him.

"I get it. You know, there are things I've wanted to do...and if it means a lot to you, you shouldn't give them up. That's the angle for this story. The bullshit about fossil fuels and stuff...I wondered what your deal was, coming in here in your fedora, building rafts. But this isn't about building rafts. This is about the frontier spirit, the can-do attitude. I'll tell you what, there's no story here right now, as far as I'm concerned. But why don't you call me when you get back from your trip, and if you make it, I think it's something people would like to read about, after all the trouble you've had."

I agreed and left the *Metroland* headquarters.

At six in the evening Mike picked me up. I loaded the batteries and charger and a backpack full of clothes in Mike's trunk, next to the big duffle bag he'd packed.

"Dude you've got to get your phone fixed, or get a new one, or stop giving people my number as a way to get in touch with you," Mike said as we drove south on Route 144. "My phone's been ringing off the hook all day. I checked my phone on my lunch break and I had fourteen voicemails." This was the period just before texting surpassed calling as the primary method of contacting people. We picked up TJ who had another two bags of clothes and toiletries, and drove to the grocery store. We bought cases of water and beer, sausages and rolls, toilet paper, toothpaste and soap, cans of stew, snack foods and ice. We had to tie the cases of water to the top of Mike's car in order to fit everything and ourselves inside his compact. By the time we got to my parent's house in New Baltimore it was a half hour past when we told our friends we'd meet them at *Yanni's*.

We were relieved to have accumulated all the supplies we needed for several days. But it was obvious that it would take the three of us several trips from the car through the woods to the creek to load the boat the next morning. Slack tide was at 9 a.m. So we set an alarm on Mike's phone for 5 a.m. in order to give us time to get breakfast, drive up to Albany, and load the provisions. Then we drove the two miles from New Baltimore to Coeymans.

The parking lot was full. This was the third time we'd had a sendoff party at *Yanni's* the night before setting sail. More people came to the bar this time than on the previous trips combined. We walked into a busy place and were met with cheers and questions. The owner, Mark Yanni, came over and shook my hand, obviously pleased with the business, and bought the crew a round of drinks. My parents bought us the next round. Many of my aunts, uncles and cousins and their friends had come down to see the boat and were disappointed that it wasn't there, but finding themselves mixed up in a crowd of people congregating for the same purpose, they overcame their disappointment and yielded to the revelry.

Mike was nearly ecstatic. Mike liked conversation and socializing but almost never sought the center of attention. For the last year he'd lived alone in a basement apartment, went to work every day, and came home.

"This is the beginning of my first vacation in my working life!" Mike announced as he came up to me with beers in both hands. "Nine days off. Time to celebrate, Captain!" We clinked our glasses and downed their contents.

"Five o'clock is going to come early," TJ cautioned.

"Hey, after tonight we've got eight days of paddling and work. That's when we have to focus. Tonight, it's time to unwind for the first time in forever!" I could hardly argue with that sentiment, and we set to work drinking pints and, now and then, shots. TJ the responsible party drove us to my parent's house at 1 a.m., where we slept for four hours.

It was, of course, very difficult to rise from bed in the dark when the alarm went off at 5 a.m., after a night of drinking which followed two days of sleeping in uncomfortable places. But it was necessary and in a way I'd trained myself for that kind of thing, because I often stayed out until early morning and forced myself out of bed at 5:30 to substitute teach. TJ had drank very little and was easy to wake. Mike was another story. He had drunk with abandon, the way we used to in college, for the first time in a year, and couldn't be roused.

"Come on, Mike, it's time to get up, we've got to go catch the tide," I said, standing over the couch where he slept. He wouldn't open his eyes. "Come on! Let's go!" Nothing. I wanted to avoid waking him physically but I saw no other choice. I shook him several times. He grunted and I shook him more.

"What!" he shouted, angrily, with his eyes closed.

"It's time to go!" Mike didn't move. I shook him again.

"What!" he shouted violently.

"We have to go get on the fucking boat, dude!"

"Let's go in a couple hours." Mike rolled onto his side.

"We can't go in a couple hours, we have to go now!" Mike knew that. He didn't move, so I shook him again. He laid still. I shook him forcefully. He growled and swatted me with his arms and pulled a pillow over his face.

"What's wrong?" TJ said upon emerging from the bathroom.

"Mike won't get up," I said.

"Shit." TJ tried talking to Mike but to no effect. I made a pot of coffee so that I could feel like I was moving things along, and we waved this in front of Mike's face. Still no response, so TJ and I shook him some more.

"Ten minutes," Mike said. I knew that would do nothing. So while hating to precipitate Mike's anger but feeling there was no other choice, we grabbed Mike's arms and lifted him into a sitting position. "What the fuck!" he shouted. Finally, he looked at TJ and I and realized who we were. We got him to stand up and wash his face, and then he started back toward the couch.

"Just go to the car with us," I said. "You can sleep in the car. TJ and I'll do most of the loading, and then we just need to push off into the tide, and you can sleep on the boat for as long as you want." Mike bitterly agreed and we loaded him into the car, where he passed out.

We parked the car in the vacant lot by the railroad tracks on the side of Route 144. The sun was beginning to rise. Mike had gained a degree of consciousness now and mechanically put his duffle bag over his shoulder. He stood with his eyes nearly closed waiting for TJ and I to lead the way. We crossed the tracks and made our way to the tree line. I found the path Jared and I had stumbled across the day before and we started down the trail.

"It'd be nice if this led all the way to the riverside," I told TJ as Mike shuffled behind us. "Yesterday we had to bushwhack our way from the boat to the road. It would sure make loading things a lot easier if this leads to the river. We could move the boat from inside the creek to wherever this path comes out."

"I thought you said this was an uninhabited place," TJ said. He pointed to several trails that crisscrossed ours. There were ATV tracks on some of them.

"I thought it was uninhabited yesterday. It looked that way from the creek bank," I said. Now it seemed ominous that there were recent foot-prints and tracks in the mud beneath our feet.

"Hey, look at this," Mike called from behind us. He was bent over looking at some multicolored fabric lying on the ground. We turned and circled back to him. "It's Old Glory!" Mike picked a tattered American flag off the ground. It was torn along the seam where the grommets pass through, as though it had been ripped from a flag pole. "Now we can have *two* American flags on our boat!"

Suddenly I felt very uneasy. Why would there be an American flag ripped up and thrown in the woods? It suggested villainy. We quickened our pace until we came to the end of the trail, which opened onto the bank of the river a little downstream from the mouth of the creek.

There was a smoldering campfire. In the ashes we saw the melted antennae of my walkie-talkies, broken glass and metal from my lanterns, and a burnt-up camping chair. I looked to my left, across the creek, and saw Mike's canoe sitting on the opposite shore. In the river, bobbing like a corpse, were a life jacket and poncho.

"Where's the raft?" TJ asked. We ran to the creek-side and looked up the shore. I saw the tree with the big branch that I'd tied the boat beneath with three different lines the day before. But *The Manhattan Project* was gone.

Back where the trail opened to the river, I scanned the water up and down, but there was no sign of the the raft. Mike reclined on the ground and closed his eyes. TJ watched me.

"Dude this is bad, this is very bad," I said.

"I'm sorry Dallas, this sucks." TJ kicked at the still-smoking fire with our supplies melted in it. "I can't believe someone stole your stuff and burned it. I guess this is the end of the trip, huh?"

"End of the trip hell! I'm not even thinking about that right now. TJ the boat is missing! The thing weighs 2,000 pounds! What happened? What if some fucking assholes set it adrift at night, without any lights on it, and some motorboat came along in the dark and hit it and somebody got killed? Jesus Christ. Or it's smashing against boats at the Albany Yacht Club? Do you know how much trouble I'd be in?"

"Well it wasn't your fault. You didn't set it adrift."

"No but I built the fucking thing and brought it here, it's my responsibility. Dude, I hate it, but we have to call the police. Mike, we're calling the police."

"Okay," Mike said, lying on his back on the ground. "I'm just gonna nap...wake me up when they get here."

TJ the Quartermaster and I sat Indian style on the side of 144 at 7 a.m. waiting for the police to arrive. We threw pebbles into a discarded Styrofoam cup to pass the time.

"Man, I hope they don't send Officer Vunck," TJ remarked.

"Who's that?" I hit the rim of the cup with a pebble.

"He's like Robocop. You never heard of this guy? He gives out more tickets than the rest of the Bethlehem Police Department combined."

"Oh Jesus Christ."

"Dude—I heard the guy gave his own wife a speeding ticket—on her birthday."

"They must have a great relationship. I got a pebble in."

"They say he sits in his car on the town line at midnight and scans license plates. He'll pull over any car that's not registered to an address in Bethlehem. He's like a savant — a walking code-book — and always finds things to give out tickets for."

"That should be illegal," I remarked.

"The *Times Union* did a story on him. He pulled over one guy and gave him 14 citations for his trailer. He always shows up to hearings and the courts always side with him. He's merciless."

"Maybe he sleeps in on Saturday mornings," I said.

Sure enough a short time later a Bethlehem cruiser pulled over next to us, and out stepped Officer Vunck.

"I don't believe it," TJ whispered.

This guy stepped out like he was General George S. Patton of the Bethlehem Police Department. Cocked hat, shiny buttons — all that was missing were a couple of ivory-handled revolvers. After giving him our names we nervously led this very serious officer back to the scene of the crime, where he asked us a series of questions, took my phone number, and told us he would return.

"That was painless," I said.

"So far..."

The officer returned an hour later with a detective from the police station who assured us that "We are taking this case very seriously." Officer Vunck retold the facts to the detective. A photographer arrived and took pictures of the campfire, as well as a turned-over cooler and a shoe print in the sand, all next to little plastic numbers for an evidence file. They even dabbed cotton swabs around the mouth of a beer can and used tweezers to put a cigarette butt in a *Ziplock* bag. Then they told us to go home while the river police combed the water for our vessel. Pointing to Mike, who slept on the ground as all this went on, the detective remarked,

"It looks like he needs a rest."

We drove back to my parent's house, then an hour and a half later we reconvened at the scene of the crime because the boat police called and told us they'd found *The Manhattan Project*. As we stood on the riverbank with the Normanskill on our left and the Hudson in front of us we watched the police come into sight from upstream, from the Port of Albany, with our raft tied to the starboard side of their police boat.

"Why do they have it tied to the side of the boat?" I asked the detective. The weight of the raft was pulling the police in wide starboard circles.

As the marine cops serpentined toward us I could see that our trip had been dealt a death-blow. The shutters and screens on the cabin were broken off, the sail was torn to shreds. On the deck I saw our paddles snapped in half. The police managed with difficulty to get the boat close enough to the shore for me to jump aboard and throw a line to TJ to tie us off. My spare clothes were missing, as was the trolling motor, all the supplies I'd loaded in New Baltimore, the ship's logbook and the medicine cabinet "dry box" of papers and documents, including my citation from the day before. Worst of all, my *Seamanship* book was gone, as was my big *Moleskinne* notebook with all the notes and descriptions I had made about Baltimore and Santina during my hitch-hiking trip. I wondered if the vandals had read the heartfelt writing I'd scribbled in that half-full notebook, and laughed, tearing out pages and burning them in their campfire.

"Well, we won't be floating downstream on this," I pronounced bitterly. "There's nothing left. No means of propulsion whatsoever."

Mike and TJ were silent. The police told me we needed to get the vessel out of the river because it was a navigation hazard. But it was impossible to drive a truck to the location and the boat was not pilotable. I asked the marine police if they'd tow it some-where with a boat launch but they said the best they could do was tow it a little ways up the creek so it would be out of the river. I agreed.

I climbed back ashore and I watched one of the silliest things I've seen on the river. I suggested to the police that they tie a towline straight off their stern through the bullnose cleat on the bow of the raft. That was the way the old man had towed me five miles.

"No, no," said a young officer with spiky blonde hair and a short-sleeve black shirt. "This is how we tow every vessel, alongside." So they left *The Manhattan Project* tied to the side of their boat.

They tried to pilot their police boat in a circle out toward the channel in order to come into the creek, which was behind them upstream. But the weight of the raft on the starboard side pulled their boat in a long, straight line, and their boat only moved downstream and to the middle of the river. Then they tried to make a starboard turn, which was easy because all the weight was there, but by now the current had pushed them past the mouth of the creek and they were unable to pilot it in.

"Something must be wrong with your raft. I can't steer the boat," the officer yelled to shore. As politely as possible I replied,

"I think the weight of it tied on the starboard side is throwing off your steering."

"No," said the cop, "this is how we always do it. There must be some piece of driftwood under your boat acting like a rudder or something. We'll try backing in."

So the cops reversed, keeping the helm straight, and that turned the boat so that they faced upstream with the raft on the side facing the center of the river. The officer tried to pilot the boat upstream and make a port turn into the creek, but was instead pulled toward the channel by the weight of the boat on the starboard side.

"Well, this is something else. I never seen anything like this," the cop said. I glanced at Mike who rolled his eyes.

Now the cop tried backing again, and they came to the exact spot they'd started from fifteen minutes before.

"How's this?" the cop asked. I told them I'd get in the water and pull the raft into the stream, and the cops agreed. I waded up to my chest and dragged the boat behind me out of the river. Then the marine policemen left, and the detective told me he'd call me when he had some leads. In the meantime we were to "get the boat out of here, however you can," which meant that we were expected to take it apart and burn it.

By then it was afternoon. We'd bought beer and sausages. Friends kept calling us for updates. Like the father in *A Christmas Story*, after his turkey is eaten by the neighbor's dogs, when he rubs his hands and declares "Get dressed; we're going out to dinner!" I suggested we bring our food to our friend Carly's parent's house (because they lived nearby) and have a barbeque.

Morgan brought Nicole. Jess and TJ and Carly joined. We drank beer and ate cheese-infused sausages cooked on a backyard barbeque.

"You must be pretty upset," Morgan said as we stood alone in Carly's back yard, drinking beer from Solo cups and listening to jazz music.

"Believe it or not, I'm not that upset."

"Really? Wow."

"I tried, and I failed. Now it's over. It could've been worse. This morning I was afraid I'd be charged with criminal negligence and go to jail. Look at the shape Mike is in. Jared isn't even here. TJ has been a nervous wreck the whole time. There's a pretty good chance I would've been abandoned by my friends and stranded, and in a worse situation than I am now."

"That's a positive way to look at it," Morgan noted. "Still you must be pretty *bilious*—GRE word, I love it, because it makes you think of the taste of bile—because you have to burn the boat after all your hard work."

"It'll be cathartic," I insisted. "When my Uncle Paul's dog got cancer and was going to die after he had him for 12 years, he walked into the woods with his shot gun and the dog followed him in, and he killed the damn dog, because it was going to die and he felt it was right that *he* do it. I guess I could never have kept this boat, so I ought to be the one to destroy it—to put her out of her misery now that she's been maimed and mangled by strangers. And then the thing will be over, and you know what I'm looking forward to doing?"

"What's that?"

"Anything other than building a raft! Like spending some quiet evenings with that blonde girl over there." I pointed to Nicole. "That's what I'm looking forward to now."

"Huh, well that's good."

"On the other trips, when it was over, my life was a disaster. I was deep in the red, living at home, relationship on the rocks, no job. Now I have a great apartment and a great roommate—you, sir, of course—I'm broke but I don't owe anyone money. And this girl likes me. So why can't I just spend my time doting on her? Don't I deserve to be able to spend my time doing that? Aren't I allowed to waste time making time with a cute girl? Isn't that the reward, the whole point behind working hard? It's time to enjoy the simple pleasures, like friends and romance and not having obligations, for a change."

"It sounds nice and normal. I wonder, though, if you can do it."

"'You can do anything if you put your mind to it, Marty,'" I quoted *Back to the Future*.

"Ha, unless quieting your mind is the issue."

I patted Morgan on the back, and waved to Nicole.

The next day Mike and I went to the riverside with a mini-keg of *Heineken*. We retrieved a hammer and a crowbar, one of the few personal items that the vandals had left on the boat, and started prying the vessel apart board by board. Mike pointed out the irony of dismantling a boat one piece at a time after it had survived storms and repeated vandalism. We made a funeral pyre and threw in piece after piece as we drank beer from the mini keg. It took 8 hours to burn my ship in a great conflagration, fire shooting twelve feet high and spewing black smoke. So much for helping the environment with our boat trips; we were under orders to destroy it. We managed to pull off the triangular bow and throw it on the pyre all at once. As we sat watching the glowing plasma burning up a summer of dreams, Mike stared and remarked,

"We should've known, when we named her *The Manhattan Project*, that she'd go up in flames."

Made in United States
North Haven, CT
20 April 2023

35658016R00254